MALAYSIAN CROSSINGS

Global Chinese Culture

GLOBAL CHINESE CULTURE

David Der-wei Wang, Editor

Michael Berry, *Speaking in Images: Interviews with Contemporary Chinese Filmmakers*
Sylvia Li-chun Lin, *Representing Atrocity in Taiwan: The 2/28 Incident and White Terror in Fiction and Film*
Michael Berry, *A History of Pain: Literary and Cinematic Mappings of Violence in Modern China*
Alexa Huang, *Chinese Shakespeares: A Century of Cultural Exchange*
Shu-mei Shih, Chien-hsin Tsai, and Brian Bernards, editors, *Sinophone Studies: A Critical Reader*
Andrea Bachner, *Beyond Sinology: Chinese Writing and the Scripts of Culture*
Jie Li, *Shanghai Homes: Palimpsests of Private Life*
Michel Hockx, *Internet Literature in China*
Lily Wong, *Transpacific Attachments: Sex Work, Media Networks, and Affective Histories of Chineseness*
Sebastian Veg, *Minjian: The Rise of China's Grassroots Intellectuals*
Shengqing Wu, *Photo Poetics: Chinese Lyricism and Modern Media*
Calvin Hui, *The Art of Useless: Fashion, Media, and Consumer Culture in Contemporary China*
A-Chin Hsiau, *Politics and Cultural Nativism in 1970s Taiwan: Youth, Narrative, Nationalism*
Michael Berry, ed., *The Musha Incident: A Reader on the Indigenous Uprising in Colonial Taiwan*

Malaysian Crossings

Place and Language in the Worlding of Modern Chinese Literature

Cheow Thia Chan 曾昭程

Columbia University Press   New York

Columbia University Press wishes to express its appreciation for assistance given by the Chiang Ching-kuo Foundation for International Scholarly Exchange and the Council for Cultural Affairs in the publication of this series.

Columbia University Press
Publishers Since 1893
New York   Chichester, West Sussex
cup.columbia.edu
Copyright © 2023 Columbia University Press
All rights reserved

Library of Congress Cataloging-in-Publication Data
Names: Zeng, Zhaocheng, author.
Title: Malaysian crossings : place and language in the worlding of modern Chinese literature / Cheow Thia Chan.
Description: New York : Columbia University Press, [2023] | Series: Global Chinese culture | Includes bibliographical references and index.
Identifiers: LCCN 2022012593 (print) | LCCN 2022012594 (ebook) | ISBN 9780231203388 (hardback ; acid-free paper) | ISBN 9780231203395 (trade paperback) | ISBN 9780231555029 (ebook)
Subjects: LCSH: Malaysian literature (Chinese)—History and criticism. | Malaysian literature (Chinese)—Appreciation. | Space in literature. | LCGFT: Literary criticism.
Classification: LCC PL3097.M3 Z416 2023 (print) | LCC PL3097.M3 (ebook) | DDC 895.13009/358595—dc23/eng/20220727
LC record available at https://lccn.loc.gov/2022012593
LC ebook record available at https://lccn.loc.gov/2022012594

Cover image: Shutterstock

For my parents,
Chan Khim Khai 曾錦凱 *and Tan Ah Moey* 陳亞妹

Contents

Acknowledgments ix
A Note on Romanization, Characters, and Translation xv

INTRODUCTION
Southern Crossings: The Covert Globality of Mahua Literature 1

CHAPTER ONE
Doubly Local: Lin Cantian and the Contrapuntal Genesis of Mahua Novelistic Fiction 31

CHAPTER TWO
Channeling Exemplarity: Han Suyin's Bifocal Writing Practice in Malaya 70

CHAPTER THREE
Cosmopolitan Visions of Drift: Wang Anyi and the Relay of Diasporic Literary Imagination 116

CHAPTER FOUR
Off-Center Articulations: Li Yongping's Transregional Literary Production 156

CODA
Always the Internal Other: Mahua Literature and the
Recognition of Alterity   195

Notes   207
Bibliography   253
Index   281

Acknowledgments

Academe prizes single-authored monographs, but no book is ever written alone. This one is no exception despite being completed amid a global pandemic that has normalized social distancing. Going through its pages feels like taking a walk through my own memory palace. I am reminded of all the locales where the kindness of many who started as strangers helped me shape fledgling ideas into reality.

My work on this book has been enabled, first, by my predecessors: the writers and scholars of Malayan and Malaysian Chinese literature. Their thought-provoking literary works related to Nanyang (Southeast Asia) and their critical commitment to the region inspired me to join their ranks. Intertwined with cultural struggles on the ground, the discourses they forged have since constituted a dynamic textual tradition, leaving a mark on the places they consider home. I stand on their shoulders as I carve out my own perspective, one that I hope will also contribute to developing local and regional cultural ecologies.

In the course of research and writing, I am further beholden to many mentors and institutions. At Yale, Jing Tsu welcomed the proposal with exceptional interest. The book's initial form would not have come together if she did not remind me, more than once, that the literary can be studied in tandem with the social in bracing ways. Her advice to anchor the study historically and to express its stakes as lucidly as possible—without seeking refuge from existing theoretical shorthand—has profoundly influenced my intellectual orientation. Peter Perdue introduced me to the thrill of archival research on the Qing dynasty and gave me the confidence to handle historical collections pertinent to my own project. I learned to analyze texts with greater care and imagination from Tina Lu's bracing approaches to reading late imperial Chinese fiction and drama. Helen Siu, Joseph Errington, and Erik Harms honed my conceptual acuity, which I have used to navigate the fascinating worlds of inter-Asian connections, and to plumb the politics of language and culture in Southeast Asia. Dudley Andrew and Haun Saussy counseled me to think more expansively. I am forever indebted to Kang-i Sun Chang's sustained support for my growth as a teacher-scholar.

My academic sojourn on the East Coast was also enriched by the company of extraordinary peers: Bo An, Rosa Vieira de Almeida, Mark Baker, Po-hsi Chen, Simone Glasl, Fu-ming Lee, Yiwen Li, Stephen Poland, Flora Shao, Shawn Ta, Mengxiao Wang, Faizah Zakaria, and Huasha Zhang. Each of them broadened my intellectual horizon immeasurably with their erudition. Erik Cronqvist, Ying Jia Tan, Gerald Goh, Jieming Chen, and Yijia Lu made those six years in New Haven equally unforgettable. My fondest memories are forged with the writing group that included Wei Luo, Yu Luo, Pengfei Zhao, and Guojun Wang, who initiated the biweekly meetings. I can never thank Guojun enough for reaching out. The camaraderie among two sociologists, two literary scholars, and one anthropologist tided me over during the isolation of those wintry years. That apartment at 407 Canner Street will always be special, for it was where we discussed our clumsy drafts, enjoyed sumptuous meals, and engaged in wide-ranging conversations. To this day I cherish the rapport we built.

From 2016 to 2018, I spent two invigorating years with Cornell University's East Asian and Southeast Asian Studies Programs. One could not have asked for a more conducive environment to reimagine the project thoroughly. It was in Ithaca that this book found both its essence and form. For the valuable experience of meeting fresh interlocutors at Cornell, I thank my hosts Andrea Bachner and Eric Tagliacozzo. The Critical Sinophone Studies Colloquium that Andrea organized was the highlight of my fellowship. During those productive sessions, I benefited from illuminating exchanges with Junning Fu, Junting Huang, Kun

Huang, Shu-mei Lin, and Elizabeth Wijaya. My stint in upstate New York was also enlivened by the spirited company of folks at the Southeast Asian Studies Program: Ryan Buyco, Alexandra Dalferro, Sebastian Dettman, Juan Fernandez, Astara Light, James Nagy, Phi-Vân Nguyen, Jinglin Piao, Chairat Polmuk, Anissa Rahadiningtyas, Matthew Reeder, Emiko Stock, Ifan Wu, Alex-Thai D. Vo, and Hoang Minh Vu. I still remember the weekly Gatty Lectures, the leisurely meals, and the summer excursions with great fondness. Beyond these two circles, Clarence Lee, Mai Shaikhanuar-Cota, Daniel Boucher, Christopher Holmes, and Jennifer Spitzer were very hospitable friends, enhancing the sense of belonging I enjoyed in Ithaca.

It would be remiss of me not to express my deepest appreciation to the librarians, archivists, and friends who helped locate research materials. At Yale, Tang Li, Michael Meng, Erlinda Pacelli, and Richard Richie tirelessly attended to my requests to track down obscure titles and to keep the relevant acquisitions updated. I miss their amazing efficiency and resourcefulness. I also wish to thank the Howard Gotlieb Archival Research Center at Boston University for facilitating access to the Han Suyin Collection, and in particular, Jane Parr, for her considerate assistance during and after my visits. At Cornell, Jeff Petersen's enthusiasm in supporting scholars' research exuded a personal touch that went beyond the customary call of vocational duty. When I was drafting the book, Dihao Zhou kindly offered lodging for research visits that took me back to New Haven. After I left the United States, Cheng Li and Yuan Ting Chan loaned and scanned requisite resources, and I am grateful for their help. In Singapore and Malaysia, several colleagues generously shared their unpublished work or sedulously gathered materials: Kuo Shiu Nue, Ina Zhang Xing Hong, Kho Tong Guan, Loo Jiaming, and Liw Pei Kien.

I feel extremely fortunate to be pursuing my academic career at the Department of Chinese Studies at the National University of Singapore (NUS). Kenneth Dean has provided unstinting support for my professional development. No junior faculty with ideals about public scholarship can ask for a better mentor than Chang Woei Ong, who not only offers guidance with compassion but inspires as well by participating in civil society. Within the larger NUS community, I appreciate the warm collegiality of Jack Chia, Chee Lick Ho, Elaine Lynn-Ee Ho, Bei Hu, Choon

Hwee Koh, Khee Heong Koh, Chien Wen Kung, Hui Kian Kwee, Lap Lam, Chee Hiang Lee, Cher Leng Lee, Hui Huan Lee, Hongxuan Lin, Chen Liu, Yuet Keung Lo, Shi Lin Loh, Shaoling Ma, Rui Peng, Guo Quan Seng, Ruiqing Shen, Jui-Lung Su, Shiao Wei Tham, Hang Tu, Charles Wong, Sin Kiong Wong, Lanjun Xu, and Sai-Shing Yung.

Many colleagues offered invaluable feedback on the manuscript at various stages of my writing. Philip Holden gave freely of his time and steered me to see the deeper layers of richness in my ideas. It would have been wonderful if we crossed paths at Kent Ridge. Nurfadzilah Yahaya pinpointed crucial gaps in the discussion that would have precluded readers from grasping the full import of my arguments. Special appreciation also goes out to my colleagues in Singapore-Malaysian literary and historical studies: Zhou Hau Liew, Siew Min Sai, Ying Xin Show, Jessica Tan, Jeremy Tiang, Nicholas Y. H. Wong, and Zhan Min-xu. Also, Mary Bagg, Ellen Tilton-Cantrell, and Kimberly Alecia Singletary provided expert editorial suggestions to make the manuscript more inviting to a wider audience. For assistance in preparing and proofreading the bibliography, I thank Shaun Choh and Goh Song Wei.

None of my intellectual adventures would have been possible without the indelible impact of selfless educators during my formative years. I am immensely obliged to Chen Yinchi and Zhang Xinying at Fudan University for their early tutelage during my undergraduate studies in Shanghai, and their support when I decided to pursue graduate studies in England and the United States. At University of Cambridge, Pei-yin Lin guided my transition to academic writing in English with patience and skill. Most significantly, in the mid-1990s when I attended Hwa Chong Junior College in Singapore, I had the fortune of meeting Sy Ren Quah and Song Hwee Lim who were exemplary teachers and mentors. Whether it was the analyses of unseen literary texts, or the production of drama performances and student literary publications, they nurtured students to think creatively, critically, and independently. Separately, Sy Ren's pursuit of meaningful connections between scholarship and civil society projects has been a beacon all these years. Aspiring to undertake similar endeavors was one of the main reasons I chose to come home after almost a decade in the United States. And of all the teachers I had, I certainly owe Song Hwee the greatest debt: he recognized my aptitude at Hwa Chong and made me believe that I could forge my own path by dreaming big and far. Over the years, his thoughtful mentorship made up for the lack of listening ears during many periods of uncertainty. I still value his advice on making a life in and beyond academia.

Research for the book received funding support from the Yale University Doctoral Fellowship, the A. Bartlett Giamatti Fellowship from the Yale University Department of East Asian Languages and Literatures, the NUS Overseas Graduate Scholarship, the NUS Overseas Postdoctoral Fellowship, and the NUS Faculty of Arts and Social Sciences Start-Up Fund. The book's publication is made possible in part by the Chiang Ching-kuo Foundation for International Scholarly Exchange's Publication Subsidy, and the NUS Faculty of Arts and Social Sciences Book Grant Scheme.

With its remarkable list of Malaysian Chinese literature in translation and global Chinese cultural studies, Columbia University Press is the perfect home for the book. Honored to join the list, I am indebted to my editor Christine Dunbar for her interest and dedication to the project since its incipient phase, and to the series editor David Der-wei Wang for recognizing the value of the manuscript. It was a true pleasure to work with the helpful editorial team that ensured a smooth publishing process. Special thanks are owed to Christian Winting for his gentle patience in responding to abundant inquiries from a first-time author. I am deeply grateful to the three reviewers whose generous engagement with my ideas and insightful suggestions helped improve the book in every way. Reaching out with warm encouragement subsequently, E. K. Tan offered uplifting kindness that I resolve to pay forward when I can. All errors that remain are my own.

An earlier version of parts of chapter 4 appeared as "Indigeneity, Map-Mindedness, and World-Literary Cartography: The Poetics and Politics of Li Yongping's Transregional Chinese Literary Production," in *Modern Chinese Literature and Culture* 30, no. 1 (Spring 2018): 63–86. I am grateful to Kirk Denton and the Ohio State University for granting permission to reprint material from the article. It has been substantially revised and expanded for this book. For permission to use images in their care, I thank Lei Ying and the Chiang Ching-kuo Foundation for International Scholarly Exchange; Chew Hui Im; Wang Anyi; and Ko Chia-cian. I also extend thanks to the literary and talent agency Curtis Brown, which allowed the publishing of material from the Han Suyin

Collection at the Howard Gotlieb Archival Research Center at Boston University.

The world has been fundamentally changed by the pandemic. What has stayed constant, comfortingly, is the unconditional love and tolerance of friends and family in Singapore. I continue to be buoyed by the friendships of Jamson Chia, Tze Pin Koh, Huay Leng Lee, Szei Ching Lim, Chun Meng Low, La Min Maung, Chee Seng Quah, Yun Huei Soh, Hwee Noi Tan, and Raymond Tan, all of whom are unremitting sources of emotional strength. My sister Tze Wan and my twin brother Cheow Pong have stood by me ever since I decided to switch careers and pursue doctoral studies. It has been lovely to reunite with my brother- and sister-in-law Tiong Eng and Lee Yong, as well as my nephews and nieces Matthias, Noel, Clara, and Calyn. I am delighted to celebrate the milestones of everyone in the family again. When I returned to Singapore, the joy was not just mine, but also my parents'. They have never fully grasped my life choices—idiosyncratic by Singaporean standards—but have nonetheless supported me wholeheartedly. It is to them that I dedicate this book.

A Note on Romanization, Characters, and Translation

The book uses standard *hanyu pinyin* (based on Mandarin pronunciation) for the romanization of Chinese sources, unless the Chinese terms or the names of places and persons are better known in alternate spellings of Mandarin and other Sinitic languages. In the notes and bibliography, because the book deals with a relatively greater amount of material produced during the Malayan period or in Taiwan, I choose to follow the scriptal presentation of the material and use traditional Chinese characters. All translations from Chinese are mine unless otherwise acknowledged.

MALAYSIAN CROSSINGS

Introduction

Southern Crossings: The Covert Globality of Mahua Literature

> To understand what world literature is . . .
> we always need to see *where* it is.
> —DAVID DAMROSCH, "WHERE IS WORLD LITERATURE?"[1]

> The way scholars position Mahua literature relates to how we treat issues of cultivating deep native knowledge. . . . If scholars in China and Taiwan . . . have their own understandings of "Mahua literature," should we, as truly active subjects, not also construct our own system of understanding? Or, are we satisfied with being inserted into conceptual frameworks such as "overseas literature in Chinese" or "world literature in Chinese" by foreign scholars?
> —CHONG FAH HING, "WHOSE MAHUA LITERARY STUDIES?"[2]

When Taiwan's National Culture and Arts Foundation organized an initiative to select the best twenty novels that appeared between 2001 and 2015 from an array of Sinitic-speaking regions, two naturalized Taiwanese writers, Li Yongping 李永平 and Zhang Guixing 張貴興, both born in Sarawak, part of current-day East Malaysia, were shortlisted. But neither author made the final cut: most of the Malaysian and the Taiwanese judges, who based their decisions on nationality and birthplace respectively, thought the other region would better categorize the writers' works.[3]

The incident reflects why the story of Malaysian Chinese literature—a literary tradition known locally as *Mahua wenxue* 馬華文學 (hereafter Mahua literature)—can be told as the story of "the unrewarded," in the sense of being overlooked for literary distinction.⁴ Benedict Anderson originally used the term "unrewarded" to characterize the absence of Southeast Asian writers among the laureates for the Nobel Prize in Literature.⁵ As the list of books endorsed by the Taiwan initiative in 2015 reveals, narrow geographical labels discount migrant writers' layered identities, which may be tied to two or more places. Besides, scholars and critics of modern Chinese literature continue to pair an author's writing practice with a single location and to perceive mobile literary actors as uncommitted to place-making.

The 2015 incident also illustrates how the literary output attributed to a place can be diminished when rigid territorial boundaries determine the size and contours of the associated literary space. In this instance, the plurality of Mahua literature is shrouded as a result of insufficient appreciation from scholars and critics for "Malaysia" as a creative venue whose borders extend beyond that of the nation-state bearing the same name. Meanwhile, institutions do not display an equal interest in all parts of the world or regard all places as notable sites of cultural production. As Anderson suggests in his essay on the Nobel committee's neglect of Southeast Asia, unrewarded writers are often linked to unrewarded regions. To be sure, some geographical areas change their fate of obscurity; for instance, Mo Yan 莫言 from China won the Nobel in 2012. Other regions, however, remain invisible or incomprehensible to prestige-granting institutions of world literature.

In the case of Mahua literature, its authors confront an existential condition of deep marginality for being associated with the Southeast Asian country. Malaysia exists as a remote site in the international cultural sphere—what Pascale Casanova calls the "world literary space"—where Europe and America are the favored regions.⁶ In the world of modern Chinese literature, the Mahua literary formation also occupies a peripheral position vis-à-vis more productive East Asian locales, including China, Taiwan, and Hong Kong. Furthermore, the Malaysian state itself relegates Mahua literature to the status of "sectional literature," since only works written in the national language of Malay are recognized as "national literature."⁷

Mahua literary actors are unrewarded from another perspective. Few now recall that they have been at the vanguard of re-regionalizing Chinese cultural areas at critical junctures. For example, Tu Wei-ming's concept of a "Cultural China" in the early 1990s, developed to eschew a singular geopolitical and cultural authority embodied by the mainland polity, originated from the ideas and cultural practices of the diasporic Mahua literary collective in Taiwan in the mid-1970s.[8] And whereas Mahua writing practices have been held out since the mid-2000s as the linchpin of Sinophone studies—a field of academic inquiry formulated to disprivilege China and reconfigure center-periphery cultural relations for a new global mapping of modern Chinese literature—the works' varied local interpretations have not received similar analytical attention.

With this book I bring due recognition to Malaysia as a vibrant literary region that produces remarkable texts as well as conceptual frameworks. *Malaysian Crossings* examines the geographical locality's understated significance for the "world-Chinese literary space," a term I use to include all Sinitic-speaking regions.[9] It aligns itself with a "located approach" of world literary studies that underscores location not only as geohistorical context but also as an important sociocultural force that actively shapes the positionalities of writers, readers, and critics.[10] In particular, it recounts Mahua literature as world literature for this extensive space by featuring the innovative ways in which authors with strong ties to the Southeast Asian country navigate their local and global concerns simultaneously, in the literary worlds they construct and the social worlds they inhabit. Such authorial interventions expand the process of "worlding" Mahua literary space to encompass not merely textual transmission and interpretive reception, as David Damrosch sees "world literature," but also rhetorical production.[11] Focusing on global perspectives within local and regional imaginaries, I examine the concrete endeavors of writers who self-identified as Chinese and who forged a distinctive literary identity for colonial Malaya or independent Malaysia. Through this examination on authorial composition, I argue for the merits of understanding the globalization of modern Chinese literature from the margins, and the value of harnessing critical thought from marginalized literary spaces.

To begin, I stress that the "Ma" in "Mahua literature" refers to postcolonial Malaysia, which gained independence in 1957, as well as to colonial Malaya, its historical antecedent. In addition, the "Ma" that stands for "Malaya" also indicates a discursive embodiment of a strong popular aspiration after World War II for a decolonized peninsula to be unified with Singapore as a nation-state.¹² Malaysia as a geopolitical unit located in Southeast Asia consists today of Peninsular Malaysia (West Malaysia) and Malaysian Borneo (East Malaysia). It is a multiracial and multilingual society whose ethnic composition in 2021 comprises 69.8 percent *bumiputera*, 22.4 percent Chinese, and 6.8 percent Indians.[13] The category *bumiputera* (sons of the soil) was created by the postcolonial state after 1963 to institute Malays and all indigenous peoples of the country as a group for preferential policy-making.[14] As a separate social category, the Chinese in Malaysia account for a minority yet constitute a politically significant Sinitic-speaking community that resides outside Macau, Hong Kong, Taiwan, and the mainland Chinese state.

In light of its colonial past and geographical location, Malaysia has long been a lively venue for migratory passages and cultural interactions that attest to the site's regional and global connectivities. The place also belongs to larger ethno-geographical imaginaries such as "Nanyang" (the South Seas) of the Chinese and "Nusantara" (the "Malay world") of the Malays.[15] Through its historical experiences, Mahua literature offers an unusual cartographical method for mapping "Malaysia" as a Chinese-language literary space that links the country's territories with other venues, including China, Taiwan, and Singapore. As an aggregated region of uneven development that sustains multiple traditions of creative writing across noncontiguous locales, the Mahua literary formation exceeds the country's geopolitical base in Southeast Asia.

From this perspective, Mahua literature refines Casanova's contention that "national literary space must not be confused with national territory."[16] Deemed nonnational by the Malaysian state, Mahua literary practices evince how all literary spaces, regardless of scale—not just national ones—should never be taken as congruent or fully associated with geographical areas under specific state control. Therefore, by indexing the divisions between literary and geopolitical realms, the analytical scale of "region"—which applies to configurations of area ranging from the subnational to the supranational—lends itself to foregrounding the flexible Mahua literary space.[17] This book, however, is concerned less with the ambiguous regionality of Mahua literature than with how that regionality is historically and rhetorically constructed. As the Mahua critic Chong Fah Hing 莊華興 suggests in the epigraph, defining the character of literary regions entails more than creating geographical compartments. Rather, the act involves subjective recognition by residents and outsiders alike who contextualize the area to achieve different discursive aims.

Malaysian Crossings presents varied perceptions of authors, critics, and scholars concerning "Mahua" as a holistic and distinctive literary region. It describes multidirectional connections among texts, ideas, and people in the "Sinophone South," my term for a largely self-sustaining corner that hosts little-explored creativity in the world-Chinese literary space. The Mahua writing practices featured in the book, spanning from the 1930s to the 2000s, throw into relief unconventional authorial identities that emerge from efforts to forge place-appropriate literary languages for portraying multilingual Southeast Asia. Negotiating between unbridled agency and absolute passivity in the margins, Mahua authors compose works whose linguistic modes register or shape the shifting boundaries of the Malayan-Malaysian literary domain. Disadvantaged but undeterred creatively, these authors are highly conscious of the transregional scales of literary address despite having only meager sociocultural capital. In delineating the "crossings," be they physical journeys, interactions among social groups, or mindset shifts that occur within and across interconnected literary spaces, the book examines the implications of the peripherized spaces' linked histories and their respective inner diversities on artistic form. Bearing signs of fluid geographical imaginaries, the resultant works reveal a unique manner of belonging to the world that is not readily discerned by literary actors in privileged locales.

NG KIM CHEW AND HIS LITERARY GALAPAGOS ARCHIPELAGO

To date, studies of world literature have not sufficiently foregrounded local and regional perspectives in maintaining the vitality of world literary systems. There is room for more scholarly work to affirm the contributions of cultural ecologies—not necessarily nation-based—that produce "literature of the world," the term that Pheng Cheah defines as stories and ideas that "seek to be disseminated, read, and received around the world so as to change it and the lives of people within it."[18] Of course, it matters not just where and how such world literature is written and read, but also where and how it is perceived. After all, as Longxi Zhang notes, world literature is always localized in practice and is "always a concept that changes in response to local needs and contexts."[19] Theories of how widespread literary configurations take on specific forms in different places, however, have portrayed local literary spaces as either inert receptacles of external ideas or undesirable situations to leave behind. In those accounts, literary spaces in the margins are often located outside of Europe, the region often deemed as the originary site of innovation. In one well-known example, Franco Moretti asserts that encounters of Western novels with non-Western contexts are "structural compromises," and proposes a triangulated formulation of world literature as a system of variations, comprising different combinations of foreign form (plot), local material (characters), and local form (narrative voice).[20]

Contrary to those theories, non-European regions are in fact vital sites for forging strategic regionalism, literary innovation, and the survival of minor literatures, all of which impact the renewal of large-scale cultural ecologies. To address scholarly indifference toward the margins, I introduce the idea of a "Literary Galapagos archipelago" (*wenxue de jialabage qundao* 文學的加拉巴戈群島) coined by the Malaysia-born scholar-cum-author Ng Kim Chew 黃錦樹. Ng is one of the most important figures in the production and the study of Mahua literature, and more broadly speaking, of the globalization of modern Chinese literature.[21] In dialogue with Pascale Casanova's conception of an autonomous literary world-system, Ng's "Galapagos archipelago" contributes an original trope to "world literary knowledges," which consist of the historically variant understandings of literature and poetics that enrich a "global repertoire of aesthetic epistemologies."[22] Notably, Ng who harbors the fundamental ambition of "not only explaining the world, but also to transform the world" through literary writing, speaks as a cultural actor with lived experiences in the geographical spaces of the symbolic archipelago he describes.[23] Through his voice we hear an actual islander whose articulations convey the historical and contemporary dimensions of marginalized Chinese literary formations in the world literary arena. Although his use of terms such as "isolation" and "margins" runs the risk of reinforcing the peripherality that Southeast Asia as a region bears in many disciplines, he does not seek to portray Malaysia as an inward-looking polity and economy. Rather, through the evocative archipelagic trope, he contemplates Malaysia's challenges in gaining external recognition as a valid literary location, and its predicament of being embedded in the fringes of multiple local and regional ecologies of culture.

Specifically, what can viewing Malaysia in terms of the "Literary Galapagos archipelago" offer us that extant analyses based on concepts of globalized literary networks cannot? Ng's striking metaphor functions like a form of what Lanny Thompson calls "heuristic geographies." According to Thompson, who analyzes symbolic representations of space in American studies, a heuristic provides "a practical method that attempts the solution of theoretical, empirical, or interpretative problems."[24] Heuristic geographies, then, are spatial configurations such as state, island, and world, each with discursive meanings that highlight the debatable assumptions of specific knowledge-producing contexts. Following Thompson's understanding, I approach Ng's archipelago-related musings as the basis of a fresh epistemological framework for analyzing Mahua literature's problematic positionality in world-Chinese literary space. Generating a new cartographic vision, Ng's "Literary Galapagos" gainsays the conventional association of margins with locational insignificance by adducing how an outlying world region can inadvertently host a sui generis ecology. In selecting a geographical area whose defining isolation and plethora of endemic species inspired Charles Darwin's theory of natural selection, his coinage casts Mahua literature as a seldom explored sociohistorical laboratory that nurtures consequential diversity for literature of and in the world despite its enduring precarity.

Ng's discursive affinity toward islands projects his position as an outsider to prevailing political and literary establishments, the coordinates of which emerge in the details of his biography, fictional writings, and scholarly concerns. Born in 1967 in Peninsular Malaysia, Ng moved north to Taiwan for college in 1986. He stayed on to pursue postgraduate studies in the 1990s, experiencing the island's transition into the postmartial law period. Now a naturalized Taiwanese citizen, he teaches at National Chi Nan University as a professor of Chinese literature. Besides his role as a scholar, he is also an award-winning author, a prolific literary critic, and an important editor of Mahua literary anthologies, working assiduously to document Mahua literary history.[25]

Citing Ng's third volume of short stories *Youdao zhidao* 由島至島 (From island to island), Carlos Rojas rightly points out that the island trope inflects Ng's creative writings.[26] In fact, if Ng had gotten his way with the publisher, the book would have been titled only in Malay as *Dari Pulau ke Pulau*, thus disguising itself as part of Malaysia's national literature, and suggesting the country's location in the Malay Archipelago.[27] From this perspective, the inter-islandic travels connoted by the 2001 volume's title indicates the concrete background of Ng's biographical and creative journey. Ng's residence in Taiwan coincided with the rise of its nativist politics whose clamors for migrants to assimilate recalls the Malay nationalism that had first driven him to leave Malaysia. What *From Island to Island* encapsulates, then, is Ng's desire to intervene in the twin literary spaces of Mahua and Taiwan—he speaks of moving "from one battleground to another battleground"—and to interrogate the parochial nativist discourses that marginalized him in both places.[28] When Ng attempted to rescale Chinese cultural regions in the mid-2000s and place Mahua creative writings beyond national frames, his double marginality prompted him to seek inspiration for inventing new horizons of literary language from the experiences of V. S. Naipaul, the Caribbean writer who felt perennially alienated from Trinidad, his place of birth in the islandic West Indies, as well as from metropolitan England where he settled down.[29]

Ng is, of course, not the only theorist of literary archipelagos. In modern Chinese literary studies, Brian Bernards channels inspiration from the Francophone critic Édouard Glissant, who works on the Caribbean, to propose that the Nanyang region (which conventionally corresponds to Southeast Asia) has inspired a multi-islandic networked cultural imaginary among ethnic Chinese writers. But Bernards focuses more on the "maritime interconnection and exchange" among regional locales than on the familiar semantic association of archipelagos with dispersed islands.[30] In a separate discursive lineage, the archipelago afforded Franco Moretti with an allusive trope to characterize European literary cultures as constituted by connected yet distinct spaces whose stylistic forms evolve apart from one another through influences across national regions.[31] Moretti's archipelagic model, however, reconsolidates a singular European canon, indicating a latent dominance of continental thought. Acting against such hierarchies of space, Brian Russell Roberts and Michelle Ann Stevens advocate "decontinentalizing" the United

States and the Americas by recasting both regions as islandic nodes in a plural archipelago.³²

Ng's spatial metaphor resonates with all these conversations, but he thinks through the archipelago in a unique way. First, Ng is rooted in the historical experiences of Malaysia—a region never regarded by local or nonlocal actors as exceptional—rather than mediated by narratives of expansive geopolitical territories such as Europe and the Americas. Indifferent to constructing any "planet-spanning archipelagic assemblage," his image of an inimitable island group does not offer a decentering model of archipelago that actively unseats the centrality of hegemonic continental formations.³³ Second, he also refrains from harnessing the multi-island trope to unify extraterritorial cultural production with the metropole, a strategy that informs Maria Rubins's vision of global Russian culture. Whereas Rubins theorizes multiply sited cultures with resonant ethnic and linguistic elements as a "polycentric" configuration that takes the form of "a chain of islands that appear independent and isolated but in fact are interconnected in space, as well as time," Ng avoids situating his Literary Galapagos archipelago in a nonhierarchical space, or seeing it as a symbol of a radically unbounded region.³⁴ On the contrary, the premise of his globalized Chinese literary space is a deeply stratified one:

> Prior to 1949, China had been regarded by Sinophone (*huawen* 華文) literature in the border regions as the literary fountainhead. To the field of international Sinology, modern Chinese-language (*zhongwen* 中文) literature has always meant only modern literature from China. China has always been the indisputable center of modern Chinese literature. Because Taiwan regarded itself as China ("Free China") after 1950, it was only in the wake of the debates over "native soil literature" that native consciousness gained traction and the cultural formation was gradually described as Taiwan literature. Besides Taiwan, the Sinophone literatures of Hong Kong, Singapore, and Malaysia have always named themselves after their own regions (such as Hong Kong literature, Mahua literature). All of them are the small islands in the Galapagos archipelago that is Chinese-language literature. They constitute what I call Sinophone literature (*huawen wenxue* 華文文學), which has always been regional and

local. Scholars from these different places deal with their own cases in silos with few attempts at integration. So configured, Sinophone Singapore and Malaysian literatures lie at the margins within the margins. (6)

Ng's Literary Galapagos archipelago elucidates the peripherality that encumbers Mahua literature (alongside the historically connected formation of Singapore Chinese-language literature). Toggling between two cartographic scales, Ng first describes modern Chinese-language literature (*zhongwen xiandai wenxue* 中文現代文學) as "the Galapagos archipelago of world literature" (*shijie wenxue li de Jialabage qundao* 世界文學裡的加拉巴戈群島) (2). He subsequently describes literatures from Taiwan, Hong Kong, Singapore, and Malaysia as "the small islands in the Galapagos archipelago that is Chinese-language literature" (*zhongwen wenxue de Jialabage qundao zhong de xiaodao* 中文文學的加拉巴戈群島中的小島) (6). Lastly, he switches the scale of his view and sets up modern Chinese literature as the global backdrop against which Taiwan and Hong Kong constitute "the small islands in the Galapagos archipelago that is Sinophone literature" (*huawen wenxue de Jialabage qundao zhong de xiaodao* 華文文學的加拉巴戈群島中的小島) (10). Following from Ng's logic, Singapore and Malaysia occupy the even smaller islands in the Sinophone Galapagos, marking a condition that he describes as lying "at the margins within the margins."

In short, the "Galapagos archipelago of world literature" in Ng's discursive map is his "world-Chinese literary system" (*zhongwen wenxue shijie tixi* 中文文學世界體系, literally "Chinese-language literary world-system") (5). Ng calls it "an independent system" elsewhere, when he describes the politics of recognition that disregards authors of modern Chinese literature in a world literary arena dominated by European languages.[35] Seen through the lens of Casanova's "world literary space," Ng's archipelagic trope of flexible scale vividly conveys the double-situatedness of the modern Chinese literary formation. In the international literary arena, Chinese-language writings are sidelined while prominence is given to works written in European languages such as French and English. Despite its store of creative works that command a global readership, the Chinese literary formation remains tangential to a world system sustained by dominant Euro-American centers, mirroring the core-periphery relations that structure the global political economy.³⁶ Yet Chinese-language literature also forms its own world-system, in which China is centered. By embodying mixed conditions of significance and insignificance, China embodies superimposed layers of globality seldom featured in world literary studies.

Likewise, Malaysia's nested marginality in the Galapagos Islands of world literature speaks to a coexistence of centrality and off-centeredness in a single location. Though scholars have also observed a similar cohabitation of varying shades of importance in the case of Taiwan, the fact that the East Asian island also regarded itself as "China" in the second half of the twentieth century disrupts my intended illustration of how a distant location hitherto seen and self-perceived as inconsequential generates an outsized value for global Chinese literary production. Overall, in this book I depart from the customary reliance on "China"—in all its historical figurations—as the universal template for contemplating the vicissitudes of modern Chinese-language literature, or the singular center that defines and moves the peripheries. Instead, I demonstrate how a place as inconspicuous as Malaysia can host its own set of overlapping core-periphery relations in the world-Chinese literary space.

Importantly, the case of Mahua literature pluralizes the circulatory patterns of world literature and refutes Moretti's claim that "movement [of forms] from one periphery to another (without passing through the center) is almost unheard of; that movement from the periphery to the center is less rare, but still quite unusual, while that from the center to the periphery is by far the most frequent."³⁷ Of crucial significance is how the transperipheral pattern of Mahua literary circumstances diverges from the accounts of successful creative mobility that world literary studies have thus far been interested in cataloguing. Whereas most discourses on world literature delineate achievements of writers and texts with wider circulation and reception, Mahua literature facilitates our understanding of the ways in which authors with limited resources and readership keep innovation alive in the literary peripheries by modulating the horizons of their knowledge and travels. Taking reference from Ng's theory of the Literary Galapagos for modern Chinese literature, and Mahua literature in particular, *Malaysian Crossings* addresses several important but unconventional questions for world literary studies: How do authors leverage the austerity of social and cultural capital to attain lasting creative outcomes in locations often forgotten by centers of cultural prestige? How do they also sustain their emotional belonging to a global literary ecology, and how do they strive to enrich it?

THE VALUE OF LITERARY MARGINALITY

Whereas Anderson contends that due to a combination of gatekeepers' linguistic and geographical favoritism, "nationalization ... means a kind of seclusion" for Southeast Asian literatures on the international stage, Mahua literature shows how its *nonnational* status has also sowed a profound sense of isolation in its authors.[38] Ng feels as if "Mahua literature is a disappearing formation," given the dire neglect on all fronts in Malaysia, from the lack of state support for Chinese-language education, to shrinking spaces for literary publication in Chinese-language newspapers, to diminishing market and critical attention.[39] Intriguingly, Ng develops his ideas about literary marginality despite an expanded reception for his creative undertakings. Although Ng's fictional works have now been translated into English and have gained tremendous popular success in the China market—at a scale far greater than in Taiwan, where most of his books are first published—he is fully aware of how linguistic and regional labels still dominate the politics of admittance in any global system of literature.[40] In his own words, "even if you think you don't wear any labels, the non-Chinese language writers will label you a 'Chinese-language writer'; or, even though you are already in the Chinese-language world, if you come from Malaysia, you will be given a 'Malaysian' label."[41] Evoking his earlier provincialization of Mahua literature in the Galapagos regions of nested world literary maps, his comment reveals the ways in which authors are subjected to sorting, labeling, and exclusion as long as they are treated as outsiders.

But rather than submitting to the lack of control over how Mahua literature is classified linguistically or geographically, Ng reflects deeply on how Mahua authors can exercise their agency—however limited it may be—through an endemism that still offers space for literary growth. To those acquainted with the history of science, it may be baffling that Ng evokes the Galapagos Islands to express the condition of literary isolation. For centuries, the region was the site of extractive exploitation and colonization, during which successive groups of Western explorers made expeditions to gather specimens for research and museum collections.⁴² As Rojas notes, Ng's interest in islands and archipelagos must be comprehended in view of his Southeast Asian background, his longstanding commitment to research on Southeast Asian Chinese literature, and the clues he inserts in his fictional works. Indeed, Ng's fascination with the cluster of equatorial volcanic islands off the Pacific coast of South America reflects his curiosity about how the splayed land formations contributed pivotal settings for the history of evolution.⁴³ Missing from the discussion, however, are the larger implications of the way he borrows concepts from evolutionary biology to interpret the spatialization of Chinese literary culture.

Although Ng first presented his idea of a Literary Galapagos archipelago at a conference in 2016, he has used this metaphor for the global development of Chinese culture since 2007.⁴⁴ Ng's geographical

FIGURE 0.1 Ng Kim Chew (seated, on the right) being introduced by David Wang (at the rostrum) and Carlos Rojas at the 2016 "Sinophone Studies: New Directions" conference held at Harvard University. The screen projects the title of Ng's keynote address: "A World Republic of Southern Letters—Our Literary Galapagos Islands: Observations from the standpoint of Mahua literature" (南方文學世界共和國—我們的文學加拉巴戈群島: 以馬華文學為立足點的觀察).

imagination is inspired by the twin theories of "adaptive radiation" (*fushe shiying* 輻射適應) and "evolution in isolation" (*geli yanhua* 隔離演化), which are commonly regarded as being responsible for the evolutionary progress of animals on the islands. He understands the former concept to mean that one ancestral species will give rise to multiple species by interacting with different ecological niches. "Adaptive radiation" would have been a fitting analogy to describe how Chinese people migrated from China to different world regions and created an array of rich cultural milieux. But in his observation of Mahua cultural realities, the dispersion of Chinese communities did not result in the flourishing of new bodies of place-based knowledge, which would have been akin to the diversification of species such as the Darwinian finches in the Galapagos Islands.[45]

Puzzled by why the process of descent with modification did not apply to the development of Chinese humanities outside China, Ng turned his attention to the forging of distinctive local characteristics for Chinese-language literature through "evolution in isolation." Tellingly, the subtitle of his 2016 talk, "Observations from the Standpoint of Mahua Literature," is evidence that the focal point of his contemplations throughout the years was always Mahua culture.[46] The stress on the local is also borne out by the ending of his 2018 article based on his earlier talk, in which he outlines a "Galapagos situation" that continues to shape and be shaped by autonomous transformations in various Sinitic-speaking regions: "Our Galapagos situation is the outcome of historical contingencies. The decline of the Chinese Empire, the isolation of the People's Republic of China, the colonization of Hong Kong, the shadows of Republican China in Taiwan and the island's repressed native experiences, the crisis-ridden Sinophone living environment of Malaysia—independent evolution occurs in those situations" (14). Here, Ng recognizes the incidental historical contexts that catalyze literary speciation through "independent evolution" that is corollary to geographical isolation. We can say that his discourse offers a paradigmatic account of literary evolution in action. According to him, the unique individual styles that result from the relative remoteness common among locales in Chinese-language literature's Galapagos archipelago evoke a shared creative principle:

Compared to China, the literatures of these islands have not been interrupted because of political interference. They have perpetuated, evolving at their own pace, producing works that could never have appeared in the Chinese mainland, such as those protean writing practices of Xi Xi 西西 and Ye Si 也斯 from Hong Kong; Ya Xian 瘂弦, Yang Mu 楊牧, and Hsia Yü 夏宇, the masters of modernist poetry from Taiwan; and, of course, the highly controversial and patently untranslatable works of fiction by Wang Wen-hsing 王文興 and Wu He 舞鶴. The "untranslatability" of texts should have been an important goal right from the start. That is the fundamental logic of the Literary Galapagos. (13–14)

Focusing on the world-Chinese literary space, Ng foregrounds the contingent emergence and delicate perpetuation of creative diversity in its literary peripheries. Citing a series of pathbreaking writers, he highlights how in off-center settings, they contribute to literary originality by "evolving at their own pace" and producing peerless accomplishments. In this way, Ng expands the approach of Yu-ting Huang, who also draws upon Darwin's experiences on the Galapagos Islands, albeit only to conceptualize Taiwan literature as "an archipelago with internal differences and comparativity."[47] Ng's commentary evokes remarks applied to Southeast Asia as well: his repeated mention of "meaningful differences" (12, 14) among works from various Chinese literary regions echoes an analogy used by Tan Swie Hian 陳瑞獻, well known for his vanguard contribution to Mahua modernist literature. Tan compared poets from Taiwan and Singapore-Malaysia to "snails that live and grow in different valleys," and whose shells "exhibit disparate colors and lines" that represent varied tastes and interests.[48]

In the extract quoted above, Ng identifies the "'untranslatability' of texts" (*wenben de "bukeyi"* 文本的"不可譯") as the raison d'être of the minoritized literary ecologies related to Taiwan, Hong Kong, Malaysia, and Singapore.[49] On the surface, his focus on the obstructed portage of language appears to restate the view of Emily Apter, who sees the concept of "untranslatability" as integral to "world forms of literature."[50] Apter contends that world literary studies should place its emphasis on observing the circulation of the "Untranslatable," which involves "words that assign new meanings to old terms, neologisms, names for ideas that are continually re-translated or mistranslated, translations that are obviously incommensurate."[51] In listing the writers' distinctive styles, Ng could well be channeling Darwin and saying, "the Galapagos seems a perennial source of new things," but his tone does not resemble the English naturalist's air of enchantment.[52] At the end of his article, Ng touches on the transient fragility of the Galapagos situation: "In time to come, when those contingent historical conditions vanish, those meaningful differences may also dissipate" (14).

Given the melancholy that permeates his article, Ng's goal is incongruent with Apter's spirited "experiment of imagining what a literary studies contoured around untranslatability might be."[53] Whereas Apter prefers comparative literary studies to provide "self-updating world-systems" that can reflect dynamic geopolitics and the attendant socioeconomic mapping,[54] Ng recruits the reality of global cultural economy to shape his description of how minor types of modern Chinese literature get by in resource-poor conditions. Echoing the "untranslatable singularity" depicted in his short story "Kebei" 刻背 (Inscribed backs), Ng's spotlight on "untranslatability" in the Literary Galapagos signals his dedication toward composing distinctive works that exploit the uniqueness of Chinese language.[55]

Ng's theory of the Literary Galapagos thus shows that the value of marginality for stimulating a literary world-system lies in aesthetic particularity, derived from both place and language. It is worth noting here that one of the novels by Wu He 舞鶴, a Taiwan writer Ng considers untranslatable, is now available in English.[56] Therefore, even though Ng contends that through the "untranslatability" of their creative peculiarities, marginalized authors indicate—in a counterintuitive manner—the merits of their worldly literary existence, it is arguably through the yet-to-be-translated rather than the untranslatable that non-China authors can provide promising contributions to world literature. While the marks of untransferable specificity can certainly be read as forms of resistance against dominant forces in the world literary space, they function more productively as invitations to understand the peripherized literary formations on their own terms. Mahua authors demonstrate that limited acknowledgment in both domestic and foreign arenas does not mean succumbing to the constraints posed by asymmetrical literary relations.

Despite their works' circumscribed reception, the indifference they encounter leads them to forge novel understandings of the worth of their writing practices for the world.

CHARTING THE SINOPHONE SOUTH

Building on Ng's spatial evaluation of modern Chinese literary production, this book assembles discourses on Chinese cultural regions and illuminates networks of interaction formerly obscured by a singular core-periphery framework in the world-Chinese literary space. It responds to ongoing discussions about the "Sinophone," the term Shu-mei Shih coined and defines as "a network of places of cultural production outside China and on the margins of China and Chineseness."[57] Shih rectifies the field's ingrained preference for the mainland state, which has resulted in uneven recognition for Chinese-language literature from other world regions. Through his historiographical effort, David Wang modifies Shih's "Sinophone" configuration to include China more comprehensively, yielding a "new literary cartography" for the "world of Chinese literature" that accommodates "multiplying individual voices, regional soundings, dialectical accents, and local expressions that are in constant negotiation with official linguistic and literary mandates."[58] His move directs modern Chinese literary studies toward addressing the inner heterogeneity of China, which resonates with a comparable approach to world literature that dehomogenizes Europe by accentuating the continent's highly differentiated internal development.[59] The discrepant views of Shih and Wang notwithstanding, Mahua literature is regarded in both scholars' formulations as an exemplar of "Sinophone literature" for its outstanding attributes that index the diversity of Southeast Asian creative writings in Sinitic languages.

But Shih's and Wang's frameworks originate from academic contexts located beyond Malaysia, with audiences who cherish different expectations for modern Chinese literary studies. Concomitantly, Malaysia has nurtured its own local traditions of assessing the link between place and literary language through native-born or on-site authors and critics who write and interpret Mahua literature differently than their colleagues in other regions. Whereas Shih and Wang render Mahua literature as part of *huayu yuxi wenxue* 華語語系文學, the same cultural formation is regarded as an instance of *huawen wenxue* 華文文學, according to the lineage of local self-understandings, which has been inadequately recognized for promoting the growth of Mahua literary ecology. Though both umbrella categories in Chinese share the rubric of "Sinophone literature" in English, the two Chinese referents are used in academic venues with differing intellectual priorities, and they have divergent implications for knowledge production.⁶⁰

In comparison to *huayu yuxi wenxue* primarily designating literary formations associated with sites that resist expansionist ambitions or the propagation of hegemonic Chineseness, *huawen wenxue* points to the actual use of the term by Mahua critics and scholars for producing locally grounded readings of a wider selection of the Mahua literary corpus. In this book, I devote greater attention to "Sinophone" (*huawen*) as sustained articulations produced in the Malaysia-related regions of the Literary Galapagos that carry either a non-China or an off-China orientation. Situating the "Sinophone" within the *huawen* rather than the *huayu yuxi* context, I treat the notion as emerging from the historical perspectives of literary actors whose discursive practices have become integral to the cultural politics of the Mahua community.⁶¹

Whether the conversations concern the scope of the Sinophone, or the extent to which local and regional discourses should be examined in tandem when Mahua literary works are interpreted, debates in modern Chinese literary studies amid its global turn since the mid-2000s indicate how the Sinophone can serve the valuable function of conceptual and locational disambiguation by advocating for place-differences. More importantly, the contest over defining the Sinophone begs a broader inquiry. In order to highlight the world-making capacities of literature related to minoritized locations, how should scholars approach the study of socioliterary formations that do not fit nation-based frameworks but allow opportunities to jointly examine the local and global aspects of those formations?

Ng's conception of a regional Sinophone literary community that amplifies the "Galapagos situation" provides a launchpad for appraising the ways in which authors tack deftly between domestic cultural politics and global literary developments. To Ng, the Sinophone (*huawen*) as a mode of literary expression also demarcates a region called the South (*nanfang* 南方), which remains outside the global centers of recognition. Ng's ideational literary community includes places such as Taiwan, Hong Kong, and Malaysia, each with varying historical entanglements with nationhood. Those sites share the "condition of occupying an external positionality," which is manifested through the "southern customs, southern topolects, and colonial experiences" that lie outside the concerns of twentieth-century China, the literary center of the world-Chinese literary space (12). There is another significant commonality: given how all three places are still finding their literary footholds by exploring the depths of their own histories, they lend themselves very well to forming a larger *nanfang huawen wenxue gongheguo* 南方華文文學共和國 (a designation that Ng renders as "Republic of Southern Sinophone Literature" in English). As an imaginary alliance "without centers and national borders," this alternative conception repurposes Casanova's divided and hierarchical "World Republic of Letters" for a utopic account of Chinese literary history (12).

On the one hand, Ng's envisioned community successfully dismantles Casanova's model of world literature, which only accommodates unidirectional migration to literary centers from the margins. Furthermore, the transperipheral linkages Ng foregrounds exist in tandem with the productive isolation that is vital for sustaining the South's literary diversity. His perspective parallels how, in the Darwinian case in the history of science, "the large number of islands in the group would allow repeated inter-island colonizations by species having achieved reproductive isolation on another island."[62] As Ng points out, Singapore and Malaysia have long been influenced by Hong Kong and Taiwan, especially in the second half of the twentieth century (6). Calling to build greater interdependence among Sinophone literary locales (14), his proposal is tantamount to contending that the "insular interlinkings" do not hinder each member locale from adapting trends external to its own local context.[63] On the other hand, Ng's take on a Republic of Letters also revises Chow Tse-tsung's sanguine appeal in the late 1980s to interpret Sinophone Southeast Asian literature in terms of "multiple literary centers" and a "double tradition" that comprises a "Chinese literary tradition" and a "native literary tradition." Chow's framework, however, does not adequately consider the reality whereby places outside of China are slotted

Introduction: Southern Crossings 19

into a taxonomy of marginalities.[64] Speculative though it is, Ng's Republic of Southern Sinophone Literature indicates the possibility of a world-Chinese literary history grounded in local and regional specificities.

Inspired by the same possibility, I translate Ng's *nanfang huawen* (Southern Sinophone) as the "Sinophone South" to emphasize the regionality that the *huawen* mode of literary language maps. Admittedly, the concept will evoke the "Global South," an analytical descriptor that has replaced "Third World" in particular references to underdeveloped nation-states after the Cold War. In literary and cultural studies, the Global South additionally delineates a postnational and noncontiguous geography of social groups that occupy the internal margins of globalized sites of affluence, and depicts transnational political subjects who recognize their common subjugation by contemporary global capitalism.[65] The critical rubric has since entered the horizon of Chinese literary and cultural studies, focusing on its promise of self-empowerment practices and transperipheral cooperation.[66]

Indeed, the Sinophone South resembles its conceptual twin insofar as they both "unhinge the South from a one-to-one relation to geography."[67] For both concepts, the "South" is installed as a special articulatory position that points toward a multiplicity of local contexts, alongside resource-poor conditions, internal diversities, and multifarious connections. What differentiates the Sinophone South from the Global South, however, is that the former is relatively limited geographically, compared to the hemispheric scale of the latter. Additionally, although the Sinophone South also emphasizes differential relations, it does not necessarily define itself through an imaginary that resists a hegemonic "North." There is no "Sinophone North" analogous to a "Global North," so to speak. Instead, "South" (*nanfang*) and "Sinophone" (*huawen*) must be understood as mutual definitions for each other. In juxtaposing the two terms and making them synonymous, Sinophone South highlights how literary actors capitalize on marginality, thus shaping distinctive local and regional cultural ecologies as the sites of an alternative globality.

Conveying a global literary vision uninterested in competing with other forms of metaregionalism in contemporary Chinese culture (such as "Cultural China" and "Greater China"), the Sinophone South projects the condition of compounded liminality and imposed provinciality, a condition shared by small-scale literatures and critical writings, as an unintended strength.⁶⁸ The Sinophone South also offers a framework that enhances the visibility of literary singularities and their interlocal ties among various peripherized sites. Leveraging the Sinophone South, I document an array of intermarginal relations without homogenizing these linkages, thus sustaining a mix of literary diversity and solidarity. By elaborating on a Mahua localism and regionalism that turns out to be consequential for creative innovation despite relative isolation, my study fashions a fresh vantage point from the margins to consider the global order of modern Chinese literary production in its totality. China remains in the analytical picture, but only as a node in a larger grid of fluid, polylocal connections.

Characterized by a judicious blend of the local and the global, the Sinophone South denotes imaginative modes of connecting with the world, expressed through Sinitic literary languages. Indexing places with the common quandary of forging locally inflected compositional practices, the conceptual rubric stages the ways in which writers situate themselves vis-à-vis resident literary fields, broader geographical regions, as well as through their own understandings of world literature. By analyzing Mahua authorial and interpretive practices at critical moments in the long twentieth century, I flip the common approach of adopting nonnative frameworks to investigate literary conceptions designated as *shijie* 世界 (world) in sites external to locales whose centralities are too often seen as given. In this regard, the Sinophone South captures a plural archive of minoritized literary and critical thought that is produced from localized Malaysian axes, which in turn rewrites literary globalization as a vernacular process with cross-regional valences. For the making of varied literary regionalities, the concept compels us to think of the local as a nonnational scale of composition and analysis, and the global as a form of cultural practice whose dynamism does not always entail traversing national borders.

THE GALAPAGOS PARADOX AND WORLD-ORIENTED CROSSINGS

To convey the artistic vitality of the Sinophone South, this book explicates three forms of literary worlding, or the process by which literary actors conceive, bridge, and adapt ideas, texts, and creative practices across time and space. The authorial acts of mediating between the local and the global—with both scales of cultural formation enfolding protean ways of literary being and repertoires of practices—constitute the "worlding" of modern Chinese literature in the first sense. Adopting this mode of worlding, Mahua authors exhibit a particular style of composition animated by concurrent concerns for situatedness and mobility. Specifically, they express a cosmopolitan identification with more than one location, the lack of wider appreciation notwithstanding. The stylistic orientation, which results in a "Galapagos Paradox," is manifest in how Mahua literature's resigned recognition of its minoritized circumstances in the world-Chinese literary space ironically becomes the impetus—rather than a hurdle—for nurturing its capacity for artistic innovation. Making the best of difficult conditions, Mahua authors wield marginality not only to serve their creative purposes of connecting with different people and places but also to overcome a dearth of readership engagement. In other words, this "Galapagos Paradox" names the covert globality of the Mahua literary formation, which simultaneously addresses local and translocal understandings of world-oriented writing practices.

To highlight the seemingly contradictory logic that drives Mahua literary production, I have developed the concept of "Malaysian crossings." This overarching theme concerns how writers in the Sinophone South maintain imaginaries of being part of the world despite encountering general disregard by composing locally specific tales that manifest inventiveness rather than pursue approval by established cultural centers. The literary isolation conveyed by the archipelagic trope of the Sinophone South projects an uneasy relationship with the world rather than a disengagement from it. It is this troubled complementarity and interdependence between the local and the global, alongside the abiding desire for community and cosmopolitan belonging of the literary actors, that I carefully evaluate through the lens of "Malaysian crossings."

With its focus on the act of creative composition, *Malaysian Crossings* foregrounds the passages of traveling or migratory authors who navigate layered spatial scales through fictional explorations. The "crossings" theme also marks how Mahua literature embodies global, local, and other regional scales of literary interests as they interact simultaneously. Figuratively speaking, Mahua literature engages modern Chinese literature not from a satellite position, but from one that generates its own matrix of multiple centers and multiple margins. Entwined with varied combinations of center-periphery relations as it overlaps with Sinitic literary production in other locales such as Singapore, Taiwan, and China, Mahua literature mediates different types of transregional ties. Depending on the historical period and discursive context, writers and critics frame Mahua literature as provincial (a subnational area of China), national (when it is treated as being from Malaysia, Taiwan, or China), or supranational (for instance, when it is invoked as Nanyang to refer to Southeast Asia). Under this focally adaptable lens, the various Chinese-Sinophone literary regions once demarcated into clear-cut territories begin to lose their edges. By elucidating the styles of imagination and composition that enable locales to become cohesive areas for aesthetic depiction and academic study, I illustrate how social actors discursively regionalize colonial Malaya or independent Malaysia as valid literary terrain.

Through their varied journeys, authors and critics of Mahua literature also show how being mobile yet regionally confined in the Sinophone South can turn out to be a potent source of worldliness. By "worldliness" I mean, primarily, the awareness Mahua authors demonstrate when they fashion works that acknowledge being situated in particular sets of geographical and historical circumstances. Remarkably, they write without the support of time-honored cultural traditions or established idioms, and yet—to borrow David Wang's gloss on literary worlding—forge their own "complex and dynamic process of ever-renewing realities, sensations, and perceptions."[69] Juggling endogenous developments and exogenous influences in the Sinophone South, the authors register the worldliness of their fictional practices by giving form to heterogenous human-interest stories that they weave into larger social histories.

Mahua literature's worldliness is also constituted, à la Edward W. Said, by the critical undertaking of "linking works to each other" and bringing "them out of the neglect and secondariness to which for all kinds of political and ideological reasons they had previously been condemned."[70] According to Said, the inclusion of erstwhile narrowly interpreted texts requires scholars to regard those texts "as literature, as style, as pleasure and illumination," the task of which involves "the restoration of such works and interpretations of their place in the global setting."[71]

The reinstitution "can only be accomplished by an appreciation not of some tiny, defensively constituted corner of the world, but of the large, many-windowed house of human culture as a whole."[72] I frame this second sense of "worlding" in my study by the concept "Malaysian crossings," which cues us to notice the Mahua literary formation's unusual connective power. In the Sinophone South, Mahua authors and critics forge the worldliness of Mahua literary works via a restorative process of mediating plural ties among texts, ideas, and people that is similar to the one Said describes. Keenly aware of their stations in the world-Chinese literary space, these actors reconfigure relations within the space and reposition neglected texts from a "corner of the world" based on their own yardsticks of artistic accomplishment, without treating them as mere "informative ethnographical specimens."[73] Being well aware of Mahua literature's marginality, they remain undiscouraged and use its liminal condition as the basis for theorizing its history of becoming an acknowledged literary formation by the reading public it addresses.

Combining Mahua literature's depictions of authors' migratory journeys as well as its twin emphases on speciation and iterative displacement, *Malaysian Crossings* joins existing studies in demonstrating a multiscalar logic of Chinese literary perpetuation that relies on peripherized formations invigorating larger cultural ecologies.[74] It shows Mahua literature negotiating its embeddedness in different geographical scales of cultural production, ranging from the subnational, to the national, as well as to the translocal and the global. Through an ongoing assessment of the inner diversity that informs Mahua literary production, the book teases out a relational dynamic in the Sinophone South whereby margins interact with other margins—or even beget their own margins—in order to forge distinction among local literary communities in the world-Chinese literary context. This dynamic illustrates an important yet unelucidated perspective on the process of worlding literature via paracentral ties: authors may choose to cultivate relationships of proximity to relatively dominant centers without submitting to cooptative terms.

Thus, we see how the literary actors' creative investment in the Sinophone South fosters a third and final sense of "worlding:" the coming into being of Mahua works (which index socioliterary spaces imagined and inhabited) as plural counterpoints to the modes of composition that occur in the central regions of the world-Chinese literary space. Adapting the hegemons' tendency to invent differences and mutually exclusive essences, "Malaysian crossings" provides an interpretive prism to track a politics of literary identity that defines a separation between centers and margins from the perspective of the latter rather than the former. Deliberately provincial in character, the separation is one that still connects, giving prominence to how literary subjectivities and solidarities are constituted in the Sinophone South, the process of which enacts the joint effects of the local and the transregional. Spatialized yet not completely unbounded, Mahua literature features a poetics of location, dislocation, and relocation that also occurs in other circumscribed constituencies of the Sinophone South. Between keeping to and being kept at the periphery, writers devise aesthetic markers of innovation for their individuated literary endeavors and in so doing, engender precious singularities for the world-Chinese literary space.

Such a world-oriented mode of relation-making holds implications for rethinking the politics of modern Chinese literary taxonomy that is often mired in parameters of language, ethnicity, and nationality.[75] Combinations of these three criteria greatly determine the legibility of literary formations in discursive, institutional, and market settings. To reclassify literature in the global age, David Porter proposes harnessing its "migratory tendency," noting that "literary history is composed not of points but of vectors."[76] His sole focus on material texts, however, elides the significance of embodied individuals engaged with creative writing. Besides texts, authors can also be regrouped according to Porter's suggested category of "trajectory" rather than nationality, and hence disrupt conventional ways of classifying Chinese-language literature.[77] Training my analytical lens on both authors and their works, I underscore the historical loci—approached as both locations and paths—of Mahua writing practices in the Sinophone South.

COSMOPOLITAN JUNCTURES

Mapping four loci generated from "Malaysian crossings," I elucidate what I call the "cosmopolitan junctures" of Mahua literary history from the 1930s to the 2000s. To avoid characterizing Mahua texts as invariably writing back against China, my study parses authorial agency during the British colonial period, as well as during times of decolonization, the Cold

War, and post–Cultural Revolution China. Throughout these periods, local and global interests cohered to spur literary production related to Malaya or Malaysia. Complementing the book's focus on spatiality, I incorporate Doreen Massey's temporalized notion of "place" as "articulated moments in networks of social relations and understandings."[78] This idea allows me to emphasize the importance of putting the linked situatedness of cultural production into historical context across locales in the Sinophone South, as well as to stress how the passage of time that is necessary for people, texts, and discourses to circulate is also integral to forge the worldliness of Mahua literature.

In other words, these significant moments of entangled histories shed light on literary worlding through a multifocal analytical method that is attentive to the cultural politics within and beyond Malaya or Malaysia as a noteworthy literary region. The method is consciously "place-based," in Arif Dirlik's sense of a locality with "a flexible and porous boundary around it, without closing out the extralocal, all the way to the global."[79] In my analyses, I shift my attention among the imbricated regional scales that are germane to Mahua literature, as the creative formation connects unevenly developed Chinese literary spaces.

Organized chronologically, *Malaysian Crossings* studies the coevolution of social locations and literary languages—including both Chinese and English—borne by stylized literary expressions. The writers' fictional worlds encode alternative visions about Malayan or Malaysian linguistic localization and place-making over the long twentieth century. Featuring inter-Asian literary relations between colonial Malaya (or independent Malaysia) and other Sinitic-speaking locales (China, Taiwan, and Singapore), the book analyzes two major proclivities: representations of multilingual social realities and metareflections on spatiality. It shows how meanings of place and language coalesce differently when Mahua writers and critics mediate local self-understandings and extralocal perspectives on the linguistic and ethnic dimensions of Malaya or Malaysia. This study thereby restores the literary region's historical locatedness in the Sinophone South's network of marginalized cultural locales, and more broadly, within a globalized Chinese literary order.

Introducing little-discussed forms of the place-language nexus that create the literary geography of Malaya or Malaysia, I bring together four case studies that pose taxonomic challenges to Mahua literature: first, an immigrant writer whose foundational text for Malayan Chinese literature was first published off-site in Shanghai (Lin Cantian 林參天); second, a sojourning Anglophone public intellectual who was misperceived as a Chinese-language author (Han Suyin 韓素音); third, a China-born writer who visited Southeast Asia to trace her heritage (Wang Anyi 王安憶); and fourth, a Sarawak-born writer who emigrated to Taiwan and resisted identifying as Malaysian (Li Yongping 李永平). Collectively, these "constitutive others" of the Mahua literary formation shape the mutual becoming of place and language as well as offer us bracing exemplars of a delicate yet also resilient globality.

In the first two chapters we see how Lin Cantian and Han Suyin developed Malayan-specific narrative strategies for the making of authorial selves and for establishing Malaya as worthy of literary depiction. Chapter 1 features Lin's pioneering practice, which fashioned him as a local insider to audiences in both China and Malaya in the 1930s. Unbeknown to many, Lin's composition of *Nongyan* 濃煙 (Thick smoke)—the first novel of Sinophone Malaysian and Singapore literary history—in Malaya was guided by the concept of the "language of the masses" that traveled from China. The transposed influence resulted in Lin's attempt to foster a place-appropriate literary language that exoticized and evoked familiarity in concert through registering Malaya's plurilinguality. On the other hand, the novel's eventual publication in Shanghai can be attributed to a circumstantial confluence: the weak Mahua cultural infrastructure could not support the publication of a full-length novel, whereas the reading public in China's premier cultural center demonstrated great interest in Nanyang in the 1920s and 1930s. Conceptually speaking, Lin's case enacts a neglected dialogue between Sinophone studies and the studies of Chinese overseas through *Thick Smoke*'s portrayal of local Chinese societies' fragmentation into "dialect groups" (*fangyan qun* 方言群). Through the lens of dialect group interaction, the novel prompts scholars to reckon with the heterogeneity of overseas Chinese communities seldom factored into literary studies.

Chapter 2 further grounds Mahua literature in its nonhomogenous sociocultural milieu by arguing that Han Suyin composed Anglophone literature as world literature in 1950s and 1960s Malaya with inspiration from Sinophone practices. Embracing both local and global perspectives, Han's writing practice was embedded in her broader cultural advocacy to affirm Malaya as a model for multiracialism, multilingualism, and multiculturalism amid decolonization in Asia. As a public intellectual based in the Southeast Asian locale, Han highlighted the sociocultural contributions of Malayan Chinese under colonial rule. Her cultural politics projected a misrecognition of her as a Chinese-language writer, which unexpectedly enabled her to extend the reach of her activism. Of particular interest are the ways in which she communicated localizing strategies across the linguistic divide that separated the Malayan Chinese literary community into the Chinese-educated and the English-educated. Most significantly, her model for the interactive adaptation of place and language was Malayan Chinese language, which appeared to her as having successfully differentiated itself from the language in China. Through composing the novel *And the Rain My Drink* and the unfinished sequel *Freedom Shout Merdeka*—two works that contain traces of Sinitic-influenced English—she gestures toward the interrelating of margins as a feasible way of reorienting cultural traffic. She also demonstrates how Anglophone literature can participate in place-making and nation-building by developing a hybrid English literary language that emulates the localizing orientation of Chinese language in Malaya.

The second half of the book highlights the place-catalyzed imaginaries and writing practices of authors who cast their literary gazes at the Malaysian region from afar. In chapter 3, we see how in the early 1990s, writers from both China and Malaysia approach their respective literary lineages as cosmopolitan cultural formations constrained by different scales of marginality. In 1991, Wang Anyi visited the Singapore-Malaysian region where her father was born. She subsequently composed the novella *Sadness of the Pacific* (Shangxin Taipingyang 傷心太平洋), which features an autobiographical narrator decoding the meanings of displaced ancestral bonds. Driven by a recurring notion that "on a map, continents are also drifting islands," the novella provincializes China by assembling a range of translocal human mobility through different characters who embody diverse routes and origins. Alongside the artistic exploration of her genealogy beyond China, Wang was searching for an ideal literary language that aims for the broadest reception. Her pursuit of what I call the "cosmopolitan Chinese literary vernacular" converged with her reflection on the travels of Chinese language in the world.

We can then turn to Wang's writing practice as an inadvertent example of literary cooperation in world literature's Galapagos Islands. Her practice pluralized the endeavors of the root-seeking literary movement in 1980s and early 1990s China by extending the group's geographical ambit; moreover, her contemporaneous nonfictional discourses about Malaysia and Singapore intersected with a localizing imperative emerging in the Mahua literary space. Relaying Wang's perception of language shift in Nanyang and her comparison of novelistic languages across China and Taiwan, Ng Kim Chew theorized *zhongwen* 中文 and *huawen*, the two interchangeable words in daily use, as a pair of terms that frames divergent linguistic modes of diasporic Chinese literature. Whereas the former relies heavily on traditional Chinese aesthetic resources, thereby indicating an unreflective reverence for the source culture in China, the latter draws on local social realities and senses of place to formulate regionally inflected poetics of literary works. This stylistic distinction Ng identified in the 1990s informs the conceptual foundation of Sinophone studies that emerged later in the mid-2000s.

Reflecting on the multisited production of Chinese literature, the last chapter uses Mahua literature in Taiwan to illuminate an organizational modality of world-Chinese literary space that does not assume dependency on China as the cultural fountainhead, but instead recognizes the power of transperipheral relations for literary world-making. By parsing the decision of naturalized Taiwanese author Li Yongping to write about his native Borneo in the 2000s, I couch Li's writing practice as a form of "off-center articulation" that entails strategic distancing from the dominant voices in both Mahua and Taiwan literary spaces. Furthermore, by comparing the China edition of his novel *Dahe jintou* 大河盡頭 (Where the Great River ends) to the original edition published in Taiwan, I delineate two coexisting textual gateways to worlding literature. When oriented toward his PRC audience, Li argues for the cosmopolitan development of the Chinese language through his use of Chinese characters to transcribe local languages in Borneo. In both editions, his worlding of Chinese as a literary language overlays his novelistic representation of Bornean indigeneity that is inspired by the flourishing of indigenous writings and studies in Taiwan since the 1990s. In Li's dual relationship with world literature, we can see how a Chinese-language writer maintains a paradoxical proximity and distance from China at once, and the striking manner in which his self-positioning straddles intranational and transregional literary concerns.

By coordinating the varying effects of native conditions alongside diasporic pressures on creative writings, the overlays of scalar connections conjured by Mahua literature in the Sinophone South thus evoke new ways of understanding the architecture of global literary relations. The Mahua literary field typifies the oft-neglected native spaces in current models of world literature, which—in spite of marginalization—are never static geographic locales passively penetrated by flows of people, ideas, and texts. Instead, these domestic spaces are shot through with global and local ties that mediate centrifugal and situated modes of social and literary belonging.

Ultimately, *Malaysian Crossings: Place and Language in the Worlding of Modern Chinese Literature* shows the paradox of how Mahua writers' grasp of their own marginality constitutes the threshold instead of a barrier to creating signature aesthetic imprints that nonetheless foster global outlooks. The book demonstrates the ways in which the fraught construction of identities in and among the literary peripheries can be as lively as the dynamics of reciprocal influence, position-taking, and community-building operating at the centers. The multiscalar transregionality thrives on asymmetry of cultural dominance, splitting and reconfiguring Sinitic-speaking communities, while also occasioning flexible constellations of Chinese-language literature. Functioning within and beyond native literary spaces that transcend established regional classifications, this foundational mechanism governs the depth and diversity of creative expression in the world-Chinese literary space.

CHAPTER ONE

Doubly Local

Lin Cantian and the Contrapuntal Genesis of Mahua Novelistic Fiction

In July 1936, Shanghai's Literature Press (Wenxue chubanshe 文學出版社) published *Nongyan* 濃煙 (Thick smoke), long hailed as the earliest novel in Mahua (Malayan and Malaysian Chinese) literary history.[1] Written by Lin Cantian 林參天 (1904–1972), the novel was included in the Literature Society Book Series (Wenxueshe congshu 文學社叢書), which featured works by luminaries such as Mao Dun 茅盾 and Hu Feng 胡風. In addition, it was advertised along with titles belonging to another series, the World Literary Repertoire (Shijie wenku 世界文庫). Both collections were distributed by the prominent Shanghai Life Bookstore (Shanghai shenghuo shudian 上海生活書店).

The marketing copy for *Thick Smoke* promoted it as a foreign tale from a distant land. Alluding to the late Qing fantasy novel *Jinghua yuan* 鏡花緣 (Flowers in the mirror) by Li Ruzhen 李汝珍, the advertisement heightened the exoticism that mainland Chinese readers associated with Nanyang 南洋—the so-called South Seas region mapping primarily onto contemporary Southeast Asia, at the center of which is Malaya and Singapore. The ad promised a reading experience that would deliver vicarious pleasure and intense thought provocation: "The author has woven in many vignettes of Nanyang's natural landscape and social customs. After perusing the novel, readers in China will feel that they have stepped into the setting of *Flowers in the Mirror*."[2]

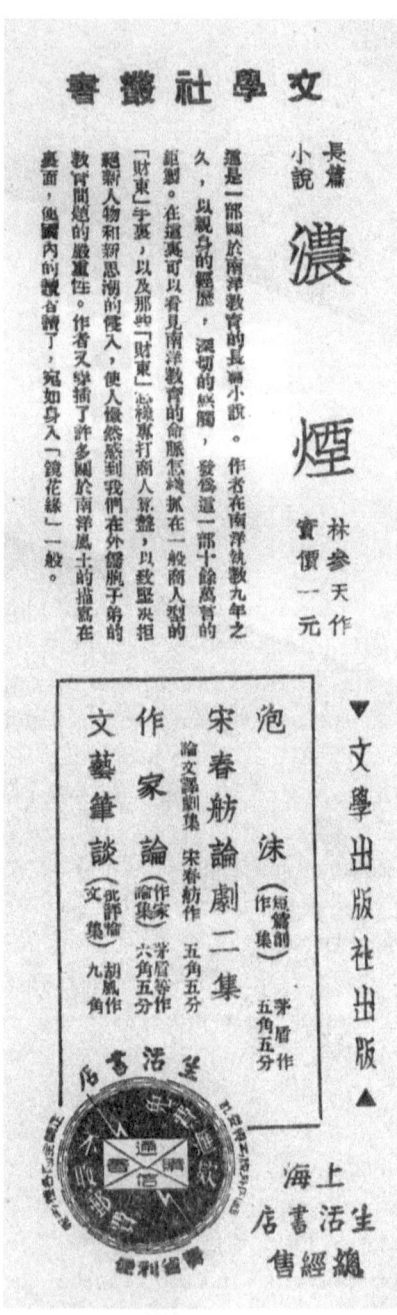

FIGURE 1.1 Advertisement of *Thick Smoke* in the literary journal *Guangming* 1 no. 6 (1936), where the novel was billed as a title in the Literary Society Book Series

The reference to Li's nineteenth-century literary work is not unfounded. His canonical novel portrays men of letters passing through strange places outside their homeland, and Lin's *Thick Smoke* portrays learned men intruding upon communities living in peculiar locations abroad. In this Mahua story, new teachers from China seek employment at a school in Malaya. Among the newcomers, the two leading characters find themselves living and working among ethnic Chinese who use an unfamiliar *fangyan* 方言 (topolect, often called "dialect" in existing social science literature on the Chinese overseas).[3] Depicting a contest between two camps, which hold conservative and reformist ideas on education respectively, the narrative describes social layers and hierarchies resulting from linguistic and native-place groupings within the local Chinese community. Semi-autobiographical in nature, *Thick Smoke* is based on the experiences of its author. Lin Cantian cotaught with the famous scholar Tan Yunshan 譚雲山 at a Chinese-medium school in the Malayan peninsula in the late 1920s.[4] According to Tan, *Thick Smoke* caused a sensation in the mainland Chinese literary arena after it was published and was widely recognized as the "only monumental work" (*weiyi juzhu* 唯一巨著) that reflects the circumstances of overseas Chinese education.[5]

Given that scholars have been tenacious in determining Mahua literature's point of genesis,[6] it is noteworthy that Lin and his pioneering authorial practice have hitherto received little critical attention.[7] Even though studies have considered Lin's work, they have not fully addressed how *Thick Smoke* embodies the intersection of contextual forces from across the Malayan and Shanghai literary fields. Striking an alternative note, this chapter offers an in-depth account of the relationship between the formal dimensions of Lin's writing practice and the historical mobility of people and ideas. I contend that *Thick Smoke* was published as a result of fortuitous, converging circumstances involving an inadequate cultural infrastructure in Nanyang and substantial interest in the Southeast Asian region among China's academics and publishers in the 1920s and 1930s. This line of inquiry entails adopting a supralocal approach that does not merely focus on a single site, examining instead the intertwining histories of Chinese-language literary spaces around the mid-1930s.

Notably, in this chapter, the geographical scale of the "local" takes on a set of coupled meanings, referring to a distinct location in the world, as well as to a subnational region of China. Bearing the doubleness of the local scale in mind, I propose reading *Thick Smoke* "contrapuntally" in the spirit of Edward W. Said's reassessment of cultural archives. Said suggests that a contrapuntal reading concerns an "awareness both of the metropolitan history that is narrated and of those other histories against which (and together with which) the dominating discourse acts."[8] And indeed, Lin's novel can be considered from the connected vantage points of the Mahua literary space and the mainland Chinese literary space in the early decades of the twentieth century. My analysis interprets the two literary ecologies in tandem, foregrounding the ways in which the cultural identity of a migrant author like Lin can be understood as a "contrapuntal ensemble" constituted by "an array of opposites, negatives, oppositions."[9]

Reading *Thick Smoke* through this interlocal approach helps us see how Lin forges the Sino-Malayan connection at two levels. First, given that the Chinese in Malaya are largely migrants from the provinces of Fujian and Guangdong in southeastern China, the novel can be studied as a social allegory of the *waijiang ren* 外江人—a category of Malayan Chinese that encompasses all non-Fujian and non-Guangdong migrants. Representing social dynamics in the Mahua literary circle, the tale intimates Lin's own suppressed status as a *waijiang ren* among southerner writers before *Thick Smoke*'s publication in Shanghai, the premier cultural center of China. The novel demonstrates how Malaya plays host to a regional tension displaced from China that gets enfolded into local interests in Nanyang. Such intracommunal tension has not been sufficiently analyzed in diasporic Chinese and Sinophone literary studies, though it has been dealt with more significantly in historical and anthropological research on displaced Chinese communities.[10] Through a rare window into an intra-China regionalism at work in a diasporic setting, readers of *Thick Smoke* can grasp how minority subgroups within an already disempowered migrant Chinese community negotiated their own daily existence in a colonial milieu populated with other ethnicities. By profiling the social world of a Sinophone literary site at a neglected resolution, the novel shifts the analysis of global Chinese creative writings from cataloguing new productive locations to the scrutiny of internal diversities in each locale.

Second, *Thick Smoke* gives form to a hybrid novelistic design that fuses the representation of local languages in Malaya and the use of narrative devices borrowed from traditional Chinese vernacular fiction. The latter falls short of the ideal of May Fourth New Literature that was regarded by the Sino-Malayan literati community then as the progressive creative modality. Besides his ambivalent engagement of the May Fourth model, Lin's compositional process was aided by the circulation of another notion from the mainland state. Specifically, the literary language of *Thick Smoke* was shaped by the idea of a "language of the masses" (*dazhong yu* 大眾語), and Lin had demonstrated familiarity with the cultural debates on the implications of adopting such a language in China's 1930s literary space. Using the concepts of "textualization," "translational mimesis," and "linguistic empathy," I examine Lin's efforts to forge a place-catalyzed literary language that represents multilingual social realities and contemplate the challenges he confronts in writing for two communities of readers in Malaya and China. Arguably, Lin's case invites broader questions of how one should study a text whose foundational status is recognized outside its place of publication, and how a text's representational strategies can be discrepantly received in different geographical contexts.

THE DIALECTICAL LITERARY SPACES OF MALAYA AND CHINA

Expanding the archive of creative personalities beyond the well-recounted examples of Huang Zunxian 黃遵憲 and Yu Dafu 郁達夫, Lin's writing practice brings the pre–World War II Mahua literary landscape into sharper focus. His reminiscences of his literary awakening provide glimpses of the cultural transformations that were emanating from urban centers in China in the early decades of the twentieth century. Although he did not engage in creative composition seriously until he reached Nanyang, his immersion in the region's cultural environment through his teaching vocation and writing avocation closely resembled that of the "southbound writers" (*nanlai zuojia* 南來作家) who enlivened the fledgling Sinophone literary circles in Southeast Asia. His biography thus still illuminates the experiences of the diasporic literary community in general.

Lin was born in 1904 in a remote rural village in the Chuzhou 處州 region (corresponding primarily with present-day Lishui 麗水 city) of

Zhejiang Province.¹¹ By the time he completed elementary school, during which he looked after his family fields in his free time, Lin had developed an affinity for reading "chapter novels" (*zhanghui xiaoshuo* 章回小說), which were works of full-length fiction written in the premodern vernacular literary language. A university student who returned to his home village after the 1919 May Fourth Movement—carrying a bound volume of *Chenbao Fukan* 晨報副刊, the Beijing newspaper's literary supplement—introduced Lin to works written in *yuti wen* 語體文, the modern *baihua* 白話 vernacular that was then promoted as the vehicle for the movement's New Literature. Lin found it refreshing to read works whose content and linguistic form were different from the chapter novels he had read previously. As he reflected on his youth, "I thought those works demonstrated the realities of life and my curiosity was piqued further."¹²

In 1922, Lin extended his studies in Hangzhou to avoid an arranged marriage.¹³ The move exposed him to a greater variety of newspaper supplements carrying New Literature, literary journals of different persuasions, and translations of foreign masterpieces. He also started voraciously reading the works of Lu Xun 鲁迅, Mao Dun, Guo Moruo 郭沫若, Ye Shaojun 叶绍钧, and Yu Dafu, among others. His urban sojourn made him realize that literature was not merely for leisurely consumption, but a powerful weapon in political and cultural spheres.

Upon graduation, mirroring the May Fourth ideal of self-determination, Lin broke away from his family to escape the imposed marriage arrangements permanently.¹⁴ Traveling to Singapore in March 1927, he arrived just before the first big wave of Chinese intellectual migration southward in the wake of the Kuomintang (Nationalist Party) split in China.¹⁵ He left Singapore soon after to teach at a Chinese school in Terengganu on the east coast of present-day Peninsular Malaysia. The school was so secluded that Lin was cut off from the Malayan and Singapore cultural circles for two years. He made his literary debut in 1929 after moving to the west coast of Malaya. It was a subsequent relocation to Kuala Lumpur, where he eventually settled down in 1932, that stoked his writing passion by giving him time to write more regularly. Except for a trip back to China to attend his father's funeral in 1935, and a hiatus during the Japanese Occupation in the early 1940s when he ran a friend's bar to avoid becoming a collaborator with the invaders, he stayed engaged with Malayan Chinese education for more than three decades until his retirement in 1964.[16]

To be sure, Lin was not the first writer to incorporate foreign text and mobilize the Chinese script to capture the aural dimension of lived realities in Malaya. Others had also adopted the strategy of transliteration in their literary works; for instance, Khoo Seok Wan 邱菽園 used Chinese characters to incorporate Malay lexicon into his poetry that describe local customs and cultures.[17] In Lin's own oeuvre, he had already devised characters freely mixing English and Sinitic languages, as well as occasionally throwing in Malay and even French phrases in his earlier dramatic works.[18] As I will demonstrate, Lin's representation of multilingualism as a mode of literary place-making must be interpreted in light of his ambivalent attitude toward his diasporic life in Malaya. Though the place provided him with abundant material for writing, it did not support a literary space for his publishing ambitions. *Thick Smoke* became the first full-length prewar novel of Mahua literature only after successfully breaking into the Shanghai market.

Thick Smoke's contingent border-crossing biography might have accounted for its scant mention in or frequent omission from current accounts of literary history. Lin only started putting pen to paper in April 1935, after having conceptualized the novel in Malaya for six years. The novel went through two drafts in six months, culminating in a manuscript that Lin brought along with him when he returned to China for his father's funeral. He never got to revise the manuscript again as he had planned, for during his return journey to Malaya, he dispatched it to potential publishers when he passed through Shanghai. Within a week, to Lin's own surprise, the eminent editor and translator Fu Donghua 傅東華 accepted it for publication as a title in the prestigious Literature Society Book Series.[19] *Thick Smoke* was subsequently made available in the book market and distributed from China's most prosperous cultural center in July 1936.

The historical juncture at which *Thick Smoke* was written and brought out encapsulated complementary structural orientations in the China and Mahua literary spaces. Lin's book pitch in 1935 encountered China's avid intellectual and general interest in Nanyang. The curiosity about the region, especially in Shanghai in the 1920s and 1930s, was facilitated by traveling Chinese intellectuals. Those intellectuals filled positions in overseas Sinophone print and educational institutions, creating a phenomenon that the historian Shelly Chan would attribute to "Nanyang circulations," which "melded new knowledge about Nanyang into Chinese narratives of the nation."[20] Back in China, a group of researchers at Shanghai Jinan University established the Nanyang Cultural and Education Affairs Bureau (Nanyang wenhua jiaoyu shiyebu 南洋文化教育事業部) in 1927, which inaugurated Nanyang studies as an academic field. The group started a series of flagship publications ranging from a scholarly journal, a current affairs periodical, and monographs. Beyond publishing activities, the bureau conducted outreach with Nanyang-based institutions and organized a large-scale Conference on Nanyang Chinese Education in 1929, whose success inspired the government to organize the Overseas Chinese Education Conference with a global outlook the same year.[21]

The spike in academic publishing paralleled a flurry of popular publications in the eclectic book market. Research and compilations of Republican-era anthologies have shown how a substantial volume of travelogues that recorded the local histories, geographical details and folk customs of Nanyang appeared in China in the 1920s and 1930s.[22] The ethos of bringing Nanyang home to China lends a certain logic to *Thick Smoke*'s appeal to Fu Donghua, since he published from Shanghai; as the leading Chinese cultural metropolis, the city was highly sensitive to scholarly trends, as well as to the tastes and interests of its general readers. Given how Lin's novel became embedded in such a context of knowledge production, it is unsurprising that Fu also ushered into Shanghai's literary space *Xiaopo de shengri* 小坡的生日 (Little Po's birthday), Lao She's 1934 novella inspired by his Singapore sojourn, through another series during the same period.[23]

There is another aspect of intellectual convergence in Fu and Lin's common imagination of the United States as a model of progressive literary growth. Lin's perception of Nanyang as literary terrain then was typical of his southbound peers who saw the Southeast Asian cultural landscape as unexplored and worthy of further development. Outlining the different areas for depictive endeavors, he envisions an American future for Nanyang:

The domain of Nanyang literary arts is still a virgin territory. The material that awaits our writing treatment, in every aspect, is truly tremendous in quantity. Folk customs, social phenomena, the daily lives of the various ethnic groups, the natural scenery of foreign lands, the unique mood of the tropics, the hard lives and glorious achievements of the Chinese sojourners who opened up Nanyang, as well as the market depression after the economic crisis.... I am optimistic about the literary arts of Nanyang.... It will shake off external literary forces of imitation and become a pure form of Nanyang literary arts, just like contemporary American literary arts, which has broken away from British traditionalism and come into its own.[24]

Lin's words signify a desire for Nanyang to take its place among culturally remarkable locales in the world by reproducing the literary temporality of the United States, which by then had achieved its independent artistic distinction vis-à-vis the United Kingdom, its colonial master. He opined that the impoverished condition of the artistic ecology in Nanyang was related to its historical development. Labeling what he called "modern Nanyang literary arts" as "immature" because "its history of producing literary arts started too late," Lin was nonetheless confident that with the joint effort of the Malays, Chinese, and writers from other ethnic groups, Nanyang literary arts would in time become unique and "radiate throughout the "world literary arena" (*shijie wentan* 世界文壇)."[25]

Lin's discourse echoed Fu's orientation toward the United States when the latter projected China's literary progress. In his 1933 article "The Future of World Literary Arts," Fu cites the exemplary traits of U.S. literature for other literary formations, including China. He characterizes U.S. literature as the vanguard of contemporary culture and predicts its future in order to infer "the general direction of literary arts in the world."[26] Clearly channeling China's emergent circumstances, Fu's analogical comparison to the United States' postcolonial trajectory conjures up a world of multiple literary temporalities in which places are not tethered to perpetual mediocrity but can innovate on the same developmental path at different paces. To be clear, it cannot be proven that Fu's discourse directly influenced Lin's perspective of looking toward America. Nonetheless, Fu and Lin's resonant aspirations, filtered through spatial inter-referencing, bespeak a shared spirit of witnessing cultural transition in their own resident literary spaces, while each space prepares for new stages of literary evolution.

Contemporaneous with how social actors in China's literary space tend to gaze beyond the mainland's borders, *Thick Smoke*'s publication outside of Malaya in the 1930s coincided with a significant period of Mahua literary history. The Mahua literary historian Fang Xiu 方修 characterizes the period as one during which intellectuals cultivated *benwei sixiang* 本位思想 (self-positioning thought) to achieve greater autonomy in developing Malayan Chinese-language literature.[27] The formulation of the literary resolve was marked by a dispute over the inadequate recognition of "local writers" (*difang zuojia* 地方作家), which broke out between 1934 and 1936.[28] According to Qiu Shizhen 丘士珍, whose article touched off the debate, Mahua literature in the mid-1930s still carried the baggage of defining its own subjectivity vis-à-vis the perceived center in China: "Local writers should stand on equal footing with writers from the center of the literary circle! In fact, the status of a writer should depend on whether their works undertake positive social responsibilities! In other words, we should not blindly value writers of Chinese literary arts who treat Shanghai as the literary center of China! We should also esteem local writers in Malaya!"[29]

Protesting the tendency in Malaya to revere writers in literary centers such as Shanghai, Qiu offered a list of "Nanyang local writers" who were committed to the validation of Malaya as worthy literary terrain. Tellingly, the list did not include Lin, who had yet to produce a representative work in his name. However, Qiu's discourse also connotes the likelihood that besides distinguishing itself from China, the Malayan literary field was divided internally among different speech groups (social clusters that spoke varied Chinese topolects) and native-place networks. Native to the Zhejiang region north of Fujian and Guangdong, Lin cuts a conspicuous figure in the literary field populated by migrant writers from those two southern China provinces. Another pioneer Mahua writer, Wei Yun 韋暈, recalls that Lin had a slightly broader face and spoke Chinese with a heavy accent from the Jiangzhe region (located south of the lower reaches of the Yangtze River). Both physical characteristics distinguished Lin from the other *wenren* 文人 (men of culture) from

Fujian and Guangdong,[30] and consequently, cast Lin as a *waijiang ren* in the eyes of other Chinese in Nanyang.

According to Zhao Rong's definition in the *Singapore-Malaysia Chinese Literature Dictionary*, *waijiang ren* is a Cantonese colloquial term that designates those ethnic Chinese who do not come from the southern provinces of Fujian, Guangdong, or Guangxi.[31] The dominance of the southerners in Malaya since the nineteenth century is well noted in the scholarship on overseas Chinese in Malaya and Singapore.[32] Outnumbered by Chinese migrants in Malaya hailing from those regions, the *waijiang ren* constituted the margins within the ethnic Chinese community which was itself a minority group in the predominantly Malay region under British colonial rule. Given the rifts among the topolectal groups and native place associations in Nanyang, Lin could well have keenly felt his relatively isolated position as a *waijiang ren* writer living in the shadows of the southerners outside China.

In apparent disregard for the "local writers" disputation, which would later be featured in accounts of Mahua literary history, Lin wrote that "1934 was an insipid period for the Malayan literary circle with almost nothing worth mentioning."[33] His curious comment appeared in the article "A Glance at the 1934 Malayan Literary Circle" alongside "The Reason for the Vapid State of Malayan Literary Arts," another essay he wrote for the 1935 New Year special supplement of *Sin Chew Jit Poh* 星洲日報, one of the major Chinese-language newspapers in Malaya and Singapore. His dismissive judgment could be related to the scope of print circulation, and/or the intense rivalry among Chinese newspapers with topolectal group loyalties, for it appears that the altercation over "local writers" was conducted in *Sin Chew Jit Poh*'s competitor *Nanyang Siang Pau* 南洋商報, a stronghold for the Hokkien-speaking group.[34]

At that time, Lin was conceptualizing *Thick Smoke* and his second novel *Rezhang* 熱瘴 (Tropical miasma), which also concerns Chinese education in Nanyang. In a review of Mahua literary arts, he implied that full-length novels—the genre in which he would soon invest his creative energies—was what the Mahua literary formation critically needed:

> The literary arts of Nanyang are usually tagged onto the rear of newspapers. There is scant space for publication, and on top of that,

> the intervals between each publication date take too long. Supplements of each newspaper are usually published once a week, and each time there is a cap of seven to eight thousand characters.... What's more, such short stories cannot be fully published in a single installment and must be divided into several sections for publication. It goes without saying that there is no chance of publishing novels. A piece of writing has its own vigor and spirit, if it gets cut up into several fragments, not only does the essay lose its sense of unity and brilliance, but readers will also find it difficult to remember the entire piece. What an immense disappointment the situation is![35]

The extract conveys Lin's state of mind when he was incubating his large-scale literary projects. Discontented with the lack of publication venues for longer fictional works, he could have written off the 1934 debate triggered by Qiu's article as a distraction from the fundamental issue that troubled the Mahua literary field. From his words one can infer the field's constitutive dynamic, which stems not only from contests over literary allegiances, but also the inadequacies of the print institutions in the region.[36]

Although *Thick Smoke* was eventually published in Shanghai rather than Malaya, it was not due to Lin hankering after the prestige and recognition of an offshore literary center. He would have been vulnerable to such a charge, considering the rising nativist cultural climate in 1930s Malaya.[37] Despite Lin's creation of a fictional world based on his lived experience in Nanyang, he was unsuccessful in finding local channels that could accommodate his work's extended narrative format. Though Lin had already chosen to stay on in Malaya, it was ultimately China's cultural metropolis with its mature publishing infrastructure that enabled him to achieve his literary breakthrough. If Lin did not revisit his native land in 1935, *Thick Smoke* might never have been brought out into the world. In this sense, Shanghai expanded genre possibilities for the Mahua literary space. Against the imbricated backdrops of struggles within the Mahua literary circle, as well as the academic and market curiosity in China about the region, the dialectical production of *Thick Smoke* demonstrates how Lin embraced a cosmopolitan outlook in Malaya by emulating America, while he also established a new category of fiction publication for Mahua literature when he engaged China's leading cultural locale fruitfully.

A SOCIAL ALLEGORY OF THE *WAIJIANG REN*

To date, readers and critics of *Thick Smoke* have focused on its thematic issues and problematic characters.[38] For those who have commented on the narrative's linguistic aspects, none have ventured beyond contending that the novel demonstrated an infusion of "local color."[39] The interpretive emphasis on geographical distinctiveness makes sense, for *Thick Smoke* was formulated after the 1927 Nanyang Color movement, which advocated writers to incorporate Nanyang's natural and social environments into their works as aesthetic markers for promoting literary self-determination in Malaya. Also, as recounted earlier, the book was developed and written amid the other polemical contest, in 1934, over the recognition of "local writers."

Based on historical records, it was only after 1937—when the anti-Japanese resistance literary movement in Nanyang was launched to support China during World War II—that substantive theorizations on the linguistic predicament of Mahua literary writings emerged.[40] Over the years, critics such as Zhao Rong 趙戎, Yeo Song Nian 楊松年, and Ng Kim Chew have unpacked those post-1937 polemics to characterize the formative period of Mahua literature since the 1920s.[41] They shape a particular impression that prewar Chinese writers who resided in the British colonies invested considerable effort in reflecting the linguistic ecology of the Malayan living world. Among the evaluative discourses, Ng's critique of Mahua writers in the early decades of the twentieth century deserves greater scrutiny for its harsh assessment. What the critic Alison Groppe construes as Mahua writers' "sociolinguistic fascination" becomes to Ng in the 1990s a manifestation of the deficiency of Chinese as a literary language that has been raised within a culturally lackluster lineage in Malaya.[42] His predecessors, Ng charges, merely viewed language as a transparent tool for didactic communication with readers and were incapable of curating distinctive literary performances. To achieve superficial authenticity through dashes of local color, they treated the unreflective transliteration of vocabulary from Chinese topolects, English, and Malay as the mimetic solution.[43] Consequently, the approach

Doubly Local 43

created "a form of 'bazaar-Chinese,' and results in the vulgarization of Chinese and not its refinement," the corollary of which is the adverse impact on literariness.[44]

A cursory read of *Thick Smoke* yields an impression congruent with Ng's critique. After all, Lin's novel is populated with textual phenomena of multilingualism, including traces of different script systems. Take, for instance, *Thick Smoke*'s evocative opening scene of a Singapore quayside, which echoes the description of the colony as "a harbor of strange tongues" by Victor Purcell, the British officer and Sinologist:[45]

"<u>*Towkay, mana pergi*</u>?" Two Indian porters ran up to ask the two young men, their hands already reaching to lift the men's luggage...[46]

"*Naiti* 耐的!" Feeling anxious, the older one blurted out an erroneous Malay sentence to stop them.

The two Indian porters rolled their eyes a couple of times, made a hand signal toward their colleagues who were running over to help, shook their heads, curled their tongues to say something in an Indian language, and the rest of the Indian porters backed off.

The Indian porters had just left when a few Hokkien boatmen came.

"Mister, *ke-dok-lok* 克篤洛?" one of them asked earnestly.

"Wait a while," the older one said, while he called his colleague to seek shelter from the blazing sun under the eaves of the quayside buildings.

"Mr. Mao, you're so capable. You can understand quite a few languages." The younger one spoke with envy.

"I'm still not there yet. But one can't get by if one does not babble a little. The languages in Nanyang are truly very complex," the older one said smilingly.

The younger one nodded his head to indicate that it was indeed rather difficult. Though he did not understand those vernaculars, he found the sounds of those strange pronunciations very intriguing. He thus began to think that he might also pick up a couple of languages if he stayed on for some time.

There were more and more travelers: the Malays in sarongs; the Arabs with their red hats; the muscular Bengalis with their thick beards and the top of their heads wrapped in white cloths; the Siamese women with floral headdresses carrying bamboo baskets on their backs, wearing *baju panjang* (*Note 1) and sarong skirts; Westerners; Chinese; all of them were streaming toward the quay.

(*Note 1): the long blouse worn by Malay women.[47]

With its multiracial cast of characters interacting in a variety of languages, the insertion of foreign text, and the transliteration of colloquial exchanges in the Chinese script, the scene features Nanyang's multicultural and multilingual setting. What makes *Thick Smoke* special is that the instances of linguistic hybridity occur not only at the lexical level, as Ng observes about the early Mahua writers, but also at the level of syntax.[48] The first sentence "*Towkay, mana pergi*?" is rendered in romanized Malay. There is, in fact, a second layer of translation, as the term *towkay* is an alphabetic transliteration of the Hokkien term pronounced as *toujia* 頭家 in standard Mandarin, which means "boss." In another part of the dialogue, Malay is represented by a transcriptive use of the Chinese script, pointing toward a second method to represent the lingua franca of the Malay world, which overlaps with Nanyang. Signaling that Lin understands enough Malay to depict "an erroneous Malay sentence," 耐的 transcribes the pronunciation *naiti*, which actually stands for the term *nanti* that means "later." Meanwhile, the logographic script is also deployed to transliterate Hokkien (克篤洛 means "Where are you going?"). As for the conversation among the Indian laborers, Lin chose direct ascription without attempting to represent the Indian language used.

Such an intricate depiction of the exuberant Malayan linguistic environment—which dramatizes social voices in all their authentic and diverse timbres—demands a fundamental re-interpretation of the narrative's rhetorical structure. In what sense can we position *Thick Smoke* within the historical interstices that have eluded Ng's sweeping judgment? Gainsaying Ng's contention of early Mahua writers' artistic incompetence, this chapter interprets the representation of multilingualism in Lin's landmark novel as indicative of a latent Sino-Malayan literary dynamic. Through my analysis of the novel's narrative form, I highlight not only the discursive linkages between China and Nanyang mediated by writers such as Lin who moved between the two regions, but also his anomalous positionality in the variegated interior of the Mahua literary space.

Illustrative of Lin's reputation as "the novelist who specializes in dramatizing problems of overseas Chinese education," *Thick Smoke* portrays the challenges besetting the noncolonial education sector around 1928, before the Great Depression in British Malaya.[49] Inspired by the historian Huei-Ying Kuo's contention that the "cleavages among Chinese speech-groups" account for internal conflicts that strongly influenced overseas Chinese nationalism, I argue that *Thick Smoke* evokes a Mahua society split along topolectal lines.[50] Whereas other ethnic groups in Malaya may perceive their Chinese counterparts to be remarkably cohesive, during the colonial period members within the Chinese community usually identified themselves with a topolectal group, known as a *bang* 幫. In the historical contexts of Singapore and Malaya, *bang* denotes "a Chinese politico-socio-economic grouping based principally on a dialect," which accounts for its alternative rendition as "dialect group" (*fangyanqun* 方言群), especially in scholarly literature.[51] Early in *Thick Smoke*, one of the main characters, Mao Zhendong 毛振東, signals his grasp of that striking aspect of Malayan society when he tells the newcomer Li Mianzhi 李勉之, who relocated from the Shanghai region: "After staying on in Nanyang, you will surely understand how ingrained the notion of '*bang*' is among Nanyang Chinese sojourners. This is a great obstacle to the solidarity of the Nanyang diaspora" 你在南洋住久了，一定會明白南洋華僑的幫會觀念是極重的。這是南洋華僑聯合的大障礙 (60). It is this factional social terrain that Lin expends substantial effort to depict in *Thick Smoke*.

Thick Smoke—which primarily uses third-person narration—recounts the experiences of several new teachers who are working at a local Chinese school in a town located on the east coast of Malaya. Conflict breaks out on many levels: among the women instructors, as well as between the Indian and Chinese instructors, over employment positions and pedagogical issues; among the principal, teachers, and board of directors over the degree of autonomy in school administrative operations; among board members in a power struggle to preserve cliquish interests; and between the teachers and students over disciplinary methods.

Among the conflicts, the clashes between the mercantile local-born Chinese who control the school's board of Hokkien-speaking directors, and the migrant educators from China who have assimilated into Malayan society unevenly, warrant renewed critical attention. Suggesting the underlying tension among Sinitic speech-groups in Nanyang, the novel explores the predicaments of the *waijiang ren* in the internally fractious Mahua community. Further intimated by the designation of Mao Zhendong and Li Mianzhi—the two *waijiang ren* characters—as the novel's protagonists, the narrative can be read as a tale about living in the margins of the dominant language of a specific place.[52] The linguistic obstacles the two men face recall the experience of the Shanghainese Li Zhongyu 李鍾鈺, who visited Singapore in 1887 and noted the social dynamics among ethnic Chinese—including both long-term immigrants and local-born residents—in his travelogue: "When members of the same social group interact, they would sometimes use Malay, at other times English or the vernaculars of Fujian and Guangdong. Those who first arrive from other provinces often respond to them like puppets" 同儕往來，時而巫語，時而英語，時而閩、廣土語，他省初到人，往往對之如木偶。[53]

As Mao remarks in the opening scene at the Singapore harbor, "the languages in Nanyang are truly very complex." The polylinguality overwhelms the newcomer Li, who hails from Shanghai. Although Mao had arrived in the region earlier than Li and can speak a smattering of Malay, neither he nor Li are conversant in Hokkien, the southern Fujian topolect dominant in the Malayan locality, which is crucial to win the support of the school directors. The linguistic disconnect creates problems, especially for Mao when he becomes head of academic affairs. As for Li, due to his relative proficiency in English, he plays a special role in the school, often helping to interpret for his Indian colleague Selvarajah, who teaches English. In the story, Selvarajah favors a conservative pedagogical approach that involves corporal punishment, in contrast to Mao and Li's liberal approach, which encourages students to be critical of authority. The two Chinese educators' checkered engagement with the Indian character eventually becomes one of the most important plot drivers of the novel.

Throughout the diegesis, tension arising from linguistic barriers to interaction constitute a recurring motif that spotlights the school's dysfunctional circumstances. The primary medium of communication among members of the school's board of directors is Hokkien. The chairman of the board dislikes *baihua wen* 白話文, the new literary vernacular that displaced classical Chinese as the main written form of the Chinese language in China (385). Interpreters are frequently required to translate between Hokkien and *guoyu* 國語—China's newly minted national language promulgated during the Republican period—for professional meetings and informal social gatherings (83, 146–47, 321, 365). In their absence, meanings are lost (331, 336) or communication becomes truncated (171, 380–82). Li privately criticizes Selvarajah for not knowing both Mandarin and Hokkien (474). On other occasions, the principal is incapable of directly addressing Selvarajah's grievances as he does not understand English (256–58), a language that is revered by the powerful Peranakan group among the local-born Chinese population.[54] While Selvarajah converses in English with some of his colleagues, he interacts mainly with his students in Malay (436–39). Ironically, *guoyu* was just being taught in Malayan Chinese schools at the time and was unintelligible not only to Selvarajah, who grows increasingly suspicious of his students using the language to criticize him for his inflexible teaching methods (235, 238, 242), but also to many local Chinese (207).

By the end of *Thick Smoke*, the two *waijiang ren* protagonists, with their educational ideals of empowering students, appear thoroughly out of place in the locale. Mao leaves the school in disappointment; Li has also made plans to depart, implying how living with people of the same ethnicity with common experiences of displacement does not necessarily lead to open-mindedness that transcends topolectal group boundaries or facilitate assimilation that offers relief from marginalization.

Lin drew on personal experiences in Malaya for his writings, so it is not surprising that he would direct his authorial gaze to examine the circumstances of *waijiang ren*.[55] Bearing in mind that native-place origins and topolects figure significantly in organizing the lives of ethnic Chinese in Malaya and Singapore in the nineteenth and early twentieth century, I read the trope of *waijiang ren* and the representations of communication challenges that result from topolectal differences as jointly contributing to a subtle metaphor for the fragmented Mahua literary space. Dovetailing with the attention Lin devotes to *waijiang ren*, the representations of multilingualism in *Thick Smoke* mark Lin's experiment of forging a place-appropriate literary language for the Nanyang masses. This rich textual phenomenon begs a more sympathetic interpretation of his authorial practice than construing it as a superficial pursuit of geographically determined realism. In her study of multilingual German literature,

Yasemin Yildiz contends that "the configuration of languages in aesthetic works shapes *how* social formations are imagined," and that "the particular *form* of multilingualism in a given cultural text encodes visions of social formations, individuals, and modes of belonging."[56] Read under Yildiz's analytical lens, Lin's novel emerges as a social allegory of the enclaves that structure the Mahua literary space, which can be segmented among the different topolectal groups, or between the China-born and the local-born Chinese. Functioning as a narrative analogue to the social milieu of Nanyang writers that was internally divided among ethnic Chinese themselves, the novel suggests a resonant continuity between the narrated world and the external world. Together, both worlds indicate that there is no unitary space of overseas Chineseness.

By implying the author's minority position in the Mahua literary space, *Thick Smoke* embodies the creative modality through which Lin carves a more durable position for himself. To produce the extended novelistic form, he employs a dualist blend of narrative strategies derived from a mass-oriented language apposite with the Malayan environment, and from the rhetorical devices of traditional Chinese fiction. At the time, intellectuals in China framed the former as an advanced medium and the latter as a regressive literary mode, but both aesthetic temporalities found a shared existence in the manuscript of a Nanyang-based writer. Fu Donghua, the editor who published the work, could have found the melded approach manifested in *Thick Smoke* appealing; he had already written about literature's current "season of hybridity" (*zaji* 雜季) in Shanghai, where May Fourth New Literature, popular fiction, martial arts novels, and foreign works translated into classical and vernacular styles coexisted in the book market and jostled for readers' attention.[57] Back in Nanyang, the multilingual and multiethnic social realities had sparked Lin's artistic imagination, leading him to invent a literary form that signifies the interaction among different kinds of linguistic consciousness and colloquial practice circulating in the British colonial territories.

ENDEAVORING TO TEXTUALIZE LOCAL LANGUAGES

The story of *Thick Smoke* unfolds in a fictional Malayan town called "The Country of Crying Children" (*ti'er guo* 啼兒國). According to a local legend, the Chinese sojourner who first arrived at the town would hear every

March and April the wailing sounds of a type of local bird that resemble crying babies (32). The town's name echoes formulations such as "The Country of Gentlemen" (*junzi guo* 君子國), "The Country of Women" (*nü'er guo* 女兒國), and "The Country of Forked-Tongued People" (*qishe guo* 歧舌國) in *Flowers in the Mirror*, the late Qing novel cited in *Thick Smoke*'s promotional materials.[58] Besides sharing the theme of travels abroad, the two narratives' intertextual association is reinforced through the diegesis of *Thick Smoke*, which is replete with detailed vignettes about the food and customs, as well as the physical and sociolinguistic landscapes of a new locality.

The novel's flavor of overseas adventure piques one's curiosity about its imagined audience. Without precise figures for *Thick Smoke*'s distribution, the more productive question is less about the book's actual readers in China and Malaya than about whom the novel was addressing. Though the novel was published in Shanghai, the omniscient narrator is capable of serving as an interlocutor to readers in both literary spaces. On the one hand, the narrator's ethnographic exposition implies a readership that is unfamiliar with the remote locale and requires introduction to its ways of life; by speaking anthropologically, *Thick Smoke* appears to posit Nanyang as an offshore extension of China on behalf of mainland readers. On the other hand, the novel can also be read as seeking resonance with Malayan readers who experienced similar orientation rituals after relocating to a new place, or who find themselves negotiating their social positions within a heterogeneous diasporic Chinese community.

Discerning Lin's bifurcated address of both Malayan and Chinese literary spaces enables us to better grasp the matrix of transregional forces—evinced through cultural infrastructure, discursive travel, and authorial psychology—that shaped *Thick Smoke*'s composition and publication. In his preface to the inaugural Shanghai edition of the novel, Lin's fashions the book as a gift to his motherland, referring to himself as a returning Nanyang vagrant.[59] His writing practice throws into relief the conflicting doubleness that resides in his words and actions. In the 1930s, he had pledged solidarity with fellow Malayan writers to enrich the local literary space, only to back down a few months later to bemoan his wasted years spent abroad, claiming that "Nanyang is not a place for me to stay on permanently. It is the tomb of the intellectual circle."[60]

Given that his disavowal of Nanyang appeared in an essay written in memory of his late father, Lin could very likely be channeling a customary sense of filial piety. But his sentiments might also have been fueled by a sense of marginalization in the Malayan literary circle, for even though the rich social and natural environments provided him with abundant resources for planning his large-scale narrative projects, he had to hustle elsewhere for his work to be published.

In David L. Kenley's interpretation of the overseas Chinese writers' psyche, he suggests that "for them, being 'Chinese' [from China] and being 'overseas Chinese' had overlapped and melded together. It is not contradictory, therefore, for Singapore's writers to emphasize their 'local colors,' while resisting 'becoming indigenous.'"[61] Lin could have conducted himself similarly. His commitment to creating a vivid Mahua literature allows him to face his Malaya-based colleagues and express independence from his native land, as well as to compose stories about foreign lands for the reading public in China. The local scale in his writing practice thus conflates the twin senses of place-specific groundedness in Malaya and extending China's regional reach across the oceans. From this perspective, Malaya is implicated in Lin's incessant calibration and recalibration of authorial distance, emotionally and narratively, which enables him to negotiate divergent modes of rapport with both places.

To take "The Country of Crying Children" as Lin's conception of the Nanyang world in the 1920s and 1930s entails examining his experiment in literary language, which enacts an artistic counterpoint to the critiques of linguistic naiveté that would later befall his writing practice. As registered in the novel's preface, Li was particularly conscious about the linguistic form of his text:

> I have adopted many popular colloquialisms and script in Nanyang. For instance, in the sentence "mana ge-gao" 嗎那格夠, "mana" is Malay for "where or how;" "ge-gao" comes from the Amoy vernacular. This will sound pleasing to the ears of the Nanyang people, but it would be baffling for the readers in the mainland. The character "峇" was originally pronounced "ke" 溘, but the people in Nanyang pronounce it as "ba" 巴, for instance "ba-ba" 峇峇, "ba-du" 峇都; all these are words that can be seen daily. The character "叻" was also

once a demotic character in Nanyang, but the *Dictionary of National Pronunciation* has now included it. Nanyang has a lot of these demotic forms of the characters. If the mainland wishes to bridge her culture with Nanyang's, then it is advisable to be acquainted with these demotic characters.⁶²

Lin attributes his use of Chinese colloquialism and differential script obliquely to an effort of connecting cultures between China and the South Seas region, and by doing so he reveals how he deliberately adopts a place-evocative mode of linguistic hybridity that calls into being a transregional readership. He implies that there is a considerable pool of Chinese characters that circulated regionally, which gives rise to various forms of linguistic misalignment. Terms that readers in Nanyang find natural may be utterly perplexing to mainland readers. Certain Chinese characters may also have discrepant pronunciation and yield different word combinations across the two cultural spaces. By pointing out that an authoritative dictionary in China included a demotic Nanyang character, he further suggests how mainland lexicographers with expansive geographical imaginaries are open to transregional input from the south.

As noted earlier, Lin was writing the novel amid the clamor to devote greater attention to "local writers" in Malaya. During this period both the terms "Nanyang literature" and "Malayan literature" circulated.⁶³ What has since faded from that familiar picture of entangled place appellations is the discursive impact on the Malayan literary circle occasioned by another contemporaneous dispute that influenced Lin's creative process more substantively. Alongside the debate on local writers, critics also weighed in on the Latinization of the Chinese script and the creation of a "mass language" (*dazhongyu* 大眾語) for Nanyang.⁶⁴

Characterized as "one of the most active promoters" of the "mass language" movement in Nanyang, Lin shows himself to have followed the local contestations.⁶⁵ In a review article, Lin relates that the "controversy between the two camps—each supporting either 'mass language' or classical Chinese—has rocked the literary circle in China," and points out how "the 'mass language movement' in Malaya caused quite a stir, but eventually subsided due to differences in social consciousness." Since "Nanyang is a modern and commercial society," he believes that "paying respect to Confucius, reading the classics, and discussing linguistic instruments (the Chinese script) cannot capture [people's] interest and attention." But "with regard to the creation of a popular script," he asks: "Has that not already been implemented in Nanyang?" Lin notes that "there are many letters among the people written in the topolects, including Cantonese and Hakka," and that "people who have received missionary training are all capable of writing letters in the topolects." He thus suggests that these letters "can be considered writings composed in the popular script."[66]

The angle through which Lin assesses the language massification movement in China speaks to his desire to find a third way between the polarizing positions of either recuperating *wenyan* (classical Chinese 文言), or promoting a language for the masses through Latinization. To him, it is impossible to revive classical Chinese in Malaya. As the site of modern commerce, Malaya is incompatible with the resurrection of the linguistic form representing feudal Chinese culture. At the same time, there is no need for Latinization since Malaya already hosts the circulation of a demotic script. Lin's question—"Has that not already been implemented in Nanyang?"—points to the pervasive employment of a mass language already in situ. Siphoning attention away from the customary cultural center of China, his remark signifies an important shift in thoughts on the dispersed usage of Sinitic script. The routes of linguistic mobility can be comprehended in terms of originally local practices that have been relocalized in different places, rather than as outcomes of dissemination from a common source.

In a separate article, "Nanyang and a Language of the Masses" (Nanyang yu dazhong yuwen 南洋與大眾語文), Lin lists several favorable social conditions that made Nanyang more conducive for forging a "mass language" than China.[67] As if to justify his long-form writing project, he indicates how Nanyang was economically more progressive. He also contends that there were more educational opportunities for the poor in the Southeast Asian region, that the topolectal situation of the Nanyang Chinese community was not as complex as that in China, and that heterogeneous communities of sojourners living in relatively closer proximity would facilitate language standardization. More importantly, there were no entrenched group interests tied to using either classical Chinese or the *baihua* vernacular advocated by the May Fourth intellectuals.[68]

Doubly Local 53

Given the temporal coincidence of his cultural commentaries and the composition of his novel, Lin must have contemplated—and eventually implemented—a literary form that employed the demotic script, which he claimed was already widespread in Malaya. He thus went further than other contributors who merely engaged in the polemics without participating in literary production.[69] In this regard, *Thick Smoke* offers a productive site to tease out Lin's thoughts on the way in which language validates the distinctiveness of a place and how the place-language nexus drives the composition of a unique literature. How then does Lin's novelistic experiment measure up to the contemporary Malayan critic Fan Cheng's 樊滕 viewpoint that a "mass language" should be one that "can be spoken aloud, understood through listening, easily written, and whose meaning is readily appreciated by the masses?"[70]

To offer a way of understanding how Lin manifests Nanyang's "mass language" in *Thick Smoke*, I posit that Lin's key method of transferring voice to print was to "textualize" the sounds of unfamiliar languages phonetically by using the Chinese script, or by incorporating the foreign script directly. In making this assertion, I borrow from Liangyan Ge's study of the sixteenth-century novel *Water Margin* (*Shuihu zhuan* 水滸傳), in which he contends that the famous Chinese tale fashions the spoken vernacular into a mature written medium for traditional Chinese fiction. Ge's concept of textualization is useful for illuminating the central authorial dilemma that shuttles between literary imagination and multilingual realities, as it implies a simultaneously "notational and compositional" process that "writes *toward*" as well as "writes *in*" the ideal place-appropriate language.[71]

Through this lens of textualization, and in view that Lin was searching for a formal solution to respond to the polemics of his times, I examine the rich representational strategies deployed in *Thick Smoke*. As the following vignette in which the Indian teacher Selvarajah explains his multilayered identity to his Chinese colleagues demonstrates, the narrative discourse is not as transparent as it seems:

"Mr Li, would you ask him for his name so that I can write it on the supervision roster tomorrow?" said the principal.

>   .... After Mianzhi translated the principal's question into English and slowly explained it to him, he broke into a smile immediately and said,
>   "<u>My name is Hassan</u>."[72]
>   "<u>Hassan</u>," this is a Muslim name. Like the Christians, the Muslims have to take on religious names such as "<u>John</u>," "<u>Mark</u>," "<u>Paul</u>." As for Muslims, they would be called "<u>Hassan</u>," "<u>Ali</u>," "<u>Aladdin</u>," "<u>Muhammad</u>." (175–76)

In the excerpt, an inefficient three-way conversation is conducted in *guoyu* between the principal and Li Mianzhi, and in English between Li and Selvarajah, who starts off in the story claiming to be "Hassan," resulting in Li's interior monologue on names associated with different religions. The underlined parts of the narrative discourse are originally rendered in the alphabetic script, suggesting indexical attempts to convey the multilingual reality in Nanyang, alongside the use of Chinese, the main representational language of the novel. By simulating the on-site linguistic milieu, Lin's authorial approach of notation and composition foregrounds a suggestive resemblance and continuity between the worlds on-page and off-page.

Lin's textualization approach can be further parsed through what Meir Sternberg calls "translational mimesis," an artistic modality that evokes "the reality of polylingual discourse through a communicative medium which is normally unilingual."[73] Sternberg would classify the type of linguistic mixing described in the above extract as "selective reproduction," which entails "the intermittent quotation of the original heterolingual discourse as uttered by the speakers."[74] Other instances in the novel feature "explicit attribution," whereby the narrator states plainly the language used in conversations to indicate linguistic diversity.[75] Besides those two representational paths, Lin also employs "conceptual reflection" in the same plot section, which illustrates the acts of cultural translation. An example of such intercultural communication can be observed in the previous scenario when Selvarajah arrives and introduces himself. After the English-speaking Li runs through his inner thoughts about religion-based names, the two men discuss the naming practices of different cultures:

"Are you a Muslim?" Mianzhi asked him.

"No," he answered.

"Why is your name Hassan?"

"My Malay friends gave it to me when I stayed at their place."

"Then what is your original name?"

"Selvarajah."

.... Mianzhi instantly took out his fountain pen from his shirt pocket to note down the name and raised his notebook to pronounce:

"Selvarajah. Is that right?"

"Yes!" He drinks a spoonful of soup and asks, "What are your names like?"

"Our names are very short, usually just three words. There are some with only two, and those with four words are very rare."

"Three or four words, how can that be short?" he exclaimed. "Mine is only one word!"

"No, there is a difference in word composition. The words in Chinese are monosyllabic; each word corresponds with a pronunciation. Sanskrit is polysyllabic, each word combines different syllables to constitute itself." (176–78)

According to Sternberg, "selective reproduction" highlights parts of the narrative that have not been homogenized by monolingual presentation, whereas "conceptual reflection" evinces "not so much the verbal forms of the foreign code as the underlying social-cultural norms."[76] The latter strategy thus enables the representation of multilingual speech to become a mode of representing the worldview of the speaker(s) in the texts. For this strategy, heterolingualism functions through "culturally typical (or typified) topics, interests, attitudes, realia, forms of address, fields of allusion, or paralinguistic features like gesticulation."[77]

The most thought-provoking remark about this mimetic aspect of *Thick Smoke* is a curious paragraph presented as a parenthetical aside, which is wedged in-between the two extracts cited above. By interrupting the diegesis, the narrator reveals himself as the author and explicates the disadvantages of faithfully reproducing Malay and English in foreign script, and of appending Chinese translations of the narrative discourse in the original languages:

The author wishes to make a special statement at this point: The Indian teacher is a foreigner; he does not understand Chinese languages. Though he is one of the protagonists in this book, if we quote his words entirely in Malay or English, not only will they be hard to read and comprehend, but they will also pose great inconveniences to typesetting. Otherwise, if translations are attached right after his original articulations, it would take up too many pages. Therefore, the conversations that involve the Indian teacher hereafter will be rendered directly in *guoyu* [the national language]. Please do not misunderstand and think that an Indian can actually speak *guoyu*. (176)

In this bracketed disclaimer, the omniscient narrator-author explains his decision to abandon translation and directly transpose the multilingual reality into the unilingual Chinese script from that point forward. The aside, which disrupts the mimetic register of the narrative discourse, contains clear signs that Lin was consciously searching for an optimal blend of local languages that would remind his readers in China and Malaya of the geographical setting of the narrative action. Augmented by such an extradiegetic dimension, the array of indexical operations undertaken by "translational mimesis" heightens readers' awareness that it is rare to read a work of Mahua fiction that exposes its own manner of composition, as does *Thick Smoke*.

Considered holistically, the disclaimer reads like Lin's defense, which seeks recourse to expressive expediency. The rendering of ensuing Malay and English dialogue directly in Chinese raises questions about the Mahua author's linguistic capacity. Lin possessed considerable English proficiency, but he had confessed his ignorance of Malay.[78] In the novel, the limited Malay dialogue transliterated in Chinese script must thus have been painstakingly invented with assistance that has not been revealed.[79] Being a *waijiang ren*, he also needed to invest considerable effort to devise the representations of Hokkien and Cantonese discourses of daily life used by the majority of Chinese migrants in Southeast Asia.[80]

Li claimed that he felt no pressure to publish, so it is unlikely that he yielded to a monolingual mode of representation because he was dissatisfied with his writing progress.[81] His dedication to writing as an avocation despite austere living conditions deepens our curiosity as to whether concern for the reader's capacity to understand foreign languages and typesetting challenges—as laid out in the ambiguous disclaimer—actually underpinned the final presentation of the narrative. Was there a Malay-literate collaborator he was able to consult but with whom he later lost touch? Did he become impatient with a certain mode of cowriting, or did the sheer scale of the remaining story make him come to terms with the impossibility of sustaining even the sporadic transcription of Malay in the Chinese script? Or did he act upon his Shanghai editor's advice?

In any case, the authorial insertion lays bare a writerly consciousness that struggles with reconciling the tension between language as representational means and social languages in Malaya as represented objects. In terms of audience reception, Li appears to better accommodate his mainland readers, as seen in how he delivers on a promise in his preface to provide "hints and explanations" for attentive readers who are alien to the "folk sayings and demotic characters" in Nanyang.[82] To that end, he employs yet another way of decoding the embedded heterolinguality: by incorporating scenarios of interpretation as part of the narrative action. For instance, Li portrays Mao Zhendong going on a weekend excursion with his colleagues and students not long after arriving at the town. Incorporating both selective reproduction and explicit attribution, Li weaves together a scene conducted in Mandarin, Malay, and Hokkien, where Mao and an old Malay woman are monolingual participants:

> They walked past the side of a hut below the coconut trees and met a hunchbacked old woman. Her skin and body were wizened like the nuts of an old pine tree. Her hair was as white as lamb's wool. She had a rickety gait and walked laboriously. Zhendong asked the plump student to inquire her age this year.
>
> "Umur berapa?" (烏木拔拉拔) the plump student walked over to the old woman and asked.
>
> "Lapan belas" (臘版拔拉土), she replied, her jowls sunken.
>
> The plump student laughed loudly after hearing her reply. Other students and the School Governor also laughed.
>
> "How old did she say she is?" Zhendong asked the student anxiously.

"She said she's only eighteen," the student replied and laughed again.

Everybody laughed.

"Ask her further: How does she count her age?" Zhendong spoke again.

"Ikut apa kira?" (以故阿巴吉拉)

"Tengok daun kelapa jatuh." (丁囉達溫克拉巴傑都)

"She said she follows the falling fronds of the coconut trees," the plump student interpreted.

"The Malays calculate their age by looking at coconut fronds that fall off. Each frond is counted as a year." The School Governor spoke in the Amoy vernacular. (126–27)[83]

As conveyed by the scene, a student who plays the role of interpreter clarifies the full meaning of the Malay encounter. From the setting readers can infer that Mao is almost completely isolated, for as a *waijiang ren* he cannot understand the Hokkien-speaking School Governor who imparts local knowledge. At the compositional level, it appears that Lin used *guoyu* pronunciation to render the Malay articulations. Such transcription of Malay into the Chinese script recalls the endeavors of Chinese migrants in late nineteenth-century Nanyang, who compiled Chinese-Malay dictionaries using similar strategies of transliteration, albeit through choosing Chinese characters based on the sounds of southern topolects such as Hokkien and Teochew.[84] By harnessing the plural depictive pathways of translational mimesis, the novel installs multilingualism not only as a governing element of the diegesis, but also as an integral authoring mechanism that constantly calibrates the critical distance from its targets of representation.

The resulting textual phenomenon is therefore not an outcome of whimsical blending to gullibly pursue a goal of mimetic vividness. In contrast to texts that present themselves as fully deciphered outcomes of translations, *Thick Smoke* harbors a translational conceit that compels readers to recognize narrative multilingualism as a formative and striking dimension of reality. The text's polylingual nature, which one Malayan reader in the 1930s judged to be furnished with insufficient explanatory footnotes, unwittingly shores up the critical effect of Lin's broad artistic design.[85] Just like in real life, the narrative discourse does not assume that readers will understand—or thoroughly comprehend—every multilingual occurrence, hence justifying the novel's incomplete referencing apparatus and its switch midway to monolingual representation in Chinese script.

MEDIATING THE BIFURCATED SENSE OF THE LOCAL

As much as *Thick Smoke* augurs an experience of a "mass language" for readers, the shift toward homogenizing its linguistic presentation also adroitly masks Lin's inadequacies. His authorial access to the polylingual Malayan social realities is uneven, for he could not effectively wield the languages and Chinese topolects he aimed to represent in his novel. Curiously, in the later years of his life, Lin spoke as if all representational modes of translational mimesis had been equally accessible to him. When he expounded on his writing beliefs, Lin couched his rhetoric in terms of artistic effect and audience consideration:

> Topolectal dialogue can convey a more vivid quality. However, topolectal dialogue also has its drawback, which is that readers who do not understand the local language will find some parts unpronounceable and unintelligible.
>
> Malaya is a multi-racial country, with a complex language situation comprising Chinese, Malay, Indian and English. If a work includes characters from all races, circumstances are such that it would be impossible to transpose all their languages. Even in the sphere of *huayu* 華語 (Chinese language), there is Hokkien, Cantonese, Teochew, Hakka, and Hainanese, five topolects in total. It will also be problematic if dialogue is represented through these topolects. To avoid damaging the effects of the works, it would be more appropriate to minimize the use of topolects.[86]

Here, Lin rationalizes his writing approach by claiming that if represented faithfully through dialogue, the diversity of *huayu*—understood in the specific conception of the time, which comprised five Sinitic topolects—will impair the intelligibility of the work.[87] He does not mention, however, the preconditions that enable a Mahua writer to materialize the full spectrum of local languages in literature. If the textualization of Malayan speech in *Thick Smoke* represents a truncated attempt to write a mass language into existence, then Lin's crossover to a different mimetic register in the middle of the novel shores up the substantial, if not insurmountable, challenge for all his creative peers. Few, if any, of the Chinese writers in Malaya were adequately multilingual to undertake literary endeavors that perform "vehicular matching," whereby multilingual literary representations perfectly correspond to multilingual folk realities.[88] Writing place-based literature in Nanyang was no straightforward task. Lin's disclaimer marks his latent recognition of the immense labor involved in transliterating Malay and representing Cantonese via the Chinese script for literary composition.

In the late 1960s, Lin reflected on writing for the masses as rectifying the undesirable disconnect between May Fourth literature and its public reception. To illustrate the attributes of a truly broad-based literary language, he looked toward traditional Chinese fiction, the genre he enjoyed when he was a child but that was later deemed regressive by proponents of the May Fourth Movement:

> The May Fourth New Literature Movement brought about a Westernized syntax and caused the literary circle to develop a foreign form of eight-legged compositions that are even more obscure than those composed in classical Chinese. This orientation caused the new literary arts to be alienated from the masses. The issue of language massification is raised precisely to critique such foreignized eight-legged compositions.
>
> The masses constitute a rich source of inspiration for literary works. What writers need to do is to get close to them, learn from and understand them in order to enrich the writers' personal experiences, as well as to distill subject matter pertaining to reality, and write about what the masses can comprehend in a succinct and fluent literary language that they find sufficiently acceptable. The authors of Chinese "chapter novels" are mostly erudite and outstanding scholars, but they can express profound content in all their works through simple language, so that readers who might have only a few years of education can also read and understand them. That these works can still circulate widely these days is a testament to their linguistic artistry....

> Shanghai was the cultural center of China. Prior to liberation, it had only published a thousand titles on New Literature and Arts. Mahua literature and arts, with its forty years of history, has only published two thousand titles. That the New Literature and Arts did not enjoy the support from a broad base of the masses is because the subject matter and literary language did not fit what the masses needed. . . . But what kind of subject matter do the masses need? Subject matter that concerns reality. What kind of literary form do they need? A form tailored for the masses.[89]

Lin's words are a poignant reversal of his admission in an autobiographical article written only a few months earlier. In that article, he shared that May Fourth New Literature opened his eyes to fresh ways of reflecting reality.[90] Here, his discursive juxtaposition of the literary spaces of Shanghai and Malaya reveals the geographical considerations in his writing practice, which echo *Thick Smoke*'s publishing trajectory. Clearly, Lin pondered an alternative model of literary communication through his narrative projects after he was introduced to the linguistic form of May Fourth literature and later, after his migration to Malaya.

Thick Smoke thus bears witness to a precious enactment of Lin's literary imagination. Lin's reflection, cited above, echoes the ideas of the Chinese writer and critic Qu Qiubai 瞿秋白, who favored the literary vernacular of popular fiction and drama of the Ming-Qing period over the May Fourth vernacular that contained palpable traces of classical Chinese and foreign language influences.[91] In all likelihood, Lin's perceived superiority of "chapter novels"—the traditional-style, long-form narratives prevalent from the Ming dynasty onward, which resonated with an expansive reading public through the use of a relatively transparent, non-elitist literary language—accounts for the way he constructs an omniscient narrator for *Thick Smoke*. The all-knowing narrator functions as the compensatory mechanism for Lin to achieve an ideal congruence with the masses, an ideal that he could not implement exhaustively via translational mimesis.

Throughout the novel, the panoptic narrator focalizes and yet maintains distance from the unfolding plot. On occasion, however, he emerges from the diegesis in a contiguous fashion, speaking in the voice of the author to address readers and provide commentaries at specific plot points. For example:

> During this meeting, the treasurer has not spoken at all, merely smiling in his seat. He would have been one of the main players attacking the directors that sided with the school. Usually, he will be sure to stand at the podium and make a rant at each meeting. Why is he so quiet and reticent this time? *Readers who recall the previously narrated incident about sending the embroidered scrolls as a wedding gift will naturally understand, I do not need to speak further.* (336)
>
> As the saying goes, misfortunes never come alone. The school has been caught up in an agitation, and its finances have fallen into difficult straits. Not only are the directors of the national school furrowing their brows, thinking that the circumstances are difficult to resolve, *even the author is also heaving a sigh for the school's future when he reaches this juncture.*
>
> *Let us not dawdle on these trivial matters and return to our story proper* (341).[92]

These examples illustrate how the narrator-author reveals himself as part of the contemporaneous social collective that also includes the characters and readers. In the first example, he assumes that readers move alongside him as the plot advances, whereas in the second, he writes as if he is recounting the events to interlocutors who share the author's time-space. It is debatable if such narratorial insertions should be seen as occurring at a hetero-diegetic level, since they are incorporated without typesetting distinctions such as parentheses on the pages. In the second example above, the author appears in the third-person narrative discourse in the same sentence that describes other characters' circumstances, as though he is a character himself. The novel therefore requires constant vigilance on the part of readers to interrogate the level at which the narrator-author is speaking and performing the focalization.

The omniscient narrative voice reminds readers, whether in China or Malaya, of the storyteller character in traditional Chinese fiction, as critics have pointed out with varying levels of approval.[93] The device creates an effect of immediacy between the narrator and his imagined audience, which in turn builds a special scenario of literary communication within and beyond the text. Commingling with the polyphony of characters from different ethnic and linguistic backgrounds, the narrator-raconteur's mode of address suggests that although the narrative has a presiding linguistic consciousness, it lacks one that is unified.

In his study of the canonical chapter novel *Water Margin*, Liangyan Ge delineates the affective precondition for creating a "literary vernacular" that "artistically presents the sum total of linguistic experience of the social community."[94] Ge contends that the creative synthesis embodied by the narrative text is underpinned by "linguistic empathy," "where the narrator endeavors to empathize with different linguistic sensibilities in the narrated world and imitates the various speech types of the characters."[95] In the case of *Thick Smoke*, creating a vernacular of the masses depends on Lin's ability to express his vicarious integration with other members of the Malayan society through various means at his disposal for literary representation. When he discontinues the mode of polylingual expression, Lin switches to a monolingual literary language to impute the thoughts, emotions, and attitudes of the people living together in the locale. *Thick Smoke*, a product of Lin's identification at large with Malaya's complex sociolinguistic condition in the 1930s, can thus be interpreted (akin to *Water Margin*) as a "textualization" of "popular orality," which indicates "the locus where different types of linguistic consciousness were registered and orchestrated."[96] Conveyed through the distinct voice of the narrator-storyteller, each character's speech is in effect "'a voice within a voice,' a speech that is wrapped up in the narrator's linguistic consciousness."[97]

It follows then that Lin's formulation of a place-appropriate literary language can be compared to the development of what Ge calls a "written vernacular." To Ge, a "written vernacular" stands in contrast to "written colloquialism." While both linguistic modalities are organic and protean, the former may not be entirely faithful to the living language of its times, as it develops eclectic combinations of stylistic shades for aesthetic pursuits.[98] Lin never fully formulated his written literary vernacular through *Thick Smoke*, but his attempt reveals a manner of authorial self-fashioning that embodies his performance of familiarity with the Malayan milieu for his geographically distributed Sino-Southeast Asian audience.

In so doing, Lin reconfigures the traffic of "linguistic empathy" mediated by the author as the nexus. Besides deploying a narrator who identifies with the gamut of speech varieties within the Mahua community, Lin also uses the narrator as implied author to solicit understanding of his representational predicament from readers in both Malaya and China. Writing for the masses then becomes a bidirectional process, a two-route experiment of not only how well an author adopts the feelings of characters in his narrated world, but also the extent to which he resonates with the reading masses who can access his equivocal creative positionality. Depending on the subjective experiences of readers, as well as where *Thick Smoke* is received, the bifurcated sense of the local can be one of familiarity or alienation, which corresponds to the disjunction between the novel's fictional setting in Malaya and its material terrain of publication in Shanghai. Perceived as either a generic site of settlement for Chinese migrants or an exotic frontier of China, the novel's Malayan setting registers Lin's differentiated performance of localization in each of the two connected literary spaces.

MAHUA LITERATURE'S TOPOLECTAL MODE OF EXISTENCE

Meir Sternberg's broader theoretical assertion is instructive in articulating the full implications of Lin's narrative practice in *Thick Smoke*. Sternberg points out that the strategies used in translational mimesis can be examined beyond their technicalities to unveil deeper contexts involving linguistic, poetic, and historical elements. To him, "the realism of polylingual discourse ... cannot be understood apart from the text's overall referential strategy, of which it is both a miniature and a part or means."[99] If Lin's use of the omniscient storyteller voice of traditional Chinese fiction and his efforts to represent Malayan multilingualism form the double thrusts of his "overall referential strategy," what overarching end did Lin hope to achieve?

Ultimately, Lin's hybrid linguistic experiment should be read as a product of, as well as a commentary on, Mahua socioliterary relations in the 1930s. Extending his artistic horizon to accommodate Chinese literary production at plural scales via his novelistic practice, Lin reveals how the translocal compatibility of Sino-Malayan literary spaces can invigorate the larger world-Chinese literary system, in tandem with the mobilization of local concerns about internal differentiation, as attested by his position as a minority *waijiang ren* writer among creative peers from southern China. Deploying the two representational modalities, he tried to carve out a distinctive authorial style alongside the coevolution of literary spaces in both Malaya and China. While the storyteller voice preserves the patina of popular resonance, indicative of Lin's command of traditional literati resources, the commitment to tailoring a language for the masses through representing literary multilingualism seeks contiguity with the locality to participate in a wider cultural project of place-making. His stylistic mingling of demotic script and the state-supported *guoyu* (the national language of China) mark his venture to accrue greater authority within the Malayan literary space by forging a place-appropriate language for the locale.

From this perspective, Lin is not as unenlightened as what Ng Kim Chew makes Mahua literary forerunners out to be. His case gives pause to Ng's confident pronouncements that the earlier generation of Mahua writers were not conscious of the language they used for literary representations, or that they were overly invested in embodying collectivity through their writings at the expense of creative individuality.[100] Looking through the amalgam of authorial beliefs, the cultural politics of the times, and the realist effects of *Thick Smoke* (which are not naively reflectionist), we can see how a writer's personal aspirations are intertwined with a rhetoric that serves the collective. But for all his public expression of committing to the Mahua literary space, Lin persevered in fostering his individuated articulations, stylizing Malaya for audiences in both China and the British colony.

Lin's supralocal positionality hence demonstrates that "place" as an analytical scale can be harnessed productively for studying the globalization of modern Chinese literature beyond merely compiling geographical venues that host Chinese-language literary production. Besides historicizing the dispersed condition of global Chinese literature, it is also important to grasp the inner heterogeneity of each locale in order to reveal the finer struggles that define the vitality within peripheral literary spaces. *Thick Smoke* allows us to observe how Lin uses creative and conceptual resources from China to address the symbiotic relationship between Malaya and the plethora of languages hosted in the locality. His literary representations give form to a language of the Malayan masses, thus underscoring a significant dimension that has been elided in the prevailing analyses of Mahua cultural polemics and literary historiography. Through the alternative lens of speech groups, his novelistic endeavor alerts us to the dynamics of intra-ethnic and inter-ethnic (mis)communication, as well as the internal differences that structure Malaya as a distinctive local Chinese society with ties to places beyond the Southeast Asian region.

Fast forward to 2015. Gesturing toward the longstanding parameter in Singapore and Malaysian Chinese studies, Ng uses the trope of topolectal group to accentuate the peripheral circumstances of Mahua literature. In a public speech, he likens literary languages of different genres such as poetry and fiction to topolects, positing that "literary enthusiasts seem to form specific topolectal groups with their own topolect-based identities."[101] Taking Mahua literature beyond its national borders thereafter, he further compares the way in which the literary formation is perceived within Taiwan's literary space to the established mode of communal organization in Southeast Asian Chinese history:

> In Taiwan, we are sometimes called "the Malaysian *bang*" (*malai bang* 馬來幫) in jest, to wit, a native-place association, representing a small community of those who use a differential language. For the sake of self-preservation, the early Southeast Asian Chinese migrants first formed cliques and factions based on bloodlines and geographical provenances. Subsequently, they organized topolectal group associations, clan associations, trade associations and other groups to unite their communities.... For this Sinophone (*huawen*) literary formation trapped within a specific communal language, it [Mahua literature] has to compete with larger communities beyond national boundaries, the result of which is that in the family of Sinitic-language literatures, it very often can only occupy the last seat, or become an appendix (within the American, Japanese and Korean academic institutions that study modern Chinese literature). That is a positionality that signifies an inconsequential positionality.[102]

What Ng describes here resonates strongly with Gilles Deleuze and Félix Guattari's concept of "minor literature," which forms the keystone of Mahua literary actors' self-imagination of their creative circumstances. In that conceptual context, "the Malaysian *bang*" as a minority group uses its special Chinese language from Southeast Asia to create a recognizable literature in cultural milieux where Chinese is the major language. In Taiwan, because Mahua literature employs an artistic language with limited users and audience, it has been ghettoized—like a small topolect-based clan association in a larger cultural ecology. By extrapolation, in the world of Chinese-language literatures, the Mahua authors of Sinophone (*huawen*) works are analogous to topolect users who gather in different small regions or under circumstances of displacement. Their writing practices lack the wherewithal to compete with other larger literary formations for academic and general readers' attention.

Ng's use of the niche social organization as a metaphor for minoritized literary collectivity represents a variation in analytical scale from his 2004 call for Mahua writers to develop their own "individualized topolect" (*geren fangyan* 個人方言).[103] *Geren fangyan* registers Ng's ideal picture of Mahua authors making conscious artistic choices about literary language so as to present varied and distinctive personal styles. Notably, the rich term contains a crucial semantic element about social location.[104] To Ng, the fundamental predicament of Mahua literature stems from Mahua authors' lack of adequate social capital, which hinders them from inventing their own signature discourses that effectively bind together person, place, and language. By emphasizing the importance of formulating nonreplicable properties of literary languages—each of which is attributed only to one person, and to a particular place—despite being constrained by larger structural forces, Ng drives home the paradox that literary provinciality can become an unexpected but worthy source of artistic singularity.

The idiomatic slant of Lin's novelistic multilingualism notwithstanding, Ng is unlikely to acknowledge *Thick Smoke* as an embodiment of the early Mahua author's dedicated stylistic choice, given Lin's stunted attempt at creating his "individualized topolect."[105] The modulative disclaimer strongly suggests that Lin could not sustain the textualization strategies of translational mimesis for the full length of the novel.

Nonetheless, I make the case that Ng's ideal type of Mahua creative writing takes after Lin's earlier artistic concerns: both their discourses—narrative or otherwise—rest upon forms of authorial agency that consider matters of style, which encode strategic considerations of writers' linguistic capacities as well as their visions of Mahua society.[106] The goals of Ng's literary predecessors share more common ground with his own aesthetically inclined aspirations for the evolution of Mahua literature than Ng admits, if only he develops greater empathy for the challenging conditions that produced a text like *Thick Smoke*.

Lin and his writing practice evince the dilemmas and trade-offs inherent in enacting place-based representations during the fledgling period of modern Chinese literature in Malaya. As I discuss in the rest of the book, writers who harbor the desire to invent a Sinophone (*huawen*) literary language that keeps pace with sociolinguistic adaptations persisted over the years. In the 1950s and 1960s, the lively linguistic representations in Mahua literary works inspired Han Suyin, an Anglophone sojourner writer who saw in those representations the parallel promise of creating a literary English evocative of Malaya. How that writer mediated the encounter between the two language streams and leveraged Malayan Chinese language for her own fictional experiment will be the subject of the next chapter.

CHAPTER TWO

Channeling Exemplarity

Han Suyin's Bifocal Writing Practice in Malaya

Since the early decades of the twentieth century, Mahua literary critics have contested writers' use of geographical specificity to produce aesthetic distinctiveness. For example, around 1927, literary actors promoted the infusion of "South Seas color" (*nanyang secai* 南洋色彩) into literature and the arts to overcome the lack of works that depicted the local milieu.[1] Prior to World War II, such concerns to cultivate local color continued in a 1939 controversy, which involved Yu Dafu 郁達夫, the famous May Fourth writer, who had just arrived in Singapore to assume editorship of the newspaper *Sin Chew Jit Poh* 星洲日報. When young Mahua writers from Penang consulted him on ways to promote Nanyang localism (*difangxing* 地方性) to wider literary spheres, Yu advised that "If Nanyang can produce a great writer who is serious about creating tens and hundreds of works that treat Nanyang as the focal point for a sustained period of time, then . . . it is only natural that Nanyang can establish literary arts with its own local sensibilities."[2] His situational diagnosis of a "great writer" (*da zuojia* 大作家) was not well-received; the local critics perceived his suggestion as valorizing a genius modality of authorship, encouraging writers to hone their craft by staying isolated from current affairs, and discounting the impact of broad-based arts and literary movements.[3]

Although Yu's discourse caused considerable pushback, after World War II the Mahua literary circle welcomed another visitor whom Yu would have recognized as a remarkable writer. The luminary figure was the Eurasian author Han Suyin (rendered in Chinese as 韓素音 or 漢素音; 1916/17–2012), now far better remembered for her enchantment with China. During the 1960s and 1970s she achieved great prominence for her role as an intellectual mediator between the West and the Chinese socialist state.[4] But she was actually first enthralled by British Malaya. Known for her work in public health and cultural advocacy for marginalized groups, Han was highly regarded in the Mahua cultural circle during her sojourn in the British territories of Malaya and Singapore in the 1950s and 1960s. In many ways, Han recalls the figure of José Rizal, the eminent author from the Philippines, whom Yu recommended to the young Mahua writers for emulation. Rizal was well-known for writing *Noli Me Tángere* (Touch Me Not), the foundational text for modern Filipino literature. As Yu notes:

> Only after this novel was published did other countries in the world know that Nanyang has the Philippine archipelago, and get acquainted with the country's politics, society, and the lives of ordinary inhabitants of the islands. Of course, Rizal did not set out to purposely emphasize the local colors of Philippines. However, it goes without saying that once the novel was published, Filipino literature was established. Although Rizal's work was originally written in Spanish, this novel has been translated into dozens of languages, and has become popular reading material in many countries.[5]

To call Han a "great writer" in Yu's sense is to highlight the ways in which she embodied the Rizal model described above. In her view, literature's role is to make a geographical location visible to the larger world. Like Yu, Han espoused that the literary history of a place should be multilingual, and that national literatures can resonate with reading publics in other national spheres via translation. As later events show, Han carved out a writing career for herself in Southeast Asia, which echoed Yu's vision of a transformative literary figure who raises the global profile of an otherwise obscured location such as Malaya. By investing her creative energy in the novelistic genre, she not only reinforced the Mahua literary circle's desire for long-form fiction but also followed Rizal in harnessing the form's panoramic capacity to represent the societal phenomena of a neglected locale, turning it into a valid terrain of global literature.

Han's Malayan writing practice was inflected by a doubled vision that habitually connected the local to the global as dynamic modes of living and analysis. While advocating for local Chinese subjectivities, she also developed a strong affective orientation toward China as it entered a fresh stage of nation-building after its civil war ended. Around the same time, as Fiona Lee demonstrates, Han's perspectives on Chinese and English as Malayan languages were profoundly influenced by the contemporaneous debates at the Afro-Asian Writers Conferences (AAWCs) held from the late 1950s to mid-1960s outside of Southeast Asia.[6] Further contextualizing the local-global resonance that Lee discerns regarding Han's cultural discourses, this chapter spotlights the Eurasian author's fiction-writing project about Malaya, which began before the mid-1950s, to posit the social realities in her place of sojourn and the intellectual work of literary representation that drew her to the AAWC discussions, and which later led her to resituate those exogenous ideas in relation to Malaya.

At the center of my analysis stands *And the Rain My Drink* (hereafter *Rain*), Han's 1956 novel about Malaya and Singapore, and *Freedom Shout Merdeka* (hereafter *Freedom*), the unfinished sequel to *Rain*.[7] Together with Rizal's *Noli Me Tángere* on the Philippines, Multatuli's *Max Havelaar* on Indonesia, and Wu Zhuoliu's *Orphan of Asia* on Taiwan, Han's larger Malayan writing project contributes to the archive of significant literary texts about the effects of colonial rule in Asia. Juxtaposing *Rain* and *Freedom* with her other nonfiction writings during the same period, I contend that she was composing Anglophone literature as world literature in late 1950s and early 1960s Malaya by adopting a bifocal approach. In both her fiction and nonfiction works, the bifocality comes through Han's twin engagement with local and global perspectives, as well as her ethnographic portrayals that function as a mode of indexing universal cultural configurations. In so doing, Han developed her nation-building vision for a Malaya that would set a precedent of interculturalism for Asia and the world as it hosts a mosaic of races, languages, and cultures.

To evaluate Han's bifocal writing method, which moves between close scrutiny of immediate Malayan realities and longer-range geopolitical prospects with global implications, I examine her endeavor to vernacularize English as an acceptable literary language for depicting Malaya. Looking to Mahua literature for inspiration, she incorporates locally inflected English in *Rain* and *Freedom* to reflect creolized linguistic habits. Though both local literary constituencies were then not fully visible to reading publics, Han introduces the efforts of the Chinese-language sphere to the English-language sphere, praising the former for mobilizing localized linguistic forms in literature to convey a distinctive sense of geographical and political community. As her spirited discourses testify, she believes in turning shared marginality into productive forces of creativity. Eluding the cultural grip of the British, Han's Anglophone writing practice in the Malayan periphery registers Sinophone inflections and demonstrates a pathbreaking approach to overcoming biases about incompatible pairings of place and language.

BECOMING AN ASIAN WRITER VIA MALAYA

Malaya represents an important station in Han's life. The Southeast Asian locale was where she transitioned from an amateur novelist to a professional author. And in the tropical British colony her writings and public image jointly projected her ideal of the culturally hybrid Asian writer to the world. Arriving from Hong Kong in Johor Bahru in 1952, Han accompanied Leonard Comber, then her husband, who worked in the Special Branch of the Malayan Police, the intelligence unit of the British colonial government. She stayed in the colonial territories for more than a decade, leaving only in 1964 due to a repressive local political climate.[8]

Throughout her Malayan sojourn, Han engaged widely with local society. As the spouse of a colonial police officer she mingled in elite social circles, becoming acquainted with wealthy Chinese entrepreneurs and other expatriates engaged at the Special Branch, the University of Malaya, and the Malayan Civil Service. That privileged circle would have resembled her social sphere during her prior residence in Hong Kong, were it not for improved financial circumstances that allowed her to drive and reach out to other communities. Being a doctor by profession, she worked initially at a government hospital and later established private medical practices in Johor Bahru and Singapore. Outside of her primary vocation, she took on a part-time job at the Singapore Anti-Tuberculosis

FIGURE 2.1 Han Suyin in her Johor Bahru home study, circa 1950s

Association to fund her voluntary services at a children's chest clinic and a "New Village," which implemented the British plan to resettle local Chinese peasants in communes placed under strict supervision and thereby cut off their logistical support for the Malayan Communist Party. House calls taught her much about living conditions in the colonies. She visited Malay villages and tin mines, stayed in rubber plantations, and expanded her contact with non-Chinese populations.

Her access to communities of different racial and class backgrounds made her sensitive to the feelings and meanings Malayans attached to various types of group belonging. In her notes for *Freedom*, she wrote excitedly about the heady experience of life in the British colony:

> Without conscious volition on my part, life had organized me, the trees and the grass, the heat and the rain became part of me. . . . I was no longer conscious of the landscape, no longer receptive to the now familiar palms and rubber trees. It was people now who wholly preoccupied me; people of all kinds and all customs, getting their

own way side by side in what appeared a tolerant chaos, preserved in their own ways like engines on rails. Perhaps the same curious blindness of familiarity insulated them, each group living its own world, in its own geometrical dimensions, occupying a similar space and time, interpenetrating, and influencing each other without knowing it.[9]

Han's evocative description of Malaya and Singapore captures the slow consequences of what John Sydenham Furnivall, the historian and ex-colonial administrator in Burma, would identify as a "plural society," where communal worlds existed alongside one another, with different groups of people exercising forbearance to create a general social order.[10] But times were changing, and those worlds in Malaya were undergoing a mutual osmosis of ideas and practices.

Stoked by the decolonizing fervor in Asia, Han launched her career as a full-time writer in 1959, closing her clinic in Singapore to focus on her literary career.[11] Building upon her literary reputation, her connections from her Yenching University days in China, and her friendship with Malcolm MacDonald—then the British High Commissioner for Southeast Asia—Han cultivated immense global social capital during her sojourn. Through her travels, she enjoyed access to many political leaders of Asia, such as the People's Republic of China's premier Zhou Enlai, the Indian prime minister Jawaharlal Nehru, the Indonesian president Sukarno, Malaysia's first prime minister Tunku Abdul Rahman; and the Cambodian monarch and later prime minister Norodom Sihanouk. As she grew into her role as a Malayan public intellectual and, subsequently, a global one, she penned current affairs commentaries on geopolitical conflicts and was frequently invited to give talks and attend cultural functions. Her international acclaim and popularity with local students led her to teach from 1959 to 1961 at Nanyang University, the first and only Chinese-medium tertiary institution ever established outside China, Hong Kong, and Taiwan. Reminiscent of how Yu Dafu was regarded as a literary mentor by young Mahua writers, Han's students went to her clinic to share "slim volumes of verses and novelettes, all of them anti-colonial, full of verve and spirit" with her, or to seek advice for their "short stories and poems, to confide their dreams of writing major novels." She also promoted local knowledge production by helping to establish and write for the Malaysian Sociological Research Institute.[12]

Insofar as she attracted major publishers in the centers of global English literary production despite being based in peripheral Southeast Asia, Han can be characterized as composing world literature during her Malayan sojourn. In 1956, *Rain* was brought out by the renowned London publishing firm Jonathan Cape, famous for its transatlantic list of authors such as Ernest Hemingway, Ian Fleming, and James Joyce. The novel was lauded in Malayan English newspapers as the first title to be released concurrently in London and Singapore.[13] By then, Han had achieved global acclaim, her fame fresh from the 1955 Hollywood film *Love Is a Many-Splendored Thing*, adapted from her earlier work on Hong Kong. The same year that *Rain* was published in the British metropole and its Southeast Asian colony, the novel also appeared in America under another distinguished publisher, Little, Brown and Company, which enhanced Malaya's visibility in the international literary arena.

In retrospect, *Rain*'s release at multiple sites in the mid-1950s did not mark a new relational modality between literary centers and peripheries. Rather than implying metropolitan publishers' optimism about a feasible readership for English-language creative writings beyond Britain and the United States—that audience gathered momentum only from the early 1960s onward—the novel's market-differentiated engagement still bespeaks Han's elevated status as an author of global appeal.[14] Hailing Han as "the most important exponent of not only Malayan but [also] Asian literature as a whole," the London-based journal *Eastern World* praised *Rain* as an "outstanding contribution" to world literature that typified how authors expressed an empathetic understanding about their local subjects.[15] The overlay of different geographical scales—Malayan, Asian, world—gestures toward Han's sociopolitical vision that combined different ranges of oversight when situating Malayan culture in the world at large. Amid the scalar variety, it was "Asia" that Han harnessed to brand her cultural politics during her sojourn. She averred that *Rain* was written "entirely from the Asian point of view," believing as she did then that an Asian writer's position gave her a unique vantage point to observe and represent what she thought were the actual circumstances in Malaya.[16]

On the local Malayan front, Han's writing practice was uniquely entangled with the Mahua literary space, for *Rain* inducted Han into the field of modern Mahua literature, even though it was written in English. In 1958, the novel was partially translated and launched the Literary Arts of Singapore and Malaya Book Series (Xinma wenyi congshu 新馬文藝叢書) published by the Youth Book Company (Qingnian shuju 青年書局), well-known for its commitment to nurturing Sinophone Singapore and Malayan literary works. Han's *Rain* was the only novel selected for two cycles of the series, each with a dozen titles. In the Southern Literature Series (Nanfang wencong 南方文叢), a separate project also sponsored by the Youth Book Company, another novel by Han—*The Mountain Is Young*, rendered into Chinese—was chosen as the lead title, ahead of the Malayan edition of Lin Cantian's *Thick Smoke* and five other novels.[17]

The cooptation of Han into Mahua literary space coincided with the rising interest in Malayan content by local bookstores and publishers after a colonial ban on publications from China and Hong Kong in 1958.[18] Her contact with Chinese school students and figures in the local Sinophone cultural circle acquainted her with the relative vibrancy of Mahua literary production, whereas her renown as an international best-selling writer would have bolstered the cachet of the Youth Book Company's Malayan publications. In terms of literary history, Han's novels contributed to the extended fictional genre, which is noticeably inadequate among the literary stock of Mahua literature, a situation brought over from earlier phases, as I discussed in chapter 1. Notably, her dedication to novelistic writing intersected with the Malayan scene's enduring reverence for the longer narrative form. Inaugurating the two book series that cultivated local consciousness, *Rain* and *The Mountain Is Young* paved the way for longer works by writers such as Miao Xiu 苗秀, Wei Yun 韋暈, and Li Rulin 李汝琳, all of whom would later become important figures in the Mahua literary circle. Furthermore, accepting Han's translated works as part of Mahua literary repertoire reinforces the scholar-critic Tee Kim Tong's proposal to recognize the role of translated literature in stimulating the growth of a lackluster body of Sinophone works. Given that *Rain* and *The Mountain Is Young* were included in each book series despite being translations from English, Han's case establishes an earlier genesis of that growth strategy than what Tee asserts for the late 1960s.[19]

Curiously, Han was fashioned as a Chinese-language writer in Malaya in the 1950s and 1960s. Ina Zhang Xing Hong 章星虹 contends that the work of the literary translator Ly Singko 李星可 (who made her novels accessible to local Chinese readers) and enthusiastic journalists from the Chinese press (who translated her public speeches) cocreated the popular misrecognition of Han as an author who wrote in Chinese.[20] The historical misrecognition raises more salient questions about place-based literary production than vexatious inquiries about the extent to which Han as a Eurasian could be considered a "Chinese" writer, and whether or not her works should be considered "Chinese" literature. In particular, the misunderstanding shows how her Chinese heritage and professional identity as an Asian writer served her purpose of promoting multilingual and multicultural exchanges in Malaya.

Importantly, the claim in the 1950s and 1960s that Han was a Chinese-language writer in Malaya operated differently from claims in China's cultural circle after the 1980s that she was one of mainland's diasporic kin. As the historian Emma Teng points out, the latter discourse relied primarily on highlighting her affective ties to Sichuan, her ancestral home, and her extended family connections in China, binding the notion of Chineseness with a territorialized identity.[21] Han's own affinity to the roots discourse, however, did not reflect a parochial mindset that precluded other Chinese from developing their roots in different places. On the contrary, she was a staunch supporter of Chinese formulating their identities in locales outside of China, such as Malaya.

As a sharp observer of cultural politics in the British territories, Han discerned the nested marginality that troubled local English literary endeavors of the ethnic Chinese. While the creative writings of colonized groups—regardless of language—were all dismissed by metropolitan centers and the colonial administration, the Malayan Chinese writers who wrote about the Southeast Asian region in English were further sidelined, as they were using a linguistic medium foreign to the majority of their ethnic community. Through her advocacy, which included *Rain*'s publication, Han mounted a simultaneous address: to the Anglophone readers in the international market, she was conveying the obscured perspectives of the segregated society under colonial governance. To the local English-literate audience, she was showing what and how to write about Malaya.

Featuring the totality of social languages through its extensive coverage of Malayan society, *Rain* was Han's most significant cultural statement on the place. Her use of Malayan English in the novel (and the uncompleted *Freedom*) documents the development of the creolizing language itself. Inhabiting the position of a Malayan writer, Han prefigures postcolonial writing that "abrogates the privileged centrality of English by using language to signify difference while employing a sameness which allows it to be understood."[22] The creative traffic between the language of representation (English) and the representation of language (Malayan English) enacts her thesis that place and language shape each other. Local or localized writers—as Han's cultural practice indicates—can foster an unblinkered sense of place by materializing a geographically specific mode of linguistic presence in literature. Moreover, *Rain* (and *Freedom*) legitimize the use of hybrid linguistic forms for cultural production. Through the novel, Han conveys that linguistic hybridity does not only connote racial or cultural intermingling, but also how social group boundaries are always in flux and never impervious. To the Eurasian author who was deeply engaged with reforming cultural mindsets in Malaya in the 1950s and 1960s, portraying the hybridity of social languages was a strategic act of allaying criticisms of linguistic impurity or inauthenticity, and emphasizing the merits of developing new linguistic forms based on heterogeneous sources. Envisioning the concurrent evolution of Malayan English in different segments of the local population, *Rain* carries Han's hope for the decolonizing locale to yield its own writers who can command a distinctly place-catalyzed literary language.

Remarkably, her forging of a locally inflected English for creative composition took reference from the exemplary localizing orientation of Mahua literature. Amid imminent postcoloniality, the history of globalizing English language in Asia was more nuanced than the familiar discursive format of writing back against the empire. Han showed how interlinguistic stimulation in the margins (between Chinese and English) could exist alongside the intralinguistic tension (among the different Englishes) that innovates Anglophone literary writing. Highlighting the oft-forgotten native dimensions of that globalized history, Han's situated literary practice in Malaya attests to how nurturing a place-based national identity entails rallying local peripheries by working across the Chinese-English divide.

BLENDING THE DOUBLE REGISTERS OF WORLD LITERATURE

After embarking on her professional writing career in Malaya, Han shuttled between a public image of deep social engagement and a private realm of detached emotions. Calling herself a "natural minority," Han told her friend Malcolm MacDonald, the British diplomat-politician in Southeast Asia: "I have a very sound perspective of my own role, which is that of observer, on the sidelines."[23] She believed that her position on the societal margins afforded her a critical distance to weave various partisan perspectives into an insightful picture about the British colony, which symptomizes a broader decolonizing movement in Asia.

Employing literature to distill local statements into larger commentaries, Han's "observer" stance feeds a compositional mode that generates trenchant descriptions about locales foreign to an author for depicting the human condition. In this light, her bifocal writing practice lends *Rain* to be read in what David Damrosch calls the ethnographic and the universal registers of world literature.[24] Damrosch's example of the well-traveled figure who navigates those twin registers with finesse is the British writer P. G. Wodehouse. Akin to Wodehouse, Han was also a "resident alien" in her place of sojourn.[25] In addition, beyond place-specific concerns, both authors wrote for an international audience, and were invested in creating fictional worlds with their own inner logics that retain signs of the external world.

Similarities aside, what warrants analytical attention is how the double registers of composing world literature for Han are not distinct—the ethnographic shades into the universal in her Malayan stories. Whereas Wodehouse portrays modern British and American life rooted in social realities of those cultures "as if from outside," Han's fiction about the British colony in Southeast Asia manifests an authorial blend of alien and native positionalities.[26] On a certain level, she succeeded at passing off as an insider of the Malayan cultures she experienced, for *Rain* was positively reviewed as an immersive work penned "for Malayans about Malayans," which accomplished a "complete merging of the writer with the people she writes about."[27] But unlike Wodehouse, who connotes the universal register by drawing on his astute observations of the social worlds he encounters, Han uses her ethnographer-like faculties to limn how widespread ethos of the times adopt specific forms in local societies.

Fundamentally, Han's rhetorical dialectics between the two compositional registers mirror the cosmopolitanism of her sojourn. Ever since she arrived in Malaya, Han found herself engrossed with its quotidian life. As she told her publisher friend Jonathan Cape, "I get into the heart of the country and am beginning to know something about it.... I never realized before how much about Asia I did not know. Going to Indian festivals, which I had never seen; having Tamil friends and Malay friends, which in China I would never have."[28] All those varied experiences acquainted her with Malayan residents of different ethnicities, inspiring her to feel "full of story material."[29] As early as 1953, she shared with Cape her plan to write an unprecedented book on her new place of residence:

> I am toying vaguely with the idea of a book on Malaya which will not be, as all books have been so far, a one-sided, European view of the thing, written from the heights of European living, but from the point of view of the squatter ... because if there is one point of view I know, it is the squatters.... I have been told here time and again by people who have been too long in Malaya ... that you cannot understand Malaya except from one point of view, that you must be pro-Malay, or pro-Chinese, or pro something or other. How wrong. At the moment the only synthesis that will make a worthwhile book is a picture of everything all together.[30]

Han's creative interest lies in constructing a social totality that transcends every Malayan resident's experiential scope. Confident of achieving the overall portraiture of Malaya from the bottom up, she inserts herself into different strata of local life. To "get the atmosphere of the real people of Singapore" and gather material for *Freedom*, she even joined the People's Action Party, a new local political party at the time, which would gain power in 1959 and govern Singapore up to the present day.[31]

To the Eurasian author, British Malaya was more than an inert setting. For the purpose of representing "the Malayan landscape of emotion and diversity," which till then was "all unexplored territory, uncharted land," Han insisted that "the whole complex pattern must unfold ... with round [sic] about 200,000 to 250,000 words," a narrative scale that she strongly suggested to be published in two to three volumes.[32] *Rain* constituted the first instalment of this proposed serialized format, and *Freedom* was supposed to follow soon after as the subsequent volume.[33] As an expatriate with intimate knowledge of the ways in which Malayan society was shaped by colonial and noncolonial forces, Han's ambiguous social position is strikingly reflected through the metafictional dimension in her larger Malayan writing project. In the project's grand narrative design, Han performs her outsider image: in *Rain*, Suyin, one of the main protagonists voiced in the first-person, shares Han's name and profession. In *Freedom*, the same character is depicted as writing a book about Malaya during her free time.[34] Suyin, the namesake who stands for the implied author, turns out to be a beginning writer collating information for her novel under preparation. Following this narrative logic, *Rain*, which represents the unfinished diptych or trilogy, actually depicts the birth of an author in Malaya. Its readers are thus looking at two worlds simultaneously: Han as both subject and object of artistic creation.

Overall, Han's Malayan writing project illuminates how she coordinates the double creative registers of ethnography and universality. In "Writing about Malaya," her article carried by *PETIR*, the organ of the People's Action Party, she elaborates on straddling the particular and the general when composing *Rain*:

> It is discouraging to find that no Malayan in these last four years produced a book about Malaya, leaving this work instead to a few transients, and by that I mean people not really born and bred in this country, and who, however interested and affectionate toward it, have come from elsewhere. . . . Where [are] the Malay, Chinese, Indian, Eurasian who belong here, who can give the feel of Malaya to the world? . . . It is only when people feel deeply about their country that a national literature is created. And it is more important to have a literature than a flag, for the things that bring people together are not legal arguments, treaties, or armies, but the fact that they read the same poems and sing the same songs and thrill to the same stories.[35]

Han has opined that expatriates can produce authentic works about Malaya if the writers show "a deep consciousness of the people they write about as part of themselves."³⁶ The nonnatives' creative orientation resembles the psychological transference of ethnographers conducting fieldwork insofar as those sojourning writers acquire the mindsets of their informants after living closely with them. But according to Han's view in the political newsletter—which in fact addressed the plurilingual Malayan public—to create a national literature, writers born and bred in the decolonizing locale should step up and undertake greater responsibilities in conveying the local ways of life to people in other countries.³⁷

By lamenting the absence of local writers of all ethnicities who would come forward and depict Malaya, Han implies that *Rain* gave "the feel of Malaya to the world." Here, the act of gifting Malaya to readers around the globe resonates with her belief that national literatures call their audiences—which include various international reading publics—into being. Asserting that "it is more important to have a literature than a flag," her use of the indefinite article "a" to index the two generic symbols of nationhood opens Malaya to a future of translocal solidarity. That future inserts the British territory into an open-ended series of locales with common struggles to achieve independence through decolonization, thereby marking an important shift in her discursive envisioning from the specific to the universal through literature.

For Han, the bracing impact of getting entangled with Malaya's decolonization struggle went beyond gaining a sense of the local. As she recalled in her twilight years, the Malayan experience "was an unshrouding, divesting me of thinking only in terms of China; making me aware of so many other cultures and peoples, and opening another door to bring me toward a certain universality."³⁸ Patently, her pursuit of that "universality" cannot be decoupled from her ambitious Malayan literary project. "I do not want to write slapdash, hasty stuff or journalese," she said.³⁹ As mentioned earlier, to depict the volatile circumstances in British Malaya, she expended immense effort to forge the most appropriate fictional form. The resultant *Rain* functions at once as a protest against the self-assured partiality that prevails in commentaries about the British colony, as well as a synthesized perspective derived from multiple sources of analysis.

Reading Han's nonfiction essays in tandem allows us to realize that her ethnographic approach to writing Malayan fiction is integral to her conception of cultural universalism. While struggling to complete

Freedom in the early 1960s, she expressed the hope that the Malayan way of life would demonstrate global exemplarity. She once commented that "we are all Eurasians culturally," which points toward there never having been discrete cultures to begin with. As she asserts, "the whole of the industrialization of Asia depends precisely upon this admixture of Eur-Asianism into all our thoughts and our modes of behavior. None of us is now purely this or that."[40] From this perspective, Malayans embody the desirable traits of being culturally fluid and mobile, which led her to conclude:

> In Malaya we have a great opportunity. We have here cultural groups that want to assimilate, that want to unite in harmony. Let us, each one of us, do our best to accomplish this, and in this way we can make Malaya a kind of pattern for the world, a pattern of how this can be achieved with the least amount of trauma, with the least amount of trouble and giving up, and with the largest share of adaptation, without rejection, of many cultures to each other.[41]

In shaping her model of a unified national culture arising from harmonious assimilation, she puts Malaya in relation to a larger world, suggesting that Malaya's particularity exist not in isolation, but in reciprocal articulation with the tide of multicultural nation-building in Asia. Put differently, Han takes the view that the local and the global have to constitute grounds for mutual enactment, in order to forge the ideal modality for cosmopolitan-minded writing. Characterizing everyone as cultural Eurasians from her vantage point in Malaya, her generalization directed the attention on embryonic national cultures in the colonies away from questions of linguistic nativity and ethnic essences to focus on place as a constitutive force of political identity.

Han's envisioning of a Malayan "pattern" predated the use of the same term in the 1970s by the postcolonial critic Edward W. Said, who described the asymmetrical relations between the East and the West. Before Said identified "the pattern of relative strength between East and West" that underpinned the hegemonic discourse of Orientalism, Han urged her Malayan audience to each become an author who "write[s] about this overwhelming country [Malaya] as he sees it, and not as he is told to see."[42] From a "complex pattern" that "must unfold"—which she conveyed privately to her publisher Cape—to "a kind of pattern for the world" in her call for Malayan residents to embrace their Eurasian tendencies, Han championed Malaya as a promising global paradigm of multiculturalism. She hoped that the place could set the standard for other countries seeking cordial cultural heterogeneity. In so doing, the decolonizing location would become the Asian archetype that embodies the successful integration of all cultural groups.

Throughout her sojourn, however, Han was troubled by the seeming incompatibility arising from her embodied spread across languages and geographical regions. As a Eurasian who spoke Chinese but lived in neither Europe nor China, she told her publisher, "One cannot deny one's roots, one's marrow. China is the marrow in my bones, and Asia is my living breath, and yet I use English. Somehow I must accommodate all this and make it all pull together. I feel, somehow, that although difficult, this can be done."[43] Clearly, the desire to suture linguistic practices and spaces widely presumed to stay apart became the driving force of her literary and extraliterary endeavors.

Han's negotiation with Lin Yutang, the famous bilingual Chinese writer who was the inaugural chancellor of Nanyang University in Singapore, bears out her determination to overcome preconceived biases about possible combinations of place and language. When Lin invited her to teach canonical "English literature" at the university, she counterproposed "an Asian type of literature" but was rejected by Lin, who did not recognize that literary category.[44] Following Lin's departure from Nanyang University, Han convened a course titled "Contemporary Literature" at the university's Faculty of Arts from 1959 to 1961. Although she lectured in a mix of English and Chinese, only English course materials were distributed. While she appeared to be recentering the West in doing so, she was actually encouraging students to exercise their own agency and master the colonial language for their own purposes. The course materials drew primarily from "books written by Asians in their own languages and translated into English."[45] She treated "the subject on a broad general basis, co-relating the history of Asian countries."[46] It was her hope that the course could "stimulate [the] curiosity of Asians about each other," as well as "open the minds of Asians more toward each other than only toward the West for everything, including literature."[47]

Han's lecturer stint at Nanyang University hence indexes her broader cultural politics, which were also manifested through her multiple public exhortations for Malayan writers to leave their monolingual moorings behind.[48] She strove to highlight how languages acquire new lives beyond hegemonic spaces that attempt to control linguistic development from afar. She took the view that places and languages evolve in concert.[49] To her, such developments in social speech heralded a new typology of place-based literature that could realistically portray the local milieu with fresh linguistic forms.

An early scene in *Rain* dramatizes her reflections on how the hidden diversity within the racial categories imposed by the colonial government poses tremendous challenges for unifying the place and its languages:

> From ward to ward . . . the sinusoid of sound pursues me. Words, words, words, all adding up to this soft cacophony, this unending flat unquietness. Words in all the dialects and languages which are spoken in Malaya. Is not so much of what happens in this country a reciprocal confusion, rooted in ignorance of each other's language and customs, producing blindness, intolerant inhumanity? . . .
>
> Chinese, Malay, Indians, three words, three sweeping generalizations out of which it has been planned to forge a new nation, to create a country called Malaya, a single people to be called Malayans. . . .
>
> The word Malay means Javanese, Sumatrans, Indonesians, people from Minangkabau and many another [sic] East Indies island, Arabs and Arab-educated Mohammedans, as well as Malays proper from Malaya itself; Chinese include half a dozen sub-groups from the southern provinces of China, by feature and emotion Chinese, but divided by dialect into Teochews, Hokkiens, Hakkas, Cantonese, Hainanese and smaller groups. Indians include Tamils, Punjabis, Sikhs, Pathans, Bengalis, and many others. In each ward the nurses must act as translators as well as nurses, and where they fail, an orderly, or an amah, must be found to interpret, with all the

inaccuracy and the florid inventiveness of the illiterate Asian. Among the doctors few can speak to all the patients. . . .

Pacing the corridors, night dark, of the hospital, I heard the poor talk, Malay, Indians, Chinese, and asked myself whether out of this babel reassembled, a pattern would emerge. (27–29)

In the interior monologue above, Suyin, the doctor-narrator who works in a Malayan public hospital, imagines the medley of translingual scenarios she encounters as a microcosm of ethnic relations in the colonial society. Given the work's autobiographical flavor, the narrator's question at the end marks Han's own curiosity. Here, the term "pattern" refers more to an ideal form of social exchange that has yet to become discernible, rather than a preexisting exemplar for emulation. This extract is particularly thought-provoking for its mirror effect: at the same time that Suyin in the story will observe first-hand if the confusion of tongues in Malaya can be "reassembled," Han the author invests great effort to delineate the challenges of unifying polylingual Malaya to serve as a model of perfect intercultural communication for the world.

Therefore, the mode of fiction-writing Han practices through *Rain* exemplifies a way of shaping geographical locations into worthy literary terrain, which is useful for contemplating complex historical and geopolitical issues. To the Eurasian author, the universal human condition can be identified in the irreducibly ethnographic. By conflating the two planes of literary composition and claiming that the ethnographic register is the universal register in Asia, Han's case extends Damrosch's discourse on the globalization of English language literature in the early decades of the twentieth century. Compared to P. G. Wodehouse in Damrosch's account, Han formulates a different dialectics between the two creative modalities. Whereas Wodehouse designs fictive and symbolic settings with no corresponding referential location in the real world as a commentary on the larger human condition, Han's characters in *Rain* repeatedly mention in deictic emphasis, "this is Malaya" (15, 25). Since "Malaya" in Han's cultural discourse can refer concurrently to the Southeast Asian locale as well as the template to nurture global multiculturalism, *Rain* is clearly meant to reach beyond representing a single location and to evoke how Malaya's replicability and modularity reveal broader world historical significance.

Damrosch's account attributes Wodehouse's global success to the author's nonpareil sensitivity to intra-English differences that won him both a transatlantic audience as well as readers in other languages through translation. Several decades later, writing amid the decolonization fervor in Asia, Han transformed English into her own culture-making vehicle. Truly, she can be seen as pioneering "postcolonial literature" *avant la lettre* and executing a compositional strategy that seeks to "replace a temporal lineality with a spatial plurality."[50] On the surface, she engages in what Bill Ashcroft would call "inner translation," which occurs when postcolonial writers shuttle between two different varieties of English, yielding works in which English becomes both the medium and target of representation.[51] Han, however, used *Rain* and her larger writing practice not just to document the features of the emerging creole, but also to participate in shaping and disseminating the intermediary language whose hybridity is still being negotiated by various social forces.

CAPTURING LINGUISTIC HYBRIDITY IN THE COLONIZED PERIPHERY

In the 1960s, Han cited *Rain* as her best work. Out of the four books she had written—namely *Destination Chungking* (1942); the popularly acclaimed *A Many-Splendored Thing* (1952); and *The Mountain Is Young* (1958)—she found *Rain* "the hardest one to write," but it had given her a "great deal of satisfaction" that involved a "play on words."[52] That wordplay patently involved the representation of an evolving Malayan English as a literary language. The novel's depiction of fictional characters dealing with an emergent creole registers a dynamic social reality in which English and Malaya coevolve to create distinct identities for each other. While writing in a localized form of a colonial language may seem unremarkable, it is helpful to remember that Han was implementing her ideas about a place-apposite language in the 1950s, well before Malayan English was recognized as a worthy topic for academic study.[53]

A condensed illustration of Malayan English occurs early in *Rain*. The traits of the language undergoing creolization are manifested through the spoken discourse of the character Doremy, a Tamil nurse who preaches an easygoing attitude toward working in the public hospital where the doctor-narrator is posted:

> Doctor must not excite herself, lah. Will get all heaty in this weather. Anger is weakening to the body. We should have a big waiting room, like the men. But what to do? Many doctors must write many, many letters to the Department before can get, lah. But patients are quite happy, doctor. They are happy so long they see women doctor. Man doctor they don't like. Before you we had poor Dr. Sandrishan. He good man doctor, but patients never let him examine them. (18)

Doremy's remarks capture various features of Malayan English that would be later identified, analyzed, and classified by scholars. For instance, Han incorporated the discourse particle "lah" at the end of sentences, a speech habit now acknowledged to be loaned from topolects in South China, thereby marking the migrant elements that shape the creole-in-the-making.[54] The novel also depicts Doremy employing many other traits of Malayan English, such as the subject-absent utterance ("Will get all heaty in this weather"), leaving the subject to be contextually determined; the omission of the linking verb "to be" (as in "But what to do?" and "He good man doctor"); and the typology of "topic-prominent" sentences ("Man doctor they don't like"), all of which illustrate a minimalist propensity and provide early records of new linguistic patterns emerging from social interaction.[55]

By portraying the hybridized linguistic habits of the people she meets, Han documents the vivid feel of a changing Malaya. In so doing, she assumes the role of a participant-observer who studies the life of a social community by partaking in its activities. One striking form of such self-representation is how she shows "Suyin," the first-person narrator, picking up social lexicon in different parts of the novel. In a scene about the Hari Merdeka (Independence Day) Parade in *Freedom*, the narrator-doctor learns about the word "serani":

> "Merdeka!" shouted Nurse Thumboo, "Chinese, Malay, Tamil and Seranis—all together in a new country. Merdeka!"
> "What does Serani mean?" I asked. It obviously referred to me.

"You are a Serani," said Amy, "a . . . what you say, 'Tsap tsung.'" She used the Cantonese word, then went into Mandarin—"Huen hsieh, mixed blood."

"Eurasian," I said. "Yes, but why do you call them Seranis?"

"It comes from Nazarenes, na-za-re-nes, zarenes—serani," said Thumboo. "Because all Eurasians are Christians, they were all going to Church, so that is what the Malay people call them, 'the Nazarenes.'"

"But anyway, what matters? All of us together, all races, all religions, together to make Malaya, no? Che Azamah?"

Che Azamah smiled politely, but I had a feeling that she did not quite agree.[56]

This scene of multiracial mixing typifies Han's interest in human plurality. Elsewhere, she conveys that she loves Malaya for its cultural diversity, finding that wherever she goes, "I am used on the street to hearing many languages spoken" and "one cannot cast one's eye around without encountering at least five or six different shades of skin, five or six different ways of dressing and eating. This is also what makes another country, more homogenous, so dull and so monotonous to me after Malaya."[57]

In the aforementioned episode composed for *Rain*'s sequel, all the characters, including the first-person narrator, are gathered in a public space to watch the celebratory procession. The ways in which the multiracial group converse, debate, and inspire one another at the locale evokes Hannah Arendt's metaphor of a table. In *The Human Condition,* Arendt uses the artifact to explicate the world where diverse communities interact: "To live together in the world means essentially that a world of things is between those who have it in common, as a table is located between those who sit around it; the world, like every in-between, relates and separates men at the same time."[58] Set up as if the characters are gathered around a communal table, the scene projects Han's vision of people regardless of race and religion cohabitating in Malaya through fostering commonalities while also preserving differences. To buttress her hopeful projection about the ideal mode of coexistence, the story depicts the Indian nurse Thumboo telling the narrator later in the scene: "One day we shall all have to mix up, in spite of all the barriers. . . . We are all human beings, doctor, and one day ... the whole world will be *Serani* ... like you."⁵⁹

The portrayal of the first-person narrator encountering neologisms created from language contact hence resonates strongly with Han's opinion that "we are all Eurasians culturally." The Malayan characters share the work of cultural translation by not merely providing the lexical equivalents in Cantonese, Mandarin, and Malay for a word that is unfamiliar to the nonnative narrator, but also by communicating the English historical morphology that gives rise to the creolized term. Framed in this manner, the snippet of interculturalism offers a lively picture of linguistic hybridity in Malaya, where no single individual or group embodies absolute cultural authority.

As the public face of Han's Malayan literary project, *Rain* offers many vignettes of quotidian interaction that double up as representations of social languages engaged in vibrant exchanges. For instance, in the novel's second chapter, "Suyin" is introduced at the hospital to her departing Euro-Indian colleague Betchine, who quirkily pronounces "her R's rolled in the fashion of the Scots University Town where she had studied" (15). To visually convey the effect of the peculiar enunciation, the way Betchine addresses "Suyin" is reproduced orthographically as "dearr girrl" (15). Afterward, through the narrative design of sharing place-specific vocabulary with a newcomer, Betchine explains a local term that indicates a unique attitudinal disposition: "We have a word for it here," said Betchine. "'Tidapathy' is the name. It's the most important word in the Malayan vocabulary, and the sooner you learn it, the quicker you'll feel at home in Malaya. *Tidapah*. It means never mind. It's compounded of *je m'en fiche* and *mañana*. It's also the Will of God. Tidapah. The less you do, the less you show up your colleagues' 'tidapathy,' and the sooner you'll get promoted" (17).

Indeed, the second chapter of *Rain* preserves Han's descriptions of the budding adaptations of everyday languages in Malaya. Staging the free-flowing interaction within a hospital setting, "Suyin" encounters interlocutors from different backgrounds. She observes the Tamil staff nurse Doremy who understands both English and Malay but has to rely on the cleaner Ah Kam to translate the multitopolectal Chinese discourses of visiting female prisoners, and Rosie Yip, the policewoman warden "who spoke six Chinese dialects, Malay, and Malayan English" (19–20). As the doctor-narrator inspects the hospital during the night, she meets a night nurse who greets her with "the pleasant Malayan English insistence on the second syllable of bi-syllabic words" (26). Toward the end of the chapter, the narrator alludes to her enigmatic positionality in the broader scheme of affairs—as someone who knows more about the insurgency than she discloses—by reporting the shifts in the linguistic preference of Chinese members of the Malayan Communist Party. When a young Chinese insurgent is brought to the hospital, she discerns the Cantonese intonation of his "standard Chinese," which she claims to be "the language which the People Inside will use, whatever dialect group they may come from" (31).

Notably, Han does not create an epistemological gap between the author and her readers by leaving words or phrases from vernacular languages or idiosyncratic habits unglossed, or by employing unfamiliar concepts or references without exposition. Instead, she depicts the author experiencing Malaya not just as a new territory but also as an unfamiliar knowledge space alongside other characters and her readers. She suggests this narrative configuration through a disclaimer before *Rain* begins proper: "This book is fiction. Any resemblance of the characters to anyone alive or dead is pure coincidence. Exception is made for the author, who insists on occasionally appearing in the chapters."[60] While the paratext presumably serves the practical function of safeguarding Han against defamation charges, it declares the participatory presence of the author amid the narrative events as well, thus highlighting an intriguing contiguity between the fictional and the external world. In fact, by using a pen name in her actual life that also refers to *Rain*'s protagonist, Han—who was born Chou Kwanghu 周光瑚—takes fictionalizing beyond the pages of her works, and blurs the boundary between the literary and the real.[61]

In other words, Han the author is positioned as a witness-participant to the events staged within the text. Registering Han's desire to become a respected interpreter of Malayan realities, *Rain* also offers a series of ethnographic vignettes written as if she were an alert linguistic anthropologist conducting fieldwork. Her descriptive method can be gleaned from her advice for young Anglophone Malayan writers, which involves going "to the people who are the creators of language and literature, and know how they live and how they talk, and write it down just as it is."[62] But the straightforward task, which frames social speech as transparent entities that can be easily transcribed, belies the way she views her writing modality as "a special reflection of reality," which was not "a photographic record," but rather, "based on the colorful and complicated picture of life."[63]

By representing how a writer lives, thinks, and engages in literary composition for her Malayan writing project, Han asserts a contemporaneity between herself as the author and her fictional characters. In emphasizing the copresence with her Malayan subjects and their cultures, she eschews the mode of perception that the anthropologist Johannes Fabian calls "allochronism," which denies the coexistence of the ethnographer and the target of his or her observation in the same timeframe, placing the latter in a separate temporality that carries negative connotations of retarded progress.[64] From Han's perspective, the reverse scenario occurs instead, whereby she the author risks being left behind by a rapidly transforming social reality. Reflecting after she published *Rain*, Han shares her steadfast effort to keep up with evolving current affairs in order to grasp how Malayan residents forge a sense of common destiny for the future through nation-building, rather than inventing a shared past:

> And now a book is done about Malaya; or rather half a book. But the story of Malaya goes on . . . the story of a land trying to find itself through many channels. . . . To write about Malaya, therefore, is to write about an ever-changing, ever-varying manscape; a kaleidoscope, altering as we look at it; a challenging, exhausting, near-impossible task to try to describe these very processes of mutation and change, to catch them as they happen, and fix them in words.[65]

Han's evocative articulation conjures up the arresting image of a writer chasing after developmental processes in the external world, having to "catch"—in both senses of intercept and capture—the ongoing adjustments of a decolonizing locale, in order to convey the truth of the times and stay true to her authorial identity. As she told a close group of friends on how writers should hone their craft: "we have to keep moving if we want to stay ourselves."[66] Interpreted in light of Han's artistic beliefs, *Rain*'s self-referential paratext not only generates the effect of historical authenticity, as Fiona Lee points out,[67] but also encourages Han's Malayan readers to emplace themselves in the story as characters—just like the author herself—who follow the historical events depicted in the fictional space. The novel hence becomes a form of nondidactic ethnography that demonstrates the ways in which one can script Malaya's biography as part of one's personal history.

In addition, the paratext foreshadows Han's interplay between the novel's first-person narration and third-person omniscient narration, which marks her ambiguous position as both a Malayan insider and outsider in real life. The bifurcation of her authorial self into "author-as-person" and "author-as-character" allows her to exercise a distinctive form of narrative control. She understands that like other Malayan subjects she encounters, her participation in Malayan society is partial. Yet her conscious effort to get in touch with an unusual range of linguistic, ethnic and occupational groups enables her to aggregate a spectrum of circumscribed perspectives, which collectively forms an all-knowing oversight in *Rain* that depicts "an account of all the inns [*sic*] and outs, and the conflict of loyalties, treachery and betrayal, which are going on at the moment."[68]

Regrettably, Han's serialized literary project did not come to fruition. As a result, her authorial vision of multiculturalism in a decolonized nation could not be fully presented through more of her fictional works on Malaya.[69] Nonetheless, her compositional orientation toward catching up with the fast-changing external world encourages us to treat *Rain* as both an embodiment of her wide-ranging ideas, as well as an enactment of her mobile consciousness. This unique sense of restlessness that informs her creative impulse is worth studying for how Han harnesses the authorial position of a concerned sojourner rather than the colonized to depict reality, represent a language in transition, and predict social changes. Her narrative practice differs from typical postcolonial literary production, which prioritizes resistance against a center, and emphasizes the distance between literary language and reality.[70] The way in which Han inserts heterolingual elements or hybridized expressions should not be read as an attempt to "maintain distance and otherness," but rather, depicts a striving for a "shared mental experience" among the author, her characters, and her readers.[71] Compared to other postcolonial writers, Han adopts a nuancedly discrepant strategy to install differences in the English crafted as literary language. Instead of defamiliarizing the colonial language that forms the linguistic base for literary expression, Han uses fiction to familiarize readers with burgeoning sociolinguistic realities in Malaya.

ANGLOPHONE MALAYAN FICTION AND ITS SINOPHONE INFLECTIONS

In *Rain*, the trope of translation is very conspicuous. As Fiona Lee contends, heterolingual rendition is "quite literally the means for telling a story set in a multilingual society to an Anglophone reader."[72] The polyglot first-person narrator often acts as the interpreter who dubs multilingual diegetic situations into intelligible forms for presumably monolingual readers. The centrality of translation in *Rain*'s narrative design, in fact, echoes Han's belief in the utility of translingual practices. In a 1961 speech to an Anglophone audience that included both Europeans and locals of different races literate in English, Han said:

> We see in the Chinese language as used in Malaya today, slight differences due to Malayanization . . . to describe new scenes, we need new images, and the preoccupation with new forms of expression is at the moment alive in writing circles. How to write stories about the new relationships, to do it with the best and the most realistic words? . . . When you have writers striving *to create new images not in one language only but in two or three*, then one realizes the effort that goes into this. We must create idioms full of local color, *with borrowings from turns of phrase of the other sectors of the population*. . . . All in all, Malayan Chinese literature is already a robust growth, its writers pioneers in achieving real harmony.[73]

Han's statement acknowledges Mahua writers' trailblazing efforts in fostering new expressive forms. Tellingly, she places great emphasis on the use of "the most realistic words," evincing her dedicated pursuit to reproduce real-life speech patterns. Her inclinations toward featuring authentic argots, colorful idioms, and vibrant turns of phrase from social groups unfamiliar to one another illustrates the sanguine scenario whereby different linguistic communities in the social margins feed off one another's lively expressions. As if she was getting ideas to create an "Asian English" in Malaya, Han observes the localizing tendencies of the Sinophone, and channels them to her own Anglophone literary practice as well as to other local English writers.

From this perspective Han's mode of composition can be seen as rooted in the mutual adaptation of place and language. Gone unnoticed by many, what drives her place-inspired creative modality is a little-discussed impetus of emulating Mahua literature and showing Malayan Anglophone writers the significance of featuring localized language in creative works. Starting with *Rain*, and extending into *Freedom*, Han underscores the strategies of linguistic localization that can be shared by Anglophone and Sinophone literature in Malaya. As she recounts in her memoir about researching Mahua literature soon after arriving in the colony: "My contacts with Chinese scholars in Malaya had made me discover that there existed an extensive body of essays, novels, criticism and poetry by Malayan Chinese authors, different in content and feeling from Chinese literature proper."[74] By the time she published the article "The Creation of a Malayan Literature," she was sufficiently confident to juxtapose the parallel localization of English and Chinese in her observations on the evolving linguistic ecology of the British territories:

> As in every other ex-colony, *English in Malaya has been enriched into something called Malayan English*, containing an admixture of local Malay words and Indian, Chinese and Malay phrasing reproduced in English. This gives the local speech a delightful flavor, until now severely suppressed in the English schoolrooms, but which is heard everywhere, in all social groups, and which happily defies the staid conventions of grammar and syntax enshrined in the textbooks imported from England.
>
> *The same change has happened to Chinese. There is a recognizable "Malayan Chinese,"* which is incomprehensible in China, but which is current in Singapore and Malaya, and which tends to blur and merge all the dialects and include Malay words into its idioms.[75]

Describing how English improves its quality by blending with other local languages beyond conservative education settings, Han characterizes the creolization of English in Malaya as a positive development. It is also evident to her that Chinese language in Malaya had undergone a very similar process of distinguishing itself through local adaptations. Later in the article, she laments the limited corpus of works "written for Malayans about Malayans, using the local people, imagery, and scenery, and even, in places, attempting to reproduce local idioms," while urging the production of a "local 'Malayan' literature" through "depicting local scenes, reproducing local imagery and tricks of speech."[76] Akin to Lin Cantian in the 1930s (see chapter 1), Han seeks to create a place-apposite literary language at a prenational juncture. The nascent sociolinguistic habits of the Malayan Anglophone populace compiled in *Rain* show how those habits take shape through organic practices and create lifeworlds in local sites where languages are used with vigor, thus upending the notion that languages travel with unmalleable structures from metropoles.

At a historical moment prior to postcoloniality, Han embodies an authorial modality that values and yet does not prioritize subverting metropolitan cultural formations. In her case, the interrelations between the imperial center and its colonies do not account for what Peter Hitchcock would have called the "logic of imbrication" that involves English, its global spread, and the British Empire.[77] Instead, Han directs the flow of literary agency within the margins of a single colonized locale. Compared to Mahua writers who were overlooked in the cultural sphere by the colonial administration, Anglophone Chinese writers had to further contend with neglect by their own ethnic community whose members mostly could not access the English language. That situation notwithstanding, Han is optimistic about potential shared marginality. She does not perceive the colonized periphery as a zone of weakness or liability, but one of flexibility and immense creativity if those in the margins can integrate their grassroots resources. Despite the paucity of cultural resources for growth under colonized circumstances, she believes in the value of identifying the Sinophone constituency's strategies to share with the local Anglophone community in hope that the latter would also develop its own grounded culture in Malaya.

Committed to innovating English as a literary language for Asia, Han stands as a precursor to writers who self-identified as Chinese and deliberately fostered individuated voices through their Sinophone-inflected Anglophone literary endeavors.[78] In a 1950s interview, she told Lian Shisheng 連士升, the famous Singapore Chinese newspaper editor and prose writer, "The reason why I can write such beautiful English is because I know the Chinese language."[79] She continued to stress her embodiment of bilingualism in the 1990s by declaring: "It is only too true that my English derives its unconscious roots from Chinese. Chiefly from Chinese poetry, which is responsible in producing a new rhythm in sentence construction in certain of my books. I found myself almost creating an English which, from its inception, is almost cliché free, since I had not learnt any clichés, nor been exposed to them."[80] By avowing Chinese as the source for the originality of her English writings, Han evokes an image of a refined individual immersed in traditional Chinese print culture. But her deep participation in Malayan everyday life, when people of different ethnicities interacted to create newly hybrid linguistic expressions, truly formed another reference for her English literary language. *Rain* and her broader novelistic project demonstrate that Han uses literature to represent the coevolution of place and language, and to serve as a role model for Malayan Anglophone writers, who in her opinion should invent the linguistic complexion of their creative works with confidence, much like their Sinophone counterparts.

What does an English-language literary text that bears Sinophone traces read like? To first speak diegetically, *Rain* portrays the lives of the expatriate communities and Chinese Malayans of different social classes during the Emergency (1948–1960), when the Malayan Communist Party fought a bitter guerilla war against the colonial armed forces. Within the narrative, two expatriate characters are integral for assisting readers to grasp the Emergency's effects on people's lives. One of the protagonists is Luke Davis, the British police officer assigned to the Special Branch. Through the depiction of Davis's psychological dilemmas over the justness of his work, as well as his interactions with other characters, readers become privy to the gamut of methods British colonial administrators employ to maintain Malaya with its rich natural resources under its sphere of influence. Besides Davis, "Suyin" (sometimes addressed as

"Doctor") also takes on the role of focalization. She adopts a first-person narrative voice while moving from scene to scene, and observes the operations sustaining the Emergency rule, including incidents at the police headquarters where captured communists are detained and interrogated; at the public hospital where injured guerrilla fighters are brought in for treatment; and in the New Villages, which are resettlement camps that prevent Chinese rural residents from providing food and other logistic support to the communists. The locus of the doctor-narrator's activities introduces readers to new characters, especially the wealthy Chinese businessmen and local politicians among the social elites. When the story moves away from the two narrators' horizons to include people beyond their social circles, it conveys the thoughts and feelings of marginalized groups such as the insurgents in the jungle and residents of the resettlement camps.

As I discuss earlier, documenting the use of Malayan English is a recurring aspect of *Rain*'s narrative discourse. But besides recording hybridized linguistic habits of the locals, Han also features nonnatives developing familiarity with foreign cultures, casting Luke Davis and "Suyin" as the two characters who are most sensitive to Malaya's sociolinguistic situation. For instance, in one section of *Freedom*, the doctor-narrator attends a Malay wedding and reflects:

> That is what I liked—a mixed party.... In mixed gatherings like this, one found that however separate the lives and different the cultures, physical propinquity itself provided, sooner or later, a melting alloy; *a tendency in conversation to ramble from one language into the next*; a knowledge of each other's quirks and habits and a good humored teasing; perhaps, also, too much good humor, a careful carelessness not to offend; but under the moon, as the talk flowed, courteous, even-toned, in the low key which is the Malay tone of entertainment, so different from the noisy raucousness of Chinese feasts, there was a sensation of tolerance and understanding, of an achievement, as if with *merdeka*, independence, truly all of us had come together at last, unseparated from each other by economics, hierarchies, and the devious paraphernalia of division and fission, to stay together, forever.[81]

Participating in a cultural-learning occasion, the narrator notes how verbal exchanges are fluidly multilingual. The observation feeds her vision of deeper social integration among the races after Malaya gains independence. Her attitudinal inclination toward linguistic blending evokes the hospital scene in *Rain*. But whereas "Suyin" was then mired in the "soft cacophony," awaiting a "Babel reassembled," here the "mixed party" was redolent with a "sensation of tolerance and understanding." Apart from "Suyin," Luke Davis too saw an emerging order amid the chaos. He becomes particularly touched from watching a group of young school-age children whose facility with code-switching signifies hope for a harmonious Malaya:

> Luke's car turned into the road, at this hour full of little girls in white shirts and blue school uniforms, going to the convent school. There were Indians with dark skin and flashing eyes and teeth, tossing their plaits and giggling..."Janiki, Vijaya, come on, hurry faster...." Little Chinese girls with serious round faces and glossy black hair crimped in the rigid locks of identical permanents, *going from various dialects into English and back again into dialect*: "I didn't do my homework, let me see yours, tolong lah...." "Eurasians with green eyes and black hair, looking Chinese, or looking European with golden hair and brown eyes...." We've got another baby, my mummy brought it home last night from the hospital after makan."...
>
> More and more little girls from Catholic or pagan India, Catholic or pagan Chinese, Catholic Eurasian and Islamic Malay families, docile, blue clad and happy little girls rippling with talk and laughter, poured into the Convent, their goal the Cambridge Overseas School certificate, *their English new and fresh and flavorful, lilting Malayan singsong English lovely to hear.*
>
> "Come, I will show you."
>
> "Die for you, lah."
>
> "I say no, Mai."
>
> Luke Davis thought: "*This is the first time I really see this little town in Malaya.*"... Perception gave him a pleasurable feel of enchanting newness, fresh as the sudden perfume of a rose. He looked and listened and saw and heard for the first time in months,

sprightly of spirit, excited by the lavishness of sound and color. Malaya was wonderful. Look at them, the little girls of the future Malaya, filing into school, so many races, so many golden shades *to melt and fuse together into one nation.* (235–36; emphases added)

This extract from *Rain* shows a remarkable moment whereby Han limns multiracial, multilingual, and multireligious sociality to forecast the coming together of a place and its people. The bustling scene shows how the aurality of Malaya, with its different shades of creolized expressions, suffuses the social picture Davis encounters in its sensuous immediacy. Significantly, out of the many characters in *Rain*, it is Davis the expatriate who feels that he is seeing Malaya anew through refreshing combinations of sight and sound that spell nation-building. His mental conception of a racially cordial future for Malaya is derived from linguistic articulations where English and various Chinese topolects commingle in myriad ways, creating the musical flavor of an English that is geographically distinctive.

Here we can recognize the way in which language mixing becomes the target of Han's "translational mimesis," the Meir Sternberg analytic I use in chapter 1 to account for the processes through which writers transpose multilingual social situations into monolingual literary discourse. In Sternberg's critical terminology, the above excerpt from *Rain* contains several instances of "vehicular matching," that is to say, the citation of speech "in its original wording so as to effect as perfect a correspondence as possible between the signified polylingualism of reality and the signifying polylingualism of the text."[82] Employing this technique of congruence, the narrative discourse marks the bilingual interference that affects the schoolchildren's speech, demonstrating how creolization reflects infusions from various local communities. The hybrid forms range from the syntax inflected by Malay, Mandarin, and Chinese topolects ("'I didn't do my homework, let me see yours, *tolong lah*"; "Come, I will show you"; "I say no, *Mai*") to the incorporation of heterolingual lexicon ("My mummy brought it home last night from the hospital after *makan*" [eating]), to the usage of discourse particles that serve pragmatic communicative functions ("Die for you, *lah*").

In undertaking such linguistic representations, Han as author-narrator of *Rain* and *Freedom* introduces the organic evolution of Malayan

English to her Anglophone readers who may not otherwise have contact with the creole-in-the-making at all, or may perceive the hybridized language negatively. Her larger Malayan writing project tracks the historical process of Malayan subject formation through the lens of linguistic belonging, especially the ways by which place-making through Malayan English gains social traction among new users. For instance, Han harnesses character development for showing how creolization inspires fondness from newcomers. The character Luke Davis starts off in *Rain* as belonging to the ruling colonial class, but gradually sympathizes with the Malayan masses, and eventually regards Malaya and Singapore as home in *Freedom*. His new perceptual framework about both places, which are intimately linked, is tied to his growing grasp of Malayan English. He finds the localized language endearing and becomes particularly impatient with his fiancée Maxine who, like most other expatriates in the region, fails to notice and follow the unique way Malayan place names are pronounced:

> It always annoyed Luke when people around him, English people, that is—mispronounced Malay words. "Johore Baroo" they said, putting the accent on the second syllable, when it should have been "Bahru" with the accent on the first syllable, like "Tar." And Maxine had all the tricks of pronunciation which the British endowed the names of places in Malaya. 'Bucket-Timah' she said, and somehow this made him wildly furious. 'Bookit' he corrected, 'like book.' . . . . Bob Stewart chortled. 'Good for you Maxine,' he said. 'Keep it up. We've to show these language experts that we can get along just as well without speaking the lingo like a native.'[83]

Immersing himself in local life, Davis has become, at this point, well acquainted with the nuanced attributes of the emerging language and Malayans' elocutionary habits. Cognizant of how locals generally pronounce place names in vernacular Malay, he stands apart from other obdurate British expatriates who refuse to adopt the grassroots manner of speaking. More than signifying linguistic peculiarities in local cultures, such metonymic instances from Luke's perspective in *Rain* and *Freedom* indicate that local languages can cross the colonial-colonized divide to make connections that strengthen the multicultural fabric of Malayan society.

Meanwhile, the doctor-character "Suyin" is also highly conscious of linguistic contact and evolution, as well as equally capable of discerning the tonal emphases in Malayan English, and the local people's inclination to switch languages casually during conversations. A vignette in *Freedom* narrated by "Suyin" further illuminates the broadening sense of local language ownership. It concerns the Hari Merdeka (Independence Day) Parade episode I discuss in the previous section. Ruminating on the ceremonial spectacle, where "processions went marching through the main streets with banners and song, demanding in Malay, in Chinese, in Tamil and in English, *Merdeka* for Malaya," she concludes that "*Merdeka*, though a Malay word, was by now, not only Malay. The Malayan Chinese Association, [and] the Malayan Indian Congress, had joined to form a great alliance of the peoples of Malaya."[84] This plot point indicates the forthcoming creation of a common national vocabulary when words from one language enter and hybridize the lexicon of other local languages, thereby generating meaning for an unprecedented range of users. Analogous to Luke Davis developing an affinity for Malayan English, the narrator's imagination of a political community is mediated by the enhanced traction of a Malay term across ethnic groups in Malaya.

Admittedly, the exemplary effect of *Rain*—in terms of its commitment toward incorporating new sociolinguistic forms into literary texts—for English writers in the region might be considered subtle. Since *Freedom* was never published, Han's compositional method, which foregrounds representations of how everyday languages in Malaya organically evolved, was not particularly appreciated by the Anglophone media and readers who focused more on *Rain*'s controversial content. The novel's emulative potential only becomes apparent when it is considered holistically in light of her nonfiction discourses, for instance, through one of Han's public speeches in the 1960s:

> The English writer must, *like some of the Chinese-language writers here*, become bilingual or trilingual. He must learn Malay, read in Malay, read Indonesian literature, and the works of his fellow countrymen, the Malays here. He must, if possible, learn Chinese too.

> *Already among the Chinese writers we have many who are bilingual and trilingual, and doing a most imposing amount of translation work. Why should our writers in the English language not do the same?*[85]

Though Han claimed elsewhere that she had no intention of comparing writers in Chinese and English in the region,[86] her rhetorical exhortation above carries a value judgment that leans toward valorizing the former. Moreover, she has argued that "writing in English in Malaya, however, lags behind other kinds of writing" and "on the whole the productions in English which we see in Malaya are not of the same caliber as, for instance, the output of the Chinese-educated, some of whom have high literary merit."[87] On more than one occasion, Han singled out Mahua authors whose dedication to translingual practices in the 1950s distinguished them as a noteworthy group within the cultural field of the fledgling Malayan nation. Her admiration for the Sinophone Malayan constituency is particularly evident in her recurring praise for the multilingual Chinese students at Nanyang University. In her correspondence with Liu Pengju, the editor of *Eastern Horizon*, an English-language journal published out of Hong Kong, she spoke zealously about the immense potential of the students who "are adapting to conditions in Southeast Asia by being bi or trilingual, thus shooting down the myth of Chinese 'chauvinism.'"[88]

In "Development of a Malayan Chinese Literature," the speech Han gave in 1961 at the Singapore Cultural Center, she commended the university students for engaging in the translation of Malay and Indonesian poetry, "introducing the *pantun* on a large scale to the Chinese speaking," and "publish[ing] many small magazines in three languages."[89] Whereas in the past she had spoken more generally of a "Malayan literature," that talk heralded Han's more striking promotion of Chinese-language writings in the British colonies, as the Nanyang University students stirred her imagination of a truly grassroots sensibility for Malayan literature. In the speech, her advocacy for the Sinophone can be discerned from how she situated Mahua literature in a sociocultural milieu dominated by colonial mindsets and introduced its accomplishments to be in sync with the development of a place-based language. Subsequently, Mahua literature and its adaptive trajectory beyond monolingual sensibilities became the implicit model that Han used to explain the merits of literature written by locally oriented writers in the British territories.

At the beginning of her speech at the Singapore Cultural Center, Han clarifies that she tailored her discourse for a socially privileged English-speaking audience that included Europeans (1). She compares the genesis of Malaya and her literatures to the antecedent example of America, whose writers became gradually "infiltrated by their environment" and began to "evolve their own style, their own way of looking, their own way of feeling and writing" (8). By asserting that there exists a substantial body of work written in Chinese that benefitted from exposure to mainland Chinese literary culture but was "Malayan in consciousness and nothing else" (10), Han remonstrates against "the impression that there is no writing done except in English . . . or that if writing is done in Chinese, it must perforce be about China" (9). In this sense, Han is mobilizing modern Mahua writers' practices to open up the close-minded conception of a national literature held by the colonial and local Anglophone communities that have yet to expand their linguistic horizons.

Han also accentuates the core of what she perceives as Mahua literature by making several deliberate distinctions. In particular, she defines what she calls "Malayan Chinese literature" by differentiating the body of literary works that draw from cultural memories and resources related to mainland China from those that focus on Malaya and Singapore:

> What I mean by Malayan Chinese literature is this: That literature, in verse, prose, drama, novel, short story, which is produced in the Chinese language, and which relates by emotion, identification, description, to the situation and to the problems of Malaya and Singapore. It excludes that literature which is nostalgic, which reminisces about China, which is about purely Chinese heroes, scenes or situations sited in China. It includes, and must include, that portion of Chinese writing, done in Chinese, which researches into the culture, folklore, customs, and literatures of other peoples living in Malaya, [and] Singapore. (3)

Here, Han unwittingly echoes the postwar controversy in the Mahua cultural sphere, which eventually affirmed "the uniqueness of Mahua literature and the arts" (*mahua wenyi dutexing* 馬華文藝獨特性) through a discursive advocacy to write the "here and now" (*cishi cidi* 此時此地).⁹⁰ To channel attention toward her "Malayan Chinese literature," she formulates "a local definition" tied to "the cultural instrument of the Chinese language" for the occasion (3–4). She is aware that her trait-based definition is "self-limiting" (3), but she defends her strategy of rhetorical funneling that excludes many groups, such as "the literary efforts of . . . Chinese speaking and writing individuals which have no bearing on the Malayan sphere at the moment" (4), Malayan literature written in Malay or by ethnic Chinese in English, as well as works written in Malaya and Singapore but focus on locales outside the colonies (4).

To introduce the nucleus of the local literary formation, she emphasizes to her Anglophone audience how Mahua literature examines an array of subjects that are non-Chinese and thus contributes to the building of national culture in a newly defined geopolitical territory. While the ethnic Chinese may address challenges particular to their group, the complexities of issues they grapple as well with apply to all other groups in Malayan society as well. Han's communicative effort attempts to remedy the situation whereby various ethnic groups are ignorant of their contemporaneity or one another's cultural practices, resulting in the marginalization of Mahua authors who are neither read nor heard except by their own linguistic constituency.

After highlighting the place of production, Han moves on to explicate her notion of what constitutes "Chinese language" in Malaya to her English-speaking audience:

> In my trips to China, I realize how the Chinese in China is different from the Chinese that is spoken in Malaya, *because the Chinese in Malaya is already becoming Malayanized.* . . . There are many turns of phraseology in Chinese writing in Malaya which are only current in Malaya and they are so because *the language is infiltrated by images and terms relating to the local setting.* In my medical practice, many patients, though Chinese, all the time use Malay words interspersed with their Chinese dialect. Penang Hokien [*sic*] is already somewhat different from Hokien as it is spoken elsewhere and the words "tolong," "sayang" and so on are used practically all

the time by [the] Chinese-speaking quite naturally. And this is also reflected in some parts of the writing. You find short stories where characters exclaim: "al ah ma" [sic], which is a Malay exclamation. (4–5, italic emphases added)

In this part of her speech, Han further deploys her contingent essentialism, which zooms in on works written in Chinese in the British colonial territories. She cites examples of translingual hybridity and interlocal differences—differences not merely within the standardized Chinese expressed in written form, but also within Chinese topolects such as location-dependent forms of Hokkien. Without getting distracted by non-Chinese linguistic strands or extralocal subject matter, her audience is afforded closer scrutiny of Mahua literary production marked by a place-catalyzed literary language that registers the adaptions of Chinese language to the unique conditions of local society.

Han insists on her broad Malaya-China distinction in order to persuade her Anglophone audience regarding the existence of Sinophone literary production that examines historical and contemporary circumstances, as well as the emotional realms of Malaya and Singapore. However, her intentionally contingent definition of Mahua literature was not completely appreciated by the bilinguals in her audience. At the talk, the Singaporean scholar Cheng Tse-yu 鄭子瑜 protested Han's definition, which he thought unduly disregards literature with yearnings for China. He urged those works to be read more sympathetically, pointing out that the nostalgic tone could have resulted from host countries rejecting the migrant writers' assimilation efforts, and should be read as the displaced people's pining for an abstract sense of home.[91] Such discrepant views between Han and Cheng raise the need for more delicate treatments of "China" as a complex sign of nostalgia in Mahua literature, a topic which has endured in subsequent Mahua literary debates.

A FRESH SUTURING OF LANGUAGE AND REGION

Overall, Han's novelistic outlook was decidedly anticipatory. She was confident that *Rain* would eventually become "the bible of people . . . who find in it the beginnings of everything."[92] Her aspiration to use literature to decolonize Malaya concerns an ideal world order yet to arrive. The "worlding" dimension in her activist fiction-writing endeavor—manifest in the interplay between the local with the extralocal—can thus be further interpreted in the temporal sense. More specifically, Han's Malayan writing project enacts the way in which both spatial and temporal aspects of worlding literature intersect in a locale beyond Euro-American cultural centers. Her literary experiment articulates the imagining of a new political community not merely as a diagnosis of the times, but also as a way of reorienting the place's culture for the future through composing fiction and tracking linguistic shifts.

In this regard, Han's authorial career in Malaya holds extraordinary sociocultural meanings for contributing to early representations of the now creolized Southeast Asian English, paving the way for the linguistic medium to gain recognition as valid for artistic exploration. Years after her Malayan sojourn, Han was proud of her prescience about diverse Anglophone expression in Asia. Reminiscing in the 1990s, Han noted the ways in which many Asian writers "could really be called Eurasian in their approach," as seen in their creative acts of employing "more vivid, immediate speech" to reflect the inherent plurality of different locales in the world.[93] She also saw herself as envisioning the possibilities for Asian English literature in mid-twentieth-century Southeast Asia, and having in turn inspired Asian American literature, while embracing her success in "putting Asian Literature on the map" through her unconventional pedagogical endeavor at Nanyang University.[94]

Examining *Rain* and Han's larger cultural practice in Malaya, this chapter focuses on her ostensive attempts to develop "Asian English," a place-inspired literary English inflected by multilingual social realities and Sinophone literary practices. In fact, she was pioneering a fresh suturing of language (English) and region (Malaysia as Asia) after recognizing how Chinese language had successfully managed to forge new connections with a locality beyond its origin in China. To Han, the Sinophone experience of linguistic de-territorialization and re-territorialization in Malaya illustrates the erosion of an established mode of expression transposed from afar, and the emergence of new idioms associated with the site of migration. The understanding also nourished her belief that constituents of literary margins are capable of engendering and channeling their own dynamic exemplarity.

Han's public discourses in the 1950s and 1960s highlight the ways in which Chinese and English coevolved to stimulate a distinctive Malayan literature and culture before national boundaries were created. In a 1958 address at Nanyang University, she told the students—whom she regards as promising young Malayan writers—to take a rooted perspective of the world, and yet not to be Malayan with a parochial outlook: "You must see things not from a narrow point of view and not from a nationalistic point of view, but from a world point of view."[95] A crucial theme in her speech was the intellectual work of "seeing," which binds a sober understanding of geopolitics and the politics of historiography for dismantling hegemonic cultural influences. A global perspective to her was not any

FIGURE 2.2 Han Suyin speaking to Nanyang University students, circa 1950s

free-floating, noncommittal oversight, but must come from a specific vantage point. Han further posited that a serious writer's "world point of view" must stem from a solid grasp of the historical relations between "the forces which come from below and which work their way up and which change governments, nations, countries and societies."[96] In the context of Cold War Southeast Asia, the apprehension of historicity would require "looking into" the underlying political economy during the colonial period, which had stirred social revolutions in the region. Such writers can then avoid becoming like their colleagues who produce "exotic literature" that "sees people only as lazy or industrious" and purveys purported essences of different cultures.[97]

Emphasizing the trope of visualization repeatedly, Han urged her student audience to always look beyond surface conclusions, and to think critically and independently. The 1958 address recalls her appeal in the political organ *PETIR* a year earlier, when she strongly encouraged her readers to face up to their own visual judgement of social developments, rather than to rely on imposed or borrowed lenses. At the heart of her counsel was the need for Malayan writers to develop different depths and ranges of vision in order to gain a thorough understanding of the historical conditions that underpin the contemporary globality, which shaped unique Malayan aesthetic forms as embodiments of universal ideals. Emblematic of her approach that mobilizes intralocal and supralocal forms of action and discourse, *Rain* represents a social totality that holds together Malaya's internal heterogeneity and contradictions.

Broadly speaking, then, Han's cultural advocacy negotiated the space for Malayans to bring forth the postcolonial world by writing as Asians. Through shaping a consensus on the artistic merits of creative works, Malayan literature instantiates an Asian mode of imagining the political becoming of nations, an imagining that can be conducted in whichever language Malayans wished. Akin to how she tried to break the entrenched association of China with the Chinese language, she stressed the importance of deactivating the conditional reflex of equating the use of English with "a colonial mentality" so that English could ultimately be regarded by the world as equally Asian.[98] By claiming that "no language is colonial in itself," she legitimized her deep affinity for the English language and a spirit of play in her narrative practice.[99] At a London event in the late 1950s, when she must have also been juggling her ambitious Malayan novelistic project, she professed her love for "the English tongue," which she saw as "only beginning on its great career" because it had "so much youth in it and so much power of new creation." Feeling that she was "only beginning to speak and to know it in all its varieties," she spoke of the "great fun" that "we Asians" have in "knock[ing] it about and chang[ing] it around and play[ing] with [its] grammar."[100]

Given Han's irreverent attitude toward normative forms of language, *Rain* can be read in terms of her stylistic representations of the Malayan sociolinguistic scenes, alongside the more conventional lens of her radical critique of British colonial rule. Apart from examining the tension among hegemonic and subjugated social actors, the novel embodies the outcome of learning from fellow enthusiasts in the grassroots literary community. When addressing local English writers, Han shows clear inspiration derived from multilingual Chinese Malayan writers. Mindset-wise, she advised the young Anglophone Malayan writers to "stop having an inferiority complex about their English" and to see English "as one of the many sources of inspiration (but certainly not the main one or the sole one) open to them."[101] On the practical level, she enjoined them to "learn Malay or Chinese or both" or "at least one Asian language," to learn about the "fields of Asian literature . . . being opened up" through translation, as well as to equip themselves with the capacity to undertake translation themselves, or read in the original languages.[102]

Han's advice for Malayan literary production may appear place-centric, but her perspective on displaced languages was never provincial. Viewing English as both a target and a source of literary influence, she commented on English literature being "indebted to other literatures, in a reciprocity of borrowings and stimulations."[103] She also compared the evolution of English in Malaya to similar processes in other colonized regions, writing that "English is a language that grows and changes and transforms itself every ten years. It is losing its grammar, its sentences are being so pulled about by so many pronunciations, different ways of thought, by African writers, Jamaican writers, American writers, that I can only see good done to it by a bit of pulling about by Malayan writers."[104] Linking an array of productive literary regions, Han used Malaya as a springboard to cast herself as the spokesperson for Malayan literature coded as Asian literature. Her adroit management of the bifocal lens enabled her audiences to shift among varied geographic scales and cultural contexts: Malaya and the world, Malaya and Asia, as well as the Sinophone and the Anglophone in the Malayan setting. Through Han's doubled surveys of spatial formations, Malaya emerged as a comparable and paradigmatic literary domain.

The nascent domain faced inherent limitations with which Han was well acquainted. Despite sharing a common quest to found a national literature amid decolonization, the Malayan literary constituencies were operating within their own insular realms. Using the Malay term *kampong* (village), Han interprets the situatedness of Malay and Mahua writers to the local Anglophone audience as such:

> Now each and every writer in the world can only write about the "kampong" he lives in, his own village, or rather, the village of his mind. Now if his mental village or kampong is very large, if it takes in, emotionally and intellectually, a big slice of the world, then his writing can never be "national" but becomes understandable on a supranational or "international" scale. But if his kampong is small and narrow, then of course he will write about a small kampong, but the human beings and their emotions are the same, whether in a big city or in a kampong, and he can make his kampong people just as universal. . . . [Malaya] is a compartmented, divided, fragmented society, and therefore in order to broaden the kampong, to advance literary output as a whole, it is imperative that we should communicate more with each other, . . . the English-speaking, although Chinese, are divided, and their problems and "mental kampong" is [*sic*] sometimes in England rather than in this country.[105]

Correlating the connectivity of writers' living environments and the scope of their worldviews, Han does not immediately impute parochialism to people's "village" sentiments, the way the Chinese intellectual Liang Qichao 梁启超 did when he described the diasporic Chinese in San Francisco at the turn into the twentieth century. When Liang encountered the Chinese overseas, he attributed their circumscribed outlooks to their *cunluo sixiang* 村落思想 (provincial mentality) rooted in their deep attachment to their native villages.[106] From Han's perspective, writers can choose to expand their "mental villages" and forge wider horizons as subjects for composition to achieve global exposure and understanding. But even if they merely take their immediate social experiences to stand for the local, their works can still transcend their narrow foci on specific racial or linguistic identities if the characters within can resonate emotionally with an extensive range of readers.

Ultimately, this chapter does not focus on Mahua literature directly, but rather on the unusual role that Mahua literature played in shaping the place-based cultural practice of a transient Anglophone writer. The peripheral literary formation provided inspiration for Han who aimed to transform the nature of English language from the colonial to the vernacular, and who imagined a multilingual national literature for Malaya. To date, although the marginalization of Mahua literature as a result of racialized governance is frequently invoked in many studies, there is scant research into instances of contact, discursive or otherwise, between Chinese literary production and other linguistic spheres. My study contemplates the import of how Han's interventions allow for a more comprehensive appreciation of Malayan literary space by juxtaposing the Sinophone and the Anglophone as two abutting local literary ecologies. Presenting a meaningful exception of rhetorical contiguity, Han's locution reminds us to revisit the Mahua archive, in order to recover missed temporal intersections as part of the intralingual and interlingual history of worlding Malayan literature, and to consider those underutilized opportunities for translingual literary integration in late colonial Malaya as potential modalities for deeper localization.[107]

Moving forward, Han's case will provide fertile possibilities for future explorations. For instance, she supported the Hong Kong–based journal *Eastern Horizon*, launched in 1960 to publish representative writings on Asia. Han played a significant advisory role in the journal's features on Malaya, which were fashioned as showcases of Asia emerging from colonialism and its decolonizing cultures.[108] The translated Malayan poems, short stories, autobiographical writings, and plays in *Eastern Horizon* that reached out to the international reading public later inspired the compilation of *Modern Malaysian Chinese Stories*

(1967), the first anthology of Malayan Chinese literature ever to be published in English. The book launched the Writing in Asia Series published by Heinemann Education Books Ltd., which curated the famous African Writers Series that nurtured the flourishing of Anglophone African literature.[109]

More significantly, Han's fiction writing should be further considered in light of other Anglophone literary writings in the British territories. Alongside her advocacy for exemplary Sinophone cultural production in Malaya that occasioned the translation of her Anglophone works, which were then incorporated into the corpus of Mahua literature, subsequent research can assess the extent to which the young Anglophone Malayan writers accepted Han as a role model for their fledgling or ongoing practices. This line of inquiry that spotlights contemporaneity will situate the Eurasian writer across the Sinophone-Anglophone divide, as well as within the realm of English-language writings in postwar Malaya. In other words, Han's writing practice highlights the need to examine both interlingual and intralingual dimensions of the Malayan literary space. During her sojourn, she encouraged Malayans to follow her in engaging with literary place-making by fostering unconventional linguistic intimacies that arose from migration and colonization. As represented in *Rain* and *Freedom*, Malayan English does not function merely as a linguistic medium wielded by an idiosyncratic author, but also as an aesthetic tool for building grassroots collectivity.

In the end, however, Malaya did not become the permanent base for Han to contemplate the world. Her vocal opinions on Asian geopolitics made her an unpopular figure with the Singapore government and caused her to depart from the Malayan region in 1964.[110] Incidentally, her departure intersected with a stage of her life when she began to cultivate a serious interest in writing about China. Reflecting on her rekindled affinity for the mainland state, Han confided in her friend Malcolm MacDonald, "I have been pursued by this great passion for a geographical continent ... but can one remain in love with geography?"[111] During tumultuous times, self-identified Chinese writers like Han imagined and lived out their own senses of global spatiality, intertwined with the specific loci of their situated expressions. Almost three decades later, another writer, born in the "geographical continent" that Han mentioned, would develop a deep curiosity about her roots in Singapore and Malaya where her father was born and raised, as that writer was searching for an appropriate linguistic form for her works on diasporic Chinese experiences. Delineating the reverse trajectory from China to Southeast Asia, the next chapter explores Wang Anyi and her entanglements, both narrative and polemical, with Mahua literature in the early 1990s.

CHAPTER THREE

Cosmopolitan Visions of Drift

Wang Anyi and the Relay of Diasporic Literary Imagination

How do writers conceive of a literary internationalism from the vantage point of an isolated place like Malaysia? In the mid-2000s, attempting to integrate the historical experiences of marginalized Chinese literary formations, Ng Kim Chew harnessed his observations of Mahua literature to propose that Taiwan literature was similarly a "Chinese-language literature without nationality" (*wuguoji huawen wenxue* 無國籍華文文學). In his view, the approach would offer stronger conceptual ground for the East Asian literary space to accommodate the Mahua literature that circulated in Taiwan.[1] Discerning Ng's ethnically and linguistically delimited motivations, the Taiwan scholar Kuei-fen Chiu 邱貴芬 countersuggested a more capacious framework by Huang De-shi 黃得時, the pioneering advocate for a multilingual, multiethnic, and transnational Taiwan literary history, who formulated five categories of works that constitute the place-based corpus:

> First, works published in Taiwan by writers born in Taiwan; second, works by writers not of Taiwan origin who have lived in Taiwan for a considerable period of time and are involved with literary activities on the island; third, works about Taiwan published by non-Taiwanese writers during their short stays there; fourth, works by writers born in Taiwan who publish their works elsewhere; and finally, works about Taiwan by writers who have never been to this place.[2]

Given Malaysia's shared peripherality with Taiwan in the world-Chinese literary space, the former location can indeed learn from the latter to devise its own mode of literary historiography by focusing on the ways in which Mahua literature is embedded in its own diverse networks of production. Replacing "Taiwan" with "Malaysia" in Huang's configuration then yields a parallel configuration of literary history, a model that is governed by links between authorial practices and the Southeast Asian country over the long twentieth century, which downplays the customary twin emphases on nativity and nationality.

Demarcating the contours of this historiographical model, the cases of Lin Cantian and Han Suyin, which I discuss in chapters 1 and 2 respectively, belong to the second category of writers born outside Malaya, who settled in the British colony for various durations and participated in local cultural activities. In this chapter I use Wang Anyi 王安憶 (1954–), the established writer from China, to illuminate the third category of works—those produced by non-Malaysian authors about their visits to the Nanyang region (current-day Southeast Asia). Wang's trip to Singapore and Peninsular Malaysia in the early 1990s harks back to the

FIGURE 3.1 Wang Anyi at the Thean Hou Temple in Kuala Lumpur, 1991

Cosmopolitan Visions of Drift 117

well-studied phenomenon of "southbound literati" (*nanlai wenren* 南來文人) and their double-facing relationships with both the China and the Nanyang literary fields from the late nineteenth century to the first half of the twentieth century. Those life stories exemplify the intersection of colonial history and sociocultural endeavors in the Sinophone South. Forming the backbone of Chinese literary development in Nanyang, those men of letters ventured abroad as diplomats of the Chinese imperial government, for employment in the education and cultural sectors, for refuge from political persecution, or to undertake covert galvanization efforts of the Chinese overseas. Unlike her male predecessors, the purpose of Wang's visit abroad was to trace her personal genealogy. When compared to Southeast Asian Chinese who traveled north in the 1980s to reconnect with their ancestral lands in the wake of the Cultural Revolution in China, her southward journey provides a counterpoint as a practice of reverse root-seeking.

More significantly, Wang's case calls attention to translocal forces that affect literary production in more than one venue in the world-Chinese literary space. The translocality pinpoints a sociospatial dynamic that emphasizes "situatedness during mobility" across different locales.[3] In this chapter, I position Wang as another unusual constituent of two literary histories by elucidating the intellectual labor her 1993 novella *Shangxin Taipingyang* 傷心太平洋 (Sadness of the Pacific) performs when read as a work of modern Chinese literature associated with China, and unconventionally, as a part of Mahua literature. Related through a first-person narrator from the mainland state on a lineage-tracking trip in Southeast Asia, the story interweaves the narrator's emotional impressions of the region with a vicarious reconstruction of her father's life in his native land of Singapore and his travels in Malaya, before he relocated to China on the eve of World War II. The novella has been neglected in existing literary histories because it never developed a durable affiliation to either Singapore-Malaysian Chinese-language literature (*Xinma huawen wenxue* 新馬華文文學) or mainland Chinese literature.[4] Whereas Singapore and Malaysian readers consider Wang's works generally as mainland texts, to readers outside of Southeast Asia her works about the region have been overshadowed by her more famous representations of settings in China, especially Shanghai. Departing from such understandings, I highlight the taxonomical ambiguity of *Sadness of the Pacific* to illustrate how Wang's depiction of its narrated world draws from two connected sociohistorical worlds that sustain global Chinese literary production.

Both intentionally and unwittingly, Wang's writing practice in the early 1990s, which includes the novella, activates several circuits of narrative representation and critical debate that I present as discursive relays. For instance, in *Sadness of the Pacific*, Wang portrays the autobiographical narrator as a reader of her father's literary works in his youth, which mirrors Wang's own interest as a reader of her father's novels written after his retirement. Those paternal compositions and the narrator's recount of genealogical memories mark what the historian Shelly Chan would recognize as "diaspora moments," that is, the episodic contributions of human displacement to unsettled sociopolitical and cultural formations (in this case, Mahua literature).[5] Reinforcing the accent on mobility, Wang's narrative does not depict diaspora as a hierarchy of locational significance but rather features typologies of Chinese migration in confluence. Figured as unending traversal rather than monodirectional relocation, the trope of diaspora embodies historical choices occasioned by generational or itinerary differences, and hence indicates Wang's authorial consciousness of a multicentered world at large.

Ranging from Chinese literati sojourners in the south, to roving Chinese leftist intellectuals, to passionate literary youths born in Singapore, to curious root-seeking descendants, the assemblage of diasporic routes in the novella will not be read simply as repeated departures from native origins, nor will the collective representation be taken only at the author's word to mean the ceaseless movements from one place to another. Instead, I interpret the various trajectories as indicative of pivotal moments that coconstitute Mahua and China's literary spaces. On the one hand, *Sadness of the Pacific* strategically expands the corpus of Mahua literature by recruiting the creative output of Singapore- and Malayan-born writers who live in China. On the other hand, in concert with Wang's other literary works written in the same period, the novella enables her to use Nanyang in the late 1980s and early 1990s for provincializing China in her global literary imagination, and for broadening the category of *xungen wenxue* 尋根文學 (root-seeking literature)—an important literary movement and creative theme centered upon writers' embrace of China's indigenous cultures—in the mainland literary space.

We can observe a second form of discursive relay in how Wang's metareflection on space and place in *Sadness of the Pacific* dialogues with her nonfictional writings on the multidirectional travels of the Chinese language. Avoiding the treatment of her narrative representations as mere expressions of ideas in her essays, I read her contemporaneous writings comprising literary and nonliterary works as two sets of mutually resonant thought that jointly allude to her search for an "abstract literary language," which forgoes the specificities of place settings and individual styles.[6] Her attraction toward such a modality of literary expression stems from her dissatisfaction with the flamboyantly individuated, the folkloric, and the period-specific linguistic styles that then flourished and became influential in the mainland literary space. Notably, her experiment with literary language splices into her reinvigorated ideals of writing, which involve setting China against a more international backdrop, and readjusting her positionality to become a mainland Chinese author working on universal themes.

Interpreting Wang's elaboration on her abstract literary language, I characterize the linguistic medium she proposes as a "cosmopolitan Chinese literary vernacular," by which I mean an all-purpose form of written language unbeholden to any social or local constituency. Wang's literary vernacular aims to connect with the largest possible readership constituted by Chinese people spread globally, all of whom are bound by a common destiny of drift. Rather than subjugate local styles of writing, Wang's written vernacular seeks to contribute to the plurality of compositional modes. In *Sadness of the Pacific* she uses her desired literary language to express a recurring notion that "on a map, continents are also drifting islands."[7] When read in tandem with her prose essays containing imageries of human and linguistic drift, we can perceive how Wang's cosmopolitanism is encoded in her act of making the two types of landmass equivalent. To Wang, the sense of cosmopolitan belonging entails liberating oneself from provincial and national attachments, in order to reevaluate the perpetual association, dissociation, and reassociation of people, places, and languages.

Alongside her fictional representations, Wang's pursuit of an ideal literary language feeds into her larger contemplation on the drift of Chinese language in the world and its attendant implications on local cultural ecologies. As a result, not only does her translocal narrative practice pluralize the endeavors of the root-seeking literary movement in China, but her fictional works and critical discourses also intersect with a localizing imperative that emerges from an expanding Mahua literary space in the 1990s. The last relay of literary connectivity appears through the ways in which Wang's ideas provide significant resources for Ng Kim Chew, who is based in Taiwan, to theorize modes of Mahua literary language. The productive crossing flags another important cosmopolitan juncture of the Sinophone South, whereby authors from different native literary spaces adapt and reference one another's ideas to envision new positionalities for themselves in the global literary order.

Driven by the same desire to innovate narrative language, Ng draws upon Wang's comparison of literary languages in China and Taiwan—as well as her commentary on the social conditions for Chinese language evolution in Southeast Asia—to reframe the localizing propensity of Mahua literature. He extrapolates Wang's ideas of linguistic shift within and beyond China to conceptualize *zhongwen* 中文 and *huawen* 華文 as two modes of literary language that index either a China-oriented or a local Chinese cultural orientation, both of which represent the choices of writers located outside or in the southern fringes of the mainland polity. These writers face the immense challenge of rendering natural speech in the south into literary representations via a written language derived from northern Chinese topolects. For Mahua literature to carve its distinctive position in world literature, Ng believes, its literary vernacular needs to formulate fresh techniques of linguistic representation that convey the unique flavor of southern languages.

But at this point Ng's pursuit of meaningful stylistic difference in literary language diverges from Wang's cosmopolitanism, which focuses on seeking human commonality. Ironically, his emphasis on particularity over universality concords with the creative orientations of Wang's peers in China who delineate local and regional attributes through their production of root-seeking literature. By constructing the *zhongwen/huawen* framework in the 1990s to highlight the shifting alliances among various literary spaces built around the two antithetical linguistic modes of composition, Ng extrapolates from the inner diversity of

Mahua literature to remap the world of Chinese-language literature. He anticipates questions that years later animate the core concerns of Sinophone studies: How do migrant writers negotiate their relationship with China and traditional Chinese literary resources? How can literature of and about a place cultivate its distinctiveness? Bracingly, his resultant configurations of alternative geographies based on varying modalities of literary language allow discrepant formations of creative writings to coexist in a single location. Wang's *Sadness of the Pacific*, as well as her contemporaneous literary works and nonfictional essays, thus demonstrate how a traveling writer from China generates ideas that spur colleagues in other locales to reorganize Chinese literary regions discursively from their own standpoints at the turn of the twenty-first century. In this instance, the reorganization makes room for the empowering possibility of an expanded Mahua literary history.

THE TRANSMITTED MEMORY OF DIASPORIC GEOGRAPHIES

Since the mid-2000s, scholars in modern Chinese literary studies have intensely debated the utility and connotations of "Chinese diaspora" for analysis. The primary point of contention is the value attached to China, often seen as the distinguished source of Chinese culture from which derivative tributaries evolve. *Sadness of the Pacific* formulates diaspora differently by portraying human mobility as a world-making activity that considers not just spatial relocation but also the temporal recurrence of translocal connections. In the novella, the narrator shares how her paternal great-grandparents migrated to Singapore in the late nineteenth century, and how two generations later, her father traveled to the mainland prior to the outbreak of the Asia-Pacific War and eventually made his destination in the north his home. Through fictionalizing the varied loci of Chinese mobilities, *Sadness of the Pacific* dramatizes a politics of contingent homeland construction that requires people's constant psychological reevaluation of places construed as points of origins.

The novella enacts the politics of home by offering a vicarious ethnography of literary youths in Nanyang before World War II. The discrepant yet coexisting homeland imaginaries that the youths construct for themselves are manifested through the life journeys of the characters "my father" (*wo fuqin* 我父親) and "Youngest Uncle" (*xiao shushu* 小叔叔). Whereas the former travels to China to fight those oppressed by the Japanese, the latter stays behind in Singapore to protect the island, thereby setting off two divergent trajectories of continual displacement in a larger history of Chinese migration.

In light of Wang's broader oeuvre, *Sadness of the Pacific* allows a reading of the China-born narrator as a diasporic subject. There is a moment in Wang's earlier short story "My Origins" (*Wode laili* 我的來歷; 1985) when the young first-person narrator called Anyi declares herself to be Singaporean after learning her father's background.[8] Extending the scope of the story, *Sadness of the Pacific* uses a resonant narrative voice—one that is anxious to "fill the void about my personal roots" (316)—to express how the narrator sees herself as part of the "history of going abroad" (*chuyang shi* 出洋史) in her family, a history that evokes a picture of the "unrestricted spread" (*manliu* 漫流) of human mobilities across the world (308).

To construct the path of "my father" in the narrated world, Wang draws upon the experiences of her own father Wang Xiaoping 王嘯平 (hereafter Xiaoping, following his pseudonym), and creates an archetypal figure for youths with a shared affinity for China. Born and bred in Nanyang, Xiaoping and his friends read literary works from China and established amateur drama groups that staged performances to promote anti-Japanese awareness among the overseas Chinese in support of China during World War II. In 1938, he joined the Malayan Chinese Roving Song and Drama Ensemble (*Mahua xunhui gejutuan* 馬華巡迴歌劇團) to perform all over Peninsular Malaya. Rousingly successful, the shows raised a substantial amount of funds for the ongoing Sino-Japanese War.[9] At the same time, Xiaoping also typifies the diasporic Mahua writer. In his twilight years, Wang's father wrote three semiautobiographical novels that scholars classify under the genre *guiqiao xiaoshuo* 歸僑小說 (novels about or by returned overseas Chinese).[10] His first two novels delineate the social and emotional upheavals that accompanied the returnees' migration to China, which they eventually regard as home.

Sadness of the Pacific marks Wang's foregrounding of this *guiqiao* route of Chinese migration, which remains little examined in modern Chinese literary studies. In the story, the narrator visits relatives, walks on the streets, and discovers the past of Singapore and Malaysia during her trip. Retracing the routes that "my father" had taken as a member of a roving drama ensemble, the narrator projects herself into several historical scenes, such as when she reconstructs the lived experiences of "my father" and his peers who were deeply passionate about literature and current affairs:

> When my father and the youths like him got together, there was another conversation topic redolent of fantasy, and that was legends about the mainland. For someone like my father who was born on the island, homeland was an abstract and remote concept. They were completely uninterested in organizations such as the native place associations. The idea of homeland failed to alleviate their sense of solitude and drift. But imaginaries about the mainland were effective remedies. Broadly speaking, the mainland was home, which catered to their romanticism. Both in their hearts and through their words, they sought identification with it eagerly. They were pro-active and passionate about learning spoken Mandarin. . . . They thought about their suffering fellow countrymen from afar. The word "fellow countrymen" made them feel extremely intimate. . . . My father thought about Japan's invasion of China through the inferior circumstances of the Malays and the Indians. At that time, they were both oppressed ethnic groups. He thought the Chinese would be relegated to the status of the Indians and the Malays if Japan occupied China. (320–21)

The distinction between "mainland" (*dalu* 大陸) and "homeland" (*guxiang* 故鄉) in this extract indicates the fundamental mindset difference among ethnic Chinese in Southeast Asia. For those China-born migrants who relocated to Nanyang, homeland and mainland are conflated concepts, which give substance to the familiar epistemology of Chinese diaspora as extensions from the originary continent. For the Nanyang-born literary youths in this scenario, however, China is not their homeland in the narrow sense of native place, but a time-honored "legend" (*chuanshuo* 傳說). The "mainland," in the narrator's imagination of the psyches of her father and his friends, connotes a different kind of "homeland": an alternative space she calls *jiayuan* 家園, which hosts a form of fictive kinship forged by common lived experiences.

The extract marks a significant moment of diasporic subject formation, as it shows that "my father" does not gravitate toward the mainland because of nostalgia for ancestral origins. Instead, he harbors imaginaries of an oppressed Chinese people whom he sees as fellow countrymen. Such imaginaries, despite the Chinese particularity, are also related to the circumstances of other oppressed ethnicities such as the Malays and the Indians in the British colony, which the narrator speculates to be the source of her father's sense of social justice. The narrator later recounts how her father wants to return "home" to Singapore after his plans to attend drama school and participate in revolutionary activities in China fall through. If the theater of World War II had not reached Shanghai on the eve of his planned return, he would have made it back to Southeast Asia. In other words, the father never considers China to be the end of his diasporic ventures. Unsurprisingly, those nuanced expressions of contingent solidarity with China can be easily taken as evidence of the Sino-centric commitment of the Chinese overseas, rather than of the ambivalent connections between one's self-defined home and motherland. Nonetheless, the father's inclination toward China as the *jiayuan*-type of "homeland" is arguably less a function of an innate identification with China as the authentic cultural fountainhead, than a response to the political appeal stemming from Western dominance over the Nanyang Chinese as a result of China's weak global standing.

Hence, by exploring the fine distinction between "homeland" as native place and "homeland" as the site of ethnic fraternity, *Sadness of the Pacific* conveys that there is no definitive relationship between the Chinese overseas and China. As Adam McKeown points out in his astute study of Chinese diasporas, "the idea of home can easily range from links to a family altar, to loyalty to a nation state, to longing for a nearly mythical site of origin, even within the mind of a single migrant."[11] In the novella, the father's diasporic consciousness highlights how such an array of connotations can be applied to every locational node that holds the potential to enable either settlement or further displacement. This inclusive diasporic network should include China as one possible station without having to privilege it as the singular source of agency. Prefiguring what Mahua critics in Taiwan in the 2000s describe as a paradoxical condition of *lisan shuangxiang* 離散雙鄉 (double diasporic homelands),[12] the father's physical and psychological trajectories show how he negotiates his self-identity between two "homelands"—that is, between Singapore, his birthplace, and China, the site of his artistic aspiration and ethnic activism.

The biographical arc of "Youngest Uncle" demonstrates an alternative path of creating a "homeland" for overseas Chinese with diasporic lineages. Like his eldest brother who eventually departs for China, "Youngest Uncle" is a *wenxue qingnian* 文學青年 (literary youth) who believes in the social function of literature. Attending the same Chinese schools together with "my father," "Youngest Uncle" is also brought up with an "inexplicable complex for the mainland" (334). Yet compared to his eldest brother, even though he is similarly driven by ethnonationalism, humanist ideals, and a deep sense of drift, he has a disparate temperament (333). Despite being emotionally aroused by the performances put on by his brother and his friends about China, he is profoundly attached to the Singapore community, which he cherishes and feels responsible toward. Pragmatic without compromising his idealism, "Youngest Uncle" is galvanized differently, as he chooses to join the Malayan Communist Party.

In this way, Wang sets up the avuncular character of "Youngest Uncle" to represent the agentive literary youth who commits himself to local institutions in times of extreme turbulence instead of traveling abroad. By portraying him as voluntarily staying in Singapore during the Japanese Occupation when most of his comrades relocated their resistance efforts to the Malayan jungles, Wang further limns a sacrificial mentality that signifies a moving devotion to place. Jointly considered with how "my father" almost returned to Singapore from Shanghai, *Sadness of the Pacific* invites readers to consider the reciprocity between contingent and intentional moorings as constitutive nodes that shape the constellations of Chinese diaspora.

As the story progresses, the novella assembles a thought-provoking range of human agency involved in a broader canvas of Chinese migration. The picture encompasses literati displaced to the south; roving members of the Chinese Communist Party; passionate Nanyang literary youths who relocated to China; and curious root-seeking descendants. Such a conjuncture of itineraries encodes multiple social visions of a global Chinese community on the move. Among these representations of Chinese mobilities, the father's fictional engagement with the "southbound literati" Yu Dafu 郁達夫 and Wu Tian 吳天, two significant figures of Mahua literary history, enables divergent interpretations of China-Nanyang relations:

> I imagined a literary youth like my father, who held a manuscript in his hands, on which the words "May Fourth" was written, who came knocking on Yu Dafu's door.... There were numerous youths who visited Yu Dafu. During his sojourn in Singapore, he was almost perpetually surrounded by these thin and tanned youths who all wore expressions of looking toward the sea. Yu Dafu was like the mainland that attracted the yearnings of scattered islands all adrift. (317)
>
> I think Wu Tian is a mysterious figure. He shuttles secretly between Singapore and the mainland, disappearing for some time only to re-emerge later. Searching for Wu Tian is also an important activity for my father during this period.... After he found Wu Tian, my father felt completely free from anxiety, as if a load was lifted off his mind. Wu Tian offered him the sense of reaching land. (336–37)

Yu Dafu, the most prominent May Fourth writer to sojourn in Nanyang, never made it back to China. Working initially as a newspaper editor and becoming a wanted fugitive during World War II, his career and life ended with his disappearance in Sumatra, Indonesia, soon after Japan's surrender. Though his body was never recovered, scholars believe that he was killed by the Japanese before their retreat.[13] Wu Tian, on the other hand, represents the peripatetic Chinese intellectual. Arriving in Malaya from Japan in 1936, he participated actively in raising anti-Japanese awareness within the local Chinese community by organizing drama performances imbued with the spirit of resistance. He joined the Malayan Communist Party in 1938 and later returned to China to escape arrest by the colonial authorities. During his sojourn, Wu engaged in literary polemics emphasizing a broader conception of "localism" (*difangxing* 地方性) that foretokens the important postwar debate on the "distinctiveness of Malayan literary arts."[14]

Glancing through the two extracts, one might first take issue with the associations arising from the asymmetrical analogies within. Yu Dafu and Wu Tian are likened to land and continents that promise security and a lofty sense of purpose, to which rudderless students, akin to vulnerable islands, are attracted. In the novella, the imagined scenes of exchange between "my father" and the cultural luminaries from the mainland can be interpreted as a novice accessing the thresholds of a literary center and its values. But by also fashioning the character of "Youngest Uncle," who was not influenced by Yu Dafu or Wu Tian, *Sadness of the Pacific* features an organic form of self-directed commitment, thereby averting the trite valorization of Chinese literary figures playing leading roles in igniting the passion of youths in Singapore. Weighing the value of place-based commitment through the contrast represented by the two brothers, Wang shows how an emotional affinity toward a mainland is no different from feeling attached to an island. At heart, "Youngest Uncle" sees Singapore as being like any mainland and as worthy as a continent for which one would be willing to lay down his life. In this view, "scattered islands all adrift" need not be distinguished from mainlands, for they all function as nodes whose interconnections are made visible through the circulation of people displaced in multiple directions who sometimes retrace their old routes or that of their ancestors.

Remarkably, the narrator's vicarious reconstruction of her father's life in Nanyang is premised upon her role as a reader of her father's literary works (325–26), which straddle Malayan and mainland literary spaces, thereby making her a reader of Mahua literature. That reconstruction mirrors how in the late 1980s and early 1990s, when Wang and Xiaoping were each penning narratives about Singapore, Malaya, and Malaysia, Wang was reading her father's works with great curiosity. When Xiaoping left Singapore for China in 1940, in part because of his participation in anticolonial activities, he was already a prolific writer who had published widely in many local newspapers and literary journals, including prose, current affairs commentary, drama criticism, and plays.[15] But his semiautobiographical novels written in his elderly years were what shaped Wang's impressions about the region. Her understanding of Xiaoping's life journey from Singapore to China turns into critical traces in *Sadness of the Pacific*, as if she is engaged in a creative relay. The intergenerational flow of creativity was not unhindered. Evidently, Wang struggles to grasp the complex psyche of *guiqiao* (returned overseas Chinese) like her father.

Doubting the sense of alienation conveyed by Xiaoping's title for his second novel, she confesses in an essay: "I have always found the word 'guest' in the title *The Guest from Nanyang* inappropriate ... because my father was no longer a 'guest' from early on. Together with other Chinese intellectuals, he experienced the surrender of the Japanese, the national liberation by the Communists, the anti-Rightist Campaign and the 'Great Cultural Revolution.'"[16]

As both reader and daughter, Wang fails to understand why her father ultimately retained sentiments of being a guest in China. In this light, *Sadness of the Pacific* embodies the ways in which Wang strives to reconcile herself with the layered emotional orientations of the social collective comprised by the returned overseas Chinese. The series of imagined events recounted from the autobiographical narrator's perspective highlights that generational gap, which is made particularly stark toward the novella's end when she evaluates the initial displacement of "my father" from his native place in Nanyang:

> The day when Singapore finally gained independence was also when my father was truly exiled. As I mentioned earlier, in the course of his life as a *zhongguoren* [man of China] my father has moved too far. He has gone deep into the outback of the mainland. The fate of him being a *zhongguoren* is immutable. When my father looked back on his life in his twilight years, he was unsure whether or not being a *zhongguoren* was a fortunate affair. I thought, however, that a romantic idealist like him could only be with people of his own *minzu* [ethnic group].... For my father, the route toward being a *zhongguoren* was rather uneven. One can say it was bumpy. He had to scramble in many ways. He would forget to wear his straw sandals on his road marches, or to load his gun when on sentry duty. On his second trip to the base area, he felt as if he was going home, his heart eager with anticipation as he walked on the road. He cast the island of my grandparents to the back of his mind. Communication between the two places stopped and the people at both ends gave up their longings. The Pacific War also seemed to be the time when my father was reborn. He began to think of himself as a real son of the mainland. (378)

That the narrator thinks of her father as becoming permanently exiled from Singapore is tantamount to seeing him as a diasporic Singaporean. In this sense, the term *zhongguoren* 中國人 (man of China) contains a poignant ambiguity. While the narrator's postulation that her father will only be safe when he stays together with his *minzu* 民族 (ethnic group) connotes a shared cultural tradition across Nanyang and China, against the backdrop of Singapore's independence, the *zhongguoren* appellation also bespeaks the involuntary shift of her father's political identity after he traveled to the mainland. Translocality hardens into transnationality when her father's agency in shaping his ideal life trajectory is circumscribed due to British colonialism and Japanese imperialism.

We can henceforth interpret *Sadness of the Pacific* not just as a narrative complementary to works by or about returned overseas Chinese, but also more importantly, as a symbolic gesture of reinserting the genre of *guiqiao* novels into the connected fields of Mahua literature and modern Chinese literature. Through the bifurcated paths of Nanyang literary youths, the novella recounts a tale of becoming Chinese in China when recognized consanguinity does not immediately promise political inclusion, as much as it constitutes a simultaneous narrative about becoming Singaporean before the British colony attained national independence. In the former context, becoming Chinese in China is not as easy as one may think, even for a person who considers himself a *zhongguoren*. The overseas imprint can be more divisive than previously imagined. For the narrator's father, the sense of shared heritage between overseas Chinese and mainland Chinese does not translate into a smooth integration experience. The mindset shift, which results in his ultimate perception of himself as a "real son of the mainland," does not inevitably occur due to some preconscious feeling or primordial sentiment of nostalgia for an abstract native place or motherland. Nor is the transformation of his worldview accomplished by the physical act of relocation often construed by many as return. Instead, the significant change in self-understanding is the outcome of a social conditioning at the personal level that requires work, both mental and physical. To assimilate in another place, he has to make substantive adjustments in his daily and vocational life, as well as forget his kinship ties with the island in the south. The experiential arc of "my father" shows how the "Chineseness of China" is not as immutable and transparent as it seems, and the sense of being Chinese can be challenged from within the self-identified community.¹⁷

Whether it is Xiaoping insisting on his sense of sojourning in China in his novels, or Wang writing about her roots in Nanyang, their stories about Southeast Asia constitute an integral part of their experiences of China. As a cross-generational palimpsest of Nanyang memories, *Sadness of the Pacific* activates a historically grounded reflection on diaspora in relation to the mainland state, which is dislodged from its superior status as the originary site of Chineseness, and where displacement can also occur, thus turning it into another site to become local.

We can then follow how Wang's particular outlook on worlding, that is, on navigating the local and the global, arises from her speculative depiction of her father's experiences in the 1930s and 1940s. Disputing critics' assertion of the book as an instance of "clan fiction" (*jiazu xiaoshuo* 家族小說) in the late 1980s, she clarifies that *Sadness of the Pacific* is thematically concerned with the "drifting fate of humanity."¹⁸ Wang's fictional portrayal of drift as the ongoing flows of people—diasporic, rootless, and unmoored—among places, rather than singular departures from origins, reaches an apex when the narrator reflects on the history of overseas Chinese in the context of a global war, leading her (and Wang the implied author) to demystify China as a continent (which shares the term *dalu* 大陸 with "mainland") at the end of the tale:

> Finally, I will repeat what I have said before, "On a map, continents are also drifting islands." All lands on earth are ocean reefs for human sojourns. In fact, humanity is a drifting community, and staying afloat its eternal fate. The archipelago in the Pacific Ocean can be likened to a miniature global landscape. The islands are truly continents. The ocean is perhaps the final settlement for humanity, the end point of man's lives adrift. (383)

The narrator's discourse resonates with critical geographers' contention that the two types of landmasses are fungibly defined because of their developmental nature. As Martin Lewis and Kären Wigen point out from a geological perspective, "continents are momentary assemblages of land that continually grow, divide, and reform."¹⁹ Clearly, the novella's narrator is not so much concerned with specifying the minimum size that differentiates an island from a mainland-like continent, as with how islands and continents interact with one another historically.

Here, the geographic commensurability evokes an underlying narrative logic articulated differently across Wang's prior works that build up to *Sadness of the Pacific*. The novella echoes its twin narrative, the 1993 novel *Jishi yu xugou* 紀實與虛構 (Documentation and fictionalization), which spins a breathtaking tale about the narrator's maternal family lineage that originates in the Mongolian steppes. In its unabridged version, the novel carries the subtitle "one method of creating the world," attesting to Wang's ambition of literary worlding. Throughout the novel, Wang interweaves the narrator's genealogical investigation in the semi-arid landscape with her struggle to feel at home in Shanghai, once described as a solitary island (*gudao* 孤島) during World War II when parts of the city were exempt from the Japanese Occupation. At one point, because of linguistic barriers in communication and an overwhelming sense of existential rootlessness, the first-person narrator compares her migrant family in Shanghai to an island.[20] Stringing urban Shanghai together with places beyond the Great Wall and across the South China Sea, Wang's fiction-writing enterprise during the early 1990s orchestrates her simultaneous interest in global, regional, national, and local spaces of Chineseness. By pronouncing an equivalence between China (the "continent") and Singapore/Malaya (the "island") in the ending of *Sadness of the Pacific*, Wang provincializes China, which she no longer conceives of as an exceptional place.

Being an island, however, does not necessarily connote parochialism. This idea is brought to the fore in *Wutuobang shipian* 烏托邦詩篇 (Utopian verses), the 1991 novella that she acknowledges was written in the same creative linguistic register as *Sadness of the Pacific*.[21] *Utopian Verses* commemorates Wang's transformative experience at the 1983 Iowa International Writers' Workshop where she first interacted with artists from all over the world. In particular, her exchanges with Chen Yingzhen 陳映真, the distinguished writer from Taiwan, led her to reassess China's position in the world, her own self-identity as an author, and how fiction-writing becomes an embodied experience of pursuing a higher faith. Touched by Chen's charisma and commitment to progressive causes in Taiwan, the first-person narrator repeatedly conveys that "a person on an island can also have the world in his heart," thereby forestalling the attachment of essentialized values of remoteness, isolation, and subordination to the smaller landmass category.[22]

Occasioning a conceptual imbrication of Singapore/Malaya, Mongolia, Shanghai, and Taiwan, Wang's writing practice in the late 1980s and early 1990s shores up a creative inclination toward flexible regionality, which maintains the possibility that every place can enter and exit continental or islandic moments of existence. In negating the exceptionality of China, she shows how local worlds of varied scales are interconnected and derive meanings by referencing one another. From this perspective, *Sadness of the Pacific* becomes more than a self-referential tale about authorial root-seeking in postcolonial Singapore and Malaysia. Rather, its repeated pronouncement that "islands are truly continents" can be interpreted as a radical act of authorial envisioning that sees universality uniquely embedded in every place that hosts Chinese migration.

At the end of the novella, the narrator ponders over the sea—instead of either category of the landmasses—as the final abode of humanity. The closing line is doubly puzzling because the narrator calls the ocean "the end point of man's lives adrift," as if it is a static container, when every large body of water so classified is rarely considered stagnant. The maritime-oriented conclusion recalls an earlier part in the novella where the narrator imagines her father on the first voyage of his life, which already suggests sea-drifting to be the fundamental leitmotif of humankind:

> The ship sailed through the vast expanse of whiteness sutured by the sea and the sky. At this instant, my father appreciated the splendor of the ship. It is home while one is adrift; it also embodies hope. It gathers all who drift along, who help one another through life and death, and steers them toward land. Land can be compared to the symbol of eternal life. I guess the ship would stop to refuel at various port cities on its route. . . . Each time the ship pulled into the harbor, my father sees it as an intimate encounter. He calibrates his distance from land, moving away whenever he gets too close, like a pair of lovers with deep feelings of gratitude and loyalty. (342)

Framing mobility as dwelling, Wang depicts the ship as a floating residence, port cities as transient stopovers, and land as places to depart from despite it also being "the symbol of eternal life." In this view, the Chinese are inexorably global because they are inexorably adrift, whereas settlement on land—whether it is a place as small as Singapore, or as expansive as China—is but a thematic variation of man's wandering destiny on the seas. Wang's description of man on maritime vessels thus signals an open-ended oceanic imaginary involving Chinese historical mobilities and lifeworlds, which underpins her fundamental grasp of Chinese diaspora. The narrative representations in *Sadness of the Pacific* assemble what McKeown identifies as two differing conceptions of scattered human connections and discourses: "diaspora-as-exile" with moral overtones of suffering and persecution on the one hand, and "diaspora-as-diversity" that connotes flows, hybridity, and multiplicity on the other.[23] In so doing, Wang liberates Chinese diaspora from prescribing essentialized ethnic or cultural bonds forged among dispersed individuals. Instead, she shapes the concept to describe historical mobility and settlement in a variety of geographical contexts by people who accessed social networks and thought resources that enabled them to negotiate discrepant modes of feeling "Chinese."

IN SEARCH OF A COSMOPOLITAN CHINESE LITERARY VERNACULAR

Around the same period that Wang was composing *Sadness of the Pacific*, she experimented with a literary language that rejected the stylistic markers of places and persons, thinking they would disrupt the work of fictional narration.[24] By then, she was completing a period of frequent overseas travel. Between 1983 and 1992, Wang shuttled between China and countries including the United States, Germany, Singapore, and Malaysia. In the 1980s Wang was also immersed in a Chinese literary scene stoked by the fervor of making cosmopolitan connections. The slogan of the times—"China must walk toward the world"—bore out the literary zeitgeist.[25] Emerging from the Cultural Revolution, many of Wang's colleagues sought to break free from the shackles of socialist ideology, which isolated Chinese literature from world literature. Scholars and critics in the 1980s were also eager to insert Chinese literature into an international sphere of cultural exchange. They reflected upon the inconspicuous position of Chinese literature in the "world literary order" (*shijie wenxue geju* 世界文學格局) that mirrored the undeveloped condition of China in the global geopolitical order and favored its premodern works.[26]

For role models, China refrained from emulating the prestige-granting cultural centers in the West. Although the younger generation of Chinese writers learned diligently from newly imported Western literary theories and works, they did not lean heavily on those creative resources for guidance. Rather, they leveraged their intermarginal solidarity with Latin American counterparts, committing themselves to uncover local customs and folk traditions as world cultural heritage lost during past decades of political turbulence. In particular, the Chinese literary circle was greatly inspired by the international success of the Colombian writer Gabriel García Márquez, who won the Nobel Prize in 1982. As Catherine Yeh notes, "the Latin American writers had not only shown a way to use traditional culture in order to create a distinct and modern literary style but also offered an example and proved to young Chinese writers that economic backwardness did not prevent a nation from producing first-class literature."[27] Subscribing to the idea that "what is uniquely national will be embraced by the world," critics and writers in the broad movement of "cultural reflection" (*wenhua fansi* 文化反思) and "root-seeking literature" enthusiastically discussed the composition of works that could be admitted into the pantheon of globally recognized texts by reviving and promoting Chinese national characteristics.[28]

Unlike her root-seeking colleagues who were rediscovering indigenous Chinese culture in their travels to China's regional peripheries, Wang ventured out of China. Her visits to foreign countries not only informed her fiction writing, but also yielded prose essays about site-specific modes of Chinese-language expression. Guided by her contemporaneous essays, I propose that the recurring emphasis on equating islands with continents in *Sadness of the Pacific* goes beyond resolving cultural asymmetries to evince Wang's ideas on her preferred form of literary language. Taken together, her two articles, "The Language of Fiction in Works from Mainland China and Taiwan: A Comparison" (Dalu Taiwan xiaoshuo yuyan bijiao 大陸臺灣小說語言比較; hereafter "Comparison") (1989), and "The Fate of Language" (Yuyan de mingyun

語言的命運) (1992), elucidate the ramifications arising from continual linguistic relocation.

For instance, Wang compares the literary languages of fiction written by authors living across the Taiwan Strait. As she contends: "Due to forty years of separation, the same language has actually developed two faces. This extraordinary reality illustrates the multiple possibilities of linguistic development."[29] In "The Fate of Language," which was written alongside *Sadness of the Pacific* after her trip to Singapore and Malaysia in 1991, Wang also observes how linguistic mobility that accompanies large-scale migration has resulted in an array of Chinese cultural ecologies in Southeast Asia. Whereas the Malaysian Chinese double down on linguistic proficiency as a key marker of ethnicity, Thailand takes the path of assimilation and Singapore chooses to internationalize through English, both places thereby attenuating their connections to Sinitic languages (226–27).[30] In particular, Wang mentions how the Singaporean interdisciplinary artist Tan Swie Hian 陳瑞獻 described those who felt isolated like him as gypsies, blaming their predicament on the local marginalization of Chinese language and culture. That image of spiritual

FIGURE 3.2 Wang Anyi after giving a literary talk in Kuala Lumpur, 1991

136 *Cosmopolitan Visions of Drift*

nomadism led her to frame "Chinese language as a place for wandering" (220). It is then no coincidence that she eventually renames the article "A Language Adrift" (Piaobo de yuyan 漂泊的語言). Rather than specifying her topic as *hanyu* 漢語 (the Han language, often used as a shorthand for Chinese language), which carries an ethnocentric ring, she keeps the use of the generic term *yuyan* 語言 (language) and ties her culturally specific observations to a general uncertainty about the effects of linguistic deterritorialization.

In addition, Wang articulates the traits of her ideal literary language obliquely through the articles. One key point she makes pertains to how the pursuits for place-appropriate literary languages, which register regional speech patterns, encounter serious obstacles. Citing China as an example in "Comparison," she describes two challenges faced by mainland fiction writers in terms of a north-south divide and a rural-urban rift. In some cases, writers of China must create a northern-based literary vernacular for portraying southern regions whose spoken languages do not match the standard written one. When read off the pages, that improvised fictional language usually sounds contrived, as most of the colloquial terms have rarely been seen in written form. Such a defamiliarization of literary language, which originally aims to convey local flavors, poses great challenges to reception, as those works require readers to perform translations in their minds based on having prior exposure to the diverse regional expressions (385–86). In other cases, mainland writers have to deal with the linguistic poverty of urban contexts. To Wang, the urban colloquialisms she encounters are not worth incorporating into narrative language, as they lack the historical depth and cultural force of the Chinese agrarian civilization, which has nurtured the aesthetics of lively literary vernaculars (386).

Toward the end of "Comparison," Wang summarizes both conundrums as the limitations of "specific languages" (*juti yuyan* 具體語言), by which she means the forms of literary language that lose their powers to shape depictions once they are divorced from the contextual specificities of the source environments or historical periods. Her proposed solution is to create and master an "abstract language" (*chouxiang yuyan* 抽象語言) (386), whose substance she elaborates elsewhere. In a conversation with literary critics, she asserts that "fundamentally, the language of fiction is the language of narration, which can also be called a language about language (*yuyan de yuyan* 語言的語言) or an abstract language."[31] In Wang's conception, the abstract language "can be used in every place: official documents, letters, fiction and prose. In fiction, it can be used for different genres of creative writing, for different forms of expression, as all stylized and individuated languages are in fact derived from it. It is the true building material for fictional worlds."[32] In other words, she intends to formulate for her fiction a kind of metalanguage from which all particularizations evolve, "a kind of language that is absent from daily life to describe the ubiquitous quotidian experiences and phenomena, which include linguistic phenomena."[33]

Her linguistic outlook results in her approach to construct narrative texts as artifices of linguistic transparency. Elaborating in terms of her writing conviction, she shares: "I aspire greatly toward writing the kind of language that is extremely plain. Such 'plainness' occurs after deliberation. . . . I feel my language has been improving these two years, especially after *Documentation and Fictionalization*, which is still a little florid; *Sadness of the Pacific* is better. In my opinion, fine literary language should be ordinary, but it can attain brilliance."[34] Here, Wang's "extremely plain" language (*henbai de hua* 很白的話) evokes the term *baihua* 白話 (literally "unadorned speech," also known as *baihuawen* 白話文) that denotes the Chinese written vernacular, commonly regarded as the linguistic foundation of modern Chinese literature. As she mentions, her desired functioning of literary language differs from transcribing the popular colloquiality of everyday life. But what is particularly noteworthy is how her textualized articulations—Wang's own *baihua*, so to speak—deviates from the conventional association of vernaculars with locality as well.

Carving out her own position in the mainland Chinese literary space, Wang distances herself from "root-seeking" writers such as Han Shaogong 韓少功, who fanned out across the country in the 1980s—especially in the rural regions—in search of remote local languages to revitalize modern Chinese literature. Also, she refrains from identifying with the urban kind of "modern street patois" (*xiandai shijing yuyan* 現代市井語言) Wang Shuo 王朔 exemplifies.[35] To Wang, literary languages that are overly invested in appearing local (*fengtuhua de yuyan* 風土化的語言) or contemporary (*shidaigan de yuyan* 時代感的語言) rely on "ready-made languages" that are like "computers with pre-set programs" to elicit reading responses.[36] Instead of inheriting the linguistic memories of a place or of an ethnic collective, she emulates the mode of literary expression exemplified by A Cheng 阿城, another writer of the root-seeking school, who defamiliarizes quotidian language by distilling it to invent a universal narrative language whose reception does not require prior experience, as its abstract nature derives from "linguistic common sense" (*yuyan li de changshi* 語言裡的常識).[37]

By claiming that her "abstract language" has widespread applications, Wang further suggests that her literary vernacular can travel. Conceptualizing the written medium of her literary endeavors in this manner challenges vernacularization processes that entail limiting the scale of linguistic circulation. The layered paradox of Wang's *baihua*, I propose, can be approached as the fostering and performance of a "cosmopolitan Chinese literary vernacular." Her vernacularization impulse has to be understood in terms of how she invests in creating a connective ground for global Chinese writing. In other words, Wang hopes to formulate a common vernacular for Chinese-language authors who share her embrace of the world as the local, an exemplary literary vernacular that represents a lingua franca for humanity.

That Wang's ideal literary language contains ecumenical shades is unsurprising, for her aspiration resonates with the sentiments she infuses in her novella *Utopian Verses*. According to its first-person narrator, the Taiwan Christian writer Chen Yingzhen imagines a time before the Tower of Babel was built when all humans live together, share a universal language, and engage in collective action (258). Despite its utopianism, the pre-Babelian imaginary does not hinder Chen from participating in grassroots social movements—of which writing is an integral component—that seek to change the world. Greatly inspired but also well aware of their differences, the narrator commits to shaping the introspective world of fiction, the realm of agency where she feels she can make the greatest difference. As the embodiment of her faith, fiction bespeaks her ideals about the world-at-large, whose operational logic influences but does not determine the world-on-page. Employed in Wang's writing practice, the cosmopolitan Chinese literary vernacular is the necessary material medium—what she calls "the true building material"—that brings the narrated world into being and gives form to the stories she tells.

On the surface, Wang's literary experiment counteracts the creative endeavors of Lin Cantian and Han Suyin that I examined in the previous chapters, as both writers attempt to bring specificities of place settings into their literary languages—a tendency I have also presented as cosmopolitan. But the apparent contradiction can be resolved if we frame Wang's case as expanding the conceptual range of universal-minded literary vernaculars. For the world-Chinese literary space, Wang's *baihua* vernacular can be seen as cosmopolitan because it participates in creating and connecting multiple site-specific cultures in a nondominant fashion, thereby contributing toward international literary-language diversity without engaging in super-imposition or domestication. While local and regional literary spaces are free to coopt her narrative poetics originating from a more expansive literary space, the resultant poetics of the local and regional literary spaces also travel, moving from Malaysia to other places such as Taiwan and Singapore, forming a dynamic ecology of intersecting centers and peripheries.

The corollary of Wang's discourse that critiques Chinese literary language soaked in localisms and modish expressions is that all writers—even those like her, from China—can be displaced from an ideal linguistic mode of literary expression. Through Wang's creative journey, we see how linguistic nativity does not preclude a simultaneous sense of linguistic alienation, which leads her to attempt restoring the senses of intimacy among people, place, and language. Strikingly, Wang's cosmopolitan Chinese literary vernacular is registered not just in *Utopian Verses*, but also in *Documentation and Fictionalization* and *Sadness of the Pacific*. The three texts form a series of works that involves crossing the geographical boundaries of China, commonly taken to be the center of the world-Chinese literary space. That the upscaling of her linguistic experimentation occurred via her diasporic literary discourses about the Chinese abroad and ethnic minorities reflects the inclusive valences of the *baihua* she formulates, as the cosmopolitan literary vernacular embodies a universality without a center.

In forging an unconventional literary language whose broad reach is impeded neither by localisms nor by knowledge of the times, Wang shapes her distinctive positionality within the group of root-seeking writers in China with whom she has been affiliated since the 1980s. Besides her peers mentioned earlier, she also compares her creative endeavors to those by Mo Yan 莫言, contending that the winner of the 2012 Nobel Prize in Literature "uses the brilliance (of literary language) to attain the brilliance (of the literary work)," whereas she uses "the ordinary to attain the brilliance."[38] Refusing to stylize her literary language according to place and person, Wang further rejects being narrowly classified as a Shanghai writer.[39] Claiming an orphan consciousness, a sensibility that recurs in Wang's works of the early 1990s, she moves beyond untethering from locality by disidentifying herself with her contemporaries and traditional Chinese cultural symbols: "I don't want to get involved in the matter of literary schools, since they are quite confusing. My attitude is that in a good piece of work, root-searching is an eternal theme. How to search for the roots is another question. Zheng Yi searched for his roots by roaming about the Yellow River district. Everybody has a different method. I grew up in Shanghai; where do I go to search for my roots? I should find my roots in myself."[40] Wang's avowal buttresses my earlier argument that the "Chineseness of China" is internally differentiated. Unlike her peers who pursue the plural origins of Chinese traditional culture to participate in world literature, she feels that her nonnative experience of growing up in Shanghai warrants an approach that is separate from reclaiming natural landscapes in China as the source of one's cultural roots. Rather than join an intellectual group, she wants to find an independent path to express her aspirations for China, which is no longer an object of obsession, but "a spot in the world."[41]

Aligned with her intention to seek her roots introspectively, her literary endeavors are influenced by her belief that texts manifest an author's personalized "world of the mind" (*xinling shijie* 心靈世界).[42] Committing to register a creative mind through writing does not mean, however, that Wang ignores the relationship between fiction writing and community building. As shown in her thoughts on the root-seeking literary movement, she is cognizant of the ways in which literature calls into being audiences of multiple scales through textual circulation. Through *Sadness of the Pacific*, Wang's cherished linguistic transparency allows readers in China and abroad to access her imaginative blend of a family history, an ethnic group's history of migration, and the vicissitudes of a global war. Featuring Wang's deployment of her cosmopolitan Chinese literary vernacular to redefine diaspora as an enduring series of movement, the novella imagines cosmopolitan connections as well, by using Nanyang's significance in mediating Chinese mobilities to de-exceptionalize China for mainland literary production and the world-Chinese literary space.

Going with Wang's logic of China being an ordinary node in the global network of Sinitic cultural production, her own *baihua* vernacular manifested through the tale loses its dominating capacity. Her compositional language's twin effects of redefinition and ending exceptionality are achieved by subtle imageries, such as when the story conveys a common mythical origin for inhabitants of both islands and continents:

> The small island in Nanyang reminds me of the legend from ancient times, the one about the world carried on a whale's back. This legend must have come from the primitive men on the island. They saw the boundless body of water surrounding them, flowing as it is, day and night. The currents gave people a sense of turbulence and drift. Indeed, one will not be mistaken to say that the world is on the back of a whale. When one looks at a map, continents also turn into islands, whereas the islands become fragments of continents, and drift along with the currents. (311)

As if to match China's long civilizational history, the narrator imbues Nanyang with a legendary antiquity about the world, which implies an enduring global community whose members are bound less by blood than by a shared sense of drift. From a whale to a map, the world is represented through two epistemic modes. The eventual shift to latter stages the organic commensurability of landmasses embedded in deep time. In this way, through what Wang considers a universal literary vernacular, the narrative poetics of *Sadness of the Pacific* urges actors in the mainland literary space to reconsider the privileging of intra-China regionalism and localism in the root-seeking movement, and to embrace the local-regional and the global as inter-changeable scales of composition and ways of being.

In the 1990s, the configuring and reconfiguring of the fit between place and language, mediated by Chinese-language literature, was not merely restricted to the mainland literary space. Alongside writers from China who considered themselves marginalized and struggled with the politics of admittance in world literature, Taiwan-based Ng Kim Chew from Malaysia contemplated the linguistic form of Mahua literature that was crucial for improving its standing in the world literary space. To Ng, the crux of the matter lies in authors effectively harnessing the disconnect between sound and script so as to invent a distinctive Mahua literary language. By parsing Ng's appropriation of Wang's commentary on the languages of fiction from Taiwan and China, as well as on the differing localizations of Chinese language in Southeast Asia, I provide in the next section an account of inter-Asia resonance between Chinese literary marginalities to contextualize the Mahua writer-cum-critic's alternative vision of rendering the Chinese literary vernacular cosmopolitan.

"HUAWEN" AND "ZHONGWEN": REWORLDING THE CHINESE LITERARY VERNACULAR

Notably, the discursive intersection between Wang and Ng illustrates the way in which the former's ideas provided conceptual grist for the latter to theorize *baihuawen* (the written Chinese vernacular) and its attendant forms of diasporic literary production related to Malaysia. The confluence also reveals how Wang's notion of a universal "abstract language" was forged under similar conditions of marginality in the larger world literary space that catalyzed Ng's perspective on Chinese literary languages in locales beyond China. Reflecting the fungibility of islands and continents articulated in the *Sadness of the Pacific*, the global and the local should be seen as interacting modes of creative existence, constantly shifting due to an ongoing dialectic of linguistic drift and settlement.

In the linguistically specific world-Chinese literary space, Ng's role models in the early 1990s were the root-seeking writers in China whose influence reached not their desired global forums, but other native literary spaces of Sinitic cultural production. Both China and Malaysia were then attempting to elevate their Chinese-language literary formations so that they can become world literature. By actively placing China against the backdrop of the world at large, Wang's writings provide differentiated insights on authors in post–Cultural Revolution China who redefined the cosmopolitan nature of Chinese literature by consciously searching for their cultural origins in less favored areas outside urban centers of political power. These authors' literary ideas and practices resonated with those of Mahua authors who confronted their own marginality vis-à-vis China and the world literary community.

Running parallel to China's obsession with the Nobel Prize for Literature in the last two decades of the twentieth century, Mahua literature also contended with the esteemed world literary institution.[43] In 1990, Ng deployed the trope of the Nobel Prize in his short story "M de shizong" M 的失蹤 (Disappearance of M) to satirize the rigid principles of classifying literary production in Malaysia, where the state only considers works written in Malay, the national language, as national literature. In the story, an anonymous author of unknown ethnicity publishes a primarily English novel that becomes the subject of an intense debate in Malay-centric Malaysia, especially on whether the work could be nominated for the Nobel Prize as the country's representative entry.[44] The Nobel Prize hypothesis appeared again in "Kaiting shenxun" 開庭審訊 (The trial), a 1992 article by Xuan Sulai 禤素萊, which describes an academic conference in Japan, where most Japanese academic specialists of Southeast Asia argue that Mahua literature should not be characterized as "Malaysian" because it is not written in the country's national language. Those scholars further propose that the history of the Mahua literary formation should be construed as "the origins and development of mainland Chinese literature in Malaysia."[45] Evoking the issues dramatized in Ng's short story, a lone defender asks his colleagues at the conference if it takes a Nobel Prize to transform the politics of recognition.[46]

Except cultural insiders, few now know that it was Xuan's report on the study of Mahua literature in Japan that triggered vigorous reflections within the Mahua literary circle in the 1990s on the literary formation's standing in the world literary arena.[47] Amid the polemics, Ng altered the course of the discussion decisively by spotlighting the topic of canonicity. He critiqued the Japanese scholars for unreflectively endorsing the ruling Malaysian government's Malay-centric rhetoric that viewed Mahua writers as unassimilated. Yet he ultimately attributed the scholars' misinterpretation to the lack of a widely recognized Malaysian literary canon in Chinese, rather than to their ignorance about multilingual postcolonial nation-states or their self-righteous immersion in Japan's own insularity. In other words, Ng thought that Mahua authors deserve the affront they received. "Without cosmopolitan (*shijie xing* 世界性) works, Mahua literature has no rights of speech in the world literary circle. The dearth also poses great constraints to creating a regional tradition," he asserted.[48] He further insisted that it was only meaningful to speak of a Mahua literary perspective after the production of comparable works that can enter the arena of world literature as a regional tradition in its own right.[49]

Coincidentally, like his root-seeking counterparts in China, Ng cited the Latin American pattern. Analyzing Latin America's success in creating its signature style of magical realism, China and Mahua writers and critics reflected on their common peripherality in world literary space, which hosted a global assembly of distinctive works that both groups of writers assumed were admitted purely through aesthetic merit. To Ng, only the Latin American literary formation "truly exhibits 'regional characteristics': mutated modes of writing and sensing, roots in specifically local cultural traditions, products of cultural hybridity. . . . It can turn around to influence its metropolitan state (Spain) and has now become one of the most noteworthy regions of world literature."[50]

The Latin American model generated different impacts on mainland Chinese and Mahua literary spaces. In China, the writers whom critics regarded as members of the root-seeking school were the ones impressed by the Latin American exemplar for creating meaningful literary diversity and committed themselves to similar undertakings. Alongside those endeavors, the root-seeking writers dissolved the dominance of what the literary critic Li Tuo 李陀 calls "the Mao-style prose" (*maowenti* 毛文体), a normative mode of expression that had curbed the organic development of Chinese vernacular speech and writing.[51] But from Wang Anyi's perspective, by eagerly imitating figures of the "Latin American literary explosion" such as Gabriel García Márquez, the root-seeking generation of authors also fell into another pitfall of homogenization.[52] As she recounts, "We saw it [Latin American literature] as the model and thought we found the direction for literature. We . . . strove sincerely for the world's recognition. For our voices to be heard, we put special effort in foregrounding difference. However, differences only exist in the past, the future was increasingly standardized, bearing identical looks. The chorus that started ahead . . . would completely swallow up our aping and immature voices."⁵³ Revealing not just the heterogeneity of ideas within the root-seeking school, Wang's evaluative recollection evinces the circumstances that limited China's success in highlighting national difference vis-à-vis the rest of the world in the 1980s due to sweeping forces of cultural globalization.

On the other hand, Ng found in the Latin American model a parallel paradigm for the world-Chinese literary space that represented how a marginalized region with a distinctive literary language could turn around to exert influence on its cultural metropole. Though he raised the notion of "regional characteristics," he was not interested in pressing those artistic features in service of nationalist agendas evident in China's Nobel Prize ambitions, given Mahua literature's fraught positionality in the Malaysian literary space. Rather than rectifying linguistic formulaicism or trying to discover indigeneity in the country's rural margins, the Mahua literary formation—in Ng's view—should be more invested in improving the creative capacity of its representational language.

To make his case for a locally inflected linguistic practice that would refine Mahua literary language, he adapts Wang's ideas explicated in her essays "Comparison" and "The Fate of Language" to compose his article "Huawen/Zhongwen: 'The South Where Language is Lost' and Linguistic Reinvention" (Huawen/Zhongwen: 'Shiyu de nanfang' yu yuyan zaizao 華文/中文: "失語的南方"與語言再造; hereafter "Huawen/Zhongwen") (1996)."⁵⁴ In his piece, Ng proposes a theoretical framework that conceptualizes *zhongwen* and *huawen* as a pair of discrepant terms that both denote the Chinese written vernacular in diasporic settings. Separately, the terms function as taxonomical labels for two types of Chinese literary vernacular employed by Mahua writers of different persuasions. Specifically, *zhongwen* refers to a "special modality of (written) linguistic practice" adopted by ethnic Chinese authors who derive resources from premodern Chinese culture, especially its textual traditions, thereby indicating a Sino-oriented cultural psyche.⁵⁵ In contrast, the use of *huawen* carries a local Chinese cultural identification. Geographically speaking, whereas the former is tied more closely to China, the latter primarily connotes the use of Chinese language in non-China contexts. Looking toward "fashioning new linguistic possibilities and developing a new linguistic culture on a new social foundation,"⁵⁶ Ng's ideal mode of the *huawen* vernacular harnesses eclectic sociolinguistic environments in every place that is invigorated by spoken topolects from south China, and by other ethnic languages, for innovations in literary aesthetics and reflections on marginality.

Recognizing that the colloquial vernacular has already taken on literary forms for centuries in China and has accumulated its own tradition of writings, Ng emphasizes the sense of place as critical to distinguishing vernacular literature of different regions within and beyond China. More than overcoming Sino-centrism, Ng wishes to contribute to the plurality of literary languages that marks different shades of Chinese cultural identity. To assess the history and future of Mahua literary language, he extrapolates liberally from Wang's aforementioned essays. Transposing the criteria that Wang uses for her China-Taiwan analysis in "Comparison," Ng elaborates on the linguistic quandary of Mahua literature: that is, to fashion a literary vernacular out of Mandarin, a northern topolect, despite the reality that the various Sinitic topolects from southern China are the true spoken vernaculars among ethnic Chinese in multicultural Southeast Asia.

Ng's dialectical framework pivots upon the conclusion he draws from Wang's comparative analysis: whether or not the social milieux and literacy levels allow authors' creative practices to foster the "unification of speech and writing" (*yanwen heyi* 言文合一) is crucial. On this criterion, Ng and Wang have both been heavily influenced by what the literary scholar Wei Shang calls "the modern view of pre-modern and early modern Chinese linguistic and writing practices." That view misrepresents the evolution of Chinese writing as a process of seeking congruence with its oral sources, when in fact, "Chinese writing is almost always at variance with the spoken language, and thus stands in a different relationship with speech than Latin does." According to Shang, the modern Chinese vernacularization movement, which sought to eliminate the structural separation of writing and speech, should be understood as part of China's nation-state building project.[57]

It is hence the common misunderstanding of Chinese writing culture shared by Wang and Ng that propelled their ideas on literary innovation. Drawing from the inaccurate but prevalent discourse—which regards the unity of sound and script as a progressive sign of literary and national modernity—Ng follows Wang and judges China to be more successful than other places in achieving the speech-writing equivalence, which results in distinct literary languages he calls *zhongwen*. Based on the purported merits of creating a colloquially inspired literary language, he delineates the challenge for the region he calls *nanfang* (the South 南方). That region has grappled with the mismatch between spoken and written vernaculars, and has produced a literary geography consisting of places that employ the *huawen* mode of literary expression:

> Taiwan, Singapore, and Malaysia resemble South China: historically, they are all regions whose spoken topolects have never been fully transformed into written language, forever banished from the writing system. On the other hand, the topolects of North China, from the outset, belonged to the same system as "Standard Mandarin." The topolectal varieties that Wang Anyi describes are in fact the foundation upon which this written language was built throughout its long historical development. Those "wonderful colloquialisms" correspond comfortably with written characters. Even their syntax is readily available and easily rendered natural in written form. The history of rendering the topolects of the South (Hokkien, Cantonese, Teochew, Hailam) in writing is by contrast extremely short. For this brief history, they can thank the May Fourth New Cultural Movement, which "transformed the fortune" of the vernacular mode. In the spate of independence movements of the emerging nations, Taiwan, Singapore, and Malaysia became relatively autonomous political entities, which necessitated their own writings in *huawen*. Yet the reference point for the so-called vernacular and colloquial spoken Mandarin is still the North China topolects, as that massive territory claimed ownership of the written language's most convenient and abundant resources. As for *the South beyond China's borders*, *huawen* writing must confront a vernacular mode that appears dull, impoverished, and strained, as well as topolects that are difficult to tame (not to mention the languages of other ethnic groups). Herein the scene of writing becomes the scene of translation. For Wang Anyi, as an author and reader of the North, those unavoidably awkward and stiff phrasings evoke embarrassment, leading her to claim: "If our writers of the South want to express the culture and life of the South, they have to adopt

the language of the North—which has dominated modes of writing and reading—and thus lose their language."⁵⁸

Alison Groppe has offered a meticulous analysis of Ng's exposition above, but misses one salient aspect: the latter's explication of Mahua writers' predicament in forging a distinctive literary vernacular provides a schema for regrouping literary regions.⁵⁹ In Ng's essay, *huawen* and *zhongwen* are initially used to map the nomenclature of Chinese in everyday life within and beyond Singapore and Malaysia, but when Ng segues into analyzing literary language, the taxonomical criteria changes from geographical location to linguistic phenomenon, resulting in a discursive reconfiguration of the world-Chinese literary space.

The slide in Taiwan's classification offers a case in point. Within the same essay, Ng designates Taiwan as a *zhongwen*-producing venue and a *huawen*-producing venue at different points.⁶⁰ Adducing the diverse creative approaches of Taiwan-based writers such as Li Yongping 李永平, Wang Wen-hsing 王文興, and Lei Hsiang 雷驤, the place starts out in Ng's discourse as one that produces the *zhongwen* modality of literary vernacular, regardless of whether the language seeks resources from premodern Chinese or foreign cultural resources.⁶¹ Ng later accentuates the geographical character of those tendencies by differentiating between the *zhongwen* within China and those beyond, calling them *jingnei / jingwai zhongwen* 境內 / 境外中文 respectively.⁶² Adopting Wang's contention that the novelistic language of Taiwan's fiction often sounds overly formal, however, he ends up assigning Taiwan to the cluster of places generating *huawen*—as seen in the extract—for he is convinced that Taiwan writers produce texts that decouple spoken and written language.⁶³

Despite appearing inconsistent, Ng is sober about the politics of worlding Chinese-language literature from the margins. When Taiwan established the World Chinese-Language Writers' Association in late 1992, he discerned the true nature of the Taiwan government's support for the organization that excludes mainland China. In his view, participants from other regions, such as the Malaysians, were accepted merely to legitimize Taiwan—which thought of itself as the Republic of China—as the center of Chinese-language literary production in another ideologically partisan "world," thereby projecting an alternative form of Sinocentrism.⁶⁴ Similarly, in Ng's article "Huawen/Zhongwen," Taiwan functions as a kind of center vis-à-vis Malaysia, while remaining marginal relative to China. The flexibility of classifying Taiwan as the host for either *zhongwen* or *huawen* writings thus signifies how an internally heterogeneous place can concurrently embody variable roles in different literary networks.

Even though Ng's article does not engage with *Sadness of the Pacific*, the instability of his linguistic categories echo the equivocal geographical categories in Wang's novella. Just like the adaptable oversight represented in the literary work that allows the imageries of islands and continents to shade into each other, the vantage point of *nanfang* in Ng's discourse on *huawen/zhongwen* is a profoundly relational one. Besides Taiwan, the positionality of South China is equally ambiguous. Ng does point out that the mainland region shares the same translational conundrum as Taiwan, Singapore, and Malaysia, but he later omits South China when naming the sites with *huawen* writings and when his discourse emphasizes "the South beyond China's borders," as if geopolitical boundaries trump other criteria in determining the modes of literary language.

In addition, Ng calls Wang "an author and reader of the North," when she is actually writing from the perspective of Shanghai—typically considered south in China—and about a "southern" condition with which Ng identifies and has turned into his own discursive niche. It is therefore ironic that the lesson Ng derives from Wang's essays—to take Mahua literature on a radical path of innovating linguistic particularity—is based on an incomplete grasp of Wang's ideas on literary language, as he does not analyze Wang's rationale for her fictional representation beyond the theories she advances in "Comparison." Despite relying on Wang's articulations to frame the predicament of Mahua literature, Ng's exclusion of South China implies his view that the literature of China's *nanfang*—be it Shanghai or China's southern provinces—has overcome the dissociation of spoken and written vernacular. Ng's oscillation between *zhongwen* and *huawen* thus yields a region-making dynamic, charting a southern literary formation outside of China that accommodates varied cases of negotiating the disjuncture between oral and written language.

In short, Ng and Wang demonstrate two divergent yet complementary attitudes toward linguistic cosmopolitanism in the world-Chinese literary space. While Ng values infusing universally recognizable forms of "literariness" into works that foreground regional particularity, thereby aligning himself with Wang's peers in China who accentuate local differences by composing root-seeking literature, Wang adopts the obverse strategy of pursuing artistic singularity by fostering the commonality proliferated by her "abstract language." In this light, the discursive encounter between Ng and Wang results in a shuffling of authorial positionalities for dispersed Chinese literary production.

At the broader level, Ng's *huawen/zhongwen* framework offers a "reworlding" of Sinitic-speaking regions, a reorganization of global and local ties that is more nuanced than the hitherto better-known notions of "Greater China" and "Cultural China," both of which frame places as inert containers of essentialized Chinese language and culture. His shifting labels of *zhongwen* and *huawen* instantiate how places are assembled and disassembled into differential coalitions in the world-Chinese literary space for the ongoing distribution and redistribution of linguistic capital. In so doing, Ng's framework considers the effects of Chinese migration that cause varied mixes of *huawen* and *zhongwen* in different localities, which in turn elucidate the entangled center-periphery dynamics fostering Sinitic cultural production in lived communities.

THE INTIMACIES OF CHINESE-SINOPHONE LITERARY REGIONS

Ng's *huawen/zhongwen* discourse initiated the evolution of his literary thought. It informs his larger conceptualization of "Chinese modernism" (*zhongwen xiandai zhuyi* 中文現代主義), which theorizes Chinese-language writers' discrepant strategies to forge their own schedules of literary progress. Through his chain of ideas, Ng delineates the modernist and modernizing ethos of a world-Chinese language literature that keeps a distance from Western centers. This non-Western global literary order subsequently provides formative inspiration to his *"nanfang huawen wenxue gongheguo"* 南方華文文學共和國, his speculative "Republic of Southern Sinophone Literature"—which I analyzed in the introduction—that constitutes the productive periphery of the world-Chinese literary space.[65]

Illuminating though it is, Ng's discourse on critical regionalization in the 1990s remained unknown except to a niche group of Chinese-language literary scholars until the coinage of Sinophone studies in the mid-2000s. When Chinese literary studies exhibited a tendency toward respatialization at the turn of the twenty-first century, Malaysia did not enter most academics' purview, as borne out by how David Wang describes "the world of Chinese literature" as an arena for "dialogical encounters of many different Chinas—in accordance with various ideological, gender, ethical, regional, and geopoetic visions."[66] Mainland China, Taiwan, and Hong Kong were then triangulated as topographical crucibles for literary production, coproducing "a discursive space of overlapping cultures and shared imaginative resources," which did not adhere to "the conventional geographical boundaries and ideological closures."[67] Chinese language, in this multisited conception, was taken as a given that did not generate friction in the places it resided or passed through, unlike the tension between the two modalities of literary language Ng configured. For his *huawen/zhongwen* framework to cohere, Ng rhetorically constructs the relative homogeneity of literary languages within China in terms of their unity of speech and writing. In so doing, his ideas prefigured the central thrust of Sinophone studies in its early phase. By conceptualizing multiculturally inflected Chinese literary production in non-China settings to propose a new cartographical method for representing the world-Chinese literary space, Ng throws into relief valuable perspectives from the margins. Concerned with overcoming the cooptive urge of Sinocentrism, he was interested in forging translocal cultural alliances, as well as in breaking away from the compelling classical Chinese textual tradition that had infiltrated authorial styles in the *nanfang* stretching from Malaysia to Taiwan.

To augment my contention that the relay of ideas between Wang Anyi and Ng illustrates the symbiotic relations within and beyond the Sinophone South, the case of Malaysia-born, naturalized Taiwanese writer Zhang Guixing's 張貴興 writing practice provides another cogent example. In the late 1990s, Ng developed the notion of "words in exile" with ideas gleaned from Wang Anyi, Yu Qiuyu 余秋雨, and Bei Dao 北島—all from China—and interprets Zhang's inventive *huawen* mode of writing in Taiwan as being driven by the uprooted sensibilities of a marginalized writer.[68]

That scholars since the 2010s have lauded Zhang's works for epitomizing the ways in which the Sinophone constitutes an autonomous off-China zone of literary creativity echoes Ng's antecedent analysis.[69] The awareness of such conceptual traffic in the Galapagos archipelago of the world-Chinese literary space can rescope the horizon of Sinophone studies to create greater common ground among different interpretations of Chinese-language literary production in neglected locales.

The imbrication of Wang's and Ng's discourses prompts the final question: How can shifting spatial imaginaries help us reevaluate Chinese literary production related to Singapore and Malaysia? The ending of *Sadness of the Pacific*, which espouses an equivalence between islands and continents, suggests that localities can relay and reshape one another's ideas without necessarily thinking of themselves as centers. In this view, Mahua literature can invert the customary move of valorizing China and incorporate works by mainland Chinese authors into its corpus. Instead of seeing Mahua literature as an overseas aspect of mainland Chinese literature, one can find diasporic specimens of Mahua literature in the latter formation. It is in this spirit that I treat Wang Anyi and her father Wang Xiaoping as diasporic Mahua authors and contend that their creative works about Singapore and Malaya or Malaysia, including Wang Anyi's critical comments about cultural production in the Southeast Asian region, should become requisite content for an expanded Singapore and Malaysian Chinese literary history.

From another interpretive perspective, the paths of Mahua literature evoked by Wang's and her father's writing practices can be cast as two historical phases in a wider process of constituting local literary terrains with ties to the Sinophone South. The egalitarian picture of islands and continents fostering a shared human destiny signifies solidarity among literary locales, but ruptures may still occur due to the misapprehension of literary relations. The misunderstood linkages are not just the relations between a center and the periphery, but those between marginalized locations as well. The mutual empathy between two islands outside the mainland state cannot be simply assumed, as evidenced by the case in which Chen Yingzhen, at a public talk in the mid-1990s organized by sojourning Malaysian Chinese students in Taiwan, criticized Mahua literature for lacking direction:

> After 1976 when the Cultural Revolution ended in China and the dream of the Malayan Chinese revolution evaporated, all the guiding images and things disappeared swiftly. Hence [Mahua literature] became confused. In addition, it suffered an onslaught of influences from Taiwan and Hong Kong. What outcomes has this brought about? Subject matters imitated those from Taiwan; otherwise, they may turn into depictions of foreign customs. For instance, I [as an imagined Mahua author] cultivate an exotic literary flavor by writing about tropical flora and climate to achieve recognition in the Taiwan literary circle. But that is after all a contrived way of representing the local flora and climate. Those elements cannot constitute subject matters derived from specific lived experiences. . . . In other words, this generation of writers does not understand the history of real Malaysia, is that right? Those who are buried under the plantations of the past might well be your ancestors. Stories of this nature, subjectivities in this relation, are gradually disappearing.[70]

One will recall that Chen appears in Wang's *Utopian Verses* as the inspirational figure who "lives on an island and holds the world in his heart." His lofty image in that novella can be compared to her depiction of the accomplished mainland authors Yu Dafu and Wu Tian in *Sadness of the Pacific* as reassuring mainlands to which unanchored Nanyang literary youths are drawn. Ironically, for all the benevolence that young literary enthusiasts from the Southeast Asian country would expect of Chen, he shows himself to be ignorant of and indifferent toward the deeper fault lines within the Mahua literary formation. To the extent that Taiwan and Hong Kong truly became significant points of cultural reference in Malaya and Singapore after the British colonial government banned publications from China in 1958, Chen's take on the sources of literary influence for Mahua literature captures the broad shift in cultural linkages among Chinese literary regions during the Cold War.[71] What I find troubling, however, is the way in which he approves of Mahua literary production in the pre-1970s for its localism built upon external cultural resources from China, and yet subsequently dismisses the positive impact of Taiwan and Hong Kong influences. Similarly, critics in Taiwan object to how Chen characterizes the younger generation of Mahua writers as disingenuously pragmatic players who replicate Taiwanese themes in Malaysia or peddle exoticism for the sake of attaining distinction in the Taiwan literary space, without committing to represent the "history of real Malaysia."[72] Misguided though he is, Chen's partial grasp of Mahua literature takes us into another terrain, crossing the threshold to enter the complex literary space of Taiwan, where the stakes of transregional connectivities are weighed differently.

CHAPTER FOUR

Off-Center Articulations

Li Yongping's Transregional Literary Production

In *The World Republic of Letters*, Pascale Casanova expounds on the delicate literary relations among nations, most of which occupy peripheral positions in a "world literary space" and share a "common condition of dependency" on dominant centers.[1] Suggesting that these peripheral literary spaces differ only in their modes of reliance on centers, Casanova's model of world literature appears to embrace plural narratives of literary transnationalism, but, in fact, constructs a singular hierarchy emanating from privileged regions in the West. Reworking the focus in Casanova's framework, Ng Kim Chew's notion of the "Literary Galapagos archipelago" reminds us that the periphery of a Eurocentric world can play host to its own varied dynamics of creativity. As my study moves on to consider such cultural undercurrents in the 2000s, this chapter explores how the expansive and interconnected world-Chinese literary space can be mapped differently. It alternately proposes that a mapping of transperipheral relations can demonstrate the critical dynamic that conditions literary world-making across social locations at multiple scales and drives the meaning-making processes in the archipelagic Sinophone South.

To this end, I take the multiscalar orientation of Mahua literature in Taiwan as a paradigm for that variant cartographic principle. The versatile nature of this displaced literary formation can be seen in how it moves fluidly among various geographical scales of interpretation,

FIGURE 4.1 Li Yongping on a 2015 boat trip through the Rajang River in northwest Borneo. He returned to Sarawak after three decades in Taiwan.

from the indigenous, the local, the regional, the national and the transnational, all the way to the global. Taking narratives by Mahua writers in Taiwan as spatially symbolic acts invigorated by authorial imaginaries of geographical affiliation and disaffiliation, I probe the tactical dimension in naturalized Taiwanese author Li Yongping's 李永平 (1947–2017) decision to write about his native land of Borneo at the turn into the twenty-first century. Not fully recognized in either the Mahua or Taiwan literary space until just prior to his demise in 2017, the Sarawak-born Li experienced marginalization in both spheres for a large part of his writing career. But he harnessed that liminality to locate himself as a constitutive outsider not just of Mahua and Taiwan literature, but also of the larger world-Chinese literary arena.[2] To delineate the cultural dynamics catalyzed by inter-Asian mobility in Li's writing practice, I examine his two-volume novel *Dahe jintou* 大河盡頭 (Where the Great River ends, 2008, 2010; hereafter *River*) and highlight figurative structures through which Li negotiates a self-positionality that not only straddles the Taiwan and Mahua literary systems but also sustains a strategic affiliation with the mainland reading public.

Framed as a semiautobiographical tale, *River* features an elderly narrator-protagonist in Taiwan who writes about his past in Borneo through an imaginary conversation with his muse Zhu Ling 朱鴒. The novel focuses on the topography of Borneo primarily via Yong-the-youth 少年永—the narrator's fifteen-year-old self—as he joins a mixed ensemble of travel companions on an expedition along the River Kapuas in search of its source on the sacred mountain Batu Tiban. Li undertakes literary worlding through *River* in two ways: by deploying the Chinese script to transcribe local and indigenous languages in Borneo, and by an allusive representation of native tribes on the island. Whereas he explicitly explains the former as a mode of linguistic cosmopolitanism rooted in the time-honored tradition of the Chinese script, the latter aspect of his narrative design enacts a bifurcated engagement with indigenous writings of Taiwan and Malaysia. In Li's bivalent relationship with the world-Chinese literary space, one can see how a writer can at once maintain a paradoxical proximity to and distance from China.

Depending on the analytical frame, Li has been read variously as a Bornean diasporic writer, a migrant writer in Taiwan, or a Sinocentric transnational writer.[3] The multiple facets of his unique positionality in world-Chinese literary space allow his works to function as what I call "off-center articulations." Masao Miyoshi first employed the notion "off center" to describe the asymmetry of historical encounters between geopolitical cultures that think of themselves as unique in different ways.[4] My study, however, focuses on literary spaces minoritized to different degrees that cultivate strategic dependence on relatively stronger formations, which often see themselves as normative. By "off-center articulations" in this chapter's context, I refer to the authorial discourses that negotiate tangent-like relations with a dominant social constituency, ranging from the nativist critics in Malaysia, to the mainstream literary community in Taiwan, to the reading public in China. Such articulations pivot upon Li's careful calibration of alterity for his geographically dispersed audiences, yielding a form of "limited strangeness"—to borrow Mads Rosendahl Thomsen's phrase—that invites rather than alienates, an attribute of foreignhood in world literature that manifests "a subtle engagement with the universal and the particular."[5]

In shaping different positions for his writing practice to embody otherness, Li's off-center articulations demonstrate a style of worldly engagement best described via the Chinese idiom *buji buli* 不即不離 (neither nearing nor departing).⁶ The form of engagement highlights the prudent manner in which writers fashion their local visibilities on their own terms in each of the multiple literary spaces they participate. Indicative of authorial agency that orchestrates transregional social relations, *buji buli* as a creative dynamic operates by emphasizing closeness and separation in tandem when writers reckon with governing markers and competing forces of various native literary spaces. Just as important, it can function as an analytical mode that illuminates the artistic innovations migrant writers produce at particular historical junctures as a result of engaging local intellectual discourses. By giving specificity to the temporality and vigor of migrant literary formations in the world-Chinese literary space, the critical term refines the enduring interpretive conceit "between two worlds," whose analytical power is limited due to its generalized connotations of cultural regions as static and stable spaces with distinct boundaries.⁷ Through Li's choice of spatiotemporal setting, his defamiliarizing employment of the Chinese language, and his concerted representation of Bornean indigeneity, he implements through *River* an approach to worlding literary relations that circumvents the national scale still dominating most accounts of world literature.⁸

Overall, my analysis characterizes *River* as Li's subtle commentary on literary regionality. My reading builds on three cartographic moments in the narrative that involve the characters' subjective appreciation of maps. In the novel, the protagonist relates the centrality of the Southeast Asian island to a larger world beyond his perceptual experience. An indigenous map plays a critical role in engendering the young protagonist's ambivalent attachment to Borneo. The recurring portrayal of such "map-mindedness" indicates a dialectic between the poetics of the novel's diegesis and the politics of Li's literary aspirations for Borneo.⁹

In this chapter, I first show the ways in which geographical parameters influence Li's authorial self-perception despite a cosmopolitan ambition that transcends regional classifications. I discuss how at the level of literary language, Li devises a hybrid linguistic form that blends various shades of Chinese (*zhongwen* and *huawen*) in order to signify his unique connections with the three literary spaces of Malaysia, Taiwan, and

China. Next, I delineate how Li derives inspiration from the flourishing of indigenous writings and studies in Taiwan but avoids coding the indigenous as the national in his tale about Borneo. By doing so, he deploys the sign of indigeneity to resist the prescriptive nativism of critics in Malaysia and to reinforce his cosmopolitan proclivity. Via unpacking the tropes of maps and indigeneity, I contend that Li's enactment of displacement in *River* does not necessarily impede his Bornean identification. The first two of the cartographic events I analyze fashion the distinctiveness of his credentials in representing the Southeast Asian island vis-à-vis his fellow Chinese-language writers in Taiwan and Sarawak who have likewise claimed Borneo as their literary terrain. To evaluate the Borneo-Taiwan route that launched Li's writing career in the world-Chinese literary space, I examine the third event cast as a culminating episode of map contemplation that sutures intranational and transnational concerns in a non-Western linguistic context.

HETEROLINGUALISM AND "THE COSMOPOLITAN DEVELOPMENT OF CHINESE LANGUAGE"

"In trying to characterize a writer's work," Casanova avers, "one must situate it with respect to two things: the place occupied by his native literary space within world literature and his own position within this space."[10] Although a country like China may be peripheral in Casanova's "world literary space," it is commonly seen as dominant in the Chinese-language context. On both counts, however, Malaysia is relegated to the margins. What makes Li's "native literary space" in the global order of Chinese literary production noteworthy is how its writers—such as Li himself—have garnered accolades even though their works also go unrecognized at the national level.[11] Having left Sarawak in 1967, four years after it joined the new polity of Malaysia, Li has repeatedly declined to be characterized in national terms, explaining:

> "I have never felt close to Malaysia in my entire life. I have never written about the Malay Peninsula, only about Borneo. . . . I grew up in a colony of the Great British Empire and held a British passport. It was only after Malaysia was established and I needed an identity that I obtained a Malaysian passport. But in my heart, I

couldn't think of myself as a citizen, as I didn't understand how this country came about."[12]

Li's sense of estrangement from the decolonized polity explains why his works do not bear the burden of national representation. As if to prevent *River* from becoming mired in issues of locality, or perhaps even to flaunt its non-Malaysian status, Li formulates a narrative design that disrupts time-space associations with the postcolonial political formation. First, the tale is set in 1962, just one year before the establishment of the Federation of Malaysia. Second, instead of situating the narrative in Kuching, his birthplace, and along the Rajang River that flows through Sarawak, Li configures the novel's action in such a way that the protagonist leaves current-day Malaysian territory and travels to neighboring Kalimantan, which belongs to Indonesia. The protagonist's ensuing rite-of-passage along the Kapuas River occurs entirely in the contiguous foreign territory of Indonesia and culminates at the peak of Batu Tiban in the frontier regions. In this way, Li's literary spotlight on the whole of Borneo island, instead of merely the Malaysian portion in the north, rejects the nation-based order of world literature and reflects his aversion toward the use of toponyms to generate literary taxonomies. In his own words:

> Why cut up world literature into so many pieces? Hong Kong literature, Taiwan literature, Mahua literature, each drawn as a small circle, one after another? Isn't it just world Chinese-language literature? I am delighted when critics classify my works as part of world Chinese-language literature. I'll be even more delighted if they call me a Chinese-language writer. Taiwan or Malaysia, it is best not to include a regional descriptor.[13]

Here, Li argues for a holistic conception of the world as an inclusive realm and reacts against the view of world literature as divided among fragmented regions. But despite his disavowal of geographical labels for his creative practice, at the 2016 ceremony for the National Award for Literary Arts, the highest official honor for Taiwan artists, Li seemed genuinely elated to be recognized as a Taiwan writer.[14] His keen attention to creating a place-appropriate literary language for *River* shows that Li still actively considers the parameters of space and place for his own literary practice located within his imagined, self-sufficient world-Chinese literary context.

For Casanova, it was the European centers such as Paris and London that conceived and promulgated the notion of literature as "pure and harmonious," as well as "nonnational, nonpartisan, and unmarked by political or linguistic divisions."[15] Li's example in another large-scale literary space in the Chinese-language context shows how the prerogative to advocate for a singular focus on literariness can also be exercised by writers moving across marginal locales. By discursively grouping Taiwan, Hong Kong, and Malaysia, Li eschews the branding of a singular, core-periphery framework that gestures toward a universal literary standard by which all works, regardless of geographical markers, should be measured.

Moreover, Li understands that choosing a language for literary composition is tantamount to choosing a community. As conveyed through the self-referential narrator in *River*, his disinclination toward Malaysia and his anticolonial stance fed his conscious choice to write in Chinese instead of English—the language of his formal education in Borneo.[16] When sought for comment on the customary treatment of his works as Mahua literature, Li's rhetorical shifts from "world literature" to "world Chinese-language literature," and then "Chinese-language literature" mark the type of sociotextual community in which he seeks a niche. Thus, to be "worldly" need not mean to attain dominance in Casanova's "world literary space." To feel as big as the world can also mean constructing personally relevant narrative spaces that transcend the dichotomous bind between the local (often taken as the national) and the global, using the tools and resources afforded by a disadvantaged language.

Li's affinity for Chinese language is well noted. As David Wang points out, the "China" to which Li is oriented is not the mainland polity, but the cultural totem that is the Chinese script, which allows Li to construct his *yuanxiang* 原鄉 (original homeland) on paper.[17] Li's fascination with the Chinese script, in fact, borders on pious devotion that undertakes literary worlding. In his view, "every character is a picture, and every picture an image. Each image, in turn, represents a microcosm of the universe."[18] That perspective of the Chinese script resonates strongly with the classical Chinese notion of *wen* 文, which governs the traditional Chinese understanding of "literariness," and can be understood—following David Wang's gloss—as "'ornamentation,' 'pattern,' 'sign,' 'artistic inscription,' 'cultural upbringing,' 'civilization,' and 'a sign of the movement of the cosmos.'"[19]

River's second volume bears the above imprint of Li's authorial thought. In its prelude, the elderly narrator discloses how the novel was composed through an intimate consideration of the Chinese script. Calling the novel a *yulin wenzi gongdian* 雨林文字宫殿 (linguistic palace about the rainforest) (2: 36), the autobiographical narrator shared in a metafictional moment:

> I had to rack my brain while selecting among the ten thousand or so logographic characters with which I got acquainted in Nanyang through my studies when I was little, in order to find the prettiest, the best-sounding and the most palatable characters.... The history of Chinese language is longstanding, its lexicon abundant, and its meanings rich. In addition, it is unrivaled in the world for being a language that bestrides the beauty of both sound and shape. To use it for describing the equally resplendent and uniquely enchanting Borneo rainforest will allow the linguistic script and the scenery to bring out the best in each other. *Where the Great River Ends* offers me, "an author whose ambition as a wordsmith is to perfect his craft," a fabulous opportunity to excavate the potential of Chinese language and display the splendid charm of its logographic script. (2: 26–27)

Voiced through the narrator, Li exudes great confidence in the expressive capacity of Chinese language in capturing the exceptional allure of Borneo's landscape, which emanates from the "South Seas spectacles and tropical customs" that are "totally different from China, the 'Divine Land and Middle Earth'" (2: 26). It is not just the bountiful physical topography that the author's literary language represents, but also Borneo's fascinating social worlds. The place's evocative topographical and human geographies are accentuated by what Rainier Grutman will recognize as "heterolingualism," which refers to "the use of foreign languages or social, regional, and historical language varieties in literary texts."[20] Notably, Li's heterolingualism is embedded in an overarching translational modality that entails Chinese language manifesting the coexistence of multiple languages in Borneo. Akin to Lin Cantian's *Thick Smoke* written in 1930s Malaya (see chapter 1), the narrative discourse shows several interlocking modes of translational mimesis. The domesticating effect is strongest when English dialogue is homogenously presented in Chinese. Through a transcriptive use of the Chinese script, both at the lexical and syntactic level, the tale further presents a plethora of other languages used in Borneo in the early 1960s, from Chinese topolects such as Hakka and Hokkien, to Malay and Japanese.

As if he is worried that the novel's hybrid linguistic style will alienate his readers in China—most of them are unfamiliar with Southeast Asia—Li pens a special preface for *River*'s mainland Chinese edition, explaining his representation of Bornean multilingualism in terms of demonstrating a form of linguistic globality:

> Nanyang is an ethnically complex and multilingual place. Fiction reflects reality. Therefore, in *Where the Great River Ends*, you will often come across lexicon from Malay, Javanese, Iban and Dayak, words that circulate in Borneo but seem to jar against the Chinese flavor of the logographic script.... The Malay words that appear through my pen have been carefully selected, most of which you must have heard frequently even if you have never visited Nanyang. Some of them have even become constituents of modern Chinese vocabulary, such as "kampong" (village), "pasar" (market), "sarong" (Malay skirt-like garment), etc. When the narrative requires the use of longer and more complete Malay phrases and sentences, I will employ subtle and artistic techniques to insert Chinese glosses to explain the Malay discourses, without affecting the tale's readability. Keen readers ... can experience a pleasantly unique Nanyang flavor.... Perhaps, at some level, the diverse linguistic representation in *Where the Great River Ends* reflects the cosmopolitan development of Chinese language.[21]

The 2012 edition of *River* was Li's first work published in China.[22] It marks the start of his triple inhabitation of not just Malaysian and Taiwan literary spaces, but also that of the mainland state. Tellingly, Li promotes his literary practice as the embodiment of "the cosmopolitan development of Chinese language" only in the edition meant for readers of the simplified script. His contact with a broader reading public primarily on the mainland occasions a discrepant mode of literary worlding, which occurs when different versions of the same title circulates at the same time in overlapping literary spheres.

As readers discover for themselves, the transcriptive heterolinguality of *River*'s narrative discourse is resolved through creative juxtaposition or collocation of words, phrases, and even sentences, sometimes in parenthesis. Through his selective transliteration of Malay and indigenous Bornean languages, Li represents the island's social polyglossia, signifying how the foreign lexical elements have become "constituents of modern Chinese vocabulary." His approach suggests that the Nanyang modality of hybrid expression has infiltrated modern Chinese language, endowing the novel with a *Nanyang fengwei* 南洋風味 (Nanyang flavor). In the view of the scholar-cum-writer Wong Yoon Wah 王潤華, Li has hence elevated the linguistic form of Mahua literature to become part of a global heritage of literary languages.[23]

To use Ng Kim Chew's analytical terms for the forms of Chinese language fostered in the Sinophone South, *River* appears to be a deliberate artifact composed in *huawen*. Besides recalling how Ng had classified Li's works as embodiments of *zhongwen*, the more China-oriented form of expression (see chapter 3), *River* constitutes a striking and thought-provoking reversal of Li's own stance on mobilizing Chinese as a literary language. After all, when he published *Jiling chunqiu* 吉陵春秋 (Jiling chronicles) in Taiwan in 1986, Li achieved critical acclaim with his spectacular mastery of a northern vernacular Chinese closer to *zhongwen*, which did not evoke any locational referent in reality.

Indeed, Li's career can be tracked through his multiple negotiations with *huawen* and *zhongwen*. Over the course of half a century, Li's exploration of a distinctive literary language went through several stages. Shortly before his death, he shared how the genesis of his linguistic experiment in fiction was tied to his search for a personal style of literary expression that extended back to his youth in Sarawak. A high school teacher from north China recognized Li's talent for storytelling but was unimpressed with his literary language; the educator considered the

Nanyang flavor in his tales odd and adulterated. Adopting his teacher's advice, Li delved into the works of the May Fourth masters such as Lu Xun 魯迅, Mao Dun 茅盾, and Lao She 老舍, in order to create another literary language that felt "purer" and "more authentic" (*bijiao chunzheng* 比較純正).[24] He used that alternative linguistic mode for the next story he sent to the local literary supplement, but the piece was swiftly rejected by the editor who criticized Li for cultivating an inappropriate style. To the editor, that externally codified form of Chinese had no real-life traction in Nanyang and was inadequate for conveying local experiences. He urged Li to use the locally specific form of Chinese language—which the latter calls *Nanyang huayu* 南洋華語—for his literary writings thereafter. Li thus resumed his use of a literary language that was "oddly flavored and deemed as inadequately pure."[25] The result was the novella *Poluozhou zhizi* 婆羅洲之子 (Sons of Borneo), which won him a 1966 creative writing competition administered by the Borneo Literature Bureau, an institution established during the colonial period. Under the bureau's sponsorship, the novella eventually became Li's first published title.

Li's subsequent relocation to Taiwan in 1967, where he encountered illustrious mentors unfamiliar with Borneo, made him change his mind again. At the National Taiwan University in the late 1960s, he met Yen Yuan-shu 顏元叔, the leading critic who introduced New Criticism to Taiwan. In an uncanny repetition of the mentor-mentee encounter in Sarawak, Yen, the authority figure, praised Li's short story "Lazi fu" 拉子婦 (The Bidayuh woman, 1968) for its narrative but dismissed Li's literary language, which he deemed peculiar. In a comment that reveals the linguistic hierarchy in Taiwan literary space, he advised Li, "If you modify your Chinese slightly, you will become an extremely outstanding fiction writer, and will be able to develop your career in Taiwan."[26] Forgetting his lesson in Sarawak, Li embarked on reforming his literary language once more. Looking back, he characterized the outcome as a "Li Yongping style," which he created by immersing himself in traditional Chinese fiction such as *Jinping mei* 金瓶梅 (The plum in the golden vase), *Honglou meng* 紅樓夢 (Dream of the red chamber), and *Xingshi yinyuan zhuan* 醒世姻緣傳 (Marriage destinies to awaken the world).[27] From the late 1970s on, he worked painstakingly to construct a "pure Chinese literary form" via the medium of a fictional northern China vernacular,[28] which he applied to *Jiling Chronicles*, the book whose intricate linguistic craftsmanship by a *qiaosheng* 侨生 (overseas student) in Taiwan astonished critics and secured Li's reputation in the Taiwan literary scene in the 1980s.²⁹

In light of his extraordinary commitment to the Chinese vernacular language, Li could well have been channeling his teacher Yen's ideas when he composed the short stories that would eventually make up *Jiling Chronicles* during his graduate school sojourn in the United States. Claiming an aversion to the contemporaneous forms of Chinese language that then pervaded Taiwan, he saw *Jiling Chronicles* as representing a literary counterpoint. The maverick work demonstrated "a reactionary and corrective attitude toward the negatively Americanized or Japonized styles of Chinese expression" that had become very popular.³⁰ At that time, he was singularly devoted to "uphold the purity and dignity of Chinese language," and hoped that "the style and ambience of *Jiling Chronicles* can better preserve the unique traits of vernacular Chinese, including its pithiness, its radiance, its lucid and lively rhythm and spirit, and its allure that makes readers linger continually."³¹

If Li's *River* provides an opportunity to consider the paratextual discrepancies between editions produced for different regions, *Jiling Chronicles* allows us to pay critical attention to the differences between reprints of the same title and reconsider the implications arising from adaptations for signifying authorial modes of belonging. The stories collected in *Jiling Chronicles* were first published in the literary supplement of Taiwan's *Lianhebao* 聯合報 (United Daily News), a significant venue for Taiwan literature, from the late 1970s to the mid-1980s, before they were collated and published under a single title in 1986. Based on Toyoda Noriko's meticulous research, we now know the substantial adaptations that Li made when the book was prepared. From the removal of specific historical references to the Japanese army in World War II, to the switch to third-person narration, to other modes of diegetic abstraction, Li dehistoricizes and delocalizes his series of episodic tales, enhancing a sense of universality via the crossing into a more enduring medium of circulation.³² As Zhan Min-xu 詹閔旭 contends, dovetailing with Li's overarching strategy of denativization is a refinement of the text's literary language.³³ From that perspective, Li's writing practice vacillates between conforming to a codified literary standard and accentuating local particularities, sustaining an iterative dynamic between *zhongwen* and *huawen*.

Whether or not the place settings of his stories are fictional, Li tailors a linguistic form for every locale he delineates as the diegetic setting. After the success of *Jiling Chronicles*, he shifted his gaze to Taipei—a place he had once spoke of exaggeratedly as "a microcosm of China" where all regional accents of China congregate—and devised another literary language to compose *Haidong qing: Taibei de yize yuyan* 海東青: 臺北的一則寓言 (East Seas turquoise: A fable of Taipei), published in 1992.[34] Returning to depict Borneo in 2002, Li brought out the novel *Yuxue feifei: Poluozhou tongnian jishi* 雨雪霏霏: 婆羅洲童年記事 (Snowfall in the clouds: Recollections of a Borneo childhood, hereafter *Snowfall*), the first part of his Borneo trilogy, in which the protagonist in Taiwan reflects upon the fundamental connection between his authorial self-identity and the largest island in Asia. Conveying a clear autobiographical effect, the episodic narrative linked by a trope of displaced wandering in urban Taipei casts a retrospective gaze on the first two decades of Li's life after the writer's more than four decades of peregrination. Starting from *Snowfall* and extending to *River* (the second part of the trilogy), the same narrator sporadically denotes his journeys via the Hokkien term *titto* 迌迌 (gallivanting), a verb excluded from most Chinese dictionaries but widely disseminated in Taiwan through folk songs (1: 32–33; 2: 32–34, 73). The term, which he describes as "two beautiful and desolate characters with a thick Taiwanese aura," allows Li to emphasize the influence of Taiwan on his literary language, especially when he faces his mainland Chinese audience.[35]

To garner literary distinction, Li negotiates—via the linguistic modes of *huawen* or *zhongwen*—the asymmetries that shape his strategic relations with various cultural centers of recognition at different junctures of his career. Li's literary practice thus bears out the effects of a "Chinese of difference,"[36] a form of blended linguistic address which may appear to be practicing tokenistic multilingualism. I contend, however, that *River*'s hybrid literary language reflects a conscious formulation of heterolingualism to enable his off-center positionality in the world-Chinese literary space vis-à-vis the intersecting loci of Malaysia, Taiwan, and China. Employing a literary language whose strangeness is adjusted to an optimal level, *River* ensures that it has a relatable linguistic dimension for each of its several audiences. Li's example shows how it is less productive to think of *huawen* and *zhongwen* as two polarized linguistic modes of literary expression that compel migrant authors to make one-off creative choices with irreversible outcomes. Rather, indexing the *buji buli* (off-center) dynamic that engages with strident forces within and across literary spaces, the two linguistic modalities should be approached as specific "stages" of writing—in both senses of the word as temporal phases and as performance venues—that authors choose to enter or exit, and which can occur within a single work such as *River*.

In view of the "mixed linguistic stew" in *River*, the novel that features heterolinguality forms a site in which transregional dynamics across Malaysia, Taiwan, and China become textualized.[37] In fact, Li also embeds intra-Southeast Asian transregionality. When Yong-the-youth and his companion Christina Van Loon arrive at the first pit stop in their ascent of Batu Tiban, he encounters a Malay village with inhabitants whose ancestors came from the Mindanao region in the Philippines (2: 312–13, 316). He notices that the villagers' accent differs from that of the Malays in Borneo or Java. Thus Chinese is not the only language suggested to be on the move, the Malay language travels as well. In the tale, the circulation of Malay language is depicted primarily through a young Mindanao female character who follows a group of American hippies and drifts from her home region in southern Philippines across the Sulu Sea to Thailand, Peninsular Malaysia, and finally reaches Borneo (1: 91; 2: 111). From another Southeast Asian island, she brings to inland Borneo a folk song about rice pounding sung in Mindanao Malay (2: 328), a language that recurs throughout both volumes and is portrayed to have spread to the Kenyah, one of the Bornean indigenous groups (2: 111). Remapping Borneo as a site that enables the dissemination of a creolized Malay, *River* thus offers a layered linguistic cartography within the multivalent Sinophone compositional framework that Li constructs.

Rather than shoring up the internal stratification of diverse speech styles within a single language, Li's experimentation in *River* builds a literary world by foreignizing his prose to create a variegated linguistic texture with a translational effect in order to demonstrate social polyglossia, that is, the commingling of two or more languages in a location.

To fully decode the contextual implications of linguistic mingling in *River*, we need to devote greater attention to analyzing the representation of indigenous languages in the narrative discourse.

THE CONCEALED SIGN OF LINGUISTIC INDIGENEITY

> Must the Hakka people only be written about in the Hakka language? Look at the Indian writers who have been colonized by the British for around two centuries, ... they have composed Indian experiences in English and have done a great job. It is of course excellent if you can use your own ethnic language to write stories about your ethnic community, but why must one insist on doing so? Why can't a common language be used? When it comes to language, one has to perhaps broaden one's horizon.[38]

In an interview after the first volume of *River* was published, Li dismissed the idea of using topolects such as Hakka, which he grew up speaking, to compose his future works, not just because he lost familiarity with the language after having left Sarawak more than four decades prior, but also because he opposed an inflexible adherence to ethno-cultural authenticity. To him, a lingua franca can also inscribe the experiences of diverse ethnic groups. At the time, his perspective seemed fully aligned with his underlying observation on Chinese linguistic cosmopolitanism, which had domesticated non-Chinese languages. But *River* actually retains translucent nodes of semi-decipherability. In the literary text, the transcriptive use of Chinese characters captures indigenous languages such as Iban—closely related to Malay—on the page.[39] The indigenous words are transcribed via Chinese characters employed as aural annotations, spotlighting terms that remain outside of the historical and contemporary Chinese lexicon.

For one thing, the Chinese characters transliterate proper nouns, such as the names of ghosts and spirits as well as the names of tribal leaders and their longhouse dwellings, all of which aim to signal Li's cultural fluency with the autochthonous dimension of Borneo's topographical and social ecologies. What deserves special scrutiny is the function of several native concepts that are elucidated in the diegesis.[40] For instance, the narrative discourse introduces *palang* 芭椰, an Iban term for the indigenous folk custom of penis piercing with a device to hold decorative items. As the tale advances, the traditional crosspiece in Borneo becomes a figural trope that underscores the protagonist's acquisition of insider knowledge about tribal customs and colonial forms of knowledge fostered by Western scholars (1: 120, 124–26, 188, 322–23, 367).

Of greater symbolic significance for the plot is the Kenyah custom of *peselai* 帕兮喇咿. Sharing his native knowledge about Borneo with his Taiwanese muse Zhu Ling, the elderly narrator explicates *peselai* in detail:

> First, get acquainted with the word *"peselai."* It belongs to the Kenyah language and refers to a "journey." This journey is not just about some person leaving home for leisurely travels or for trade outside one's home region. It is a form of spiritual cultivation—the men of Borneo tribes must travel on their own at least once in their lifetime, for a week-long trip to the wilderness in the Central Highlands and the upstream of the Great River, and return with a few human heads.... The Westerners call it a "coming-of-age ritual," akin to the young men of the Australian aboriginal peoples who have to wander through the outback on foot before they attain adulthood. There is, however, one difference. The natives of Borneo who undertake the faraway journey have got the canoe, a unique mode of transport bestowed by their gods, which their distant cousins in Australia do not have. (2: 73–74)

Calling the *peselai* "a rather appealing custom of the Borneo indigenes" (2: 73), the narrator's knowledge matches ethnographic accounts of "rite[s] of passage with deep roots to the land" undertaken toward distant territories in search of new cultures. These journeys were "closely interlinked with economic and ritual needs, manhood and social status" and thus counters the common misconception of *peselai* as mere trading expeditions.[41] Remarkably, the elderly narrator frames *peselai* as a common custom for the males of all Borneo tribes, highlighting especially the practices of the Kenyah, the Iban, the Kayan, and the Bidayuh (2: 74–75). Later on, the narrator, who is ethnically Chinese, also explicitly describes the voyage he undertook when he was fifteen as a *peselai* trip

(2:93), thereby marking the indigenous dimension of his compositional thoughts. This narrative thrust, built on a representative notion of the Borneo indigenes, overlays how the elderly man used to perceive the indigenous peoples' ways of life through an extralocal lens. In the first half of the tale, he prefigures the imbrication of Chinese and indigenous epistemes by depicting the tribal groups' night activity using the Taiwanese (Hokkien) term *titto* (gallivanting), when they leave the jungles temporarily and throng the streets of Sanggau in West Kalimantan with groups from other communities also moving toward the local Chinese temple to celebrate the Hungry Ghost Festival (1: 136).

Li's hybrid literary language in *River* thus embodies a delicate balance between shared intelligibility and exoticized authenticity. The lingering lexical traces of indigenous otherness do not undermine the assimilating power of Chinese language, but rather, anchor the author as a native informant of Borneo familiar with the island's landscape and indigenous cultures. The insertions of these terms are acts of knowledge production and dissemination, given how the vast majority of the Chinese-reading public is foreign to the ideas of Bornean indigeneity. Lin's linguistic address opens up the literary world rooted in the frontier regions of the Malaysian-Indonesian border on the island and draws attention to the ways in which the new knowledge in Chinese is communicated via literary representation.

In *River*, the elderly narrator conveys the practice of *peselai* to his muse by comparing it to the peripatetic rite of passage of the Australian aborigines. That link with global indigenous cultures, however, belies the covert lessons Li derives from Taiwan indigenous writings that have flourished since the 1990s. As I will show, his literary indebtedness to Taiwan's sociocultural milieu goes beyond the island's Hokkien dimension, which he freely acknowledges. The indigenous literary discourse in Taiwan plays a largely undiscerned role, but truly functions as a resource for critical adaptation by Li who reclaims his creative rights to limn Borneo from afar.

Notably, Li's evolving novelistic subject matter parallels the ideological shifts in the Taiwan literary space. Since the late 1980s, indigenous literature gradually became a defined field of cultural production in Taiwan, contributing to a pluralist cultural scene that emerged after martial law was lifted in 1987. Massive social changes extended into the 1990s, fueled by grassroot political forces that included feminism, sexual minorities, trade unions, and indigenous movements. Literary works appeared in an unprecedented variety of genres and styles, of which indigenous writings constituted a distinct category. With the rise of nativist discourse in the 1990s, indigenous literature offered an attractive venue for the nativist movement to advocate a separate Taiwanese subjectivity by pointing to an Austronesian oceanic cultural genealogy that pulls the island away from China's continental grip. According to Kuei-fen Chiu, it was in the late 1990s when discourses of indigeneity began to straddle the condition of cultural otherness vis-à-vis the dominant Han culture and the quintessential "Taiwanese self" rooted in Austronesian cultural heritage.[42]

Over the years, Li has shown himself be a keen observer of the island's political and social vicissitudes.[43] When he developed his own literary ideas on indigeneity, he was likely inspired by the turn since the 1990s in Taiwan's cultural discourse and political economy. Moreover, not only did he live through the era of the island's indigenous social movements, he also was immersed in the physical and intellectual environments of Taiwan's indigeneity when he incubated and started composing his Borneo Trilogy. In 2000, he began teaching in east Taiwan at the National Dong Hwa University in Hualien 花蓮, one of the main living areas of indigenous tribes on the island. The Dong Hwa campus housed the country's first college of indigenous studies within a tertiary institution.[44] Living, teaching, and writing amid the school's unique location in the Hua-tung rift valley—nestled among mountains and water features—must have greatly stimulated Li's creativity.[45] Reflecting authorial circumstances at the metadiegetic level, the elderly narrator frequently reminds readers that he is composing the novel while facing the undulating terrain of east Taiwan. The recurring reminders are often a variant of the following description:

> When this journey of remembrance along the Great River—this book—began, I had just arrived to teach at a new university in east Taiwan and was living in the brand new faculty hostel. Once, I woke up around midnight and sat idly under a table lamp, which

emitted a pale white light in the desolate campus that resides in the valley.... A thought struck me suddenly. I hurriedly found some manuscript paper and picked up a pen. Facing Mount Qilai, the dark, steep and silent sacred mountain of the A-mei tribe, which towers outside the window and under the curved moon... I started calling for your spirit. Zhu Ling!... Please listen to me once more, as I recount something that happened to me in Nanyang when I was little.... Please help me purge the nightmare that is Batu Tiban, which has been hiding in the depths of my heart, and from which I cannot and do not wish to extract myself. (2: 16)

Significantly, the mentioning of the two sacred mountains of the indigenous tribes in different regions reveals the imagined contiguity of Taiwan and Borneo's landscapes in Li's authorial mind. His choice of indigeneity over Chineseness as the overall organizing principle of *River* is patent in the way he designs the novel's doubly nested diegesis. The literary text begins by adopting the overarching structure about an elderly narrator (the implied author) who pens his memoir about his youth in Borneo. The memoir replicates the frame of an old man reminiscing about his past on the Southeast Asian island. Midway through the adventurous tale of his youth, the elderly narrator discloses that he was inspired to begin composition in Hualien while facing Mount Qilai 奇萊山 (2: 16), the scared mountain of the local indigenous tribes. That setting of writing in a mountainous region of Taiwan turns out to constitute the premise of the primary plot, rendering *River* a metanarrative. At the metadiegetic level, the narrator subsequently reveals that he experienced writer's block not long after staying in Hualien, which he only overcame after moving northward to Tamsui 淡水. One night in his new house, he resumed writing, inspired by the sight of Mount Guanyin 觀音山 outside the window (2: 18–20). Strikingly, he does not change the circumstances of his memoir's narrator and continues to depict him autobiographically as a university teacher in East Taiwan writing his memoir while facing Mount Qilai (2: 132, 296).

To clarify, Li's intervention does not adopt the tactics of Taiwan's indigenous writers, which Kuei-fen Chiu has identified as entailing the use of "indigenous words in romanization to interrupt the smooth flow of Chinese in the construction of a literary text."[46] *River* invites comparison with contemporary indigenous literature in Taiwan because of its affinity with several other thematic and stylistic features, including the choice of an autobiographical first-person perspective, the conspicuous ethnographic dimension in the writings, and the deployment of a homecoming trope.[47] In the case of Li's differential approach, he selects the genre of fiction rather than prose essays, which forms the majority of Chinese-language works written by indigenous authors in Taiwan. Besides, he substitutes the first-person narration rooted in indigenous authors' tribal identities with an autobiographical character (the implied author), also speaking in the first person, who gravitates toward acquiring the indigenous habitus. Finally, Li adapts the homecoming trope. Instead of a physical return, homecoming in *River* becomes a symbolic journey undertaken through the act of composition beyond Borneo and in Taiwan, immersed in the topographical and cultural milieux of an alternative indigeneity. Depicting the elderly narrator as capable of conveying Borneo's rich native landscape and sociality to Zhu Ling, Li shows the enduring impact of Borneo's indigeneity on the protagonist, which is dissimilar from Taiwan's indigenous writers portraying themselves as having to get reacquainted with their native way of life.[48] Thus, migrant Mahua literature under Li's direction is inspired by, but neither reproduces nor radically alters the fundamentals of indigenous literature in Taiwan.

The latent mixing of Mahua literature and Taiwan's indigenous literature, two peripheral constituents of Taiwan literary space, also points to a wider context of reconfiguring the elements in Taiwan's indigenous literary discourse. More broadly speaking, the blending contributes toward a doubly situated cosmopolitanism of Li's writing practice in the 2000s. *River*'s narrative discourse folds itself into webs of literary relations and shows how indigeneity as a creative parameter rests upon a scalar politics of discrepant regionalities that connects the local to the global. Operating transregionally, Li seeks to ally with indigenous writings in Taiwan while fashioning indigeneity from a diasporic position in the eyes of his Borneo-based colleagues. His meticulous interweaving of indigenous and diasporic tropes critiques a fundamentalist form of Bornean literary nativism by advocating reconnection from a distance, thereby making "Malaysia" an open literary space.

Moving forward, I address Li's "world Chinese-language literature" from the superimposed vantage points of Borneo and Taiwan that the author embeds in *River*. To explicate how the novelistic form refracts his unique situatedness in the world-Chinese literary space, I use the trope of indigeneity and scenes of map-mindedness to interpret Li's reawakened yearning for his native land of Borneo. I build on Kuei-fen Chiu's insight about his "simultaneous inhabitation" in Mahua and Taiwan literary spaces in the 1970s and 1980s to show how Li's diasporic imagination still contains a divergent signification in both arenas in the 2000s, but it makes a significant shift toward representing indigeneity rather than Chineseness. Chiu argues that Li, in the earlier period, harnesses the symbolic value of the Chinese diaspora to stress the legitimacy of his Chinese cultural identity in Malay-centric Malaysia, while striving to prove the authenticity of his Chinese-language writings as an "overseas" writer in Taiwan.[49] I contend that more than two decades later, in the Taiwan context, the double-faceted indigenous literary imaginary in *River* puts Li in dialogue with other Chinese-language writers who are also invested in fashioning Borneo as a prominent literary locale, whereas in the Malaysian context, the same literary imaginary signals a Bornean authenticity alongside Li's own diasporic discourse.

In the next two sections, I focus on how the critical reception of Li's works in his native literary space of Malaysia, which has hitherto been neglected by critics, actually shapes his self-fashioning as a Chinese-language writer of the world. Li's use of emplotment in *River* can certainly be examined in terms of literary relations across regions that are peripheral to the cultural production of mainland China. My interest, however, lies in deciphering the built-in yet obscured intra-Malaysian dynamic that is stretched geographically beyond the postcolonial nation-state so as to reveal how that interactive principle fuels Li's writing practice in Taiwan, the place where he confronts the globalization of Chinese-language literature.

THE PEDAGOGY OF MAPS AND THE USES OF INDIGENEITY

Historians of Taiwan literary space have come to acknowledge Mahua literature as a valid constituent of Taiwan literature.[50] In the late 1980s and early 1990s, however, amid the unusual mix of fervent interest in mainland literature and the increasing impact of nativist tendencies on Taiwan literary space, both Li and Zhang Guixing 張貴興, another Sarawak-born writer who also adopted Taiwanese citizenship, were relegated to its margins.[51] From the 1990s to the 2000s, many Mahua authors in Taiwan chose to attenuate the Malaysian color of their works in order to achieve distinction via literary contests in their nonnative literary sphere on the East Asian island. Their strategy stands in contrast to that of the contemporaneous Taiwan's indigenous authors who foregrounded their ethnic identity in their writings to advocate for the visibility of their communities.[52]

Li's conscious decision to limn Bornean indigeneity for publication in Taiwan at the turn of the twenty-first century thus begs further analysis. Unlike his Taiwan colleagues who mobilized indigeneity to construct national legitimacy, Li adopted a denationalized conception and deployment of indigeneity. Expressing his personal sense of authorial agency, Li has said: "I face this appalling world which I cannot change as a man of letters. What I can do is to create an order for this chaotic world with my writing. That order is none other than works of art."[53] His ideal of an artistic "order" invites us to analyze the thoughtful recurrence of compositional features in his creative output. In the case of *River*, Li structures the plot using a series of cartographic visions of Borneo that shows how novelistic discourses can rationalize the life trajectories of writers as well as register competing forms of geographical knowledge. The depictions lead readers to note the ways in which he imagines and mediates spatial divisions in the world-Chinese literary space through the text.

To be sure, *River* is not Li's first attempt at employing the narrative device of cartography.[54] His strategies in *River* bear fruitful comparisons to his earlier work, *East Seas Turquoise*, in which Taipei's urban environment is mapped onto mainland China's historical geography.[55] Similarly, Li inserts an underlying cartographic design in *Snowfall* by charting a route undertaken by the senior Yong, the same protagonist as in *River*, along an inner-city river in Taipei. The spatial consciousness in *River*, however, does not signify the progenitive relationship between China and Taiwan that Carlos Rojas interprets as being established and redeveloped concurrently in *East Seas Turquoise*.[56] Nor does it reflect Li's layered nostalgia for his original homeland in Sarawak that Alison Groppe discerns in *Snowfall*.[57] Instead, *River*'s map-minded disposition manifests a strategic dynamic of ironic distancing from relative centers that produces and maintains a native literary space incongruent with its actual geopolitical position on the world map.

River begins with a metadiegetic prelude in which the elderly narrator kickstarts his writing project in Taiwan through an imaginary conversation with his muse Zhu Ling. Significantly, the narrator-writer introduces Borneo by poring over a map: "My girl, open up a large world map and take a look! Isn't there an island lying above the equator, at the intersection of the 115 degrees east longitude and the zero degrees latitude?" (1: 28). The use of precise coordinates to locate the island suggests a form of cartographic representation that incorporates European measures and the Western conception of Earth as spherical. Since the discursive close-up is performed on the equatorial Southeast Asian island without reference to Malaysia, the narrative oversight implies an authorial outlook that frees Li from viewing places through a national lens.

The geography lesson is the first instance of the map device in the novel. As the narrator, the senior Yong invokes the history of a Borneo populated by European missionaries, Arab merchants, Dutch bureaucrats, Japanese soldiers, American hippies, and Chinese coolies (1: 28). The native inhabitants are curiously absent from his enumeration, but the elderly narrator hints at the significance of indigeneity for his tale by opting from the outset to follow the Dayak in calling the topographical feature "Great River" (rendered as *Dahe* 大河 in the text), rather than "River Ka" (*Kajiang* 卡江) spoken by the local Chinese or "Kapuas" (transliterated as *Kabuyasi* 卡布雅思) by the Indonesians (1: 28).

The native groups' conceptions and perceptions of landscape ultimately enter the novel in ways that profoundly impact the unfolding diegesis. Constituting a striking leitmotif in the novel, Yong-the-youth's interaction with the indigenous tribes activates a "cognitive mapping"—the mental representation of geographical relations—of the transregional Chinese-language literary space connecting Malaysia and Taiwan. As the narrative develops, its emplotment configures greater differentiation among various native tribes, such as the Iban, the Kenyah, the Punan, and the Bidayuh. In other literary and nonliterary situations, it is common to refer to all of these non-Muslim tribes collectively as "Dayak."

But in Malaysian Borneo, the generic term "Dayak" has a smaller semantic scope limited to the Iban (once known as the "Sea Dayak") and the Bidayuh (once called the "Land Dayak").[58] Although Li launched his writing career with shorter stories that focused thematically on single indigenous tribes, the ensemble of native groups in *River* provokes deeper interpretations that might initially seem justified by the longer narrative format.[59] For one thing, the depiction in *River* sets up a contrast with the configuration of ethnic diversity in *Poluozhou zhizi* 婆羅洲之子 (Sons of Borneo), the novella that marked his literary debut in the 1960s. Also speaking in first-person narrative, the mixed-race protagonist of the latter invokes the categories of generalized ethnicities that underpin his desire for intercommunal harmony: "There are the Chinese, the Dayak and the Malay on this land."[60] Furthermore, *River* departs from the representations in *The Bidayuh Woman*, Li's literary debut in Taiwan, insofar as the indigenous characters the novel depicts are no longer "nameless and voiceless," or with "vague countenances."[61]

Of what significance, then, is Li's recourse to a finer-grained portrayal of indigeneity? To date, the variegated descriptions of the diverse native communities in *River* have not been adequately interpreted. In Ng Kim Chew's view, Li constructs a distinctive Borneo literary "nativism" (*bentu xing* 本土性) "that is different from Taiwan's Chinese-language literature and Malaysian Chinese-language literature" by investing in the representation of indigenous cultures.[62] Whereas this perspective may be persuasive, Ng's homogenization of the various native groups in Borneo under the umbrella rubric of "Dayak" fails to consider the strategic value of distinguishing the plural autochthonous elements in *River*.[63]

Although Li indeed sidesteps the depiction of Chinese settler colonialism to foreground the indigenous presence,[64] I contend that he does so to prevent *River* from overlapping excessively with the fictional worlds created by Zhang Guixing. Since the 1990s, Zhang has cultivated the tropical rainforest of Borneo as his trademark motif and established the island as the metonymical trope for Mahua fiction in Taiwan's Chinese-language literary space.[65] His intriguing tales of Chinese family histories—such as *Qunxiang* 群象 (Elephant herd, 2006) and *Houbei* 猴杯 (Monkey cup, 2000)—have been recognized by literary awards and media institutions. Li had once expressed interest in a scholarly contention that Zhang's rainforest narratives have become trite, showing how he clearly followed his colleague's writing career in Taiwan, but he consciously declined to comment on Zhang's writings about Borneo.[66] From this perspective, the finer ethnic contours in *River* enable him to distance himself from and yet remain connected to the Borneo rainforest imaginary that circulates in the Taiwan literary space primarily through Zhang's novels, in which indigenous characters are portrayed as either just "Dayak" or "Iban."[67] Moreover, as Ko Chia-cian points out, unlike Zhang who employs vivid imageries of flora and fauna to mark the alien jungle motif, the exoticism of Li's fictional rainforest is channeled through indigenous folk customs that are treated as myths and spectacles.[68] By developing a veritable ethnography of inland Borneo and showcasing a greater spectrum of human diversity on the island, *River* foregrounds its writer as someone with deep local knowledge who attempts to represent Borneo more authentically than Zhang.

River's array of indigenous tribes hence allows Li to carve a niche for himself in the literary spaces of Taiwan and Malaysia that is both different from and complementary to that of Zhang. That dialectical operation risks being overlooked in Casanova's model of world literary space, fixated as the model is on asymmetrical international dependencies. But in the world-Chinese literary context, the subtle process can be detected through Li's emblematic writing practice and in the way that *River*'s publisher in Taiwan packages the novel as "a canonical *magnum opus* about Malaysian indigenous tribes."[69] The advertisement, by one of Taiwan's leading literary publishers, not only shows a bewildering disregard for the story's Indonesian setting, but also reveals the mindset of important literary stakeholders in Taiwan who still fail to distinguish between Li and Zhang, even though both of them have been Taiwanese citizens for more than three decades.

At the other end of the transregional articulation, nativist critics in Malaysia also negotiate with literary representations by emigrant writers. These critics group Li and Zhang together as writers alienated from their birthplaces, perceiving them as incapable of depicting the "real Borneo." In the Sarawak critic Tian Si's 田思 words, "The truly authentic writings on Borneo have to perhaps still rely on us, the people of Borneo who were born, grew up, and have lived here, and who are willing to treat this place as our home."[70] Tian Si also remonstrates against the emigrant writers' exoticization of Borneo: "We should not deliberately distort the [native] cultures to court readership, or pander to people's mentalities to seek novelties."[71] On the surface, Tian Si's objections point toward a dispute over who can best represent Borneo accurately to the larger world of Chinese readers, but his opposition also betrays an anxiety among Sarawak-based writers and critics that their literary locale will be primarily produced and promoted by translocal forces.

The polemics among the players of the Sarawak Chinese literary circle is overlaid with an additional layer of contestation. Since the 2000s, the issue of representing non-Chinese marginalized ethnicities in Mahua literature has gained traction in its native literary space.[72] Given *River*'s spotlight on Borneo's indigenous groups, critics in Malaysia may analyze the novel under the rubric of *shaoshu zuqun shuxie* 少數族群書寫 (writings by or about minority ethnic groups). To Malaysia-based critic Chong Fah Hing 莊華興, however, that mode of reading via depictions of the non-Chinese in the margins obscures the fact that Chinese in the Southeast Asian country constitute an ethnic minority category themselves. The Mahua literary works that purport to represent minority ethnic groups—as well as most attendant interpretations—often speak with an underlying sense of ethnic-Chinese centrism that perpetuates asymmetrical, intermarginal dynamics. Chong prefers to focus on the multifarious interactions among different ethnic groups in Malaysia and read the depictions of Chinese-indigenous relations as indicative of *kuazuqun shuxie* 跨族群書寫 (transethnic writings).[73] As Chong contends, in the postcolonial phase, the indigenous question of Malaysian Borneo has to be examined in tandem with the history of nation-building. The analysis must be directed at the structure of the region's political economy, especially the way in which the region's abundant resources have been dominated by oligarchic families not unlike what occurred during the reign of the Brooke Raj (1841–1946). In Chong's view, however, Mahua literature has failed to perform its function of social critique effectively, as writers and literary critics have channeled their energies elsewhere. On the one hand, some of them—including Tian Si and his colleagues who were disturbed by the attenuation of Mahua literary realism in Taiwan—mounted the nativist "Writing Borneo" initiative, hoping to rectify what they perceived as flagrant misrepresentations of the island by penning purportedly more authentic works for the literary market.[74] On the other hand, other Borneo writers composed works that have been subsumed under alternative interpretive rubrics such as "literature about environmental protection," "rainforest literature," or "nature writing." Neither orientation has fundamentally addressed the complex structure of transethnic relations that involve the intersecting forces of hegemony and subaltern solidarity. Instead, the Mahua literary writings that depict minority groups risk slipping into exoticism or indulgent sentimentalism, vaguely lamenting the destruction caused by natural calamities or human avarice.[75]

Against this contentious backdrop, the equivocal manner in which Li engages the aforementioned misgivings deserves attention. Faced with the charge of inauthenticity, Li foregrounds his experiential credentials by acknowledging that *River* is based on a trip he took to Indonesia's Kalimantan when he was little. He also asserts that the landscapes and indigenous customs portrayed within the novel are extrapolated from his past experiences in Sarawak.[76] Transposing his ideas into the narrative world, Li arranges for Yong-the-youth and Christina Van Loon, his Dutch travel companion, to meet a Kenyah tribal elder who had embarked on several *peselai* journeys across the island. The elder's extensive travels evoke curious affinities with the bildungsroman that underpins Yong-the-youth's transnational voyage in the Borneo rainforests and suggests an authorial appreciation for the peripatetic Kenyah men as figures who retain their native identities despite their mobility.

By inscribing indigenous folk customs that involve practices of border-effacing mobility and nomadism, the *peselai* trope counters the colonialist imaginary of the confined native who does not travel in search of adventure like the metropolitans.[77] The colonially inflected notion about immobile natives has a residual presence in the mindsets of critics such as Tian Si who emphasize an exclusive concatenation of birth, formative experience, and permanent settlement as essential for presenting Borneo realistically. Through the evocative tale of *River*, however, in which a traveling Chinese protagonist from Kuching meets periodically itinerant tribes that traverse the entirety of Borneo, Li turns such rigid Malaysian nationalist nativism on its head. His nonconforming stance is attested by the way in which he devises a second map-learning encounter that challenges the nativist Sarawak critics who valorize writers as authentic artists only if they do not leave their place of birth.

Featuring the indigenous peoples in their own cartographic moment, the second map scene involves the Kenyah tribal elder who accrues wisdom about the island's geography through his periodic itinerancy. After the elder fails to dissuade Yong-the-youth and Christina from climbing the sacred mountain, he draws a charcoal map that details the legendary topography of the indigenous landscape. According to that hand-drawn map, five major lakes inhabited by the souls of the dead lay at the foot of the mountain. Remarkably, the aboriginal legend keeps pace with changing social realities by incorporating a sixth lake that accommodates a rising number of souls of foreigners who have traveled upriver toward Batu Tiban (2: 310–11). That pedagogical setting echoes the first map-studying scenario. Just as the senior Yong tells a story about his remembrances of Borneo's rivers and mountains at the metadiegetic level, the Kenyah elder delineates the landscape using his memory and belief system.

As a means of geographic pedagogy, map learning in this instance heralds the absorption of native elements into the habitus of Yong-the-youth. The transmitted indigenous knowledge subsequently recurs through the protagonist's recall, application, and perception thereof, which indicate Yong's internalization of the tribal map's worldview. In the key plot arc, signifying his induction into the preternatural world of Borneo, Yong-the-youth witnesses the procession of empty canoes making their annual pilgrimage up the sacred mountain (2: 430–38). His spectatorship corroborates what he has learned earlier from both the Kenyah elder and his Bidayuh friend (1: 313), and it renders him a cultural insider. By becoming privy to the surreal pilgrimage, he melds himself with a native tradition that represents the local collective whose beliefs are deeply bound to Borneo's landscape.

Admittedly, Li does not go to the extent of creating a miscegenated protagonist whose protonational consciousness corelates with the desinicizing of narrative perspective. That approach to character construction was undertaken by the Sarawak-based writer Liang Fang 梁放 in his novel *Woceng tingdao nizai fengzhong kuqi* 我曾聽到你在風中哭泣 (I once heard you crying in the wind).[78] Meanwhile, Li does not foreground Chineseness in *River* as well. He refrains from carving out any special vantage point for Yong-the-youth to interact with the autochthonous minorities as a Chinese person, just as he avoids fashioning the protagonist to demonstrate forms of Chinese-centrism that will incur Malaysia-based critics' negative appraisal. As critics have noted, while the ethnocultural attribute of Chineseness is embodied primarily by Yong-the-youth, its presence is muted, for the multilingual diegetic world features English and indigenous languages of Borneo. Furthermore, Li eschews limning the history of collusion between the Chinese and British colonialists.[79] Following an alternative set-up, Li portrays the tale's protagonist as a stranger stepping into the organic living environments of the indigenous tribes, as well as into their ethical and psychological worlds, which leads him to appreciate the indigenous Other as agentive subjects with their own epistemes.

Through charting the path of Yong-the-youth, Li also responds to the critique of Shi Wenting 石問亭, another of his Sarawak colleagues, by dissolving the clear boundary that separates Chineseness and indigeneity in his earlier short stories.[80] In particular, Li appears to be forging an "insider point of view," a creative orientation that should have pleased the critic Chong back in Malaysia, who hoped that emigrant writers could focus on societal issues about their homeland.[81] Initially encouraged by Li's foregrounding of his Bornean heritage in his works, which suggested a renewed commitment toward his native land, Chong is ultimately disappointed by the symbolic connotations of *River*'s ending, when Yong-the-youth realizes that the sacred summit—touted as the source of life—is a site of desolate rocks associated more closely with death and copulation. To Chong, the denouement suggests the impossibility of Sarawak's historical and literary subjectivities, as if Sarawak could never forge its own aesthetic epistemology.[82]

True enough, the novel portrays Yong-the-youth as eventually failing to absorb the indigenous structures of consciousness shared with him by native inhabitants. But Chong fails to discern how Li's narrative design adroitly evades the polemics on how East Malaysian and Peninsular Malaysian writers forge discrepant representations of non-Chinese ethnic groups in the national context. According to another Malaysia-based scholar, Ngu Ik Tien 吳益婷, a postcolonial Sarawak Chinese literary approach avoids using depictions of interethnic ties as commentaries on state policies or on relations between ethnic Chinese and the state or public authority. By contrast, Peninsular Malaysian authors reproduce the state logic of maintaining strict ethnic and religious boundaries in their works even if the stories critique the state's rigid social policies.[83]

It thus bears reiterating that *River* circles back to Li's earlier works on Borneo in the 1960s and 1970s, which are set in Malaysia's prenational phase. His choice of historical period for *River* enables him to skirt the discussion on the nation-building elements of Mahua literature. Under his pen, the trope of indigeneity does not become a convenient sign of nullifying diasporic values or a naive nationalist celebration of landedness/rootedness. Once again, he crafts his message through events involving the characters' map-mindedness. In *River*, Yong-the-youth's repeated encounters with Maria, the apparition of a young Kenyah girl, develops in him a profound attachment to the east lagoon at the foot of the mountain. The night before reaching the summit, Maria makes him recount the aboriginal topography that corresponds to the tribal elder's cartographic demonstration. Calling the east lagoon "their home," Maria tries to persuade Yong-the-youth to settle down with her, a gesture that can be read as inviting him to fully embrace Borneo's indigenous landscape. He almost yields, but Maria releases him at the last moment, predicting that he will return to the lake district after completing his life journey, thereby also severing his newly forged connection with the indigenous episteme (2: 483–97).

Yong-the-youth's symbolic break with the indigenous way of living and thinking should be construed as integral to *River*'s overall referential strategy, which shows how one can feel native even from afar. Legitimizing his own creative effort amid the cultural politics of the Mahua community, Li frames Borneo as homogenous in order to write about the adjacent Indonesian region:

> Borneo as a whole is divided into three main areas. Sarawak lies to the northwest; the tiny territory in the north is Brunei; Sabah is in the northeast. These three places occupy one quarter of the surface area of Borneo. The remaining part in the south, which constitutes the other three quarters . . . is called "Kalimantan." There is this political division, but the geographical landscape, folk customs, and ethnic groups are all identical . . . they only become wider in scope

in south Borneo...and the jungle even more primitive and more savage.[84]

Given Borneo's well-documented diversity, Li's remarks are perplexing, but his essentializing logic allows him to elide fluid differences within the island for the sake of justifying *River*'s formulation, in which the island is fashioned as a uniform locale that holds meaning for its inhabitants as a nonnational space. To Li, Borneo's actual landscape presents negligible disparities of topographical scale and degrees of "primitivity." That authorial stance is incongruous with the tribal variations he maintains in the novel's diegesis. That said, for a literary construct, the narrator demonstrating how those communal categories shape his mind, body, and actions matters more than whether the distinctions among the native groups employed by the author are anthropologically rigorous or even terminologically consistent.[85] *River* should thus be read less to discern Li's stance on indigeneity than to observe how he uses indigeneity to negotiate his bifurcated authorial identity.

MAP-MINDEDNESS AND MULTISCALAR LITERARY RELATIONS

It follows then that Li's judicious manner of inserting his representations of Borneo into the world-Chinese literary space, as well as his denationalized approach to literary culture, set the stage for a concordance and dissension of authors' and critics' subnational, nonnational, and transnational imaginaries. Indexing how flexible national literary spaces are invigorated from within through nuanced calculations about sociality, his creative practice triangulates literary relations among noncontiguous areas of Mahua literary production. These embedded relational comparisons are usually concealed within the world-Chinese literary context, which highlights international dialectics. As the fraught relationship between the nativist critics and emigrant writers reveals, the native literary space of Malaysia is not quite the "literary federation" that Chan Tah Wei 陳大為 theorizes. Under that organizational rubric, he includes three "autonomously developing regions"—namely, Peninsular (West) Malaysia, East Malaysia (of which

Sarawak is a constituent territory), and Taiwan—which jointly conjure up an idealized egalitarian picture of co-production where no one region is subsidiary to another.[86]

Given Peninsular Malaysia's general standing as the postcolonial nation's cultural mainstream, the way in which Li invokes Borneo as a singular literary space, by sublimating the trope of indigeneity with mobility, represents an alternative logic of peripheral relations. The nativist critics in Sarawak also employ this logic, which foregrounds deeper fissures that are unaccounted for by national boundaries, when they articulate the uniqueness of local literary production. For example, in Tian Si's words:

> After joining Malaysia, a barrier still exists between East Malaysia and West Malaysia, both sides have not engaged in adequate interaction ... so although we are also Mahua writers, what we write is not that familiar to the majority of West Malaysian writers and readers. To evaluate other Malaysian states in this regard, for instance, to now promote Johor literature and Penang literature is meaningless, for the cultural and societal circumstances from south Peninsular Malaysia to north Peninsular Malaysia, or even to central Peninsular Malaysia, are virtually identical. Those areas lack the conditions to create a regional literature. Except for our Sarawak, which not only constitutes a part of Borneo, but also has a long literary tradition since the 1950s.[87]

Like Li, Tian Si advocates Borneo as an exceptional literary locality. But in using Sarawak to justify his "Writing Borneo" initiative—which seeks a worldwide audience—Tian Si flattens internal differences and denies the possibility of regional literatures in Peninsular Malaysia. His discourse in effect leverages the transnational to shrewdly reorder structural relations in the uneven intranational sphere. On the one hand, it accords greater visibility to Sarawak through critiquing representations by Mahua literature in Taiwan; on the other hand, it continues to sideline the abutting state of Sabah within East Malaysia's literary community.[88] Such negotiations within the malleable native literary space of Malaysia vis-à-vis "foreign" writers (such as Li and Zhang) show the pragmatic mode of interdependence among sites of literary production peripheral to China.

By insisting on writing Borneo from Taiwan, Li's transregional move disguises a discursive strategy—arguably shared by Tian Si as well—of juxtaposing nodes of literary production in the Sinophone South, the dialectical mechanism of which allows writers to become more visible and accrue greater legitimacy to perpetuate their own creative positions. In order to promote its own growth that had been stunted by past marginalization, a less significant node in the network may use another node with greater cultural capital to foster productive interplay. In the case of nativist critics like Tian Si and Shi Wenting, who take issue with offshore Sarawak-born writers, what appears as competition between different locales of literary production belies an iterative dynamic of unexpected collaboration to refresh the chronotope that is Borneo for the Chinese reading world. To appreciate the finer workings of how such interlocal and intranational dynamics are as unifying as they are divisive, then, is to grasp the "off-center articulations" that give sustenance to literary production at the scale most desired for different players who foster their own imaginations of the native literary space.

The thought-provoking locus of Malaysia—apprehended not just as positionality but also as trajectory—through which Li constructs the transperipheral mode of literary world-making, is ultimately borne out by the protagonist's final encounter with map imagery. The episode, in which a persistent tendency toward mobility forges connections with new places outside of Borneo, occurs near the end of the novel when Yong-the-youth scrutinizes a Japanese map he has salvaged along the journey. Confronting a "brand new world that is once strangely exotic and yet also very familiar" (2: 409), he recalls:

> Growing up in the British territory of Sarawak, I saw, daily and inescapably—in school or on the walls of government agencies, in public places, and even in my own living room—world maps annotated in Dutch or English, which used the primary colors of red, blue, and white to demarcate the huge spheres of influence of the various empires. The Atlantic Ocean occupied the center. Europe and America constituted the main axes that configured the earth

and presented it holistically and compellingly to the colonized people. (2: 409)

In the European maps that Yong perused as an elementary school student, China, Japan, and Borneo were all relegated to the margins, or remained in the shadows of other regions. The pictorial order shown on the Japanese map, however, is radically different. The Pacific Ocean occupies center stage, with Japan presiding at the center top, China conspicuously featured on the western rim, and Asia as "the central region of the globe" (2: 410). In an epiphanic moment, Yong-the-youth notices that the island of his birth, Borneo, is at the center of the map, which implies its inimitable position in the world. The discovery facilitates the emotive relation of that tacit knowledge with his own physical presence in the heart of the island (2: 411).

The affective impact of the third map strongly emerges once more in a subsequent scene of self-reproach, when Yong-the-youth laments his failure to appreciate the physical and human landscapes of Borneo:

> I was an unfilial son, who took her [Borneo's] nurturing since I was little for granted... After I grew up, I devoted myself wholeheartedly to escape from her warm, humid, and sickening miasma... to leave home alone, and truly explore what in my imagination was the vast, bustling, raucous and magnificent world out there. But now... I gaze blankly at the map on my lap and think about the past... and my heart cannot help becoming forlorn. (2: 413–14)

The Japanese map evokes an intriguing moment of cartographic melancholy, a pensive sadness arising from the perceived misalignment between Yong-the-youth's keen desire to leave Borneo and his poignant realization about the existential meaning of the place for him. This is a stark reversal of the elderly narrator's confession in the metadiegesis that his "ignorant" self never deciphered the significance of the voyage in the past (1: 33). Although the novel finally shows the senior Yong to have developed a more profound awareness of Borneo's place-based indigeneity— the narrative discourse essentially parlays his reflections on four decades of displacement into an extended experience of enlightenment at the age of fifteen—the embedded tale does not depict Yong-the-youth staying on the island, which would have posed a meaningful counterpoint to Li's actual authorial path. There is no alternative script of life events in the fictional world. Impelled by his ardent desire to explore a world he can call his own, after the voyage, Yong-the-youth would still leave his "motherland" for Taiwan.

The recurring deployment of map images in this way maintains the reader's sensitivity toward Li's assessment of his own writing practice. Calling for an allegorical reading of Li and his relationship with globalized Chinese-language writing, *River* projects an author's search for his self-positionality in an ever-expanding literary space. The idiom of map learning, particularly as it percolates through the trope of navigating an organic indigenous realm, sets up Li's self-exoneration through the figure of the elderly narrator, who ultimately embraces the idea of constructing Borneo as a literary world. While the second map limns the topography of the island to attract Yong-the-youth to stay, the protagonist's ruminations about the final map bespeak topological concerns over the placement of Borneo in relation to other sites in the world. The overarching plot of the elderly narrator as he recounts his past marks the prioritized connection to Taiwan, the metadiegetic setting of the novel. Inferred from the plot, the East Asian island is veritably the spring of the narrator's world-making literary orientation that eventually groomed his younger self—"Yong-the-youth"—into a mature writer.

Unbeknownst to the Li, who first arrived in Taiwan in 1967, the island north of Borneo would transform the geometry of the Mahua literary space. On the occasion of *River*'s publication in 2008, Li disclosed that he had ignored the scholar-critic Joseph Lau's advice to develop his oeuvre by writing a series of novels set in Sarawak, or he might have "created a Faulknerian world of the American South in the Nanyang archipelago."[89] Besides ruing how he failed to act on Lau's foresight to engender a trademark regionalism through Borneo à la the American Nobel Prize winner, his regrets also extend to the realm of literary language.[90] For that aspect of composition, Li admires Mark Twain, renowned for crafting a unique vernacular style through the vivid use of several American dialects in his *Adventures of Huckleberry Finn*, who by doing so made a seminal contribution to the literary language of modern America. Li realized, belatedly, that there was no such thing in the world as a pure language for literature. If given the opportunity to turn back the clock, he would have disregarded his university mentor Yen Yuan-shu's counsel and doubled down on the language he formulated in "The Bidayuh Woman," the first short story he published in Taiwan. He would have insisted on developing the spoken *huayu* in Nanyang—which is seen by many as impure, inauthentic, and tainted by a strange flavor—and distill it into a novel literary language that would have afforded him greater success as a writer.[91]

We now know what made him renounce the Nanyang accent of his earlier works. Reflecting on his shift of creative emphasis away from Malaysia after publishing the short story collection *The Bidayuh Woman* in Taiwan in 1976, Li divulges a latent competitive inclination that originated much earlier than previously known:

> In hindsight, the real reason why I did not develop this [Malaysian] subject matter is because . . . I wanted to expand my literary themes in order to construct a more extensive literary world. Discontent with just writing about Malaysia, which had already been covered by many Mahua writers, and yearning to find a broader literary path, that was the most fundamental reason. I wanted to confront a new challenge, as very few Mahua writers select Taiwan as the subject matter for their works.[92]

Li's initial wish to transcend the literary world centered on Borneo can, of course, be construed as a form of self-challenge. What is remarkable about his retrospective rationalization, however, is the way in which he frames the challenge in terms of distinguishing himself from other Mahua writers by directing his creative energy toward the offbeat topic of Taiwan. His reference to "Mahua writers" and his subtle inclusion of himself as part of that community shore up how, despite repeated negations of his Malaysian identity, he still requires the national label, if only to eventually refute it, so that he can remain intelligible in a large-scale literary order premised on nationality. In so doing, Li resembles other Chinese-language writers displaced from and critical of their homelands, such as the Nobel Prize winner Gao Xingjian 高行健, whose novels feature fictional protagonists in "oppositional symbiosis with the nationstate."[93] Although these writers benefit from being associated with specific

Off-Center Articulations 191

native spaces in the global fold of Chinese-language literary production, they calibrate their own dialectics of association. For Gao and Li, they profit more from nimble synecdochical collocation than from becoming pigeonholed in national metonyms. Keeping in mind Li's own cosmopolitan preferences and his unfulfilled Faulknerian ambition, his narrative return to Borneo through mediating indigeneity in *River* must be read as his gaining a new foothold in the global circuits of recognition.

THE POETICS AND POLITICS OF TRANSREGIONAL LITERARY PRODUCTION

When read holistically, Li Yongping's long-distance recommitment to his native place is an act of worlding that emanates from within the artistic order he configured for the tale of his youthful travels. Revolving around the choices he made and remade when he could not predict the outcomes at various stages of his writing career, Li's literary biography throws into relief his off-center articulations as a creative subject. His artistic discourses are driven by the *buji buli* dynamic that keeps him away but not too distant from the centers of the world-Chinese literary space. Between staying put and pursuing, between holding on and letting go, Li's journey spotlights the role of place in the forging of Mahua literary language, and how way before his demonstration in *River*, he had already tried turning Chinese language in Nanyang cosmopolitan by using the Chinese script to convey Nanyang social realities.

Li's design of linguistic deterritorialization and reterritorialization—which is predicated on representing indigenous expressions—results in a stylized polyphony manifested through the author's distinctive novelistic language in *River*. As a tale about peripatetic movements among different locales, the novel demonstrates how the narrator as implied author does not relinquish his grasp of native ecologies, places, and histories. By harnessing knowledge from and about Southeast Asia, the narrator-author dialogues with representations of indigeneity in both Borneo and Taiwan, thus establishing himself as an embodiment of alterity for the two places. Explicating the strategic distribution of narrative events depicting indigeneity and "map-mindedness," this chapter also elucidates the poetics in Li's *River*—its plot about the belated self-recognition and fateful reversals that occasion departures rather than settlement—and traces its suggestive continuity with an unconventional mode of literary worlding that gravitates toward relative centers through sustaining fragile ties from the margins. In itself, that modality is emblematic of how writers and critics from minor locations orchestrate their politics of belonging amid varying registers of literary ideas about Borneo. The interlinked tropes of maps and indigeneity in *River* are not just aesthetic signification; they go beyond promising the fecundity of difference in terms of literary language and topographical setting to emphasize the active social dimension of literary worldmaking. The protagonist's cartographic impulse is vitalized by an iterative process of mutual engagement between the intranational and the transnational, which mirrors how Li works within and against the parochial limits of nativist expectations. From this perspective, Li's case goes further than gainsaying the fundamental binary between "dominant and dominated literary spaces" in Casanova's account, because it ushers the consequential politics of subnational and transregional Chinese cultural identities into the globalized horizon of modern Chinese literary studies.[94]

Demonstrative of the global, regional, national, and local literary interests simultaneously in play, the multiscalar Mahua literature in Taiwan in the 2000s thus illuminates the implications of literary relations among marginal locales in the world-Chinese literary space. As a migrant writer in Taiwan, Li displays a heightened sensitivity to the forces of canonization and the book markets, as well as to critical reception and literary historiography. In Li's literary return to Borneo, we see how he favors the use of the indigenous scale over the national to function variously as the local, the regional, or the global mode of identity performance. Orchestrating a scalar flexibility rarely seen in formulaic local-global discursive struggles, his move provides a corrective complement to Casanova's conception of world literature, which pivots on a nation-centric hierarchy of cultural capital. Instead of unseating conspicuous hegemonic centers, which in the case of Malaysia involves resisting the Malay-partisan definition of national literature and/or writing back against the dominant influence of China, we see in Li's writing an innovative superimposition of indigenous and diasporic elements. Through *River*, we discern how the incessant desire to differentiate is also inherent within domestic contestations that are resolutely part of the transregional purviews of writers inhabiting the world-Chinese literary space. Whereas the "world" in Casanova's *The World Republic of Letters* strangely belies its own provincialism, Li Yongping's case demonstrates the reverse scenario of how representations of indigeneity can harbor a tacit claim to literary cosmopolitanism, as well as how multiple geographies and temporalities overlay one another in the scripting of global Chinese literature from the margins in the Sinophone South.

Coda

Always the Internal Other: Mahua Literature and the Recognition of Alterity

In 2019 and 2020 respectively, the Mahua author Ho Sok Fong's 賀淑芳 short story collection *Humian rujing* 湖面如鏡 (Lake like a mirror) was published in translation by Granta Books in the United Kingdom and Two Lines Press in the United States.[1] Representing a breakthrough for Mahua literature, Ho's transatlantic debut in the English-reading world marked the first time non-university presses selected a Sinophone Malaysian title for publication. Although Mahua novels and collections of short stories had previously appeared in English, those works (by Li Yongping, Zhang Guixing and Ng Kim Chew) were published because of scholarly recognition of their importance for research and higher education curricula, rather than their expected appeal to a general market.[2] Now available beyond the Chinese-reading public, Ho's tales about women related to Malaya and Malaysia index the book's broader reach beyond academe, giving rise to new zones of contact between Mahua literature and its Anglophone audience.

In acquiring a new linguistic face, *Lake Like a Mirror* enters what Julia Lovell calls the "world literary economy," which regulates an "international politics of publishing, translation and reception" that influences the market success of non-Anglophone literature.[3] As Michael S. Duke points out, "the international reputation of modern and contemporary fiction written in Chinese anywhere in the world is chiefly dependent upon English-language translations of that fiction." His 1990 remark still holds true, but general opinions on modern Chinese literature in the English-speaking world have vastly improved due to the increased variety—in terms of themes, styles, and geographical settings—offered by a more diverse group of translators.[4] Extended by translation, Ho's trajectory represents another form of "Malaysian crossings," a conceptual trope I have delineated throughout this book. The trope frames the production of Chinese literary worldliness as the composite process of authors fashioning fictional worlds and navigating imbricated socioliterary spaces by responding to variegated combinations of local and global cultural relations. Although translated literature remains extremely peripheral in the Anglophone publication industry,[5] *Lake Like a Mirror*, with its focus on the widely resonant theme of gender, nonetheless signifies a new, more market-oriented and public-facing type of "cosmopolitan juncture" for Mahua literature. The publishing headway helps to foreground the Southeast Asian region hitherto unfamiliar to many readers in the world literary space.

Keeping in mind Chinese literature's marginal status in the larger world literary economy, in *Malaysian Crossings* I use Mahua literature in the world-Chinese literary space to illustrate the disparate yet homologous forces that account for the neglect of local and regional spaces of creativity and currents of literary thought. By elucidating the worldliness of Mahua authorial imaginaries and practices from a Southeast Asian perspective, this book makes four contributions to remapping modern Chinese literary production. First, the case of Mahua literature shows how a global scale of creative writing and analysis must also pay attention to how the local scale is coconstructed in specific places. For "place" as a concept to better highlight the diversity of global Chinese literature and culture, we need to historicize local and translocal connectivities in tandem. Whether the work is about forging a Malaya-Shanghai connection (chapter 1), dismantling the barriers between Sinophone and Anglophone cultural spheres in Malaya (chapter 2), circulating cosmopolitan linguistic and literary imaginaries from China to Malaysia and beyond (chapter 3), or representing indigeneity for audiences in Malaysia, Taiwan, and China (chapter 4), the varied linkages spotlight Mahua literature as a scalable modality that will be useful for interpreting other area-based labels of modern Chinese literature.

Scaling downward, the modality evokes the survivalist spirit of more peripherized locales such as Macau. Mahua literature's ambivalent understanding of its importance for larger literary ecologies constitutes the obverse side to the thoroughly noncompetitive approach adopted by Macanese authors. Those Macanese writers, as Rosa Vieira de Almeida shows persuasively, foster a purposive style of inconsequentiality for Sinophone Macau literature built upon the site's even more marginal position than that of Mahua literature in the world-Chinese literary space.[6]

Scaling upward, the flexible Mahua literary formation can inform renewed attention on regionality in mainland Chinese literature.[7] For instance, David Wang has called for establishing "Dongbei studies" (*dongbeixue* 東北學) to exist alongside recognized intellectual rubrics such as Shanghai studies, Beijing studies, and Jiangnan studies, as he emphasizes the cruciality of the mainland's northeast region for imagining China as "native soil" (*xiangtu* 鄉土).[8] The salient dimensions of Mahua literary studies can provide fruitful pointers for grasping the literary-cultural phenomena of northeast China. The pertinent facets range from the layered personal histories of mobile authors who write about their shared homeland from afar, to the shifting boundaries of a literary space that is not coextensive with the geographical region bearing the same name, to the politics of representation that occurs among local-regional and national interests. These common aspects remind us that dominant Chinese literary formations are also infused with heterogeneity, shaped as they are by similar forces that create their marginalized counterparts but with differing implications for the world-Chinese literary space.

Extrapolating from the Mahua example, then, each place—be it Malaysia, Taiwan, or China (each addressed directly in the book), or other sites such as Singapore, Indonesia, Hong Kong, and Macau—stands as an embedded locality dealing with its own set of centers and margins based on diverse historical senses of literary regionality.[9] Interacting with local cultural ecologies that host both rootedness and mobility, the site-specific experiences reveal how literary hierarchies are always in flux, giving rise to nodal regions that exhibit differentiated core-periphery nexuses over time.

The book's second contribution lies in its reminder that the local need not be always treated as the national. Instead, we can consider the local as operating on different regional scales. From showing how global discourses take on site-specific forms, to demonstrating how representations of indigeneity mediate off-site concerns, the authors I examine in the book cultivated translocal practices that straddle plural literary histories. Underscoring the importance for world literary studies to accommodate artistic practices that inhabit double or even multiple literary spaces, the writers provide depictions of Malaya or Malaysia that may not necessarily be vehicles for nation-building. Han Suyin in chapter 2 appears to be an exception, given the author's use of English and her fervent aspirations for Malaya to become an exemplary nation for the world. But what the chapter really conveys is the extended ground of Sinophone (*huawen*) Malayan literature, which occasioned remarkable contact between Sinophone and Anglophone literary histories in a single locale.

In turning Mahua literary history into a multisited and bilingual configuration, *Malaysian Crossings* assembles authorial practices and cultural developments conventionally not thought to belong together, and in so doing, presents Malaya and Malaysia as historically open and fluid spheres for inventing narrative modalities of localization. In view of Malaysia's multiracial and multilingual societal composition, the concept of "crossings" can undergird collaborative projects that incorporate studies on Malaysian literature written in Malay and Tamil. Furthermore, "crossings" as an analytical method will benefit studies on other multicultural sites in Southeast Asia that are embedded in polylocal networks of creative writings by ethnic Chinese in multiple languages.

Third, the book's analytical framework of twinning the local and the global can be applied to other genres, such as prose and poetry, as well as to other modes of cultural production, such as film and popular music. For example, the approach will illuminate the contributions of Tan Swie Hian 陳瑞獻, best known for his pioneering work that introduced Western literary modernism to postcolonial Singapore and Malaysia. Tan's multifaceted practice in the late 1960s and early 1970s—which spanned journal editorship, translation, and creative writing of both fiction and poetry—highlights the cosmopolitan energies that flowed across new national contexts from Singapore to Malaysia. At that time, the two Sinophone literary spheres were still imagined as unified via literary supplements shared between Chinese-language newspapers of the two countries.[10] Looking beyond literature, the growing prominence of Southeast Asian Chinese cinema in Taiwan's film ecology since the 2000s does not just throw into relief the shifting geopolitics of a Sinitic-speaking world where China plays an increasingly influential role in defining the scope and visibility of Chinese culture. The phenomenon also accentuates the strategies through which self-identified Chinese filmmakers carve their footholds in transregional cultural spaces as constitutive members, foregrounding different aspects of their craft in the various sites where their works circulate.[11] The realm of acoustic arts also demonstrates a similar interplay of intranational and transnational forces. As it is, the story of how *xinyao* 新謠 (Sinophone Singapore popular music) evolved from a homegrown grassroots creative movement in the 1980s to engage and influence the popular Mandarin music scenes of Taiwan and China, from the 1990s to the current times, awaits scholarly updates.[12]

Fourth, in advancing the call of Sinophone studies to feature the construction of place through literary writing, *Malaysian Crossings* engages Chinese diaspora studies in a more grounded manner by addressing the dynamics among topolectal groups in one location. Future research on globalized-cum-localized Sinitic cultures can inquire further into the inner complexities within each topolectal group, as they will evince parameters of analysis that are inadequately explored. For instance, studies of the Chinese overseas have shown how social class affects the type of cultural commodities that members of the same topolectal group consumed. Specifically, the Teochew (潮州; also rendered as Chaozhou) merchants in Singapore before World War II preferred watching *waijiang xi* 外江戲—a form of traditional opera that is nonnative to their home region of Chaoshan 潮汕—because the theatrical form was perceived to be culturally more sophisticated than the performances staged in the Teochew topolect.[13] Given this case whereby the Teochews did not necessarily consume Teochew opera in order to exhibit cultural distinction, the class divide manifested through differences in artistic taste indicates the nuanced diversity *within* (rather than across) Sinitic-speaking societies in Southeast Asia.

MINOR REGISTERS

Equally important to discerning the multiscalar Mahua literary relations are the frames employed to explicate how the literary formation evolves. After all, geographical spaces get localized not merely via historical and material processes on the ground, but also through conscious acts of scholarship. As Eric Hayot notes, a global assembly of critical viewpoints cannot exclude the interpretive perspectives from the places where Chinese-language texts are initially produced:

> The critique of nationalism, national languages, and national literary studies, if it wishes to be truly global, must launch itself *from* those [Chinese] shores as well, lest its postnationalism either minimize "the conflict among the interests of the monocultural states and multilingual communities" or promote "generic critical lexicons that presume universal translatability or global applicability." To do so, such a critic needs the help of scholars in Chinese ... to wreak upon the coming transformations of *global* literary thought the effects of their particular difference.[14]

Following Hayot, a critique of Mahua literature and its entanglements with nation-based literary histories must likewise depart from the "shores" associated with colonial Malaya and independent Malaysia. *Malaysian Crossings* presents a globalized Mahua literary studies that not only values imaginative texts, but also reckons with critical discourses from Malaysia and its associated venues. In lieu of conveying the impression that Malaysia—or Mahua, for that matter—is simply an empty epistemological space devoid of its own theoretical ideas, this book helps to build a repertoire of world-Chinese literary thought that is attuned to how literary actors in peripherized locales grasp the historical dimension of their subjectivities.

Indeed, besides creative works that lend themselves well to supporting exogenous concepts, the Mahua literary formation also offers insights on place-based communities forming their own interpretive traditions.[15] These insights should be given due attention in world literary studies, not least because the ways in which Mahua scholars have domesticated Western critical theory to interpret the autonomous and inflected developments of Mahua literary production constitute another mode of creating worldliness. One key example of how these scholars have mediated local and extralocal intellectual references is the Mahua vernacularization of "minor literature" since the early 1990s to explain Malaya- or Malaysia-born authors' experiments in literary language.

Mahua scholars' situational adaptation of the concept is captured in the dual translations of "minor literature" into *xiaowenxue* 小文學 (small literature) and *shaoshu wenxue* 少數文學 (minority literature). The French thinkers Gilles Deleuze and Félix Guattari had coined the seminal idea to account for minorities writing in a major language that transcends national borders. For Lim Kien Ket 林建國 and Tee Kim Tong 張錦忠, who opt to render the concept as *xiaowenxue*, they scrutinize the implications of Mahua linguistic de-territorialization and re-territorialization—à la Deleuze and Guattari—against the backdrop of a wider Chinese literary space where mainland Chinese and Taiwan occupy superior positions. They thereby direct their common analytical focus to the asymmetrical relationship between the Chinese language used in Southeast Asia and in the more mature environments of Greater China. By comparison, Ng Kim Chew uses *shaoshu wenxue* to indicate the specific background of Mahua literary production through the term's resonance with the historical studies of the Chinese overseas. To Ng, this second translation of "minor literature," which capitalizes on marginality arising from the minority status of ethnic Chinese in most Southeast Asian states, represents a progressive mode of creative linguistic expression that Mahua literature can aspire toward for attaining literary modernity.[16]

Malaysian Crossings builds upon such localized understandings to show how the nested conditions that make Mahua literature a "minor" literary formation, in the double registers of "small literature" and "minority literature," also produce its worldliness. Mahua literature comes into being, after which it moves on to connect and modulate ideas and texts, through literary actors who search for avenues to innovate their literary language-in-the-making. Enacting their creative experiments at various "cosmopolitan junctures," Lin Cantian, Han Suyin, Wang Anyi, and Li Yongping exemplify how Mahua writings become "world literature"— that is to say, literature that exists in the world and waits to be read—by becoming minor. From writing in or about displaced settings against a dominant ideal of Chinese expression (Lin, Wang, Li) to connecting parallel undertakings within a minority ethnic community amid political transition (Han), these writers perform the worlding of Chinese literature in the margins by simultaneously looking far and staying near.

Yielding a historiographical approach that can be applied to Anglophone, Francophone, and other iterations of world literary studies, Mahua literature then gestures toward a new heuristic classification for world literature. This new taxonomical category stands for minor literatures tied to multifarious projects of regional disarticulation and rearticulation from the periphery rather than to the sole labor of decentering asymmetrical cultural relations.[17] As we can see in *Malaysian Crossings*, in trying to place Mahua writings into alternative spheres of influence through strategies of circulation (Lin), channeling (Han), relay (Wang), and simultaneity (Li), the authors contend with circumstances that are far from optimal. They find themselves having to always fortify their writing practices with resources elsewhere, while recognizing the impossibility of being admitted into the core of any world literary formation. Works in the same category as Mahua literature are unlikely to be widely read or studied, but the tendency for their associated literary formations to create inner centers and peripheries demonstrates the merits of sustaining multiplicities of various scales for global literary pluralism.

ANTIPODAL ARCHIPELAGOS

Unlike the conceptual biography of "minor literature" in the Mahua context, Ng Kim Chew's notion of the Literary Galapagos moves beyond adapting Western frameworks to offer an original figuration of literary thought. Developing Ng's metaphor in *Malaysian Crossings*, I call this remote archipelagic region in the world-Chinese literary space—which hosts significant artistic innovation despite its underresourced conditions—the "Sinophone South." The ways in which Mahua literature's extended periods of isolation ironically nourished its inventiveness in the Sinophone South exemplify what I have described as the Galapagos Paradox. This seemingly conflicted form of literary existence dramatizes a mode of claiming global belonging that goes unvalidated by the centers as having fully integrated with the world. Coming to terms with historical inattention and geolinguistic limitations, Mahua authors seek to establish themselves by persisting to write with a difference while deferring the normative possibility of their creative practices. Literary worlding, in this view, spotlights an unobtrusive global connectivity through the remote pathways of people, ideas, and texts. Such connectivity in the Sinophone South shapes "Malaysia" into a multilocal and multitemporal frontier of development for the world-Chinese literary space.[18]

What Ng does not realize about his pairing of the Galapagos Islands and Malaysia (which includes Singapore, given the historical Malayan connection) is that the two regions constitute a symbolic pair of antipodes.[19] The regions' diametric opposition through Earth's center marks the South American islands as the place farthest away from Singapore-Malaysia. In framing the globality of Mahua literature in terms of its antipodal relation, Ng's Galapagos trope not only elicits a comparison across biology and literary studies, as I have laid out in the introduction, but also suggests the ways in which Mahua authorial practices located mainly in archipelagic Southeast Asia can be perceived as exotic and inaccessible endeavors. The situation is as if the writers have gone as far as the other side of the world to produce their works but still encounter the same limiting judgment.

Given the locational correspondence across the globe, my concept of "Malaysian crossings" and Ng's "Literary Galapagos" jointly illustrate how ostensibly peripheral authorial pursuits contribute to the collective of local singularities that invigorate the world-Chinese literary space. Yoked to its imagined antipode, Mahua literature reluctantly serves as the epitome of an involuntary state of being minor, a condition that represents all Chinese-language literatures figured through the geographical trait of "islandness." Once again, it is Ng who offers vivid exposition on this paradigmatic circumstance as an insider-participant in two literary ecologies. Spurred by the multi-islandic similarity between Malaysia and Taiwan, Ng describes the reproducibility of Mahua literature's existential dynamic, which echoes the Sinophone South's archipelagic configuration, as follows:

> Just like Taiwan literature, it [Mahua literature] is propped up by concerns of (political, cultural, personal) identity.... "Mahua literature"... as a metaphor for Taiwan literature and its existential condition... is a symbol for all forms of Sinophone (*huawen*)

minor literature. *In time to come, Taiwan literature may also "become" Mahua literature....* To adapt a line from Lim Kien Ket's article "On Fang Xiu" (2000): "Such literatures that are deficient in resources, resulting in hopeless prospects of development, whatever their original names, can all be called 'Mahua literature.'"[20]

As Ng makes clear, he is elaborating on fellow Mahua scholar-critic Lim Kien Ket's characterization of how the writing of Mahua literary history reflects the larger predicament of Third World intellectuals who can only rely on meager conceptual resources to make sense of their cultural circumstances.[21] Outside of the Mahua interpretive tradition, Ng's articulations bear an alternative resonance. The Mahua literary formation in the Sinophone South, which yearns for an uncentered and borderless regional order, resembles what Antonio Benitez-Rojo would have recognized as the trope of the "repeating island." According to Benitez-Rojo's famous theorization of the Caribbean, the "repeating island" is "an island that proliferates endlessly, each copy a different one," located as it is within "a cultural meta-archipelago without center and without limits."[22] In contrast to Benitez-Rojo's generic descriptor, which conveys his creative vision of a highly fertile cultural region enlivened by migratory histories and symbolic similarities, the evocative attribute of a "repetitious islandness" in Ng's discourse is encapsulated in the specific rubric of "Mahua literature" and points to an alliance of local literary spaces in the making.

Ng's approach hence enriches global literary knowledge in a distinctive way. Although it is in fact Mahua literature that migrated and turned into Taiwan literature, Ng inverts the historical trajectory of literary becoming: his bold conflation of Mahua and Taiwan builds on the connective poetics of the Sinophone South, thus developing the holistic inter-referencing of literary formations to represent the challenging constitution of place-based literary histories. His approach also reflects how he prioritizes cultivating immediate literary milieux, rather than seeking acknowledgment in world literary contexts that is desired but elusive.

Negotiating local and global critical contexts, Ng appears to proclaim Mahua literature as a superior label for a new regional classification that erases spatiotemporal specificities. Nonetheless, though he gains control over the naming prerogative usually exercised by exogenous scholars, his proposal lacks the strength of an assertion since he perceives the Sinophone South—where meaningful differences flourished only because of historical contingencies—as fleeting, precarious and thus likely to be impermanent. Ng's discourse of Mahua replicability is underpinned by poignance rather than pride, as he notices how the parochialism of Mahua literary actors who insist on gate-keeping membership through nationality is refigured in Taiwan's nativist ideologies, which cast Mahua literature as the "internal Other of Taiwan literature."[23] Embodying an "absolute heterogeneity" wherever it undertakes creative labor, Mahua literature signifies the enduring condition of embedded "outsideness" (*waizaixing* 外在性) that feeds literary actors' lived experiences of any minoritized formation.[24] It is on this basis that "Mahua literature" becomes the discomforting byword for all "literatures that are deficient in resources, resulting in hopeless prospects of development."

In other words, Mahua literature's increased currency in global Chinese cultural studies belies its existential position as the outsider within larger literary formations. David Wang once identified the alterity residing within Mahua sociohistorical and literary circumstances—doing so, in fact, by analyzing Ng's writing practice—to formulate his tripartite theory of othered figures (the alien-*yimin* 夷民, the migrant-*yimin* 移民, and the loyalist-*yimin* 遺民) who catalyze Chinese-language literary production beyond mainland China.[25] Through the strength of his own perceptive analysis, Ng hereby reminds us that Mahua literature no longer acts merely as an example or springboard for compelling abstractions generated from afar. The literary formation has come into its own, standing for a distinct conceptual category of global Chinese literature with its modular specificity as the inner constitutive other of multiple scales.

By drawing on Mahua literary thought, *Malaysian Crossings* hence steers world literary studies toward examining the situated particulars of creative composition and critical debates in and among peripherized locations, instead of tracking the unidirectional impact of ideas exported from dominant centers. While underscoring Malaysia's sensitive positionality in the world-Chinese literary space, the book also installs a useful native perspective for grasping the discursive styles of writers and critics who globalize modern Chinese literature from the margins by nursing their quiet ambitions. Despite being geographically constrained, these literary actors remain agents of physical journeys, social interaction, and conceptual engagement. Their individuated imaginaries and practices of literary regionality restore site-specificity below, above, or unrelated to the national scale, producing insights—not only about the commitments to sustaining fragile creative traditions but also about the possibilities of forging collaborative ties across neglected literary terrains with limited cultural capital.

Notes

INTRODUCTION: SOUTHERN CROSSINGS

1. David Damrosch, "Where is World Literature?," in *Studying Transcultural Literary History*, ed. Gunilla Lindberg-Wada (Berlin: De Gruyter, 2012), 214.
2. Chong Fah Hing 莊華興, "Shuide Mahua wenxue yanjiu? Ping Xu Wenrong de *Nanfang xuanhua: Mahua wenxue de zhengzhi dikang shixue*" 誰的馬華文學研究？評許文榮的《南方喧嘩：馬華文學的政治抵抗詩學》 [Whose Mahua literary studies? On Khor Boon Eng's *Uproar in the South: The Poetics of Political Resistance in Mahua Literature*], *Taiwan dongnanya xuekan* 臺灣東南亞學刊 [Taiwan journal of Southeast Asian studies] 3, no. 1 (2006): 106.
3. The initiative was titled "Xiaoshuo yinli: Huawen guoji hulian pingtai" 小說引力：華文國際互聯平臺 [The gravitational force of fiction: An interlinked platform for the Chinese-language international]. For a trenchant analysis of this incident, see Zhan Min-xu 詹閔旭, "Duodi gonggou de huayuyuxi wenxue: Yi Mahua wenxue de Taiwan jingyu weili" 多地共構的華語語系文學：以馬華文學的臺灣境遇為例 [Sinophone literature as multiple forms of place-based production: On the predicament of Mahua literature in Taiwan], *Taiwan wenxue xuebao* 臺灣文學學報 [Bulletin of Taiwanese literature] 30 (2017): 84–85.
4. Scholars have proposed "Mahua literature" as a viable analytical category for modern Chinese literary studies. See Carlos Rojas, "Language, Ethnicity, and the Politics of Literary Taxonomy: Ng Kim Chew and Mahua Literature," *PMLA* 131, no. 5 (2016): 1316–327; and Brian Bernards, "Malaysia as Method: Xiao Hei and Ethnolinguistic Literary Taxonomy," in *The Oxford Handbook of Modern*

Chinese Literatures, ed. Carlos Rojas and Andrea Bachner (Oxford: Oxford University Press, 2016), 811–31.

5. Benedict Anderson, "The Unrewarded: Notes on the Novel Prize for Literature," *New Left Review* 80 (2013): 99–108.

6. Pascale Casanova, *The World Republic of Letters*, trans. M. B. DeBevoise (Cambridge, MA: Harvard University Press, 2004), 82–125.

7. See Alison M. Groppe, *Sinophone Malaysian Literature: Not Made in China* (Amherst, NY: Cambria Press, 2013), 2.

8. See Zhang Hongmin 張宏敏, "'Wenhua Zhongguo' gainian suyuan" "文化中國" 概念溯源 [Tracing the concept of "Cultural China"], *Shenzhen daxue xuebao* 深圳大學學報 [Journal of Shenzhen University] 28, no. 3 (2011): 57; and Tu Wei-ming, "Cultural China: The Periphery as Center," in *The Living Tree: The Changing Meaning of Being Chinese Today*, ed. Tu Wei-ming (Stanford, CA: Stanford University Press, 1994), 1–34.

9. Different interpretive locations support different articulations of world literature. My all-inclusive concept of "world-Chinese literary space" must be distinguished from the notion of *"shijie huawen wenxue"* 世界華文文學 (world Chinese-language literature) coined by PRC scholars in the early 1990s. The latter excludes China from this nominally global literary order. For more on the study of Chinese-language literary formations outside mainland China, see Chen Liao 陳遼, "Huawen wenxue yanjiu sanshinian" 華文文學研究三十年 [Studies of literatures in Chinese: A thirty-year review], *Huawen wenxue* 華文文學 [Literatures in Chinese] 2 (2008): 10–14.

10. Francesca Orsini and Laetitia Zecchini, "The Locations of (World) Literature: Perspectives from Africa and South Asia: Introduction," *Journal of World Literature* 4, no. 1 (2019): 10.

11. Damrosch defines world literature not as "an infinite, ungraspable canon of works but rather a mode of circulation and of reading." See David Damrosch, *What Is World Literature?* (Princeton, NJ: Princeton University Press, 2003), 5.

12. For an explication of how Malaya as an administrative unit of colonial governance became intertwined with Malaya as a construction of grassroots, everyday consciousness, the latter of which usually includes Singapore, see Edwin Lee, *Singapore: The Unexpected Nation* (Singapore: Institute of Southeast Asian Studies, 2008), 21–22.

13. The remaining 1 percent of the population is classified as "Others," which includes primarily Eurasians. See Department of Statistics, Malaysia, "Press Release: Current Population Estimates, Malaysia, 2021," July 15, 2021, https://www.dosm.gov.my/v1/index.php?r=column/pdfPrev&id=ZjJOSnpJR21sQWVUcUp6ODRudm5JZz09.

14. Barbara Watson Andaya and Leonard Y. Andaya, *A History of Malaysia (Second Edition)* (Honolulu: University of Hawai'i Press, 2001), 341–42.
15. On the Sanskrit roots of "Nusantara," and how the terms are glossed differently in Indonesia and Malaysia, see Hans-Dieter Evers, "Nusantara: History of a Concept," *Journal of the Malaysian Branch of the Royal Asiatic Society* 89, part 1, no. 310 (2016): 4, 8. For a meticulous study on "Nanyang" as a vibrant mode of Chinese and Sinophone literary imagination, see Brian Bernards, *Writing the South Seas: Imagining the Nanyang in Chinese and Southeast Asian Postcolonial Literature* (Seattle: University of Washington Press, 2015).
16. Casanova, *World Republic of Letters*, 206.
17. Studies that examine inter-Asian regionality are rare. Two notable exceptions include: Margaret Hillenbrand, *Literature, Modernity, and the Practice of Resistance: Japanese and Taiwanese Fiction, 1960–1990* (Leiden: Brill, 2007), and Caroline S. Hau, *The Chinese Question: Ethnicity, Nation and Region In and Beyond the Philippines* (Singapore: NUS Press, 2014).
18. Pheng Cheah, *What Is a World? On Postcolonial Literature as World Literature* (Durham, NC: Duke University Press, 2016), 210. A remarkable exception that demonstrates the merits of adopting a non-national lens for literary studies is Jing Tsu's "Weak Links, Literary Spaces, and Comparative Taiwan," in *Comparatizing Taiwan*, ed. Shu-mei Shih and Ping-hui Liao (New York: Routledge, 2015), 123–44, which examines the understudied literary relations among Taiwan, Hong Kong, and Macau, and the struggles of minority languages within Taiwan.
19. Longxi Zhang, "Epilogue: The Changing Concept of World Literature," in *World Literature in Theory*, ed. David Damrosch (Western Sussex: Wiley-Blackwell, 2014), 522.
20. Franco Moretti, "Conjectures on World Literature," in *Distant Reading* (London: Verso, 2013), 54, 57.
21. Ng Kim Chew 黃錦樹, "Nanfang huawen wenxue gongheguo: Yige chuyi" 南方華文文學共和國：一個芻議 [Republic of southern-Sinophone literature: A proposal], *Zhongshan renwen xuebao* 中山人文學報 [Sun Yat-sen journal of humanities], issue no. 45 (2018): 2. Subsequent quotations will be cited in the text by page number.
22. Revathi Krishnaswamy, "Toward World Literary Knowledges: Theory in the Age of Globalization," *Comparative Literature* 62, no. 4 (2010): 401.
23. Ng Kim Chew, "Fen yu lu—Chongshen kaiduan, chongfan 'weishenme Mahua wenxue'" 墳與路—重審開端，重返"爲什麼馬華文學" [The grave and the road—Reassessing the genesis, returning to the question of "Why Mahua literature"], in *Huawen xiaowenxue de Malaixiya ge'an* 華文小文學的馬來西亞個案 [Minor literature in Chinese: The case of Malaysia] (Taipei: Maitian, 2015), 93.

24. Lanny Thompson, "Heuristic Geographies: Territories and Areas, Islands and Archipelagoes," in *Archipelagic American Studies*, ed. Brian Russell Roberts and Michelle Ann Stephens (Durham, NC: Duke University Press, 2017), 57.
25. See the list included in the front and back matter of Ng Kim Chew, *Youling de wenzi* 幽靈的文字 [The script of the spirit] (Kaohsiung: Center for the Humanities, National Sun Yat-sen University, 2019).
26. Carlos Rojas, "A ~~World~~ Republic of Southern [Sinophone] Letters," *Modern Chinese Literature and Culture* 30, no. 1 (2018), 52 [strikethrough part of original title].
27. Ng Kim Chew, "Fulu san: Yu Luo Yijun de duitan" 附錄三：與駱以軍的對談 [Appendix 3: A dialogue with Lo Yi-chin], in *Tu yu huo: Tanah Melayu* 土與火 [Earth and fire: Malay land] (Taipei: Maitian, 2005), 314–15.
28. Ng Kim Chew, "Fulu san," 317.
29. See Ng Kim Chew, "Huawen shaoshu wenxue—lisan xiandaixing de weijing zhi lü" 華文少數文學——離散現代性的未竟之旅 [Minor Sinophone literature: Diasporic modernity's incomplete journey], in *Huawen xiaowenxue de Malaixiya ge'an* 華文小文學的馬來西亞個案 [Minor literature in Chinese: The case of Malaysia] (Taipei: Maitian, 2015), 115–19.
30. Brian Bernards, *Writing the South Seas*, 15.
31. See Franco Moretti's "Modern European Literature: A Geographical Sketch" in *Distant Reading*, 1, 12, 18, where he explicitly refers to the European literary formation as an archipelago.
32. Brian Russell Roberts and Michelle Ann Stephens, eds., *Archipelagic American Studies* (Durham, NC: Duke University Press, 2017).
33. Brian Russell Roberts and Michelle Ann Stephens, "Archipelagic American Studies: De-continentalizing the Study of American Culture," in *Archipelagic American Studies*, 29.
34. Maria Rubins, "A Century of Russian Culture(s) 'Abroad': The Unfolding of Literary Geography," in *Global Russian Cultures*, ed. Kevin M. F. Platt (Madison: The University of Wisconsin Press, 2019), 24.
35. See Jingzi 鏡子, "Fulu: Malaixiya huawen wenxue suishi keneng xiaoshi, erwo ganghao shenzaiqizhong" 附錄：馬來西亞華文文學隨時可能消失，而我剛好身在其中 [Appendix: Mahua literature may disappear anytime, and I happen to be in the midst of it], in Ng Kim Chew, *Minguo de manchuan* 民國的慢船 [Slow boat to Republican China] (Petaling Jaya: Got One Publisher Sdn. Bhd., 2019), 248.
36. The contrast between the metaphorical scale of the remote archipelago and the actual scale of the literary formation is stark. Rojas points out that "Chinese has a global readership of well over a billion people, which is to say approximately one-seventh of the world population." See Carlos Rojas, "A ~~World~~ Republic of Southern [Sinophone] Letters," 44 [strikethrough part of original title].
37. Franco Moretti, "More Conjectures," in *Distant Reading*, 112.

38. Benedict Anderson, "The Unrewarded," 106.
39. Jingzi, "Fulu."
40. Jingzi, "Fulu," 236. For English renditions of his work, see Ng Kim Chew, *Slow Boat to China and other Stories*, trans. Carlos Rojas (New York: Columbia University Press, 2016).
41. Jingzi, "Fulu," 248.
42. J. A. González, C. Montes, J. Rodríguez, and W. Tapia, "Rethinking the Galapagos Islands as a Complex Social-ecological System: Implications for Conservation and Management," *Ecology and Society* 13, no. 2 (2008): 13, accessed June 29, 2020, http://www.ecologyandsociety.org/vol13/iss2/art13/. On the longest expedition and the largest specimen collection exercise, see Matthew James, *Collecting Evolution: The Galapagos Expedition that Vindicated Darwin* (New York: Oxford University Press, 2017).
43. Carlos Rojas, "A ~~World~~ Republic of Southern [Sinophone] Letters," 51–54 [strikethrough part of original title].
44. See the following essay, written in 2007, by Ng Kim Chew, *Women de yanhua* 我們的演化 [Our evolution], in *Shicha de zengli* 時差的贈禮 [The gift of time-lags] (Taipei: Maitian, 2019), 214–18. Rojas has analyzed Ng's keynote speech at the 2016 "Sinophone Studies: New Directions" conference, which first features the archipelagic trope. See Carlos Rojas, "A ~~World~~ Republic of Southern [Sinophone] Letters."
45. Ng Kim Chew, *Women de yanhua*, 217.
46. Ng's keynote address at the "Sinophone Studies: New Directions" conference held at Harvard University, October 15, 2016, accessed 2 October 2021, https://soundcloud.com/fairbank-center/ng-kim-chew-sinophone-studies-new-directions.
47. Yu-ting Huang, "The Archipelagos of Taiwan Literature: Comparative Methods and Island Writings in Taiwan," in *Comparatizing Taiwan*, 96.
48. Tan Swie Hian 陳瑞獻, "Dakewen" 答客問 [Interview by a guest], in *Chao Foon* 蕉風, no. 225 (1971): 9–10.
49. Notably, Ng dramatizes this attribute of untranslatability of an exceptional Mahua literary text that nonetheless garnered international acclaim in his famous short story "The Disappearance of M." See Ng Kim Chew, *M de shizong* M 的失蹤 [The disappearance of M], in *Meng yu zhu yu liming* 夢與豬與黎明 [Dream and swine and aurora] (Taipei: Jiuge, 1994), 10–42.
50. Emily Apter, *Against World Literature: On the Politics of Untranslatability* (London: Verso, 2013), 16.
51. Emily Apter, *Against World Literature*, 35.
52. Darwin Manuscript Collection (Cambridge University Library) 114, letter no. 63, dated July 1846, quoted in Frank J. Sulloway, "Darwin and the Galapagos," *Biological Journal of the Linnean Society* 21, no. 1–2 (1984): 55.
53. Emily Apter, *Against World Literature*, 18.

54. Emily Apter, *Against World Literature*, 40.
55. Ng Kim Chew, "Inscribed Backs," in *Slow Boat to China and other Stories*, trans. Carlos Rojas, 270. The English rendition is Rojas's for Ng's phrase "buke fanyi de yicixing" 不可翻譯的一次性.
56. Wu He, *Remains of Life*, trans. Michael Berry (New York: Columbia University Press, 2017).
57. Shu-mei Shih, *Visuality and Identity: Sinophone Articulations across the Pacific* (Berkeley: University of California Press, 2007), 4.
58. David Der-wei Wang, "Introduction: Worlding Literary China," in *A New Literary History of Modern China*, ed. David Der-wei Wang (Cambridge, MA: Harvard University Press, 2017), 24–25.
59. Regarding the notion of the "European literary periphery" that parallels Wang's move to provincialize China, see Warwick Research Collective, *Combined and Uneven Development: Towards a New Theory of World-Literature* (Liverpool: Liverpool University Press, 2015), 115–42.
60. On how America-based scholars use "Sinophone" to translate *huawen* 華文, which originated from Mahua literary thought, and yet translate "Sinophone" back into Chinese as *huayu yuxi* 華語語系, thus privileging the Western context of knowledge production and obscuring the antecedent Mahua dimension, see Hee Wai Siam 許維賢, *Huayu dianying zai hou-Malaixiya: tuqiang fengge, huayifeng yu zuozhelun* 華語電影在後馬來西亞：土腔風格、華夷風與作者論 [Post-Malaysian Chinese-language film: Accented style, Sinophone and auteur theory] (Taipei: Linking Publishing, 2018), 51–52. Notably, Ng accepts "Sinophone literature" as a suitable translation for his coinage *huawen wenxue*. See Ng Kim Chew, "Nanfang huawen wenxue gongheguo," 5.
61. In the book, I use both "Sinophone" and "Chinese-language" to render *huawen* 華文 and the spoken form *huayu* 華語. The latter term foregrounds historical realities that occurred before the former term was adopted by writers and critics to mark differential creative identities and academic research topics not necessarily related to China. Having become keywords in the Mahua cultural vocabulary, *huawen* and "Chinese-language" are used in publications, events, and institution names as the customary translations for each other. In the instances that I draw on "Sinophone" to translate *huawen* and *huayu*, it will be clear from my discussion that I intend to disengage from associations with mainland China, or to parallel the use of "Anglophone" that indicates off-center cultural practices.
62. Frank J. Sulloway, "Darwin and the Galapagos," 52, fn. 21.
63. I borrow this pithy phrase from Brian Russell Roberts and Michelle Ann Stephens, "Archipelagic American Studies," 29.
64. Chow Tse-tsung 周策縱, "Zongjieci" 總結辭 [Closing remarks], in *Dongnanya huawen wenxue* 東南亞華文文學 Chinese literature in Southeast Asia], ed. Wong

Yoon Wah 王潤華 and Horst Pastoors (Singapore: Goethe-Institut Singapore and Singapore Association of Writers, 1989), 359–62.
65. Anne Garland Mahler, "Global South," *Oxford Bibliographies in Literary and Critical Theory*, ed. Eugene O'Brien (New York: Oxford University Press, 2017), accessed December 27, 2019, doi: 10.1093/OBO/9780190221911-0055.
66. See Zhan Min-xu and Wu Chia-rong 吳家榮, eds., Special issue on "Quanqiu nanfang huawen wenxue" 全球南方華文文學 [Global South and Sinophone literature] in *Zhongshan renwen xuebao* 中山人文學報 [Sun Yat-sen journal of humanities], issue no. 51 (2021), 1–154.
67. Anne Garland Mahler, "Global South."
68. On the notion of "Cultural China," see note 8. On "Greater China," see "Special Issue: Greater China," ed. David Shambaugh, *The China Quarterly*, no. 136 (December 1993).
69. David Der-wei Wang, *A New Literary History of Modern China*, 13.
70. Edward W. Said, "The Politics of Knowledge," in *Reflections on Exile and Other Essays* (Cambridge, MA: Harvard University Press, 2000), 382.
71. Edward W. Said, "The Politics of Knowledge," 382.
72. Edward W. Said, "The Politics of Knowledge," 382.
73. Edward W. Said, "The Politics of Knowledge," 382.
74. See for instance Jing Tsu, "Weak Links," and Li Yang 李揚, "'Chengdu moshi' yu wenxue yanjiu shiye de difanghua" "成都模式"與文學研究視野的地方化 [The Chengdu model and localizing the horizon of literary studies], *Dangdai wentan* 當代文壇 [Contemporary literary criticism], no. 2 (2020): 91–96.
75. On the conundrums of classifying Chinese literature, see Carlos Rojas, "Language, Ethnicity, and the Politics of Literary Taxonomy."
76. David Porter, "The Crisis of Comparison and the World Literature Debates," *Profession* (2011): 254–55.
77. David Porter, "The Crisis of Comparison," 253.
78. Doreen Massey, "Power-Geometry and a Progressive Sense of Place," in *Mapping the Futures: Local Cultures, Global Change*, ed. Jon Bird, Barry Curtis, Tim Putnam, George Robertson, and Lisa Tickner (London: Routledge, 1993), 66.
79. Arif Dirlik, "Place-Based Imagination: Globalism and the Politics of Place," in *Places and Politics in an Age of Globalization*, ed. Roxann Prazniak and Arik Dirlik (Lanham, MD: Rowman & Littlefield, 2001), 22.

1. DOUBLY LOCAL

1. For instance, *Thick Smoke* is identified as the only pre–World War II novel in Miao Xiu 苗秀, "Daolun" 導論 [Introduction], in *Xinma huawen wenxue daxi diwuji: Xiaoshuo (er)* 新馬華文文學大系第五集：小說（二）[Compendium of

Singapore, Malayan, and Malaysian Chinese-language literature, vol. 5: Fiction (part 2)], ed. Miao Xiu (Singapore: Jiaoyu chubanshe, 1971), 1, 7.

2. This advertisement appears in the front matter of the literary journal *Guangming* 光明 [Light] 1, no. 6 (1936). It appeared alongside another advertisement that promoted the World Literary Repertoire Book Series.

3. To highlight the bind between language and territoriality, I follow Victor Mair in using "topolect" over the more ideologically charged "dialect" to translate the Chinese term *fangyan*, despite "dialect" being the customary term used in the studies of Singapore and Malayan Chinese. See Victor Mair, "What is a Chinese 'Dialect/Topolect'? Reflection on Some Key Sino-English Linguistic Terms," *Sino-Platonic Papers*. 29 (1991): 1–31.

4. The archetype for the protagonist Mao Zhendong 毛振東 was Tan. The other main character Li Mianzhi 李勉之 is likely to be Lin's own self-projection. See Ma Lun 馬崙, *Xinma huawen zuojia qunxiang, 1919–1983* 新馬華文作家群像, 1919–1983 [Biographies of Singapore, Malayan, and Malaysian Chinese writers, 1919–1983] (Singapore: Fengyun Publications, 1984), 12.

5. Tan Yunshan 譚雲山, "Fu *Nongyan* tiju (youba)" 附《濃煙》題句（有跋） [Attached to poem about *Thick Smoke* (a postscript)], *Shenzhen daxue Yindu yanjiu tongxun* 深圳大學印度研究通訊 [Newsletter for Indian studies at Shenzhen University] 2 (2010): 33.

6. In the most recent attempt, Quah Sy Ren identifies the formation's genesis in the first drama performance in the *baihua* 白話 vernacular staged in Singapore in 1913, more than six years earlier than what preceding scholars Fang Xiu 方修 and Miao Xiu averred. See Quah Sy Ren 柯思仁, *Xiju bainian: Xinjiapo huawen xiju, 1913–2013* 戲聚百年：新加坡華文戲劇, 1913–2013 [SCENES: A hundred years of Singapore Chinese-language theater, 1913–2013] (Singapore: Drama Box and National Museum of Singapore, 2013).

7. Fang Xiu 方修 points out that Lin's fictional works had fallen off the radar of the literary circle by the end of the 1930s. See *Zhang Tianbai zuopinxuan* 張天白作品選, ed. Fang Xiu (Singapore: Shanghai shuju, 1979), 1. Zhao Rong has also remonstrated against the neglect of Lin and *Thick Smoke*'s contribution to Mahua literary history. See Yi Duo 以多 (Zhao Rong 趙戎), "Lun Lin Cantian de xiaoshuo" 論林參天的小說 [On Lin Cantian's fictional works], in *Xinshengdai (hedingben)* 新生代（合訂本） [Compilation of the "New Generation" literary supplement], ed. Xie Ke 謝克 (Singapore: Xinshengdai chubanshe, 1968), issue no. 61.

8. Edward W. Said, *Culture and Imperialism* (New York: Vintage Books, 1994), 51.

9. Edward W. Said, *Culture and Imperialism*, 52.

10. For historical overviews on intracommunal relations among the Chinese overseas, see Huei-Ying Kuo, *Networks beyond Empires: Chinese Business and Nationalism in the Hong-Kong-Singapore Corridor, 1914–1941* (Leiden: Brill,

2014), 1–17, and Goh Leng Hoon 吳龍雲, *Zaoyu bangqun: Bincheng huaren shehui de kuabang zuzhi yanjiu* 遭遇幫群：檳城華人社會的跨幫組織研究 [Encountering dialect groups: A study of cross-*bang* organizations in Penang Chinese society] (Singapore: National University of Singapore Department of Chinese Studies and Global Publishing, 2009), 1–20.

11. Lin Cantian, "Jinian xianfu (san)" 紀念先父（三） [In remembrance of my late father (part 3)], *Sin Chew Jit Poh*, May 10, 1935.
12. Lin Cantian, "Wo yu wenxue" 我與文學 [My relationship with literature], in *Xinshengdai (hedingben)*, issue no. 20.
13. Lin Cantian, "Jinian xianfu (wu)" 紀念先父（五） [In remembrance of my late father (part 5)], *Sin Chew Jit Poh*, May 13, 1935.
14. Lin Cantian, "Jinian xianfu (wu)."
15. Fang Xiu outlined the different cohorts of the southbound writers in his *Mahua wenyi sichao de yanbian* 馬華文藝思潮的演變 [The development of Mahua artistic and literary thought] (Singapore: Wanli wenhua qiye, 1970), 45.
16. The biographical information in the rest of this paragraph is assembled from Li Jinzong 李錦宗, *Yunluo de wenxing* 殞落的文星 [The fallen literary stars] (Selangor: Caihong chuban youxian gongsi, 1999), 23; Wei Yun 葦暈, "Xie *Nongyan* de Lin Cantian" 寫《濃煙》的林參天 [Lin Cantian who wrote *Thick Smoke*], in *Wenyuan sanye* 文苑散叶 [The scattered leaves in the literary world] (Kuala Lumpur: Tieshanni chuban youxian gongsi, 1985), 16–17; and Lin Cantian, "Wo yu wenxue."
17. See Ko Chia-cian 高嘉謙, *Yimin, jiangjie yu xiandaixing: Hanshi de nanfang lisan yu shuqing (1895–1945)* 遺民、疆界與現代性：漢詩的南方離散與抒情（1895–1945）[Loyalists, boundary and modernity: Southbound diaspora and lyricism of classical-style Chinese poetry (1895–1945)] (Taipei: Linking Publishing, 2016), 424–33. For other examples of similar transliteration in fiction and poetry, see Yeo Song Nian 楊松年, *Zhanqian Xinma wenxue bendi yishi de xingcheng yu fazhan* 戰前新馬文學本地意識的形成與發展 [The formation and development of local consciousness in prewar Singapore and Malayan literature] (Singapore: National University of Singapore Department of Chinese Studies and Global Publishing, 2001), 76–82.
18. See three short plays written by Lin in *Mahua Xinwenxue daxi V.Xiju ji* 馬華新文學大系（五）·戲劇集 [Compendium of modern Mahua literature, vol. 5: Drama], ed. Fang Xiu (Singapore: Shijie shuju, 1972); "Nanyang de nüpengyou" 南洋的女朋友 [Female friends in Nanyang], 133–50; "Jinbiao" 金錶 [The golden watch], 151–63; "Yintong" 隱痛 [Hidden pain], 164–72.
19. Lin Cantian, "Wo yu wenxue."
20. Shelly Chan, *Diaspora's Homeland: Modern China in the Age of Global Migration* (Durham, NC: Duke University Press, 2018), 50.

21. See Leander Seah, "Between East Asia and Southeast Asia: Nanyang Studies, Chinese Migration, and National Jinan University, 1927–1940," *Translocal Chinese: East Asian Perspectives* 11, no. 1 (2017): 32, 41–50.
22. Chong Yee-Voon 鍾怡雯 offers a brief but similar argument in "Zhongguo nanyou(lai) wenren yu Mahua sanwenshi" 中國南遊（來）文人與馬華散文史 [Southern-touring (incoming) scholars from China and the history of Mahua prose], *Zhongguo xiandai wenxue* 中國現代文學 [Modern Chinese literature] 25 (2014): 173. See also volumes 17–20 on Nanyang and the Malay Archipelago in the 39-volume *Jindai yuwai youji congkan* 近代域外遊記叢刊 [A series of foreign travelogues in modern times], ed. Wang Qiang 王強 (Nanjing: Fenghuang chubanshe, 2016). Recent scholarly attention on China's interest in Nanyang during the Republican period include Shelly Chan, *Diaspora's Homeland*, 48–74; and Chen Ying 陳穎, "Xiandai Zhongguo zhishi puxizhong de Nanyang, 1911–1937" 現代中國知識譜系中的南洋, 1911–1937 [Nanyang in modern China's knowledge system, 1911–1937], PhD diss., Nanyang Technological University, 2018.
23. See the advertisement in the back matter of Fu Donghua 傅東華, *Shanhutao ji* 山胡桃集 [The hickory collection] (Shanghai: Shenghuo shudian, 1935). It should be noted that Fu published *Little Po's Birthday* as a single title, but the novella was first serialized in 1931 in the journal *Literary Monthly* (Xiaoshuo yuebao 小說月報), also based in Shanghai. See Brian Bernards, "From Diasporic Nationalism to Transcolonial Consciousness: Lao She's Singaporean Satire, *Little Po's Birthday*," *Modern Chinese Literature and Culture* 26, no. 1 (2014): 11.
24. Lin Cantian, "Malaiya wenyi chenji de yuanyin" 馬來亞文藝沉寂的原因 [The reason for the vapid state of Malayan literary arts], in *Mahua Xinwenxue daxi I·Lilun piping yiji* 馬華新文學大系（一） 理論批評一集 [Compendium of modern Mahua literature, vol. 1: Theory and critique, part 1], ed. Fang Xiu (Singapore: Shijie shuju, 1972), 481. Lin was not the only member of the literary circle who considered the United States as the model for Malayan Chinese literature. See Lianqing 鍊青, "Bianzhe di'erci de xianci" 編者第二次的獻辭 [The editor's second pledge], in *Mahua Xinwenxue daxi X · Chuban shiliao* 馬華新文學大系（十）· 出版史料 [Compendium of modern Mahua literature, vol. 10: Historical material on publications], ed. Fang Xiu (Singapore: Shijie shuju, 1972), 124.
25. Lin Cantian, "Malaiya wenyi chenji de yuanyin," 478.
26. Fu Donghua 傅東華, "Shijie wenyi de qiantu" 世界文藝的前途 [The future of world literary arts], *Qiantu zazhi* 前途雜誌 [Prospect] 1, no. 1 (1933): 1–2.
27. Fang Xiu, *Mahua wenyi sichao de yanbian*, 10.
28. For an outline of the waves of literary movements striving for autonomy, see Fang Xiu, "Daoyan" 導言 [Introductory remarks], in *Mahua Xinwenxue daxi I·Lilun piping yiji*, 16–19.

29. Feiming 廢名 (Qiu Shizhen 丘士珍), "Difang zuojia tan" 地方作家談 [On local writers], in *Mahua Xinwenxue daxi I·Lilun piping yiji*, 260.
30. Wei Yun, "Xie *Nongyan* de Lin Cantian," 15.
31. *Xinma huawen wenyi cidian* 新馬華文文藝辭典 [Dictionary of Singapore-Malaysia Chinese literature], ed. Zhao Rong (Singapore: Education Publications Bureau, 1979), 246. For a cognate exposition worth documenting: "The Chinese who come from the provinces north of Fujian and Guangdong are generally called in Singapore, *Waijiangren*, i.e., 'people beyond the Changjiang [the Yangtze River],' or Sanjiang ren, i.e., 'people of the three jiang' (Jiangxi, Jiangsu and Zhejiang)"; see Cheng Lim-Keak, *Social Change and the Chinese in Singapore* (Singapore: Singapore University Press, 1985), 22. Colloquially, the term *waijiang ren* is also interchangeable with "Shanghainese," another blanket category for migrants from northern and central China. See Shen Lingxie, "The Sanjiangren in Singapore," *Chinese Southern Diaspora Studies* 5 (2011/2012): 175–81.
32. See, for instance, Yen Ching-hwang, *A Social History of the Chinese in Singapore and Malaya, 1800–1911* (Singapore: Oxford University Press, 1986), 42, 76; Mak Lau Fong 麥留芳, *Fangyanqun rentong: Zaoqi Xingma huaren de fenlei faze* 方言群認同：早期星馬華人的分類法則 [Dialect group identity: A study of Chinese subethnic groups in early Malaya] (Taipei: Institute of Ethnology, Academia Sinica, 1985), 124. For more on the prominence of the *waijiang ren* in the book trade despite their minority status in the Singapore Chinese community, see Shen Lingxie, "The Sanjiangren in Singapore," 195.
33. Lin Mang 林莽 (Lin Cantian), "Yijiusansi nian Malaiya wentan yipie" 一九三四年馬來亞文壇一瞥 [A glance at the 1934 Malayan literary circle], in *Mahua Xinwenxue daxi X · Chuban shiliao*, 450. See Ma Lun, *Xinma huawen zuojia qunxiang, 1919–1983*, 12, which notes Lin's pseudonym.
34. A local critic corroborated that the debate over "local writers" and the controversy over "mass language" were indeed conducted in *Nanyang Siang Pau* and *Sin Chew Jit Poh* respectively. See Ge Kong 哥空, "Yijiusanwu nian Malaiya wentan" 一九三五年馬來亞文壇 [The 1935 Malayan literary circle], in *Mahua Xinwenxue daxi X · Chuban shiliao*, 468. For a sense of the inter-newspaper rivalry related to topolectal divides and native place loyalties, see Chui Kwei Chiang 崔貴強, *Xinjiapo huawen baokan yu baoren* 新加坡華文報刊與報人 [The Chinese newspapers and newspapermen of Singapore] (Singapore: Haitian wenhua, 1993), 142–44.
35. Lin Cantian, "Malaiya wenyi chenji de yuanyin," 479–80.
36. The novel's border-crossing biography did not end then. Due to the onset of World War II, the Shanghai edition did not circulate widely. In 1959, the Youth

Book Company—a publishing enterprise based in Singapore and later known for nurturing regional Sinophone literary works—produced a Malayan edition after the colonial government imposed a wide-ranging ban on publications from China and Hong Kong in 1958. See Lin Cantian, *Nongyan* [Thick smoke] (Singapore: Xinjiapo qingnian shuju, 1959).

37. The critic Liang Shan 梁山 lamented in 1934: "The community of Nanyang writers constantly harbors the erroneous view of making it big by ingratiating themselves with the Shanghai literary world. Why do they pursue such an overly ambitious goal? Isn't it true that Nanyang has a great and beautiful literary field? It is truly an erroneous view that they have, to refuse investing effort in opening up [the local literary space] and forsake what is near for what is faraway." See C Jun C 君 [Mr. C] (Liang Shan), "Difang zuojia jieshao de shangque" 地方作家介紹的商榷 [A deliberation on the introduction of local writers], in *Mahua Xinwenxue daxi I·Lilun piping yiji*, 263. Ma Lun notes Liang's pen name in his *Xinma huawen zuojia qunxiang, 1919–1983*, 15.

38. On the historical reception of *Thick Smoke* in the 1930s, see Kuo Shiu Nue 郭秀女, "Changpian xiaoshuo *Nongyan* de duocengmian yiyi" 長篇小說《濃煙》的多層面意義 [The multifaceted significance of the novel *Thick Smoke*], in *Xinma huawen wenxue yanjiu xinguancha* 新馬華文文學研究新觀察 [New observations on Singapore and Malaysian Chinese literary studies], ed. Luo Futeng 羅福騰 (Singapore: UniSIM Centre for Chinese Studies and Global Publishing, 2012), 135–76.

39. See, for instance, Mo Yimei, *Local Color in Malayan Chinese Fiction: A New Approach, 1920–1937* (Bochum: Brockmeyer, 1992), 80–94.

40. These materials are compiled in the two authoritative anthologies: Fang Xiu ed., *Mahua Xinwenxue daxi* 馬華新文學大系 [Compendium of modern Mahua literature], 10 vols. (Singapore: Shijie shuju, 1971–1972); and Xinshe *Xinma huawen wenxue daxi* bianji weiyuanhui 新社新馬華文文學大系編輯委員會 [Editorial Committee for *Compendium of Singapore, Malayan, and Malaysian Chinese-Language Literature*, Journal of the Island Society] ed., *Xinma huawen wenxue daxi* 新馬華文文學大系 [Compendium of Singapore, Malayan, and Malaysian Chinese-language literature], 8 vols. (Singapore: Jiaoyu chubanshe, 1971).

41. Yi Duo (Zhao Rong), "Lun Lin Cantian de xiaoshuo," issue no. 61; Yeo Song Nian, *Zhanqian Xinma wenxue bendi yishi de xingcheng yu fazhan*, 82–83, 163–64; Ng Kim Chew, *Mahua wenxue yu Zhongguoxing* 馬華文學與中國性 [The spirit of China in Malaysian Chinese literature] (Taipei: Yuanzun wenhua, 1998), 55–56.

42. Alison Groppe, *Sinophone Malaysian Literature: Not Made in China* (Amherst, NY: Cambria Press, 2013), 70.

43. Ng Kim Chew, *Mahua wenxue yu Zhongguoxing*, 56–58; 77–78.

44. Ng Kim Chew, *Mahua wenxue: Neizai zhongguo, yuyan yu wenxueshi* 馬華文學: 內在中國、語言與文學史 [Mahua literature: Internal China, language and literary history] (Kuala Lumpur: Huazi Resource and Research Centre Bhd., 1996), 22.
45. Victor Purcell, *Basic English for Malaya* (Singapore: Lithographies Limited, 1937), 7.
46. Here, and for the rest of the extract, I use "Indian" to render the Chinese term 吉寧 which actually corresponds more closely to "Keling," an offensive term today with derogatory connotations.
47. Lin Cantian, *Nongyan* [Thick smoke] (Shanghai: Wenxue chubanshe, 1936), 3–4, 14. Subsequent citations from the novel will be included directly in the text in parentheses. The underlined sentence in this excerpt denotes that it was originally rendered in the English alphabet. I insert Chinese characters to mark the places where Lin uses Chinese characters to transcribe non-Mandarin and non-English speech. The "(*Note 1)" in-text annotation indicates the chapter's endnotes in the original text.
48. Other sentence-level formulations can be found in many parts of the novel. See Lin Cantian, *Nongyan*, 11, 20–22, 67, 115, 126–27, 170, 174–76, 244, 314, 487–88.
49. Yi Duo, "Lun Lin Cantian de xiaoshuo," issue no. 61.
50. Huei-Ying Kuo, *Networks Beyond Empires*, 3.
51. Cheng Lim-Keak, *Social Change and the Chinese in Singapore*, xvi.
52. Notably, the *waijiang ren* figure appears again in Lin's second novel, also as a new member of a school's teaching staff. See Lin Cantian, *Rezhang* 熱瘴 [Tropical miasma] (Singapore: Qingnian shuju, 1961), 8, 117, 267.
53. Li Zhongyu 李鍾鈺, *Xinjiapo fengtuji* 新嘉坡風土記 [A record of the local customs of Singapore], in *Zhongguo gujizhong youguan Xinjiapo Malaixiya ziliao huibian* 中國古籍中有關新加坡馬來西亞資料彙編 [A compilation of materials on Singapore and Malaysia in ancient Chinese books], ed. Yu Dingbang 余定邦 and Huang Chongyan 黃重言 (Beijing: Zhonghua shuju, 2002), 190.
54. For an account of the communities of acculturated Chinese also known as the Baba-Nyonya, see Tan Chee Beng, *Chinese Peranakan Heritage in Malaysia and Singapore* (Kuala Lumpur: Penerbit Fajar Bakti Sdn. Bhd., 1993).
55. Lin Cantian, "Tan wode xiezuo" 談我的寫作 [About my writing practice], in *Xinshengdai (hedingben)* [Compilation of the "New Generation" literary supplement],), issue no. 99. Original emphases.
56. Yasemin Yildiz, *Beyond the Mother Tongue: The Postmonolingual Condition* (New York: Fordham University Press, 2012), 25. Original emphasis.
57. Fu Donghua, "Shijie wenyi de qiantu," 8.
58. The May Fourth writer Lao She 老舍 adopted narrative strategies that resemble Lin's. In his 1931 novella "Xiaopo de shengri" 小坡的生日 [Little Po's

birthday]—also set in Nanyang—he calls the young protagonist Xiaopo's dreamscape "Shadowland" (ying'er guo 影兒國). Lao She's only work on Singapore, where he sojourned in 1929, also captures the divisions within the local ethnic Chinese community. Early in the tale, Xiaopo claims that the Malays must be from Shanghai because he notices the similar ways in which his father, who is from Guangdong, looks down on the "Shanghainese" (a shorthand for waijiang ren, see note 31) and the Malays. See Lao She, "Xiaopo de shengri" 小坡的生日 [Little Po's birthday], in Lao She wenji: Di'er juan 老舍文集：第二卷 [An anthology of Lao She's works] vol. 2, (Beijing: Renmin wenxue chubanshe, 1980), 14, 94.

59. Lin Cantian, "Zixu" 自序 [Self-preface], in Nongyan, 3.
60. Lin Cantian, "Jinian xianfu (yi)" [In remembrance of my late father (part 1)], Sin Chew Jit Poh, May 8, 1935.
61. David L. Kenley, New Culture in a New World: The May Fourth Movement and the Chinese Diaspora in Singapore, 1919–1932 (New York: Routledge, 2003), 183.
62. Lin Cantian, Nongyan, 2–3. I include Chinese characters to show how Lin uses them to transcribe non-Mandarin articulations, as well as to indicate the specific Chinese characters he cites as examples for his argument.
63. See Yijiao 一礁, "Lingling suisui: Gei Zeng Aidi xiansheng" 零零碎碎—給曾艾狄先生 [Some miscellaneous issues: To Mr Zeng Aidi], in Mahua Xinwenxue daxi I·Lilun piping yiji, 310.
64. For articles on the debate over "mass language" and the Latinization of the Chinese script in Malaya, see Mahua Xinwenxue daxi I · Lilun piping yiji, 332–64; Mahua Xinwenxue daxi X · Chuban shiliao, 454, 467, 495–96. The debate is omitted from Lin Jin 林錦, Zhanqian wunian xinma wenxue lilun yanjiu, 1937–1941 戰前五年新馬文學理論研究, 1931–1941 [A study on prewar Singapore-Malayan literary theory, 1937–1941] (Singapore: Singapore Tong An Association, 1992), the usual guide to literary criticism of that period. It is also missing from Tee Kim Tong's bilingual expositions, neither mentioned in "Sinophone Malaysian Literature: An Overview," in Sinophone Studies: A Critical Reader, ed. Shu-mei Shih, Chien-hsin Tsai, and Brian Bernards (New York: Columbia University Press, 2013), 304–14, nor in Malaixiya huayu yuxi wenxue 馬來西亞華語語系文學 [Sinophone Malaysian literature] (Selangor: Got One Publisher Sdn Bhd, 2011), 149–51.
65. Li Jinzong, Yunluo de wenxing, 24.
66. All quotations in this paragraph are extracted from Lin Mang (Lin Cantian), "Yijiusansi nian Malaiya wentan yipie," 454.
67. Lin Cantian, "Nanyang yu dazhong yuwen" 南洋與大眾語文 [Nanyang and a language of the masses], Sin Chew Jit Poh, February 7 and 8, 1935. Located within the British Library holdings, the article fills the gap in the combined microfilm

collections at the National Library Board (Singapore) and the National University of Singapore. The piece, which has been excluded from Fang Xiu's magisterial compendium, was written a month after Lin's double commentaries in *Sin Chew Jit Poh*. All three pieces were written just right before Lin set *Thick Smoke* to paper.

68. Lin Cantian, "Nanyang yu dazhong yuwen," *Sin Chew Jit Poh*, February 8, 1935.
69. There was palpable concern among critics for a specific method of implementation to produce concrete works termed as "*huose*" 貨色 (goods). See for instance Du Can 杜殘, "Santan dazhongyu" 三談大眾語 [On mass language (part 3)], in *Mahua Xinwenxue daxi I·Lilun piping yiji*, 347–49.
70. Fan Cheng also suggested the promotion of specific topolectal expressions that have gained popular traction to enrich the "mass language," which functions as the lingua franca. See Fan Cheng 樊塍 "Wo duiyu dazhongyu wenxue de yijian" 我對於大眾語文學的意見 [My views on literature written in "mass language"], in *Mahua Xinwenxue daxi I · Lilun piping yiji*, 338–39.
71. Liangyan Ge, *Out of the Margins: The Rise of Chinese Vernacular Fiction* (Honolulu: University of Hawai'i Press, 2001), 7. Original emphases.
72. The underlined parts in the excerpt are rendered in English in the original text.
73. Meir Sternberg, "Polylingualism as Reality and Translation as Mimesis," *Poetics Today* 2, no. 4 (1981): 222.
74. Meir Sternberg, "Polylingualism as Reality," 225.
75. Meir Sternberg, "Polylingualism as Reality," 231–32.
76. Meir Sternberg, "Polylingualism as Reality," 225, 230.
77. Meir Sternberg, "Polylingualism as Reality," 231.
78. Lin's English proficiency can be inferred from how he translated and published an excerpt from Allardyce Nicoll's *An Introduction to Dramatic Theory*. See Allardyce Nicoll, "Xiju piping gaiguan" 戲劇批評概觀 [An introduction to dramatic theory], trans. Lin Cantian, *Sin Chew Jit Poh*, May 20, 1934. In a 1935 article, he mentioned that he could not read Malay, but had read Malay love poetry through English translations. See Lin Cantian, "Malaiya wenyi chenji de yuanyin," 478.
79. Lin depicts his writing endeavor as a solitary activity of his frugal life. See Lin Cantian, "Tan wode xiezuo," and Chen Zhengyan 陳征雁, "Mahua xiaoshuojia tan chuangzuo zhi'er" 馬華小說家談創作之二 [Mahua fiction authors on creative writing (part 2)], in *Xinma huawen wenxue daxi dibaji: Shiliao* 新馬華文文學大系第八集: 史料 [Compendium of Singapore, Malayan, and Malaysian Chinese-language literature, vol. 8: Historical material], ed. Zhao Rong (Singapore: Jiaoyu chubanshe, 1971), 263. However, the incorporation of Malay and Chinese topolects unfamiliar to him casts doubt on the veracity of his discourse.

80. For Hokkien discourses, he either used the Chinese script as a pronunciation-annotating tool for transcription or made explicit attributions, unlike Cantonese, for which Lin drew upon its special Chinese characters to render the novel's ending, which features a dialogue between Li and a Cantonese-speaking school helper (487–88). For a comprehensive list of such topolect-related renderings, see Kho Tong Guan 許通元, "Yanshao de huajiao *Nongyan*: Lin Cantian shoubu changpian de Mahua wenxue 'jingdianlun'" 延燒的華教《濃煙》：林參天首部長篇的馬華文學"經典論" (The ongoing *Thick Smoke* in Chinese education: Rethinking the discourse of canonicity in Mahua literature through Lin Cantian's first novel), *Nanfang yanjiu baogao xilie* 南方研究報告系列 [Southern working paper series] 2 (2016): 18–22.
81. Lin Cantian, "Tan wode xiezuo."
82. Lin Cantian, "Zixu," 3.
83. To show Lin's transliteration approach beyond rendering lexical items, I include the Chinese characters he adopted to transcribe Malay dialogue.
84. One well-known example is the earliest Chinese-Malay dictionary *Huayi tongyu* 華夷通語 [Language bridger between the Chinese and the non-Chinese] compiled by Lin Hengnan 林衡南, which was printed in Singapore in 1877. The dictionary can be browsed at "BookSG: A digital collection of Singapore and Southeast Asia's print heritage," accessed September 11, 2019, http://eresources.nlb.gov.sg/printheritage/detail/3b07f148-8b6f-492f-b2fa-7c1c3dc1f188.aspx.
85. Meimei 梅梅, "*Nongyan* duhou"《濃煙》讀後 [Reflections after reading *Thick Smoke*], *Sin Chew Jit Poh* 星洲日報, January 18, 1937.
86. Lin Cantian, "Tan wode xiezuo."
87. This capacious conception of *huayu* (Chinese language) that includes Sinitic topolects was also prevalent among ethnic Chinese in Singapore and Malaya in the 1950s and 1960s. On this important discovery through elucidating the forgotten lineage of *huayu* cinema in Southeast Asia, see Hee Wai-Siam 許維賢, *Huayu dianying zai hou-Malaixiya: Tuqiang fengge, huayifeng yu zuozhelun* 華語電影在後馬來西亞：土腔風格、華夷風與作者論 [Post-Malaysian Chinese-language film: Accented style, Sinophone and auteur theory] (Taipei: Linking Publishing, 2018), 36–43.
88. Meir Sternberg, "Polylingualism as Reality," 224.
89. Lin Cantian, "Tan wode xiezuo."
90. Lin Cantian, "Wo yu wenxue."
91. For a discussion on Qu Qiubai's stance on vernacularization and mass reception, see Paul G. Pickowicz, *Marxist Literary Thought in China: The Influence of Ch'ü Ch'iu-pai* (Berkeley: University of California Press, 1981), 157–59.

92. Emphases in italics in both excerpts are mine. The second half of the novel sees several more instances of this technique (318, 335, 368, 394).
93. Tan Yunshan commented in the 1950s on the occasion of the reprint of *Thick Smoke* that the novel was written in the form of "popular arts" (*tongsu wenyi de xingshi* 通俗文藝的形式). See Tan Yunshan, "Fu 'Nongyan' tiju (youba)," 33. Writing under his pen name, the critic Zhao Rong regards the intrusive narrative voice as "superfluous parts" that resemble the narrative device in traditional "chapter novels." See Yi Duo, "Lun Lin Cantian de xiaoshuo," issue no. 63.
94. Liangyan Ge, *Out of the Margins*, 197.
95. Liangyan Ge, *Out of the Margins*, 192.
96. Liangyan Ge, *Out of the Margins*, 186.
97. Liangyan Ge, *Out of the Margins*, 192.
98. Liangyan Ge, *Out of the Margins*, 21.
99. Meir Sternberg, "Polylingualism as Reality," 233.
100. Ng Kim Chew, "Huawen shaoshu wenxue—lisan xiandaixing de weijing zhilü" 華文少數文學——離散現代性的未竟之旅 [Minor Sinophone literature: Diasporic modernity's incomplete journey], in *Huawen xiaowenxue de Malaixiya ge'an* 華文小文學的馬來西亞個案 [Minor literature in Chinese: The case of Malaysia] (Taipei: Maitian, 2015), 109–11.
101. Ng Kim Chew, "Meiyou weizhi de weizhi" 沒有位置的位置 [A position that is an inconsequential position], in his prose collection *Huo xiaole* 火笑了 [The fire smiled] (Taipei: Maitian, 2015), 286–87.
102. Ng Kim Chew, "Meiyou weizhi de weizhi," 287.
103. Ng Kim Chew, "Huawen shaoshu wenxue," 110.
104. My translation is modified from Ng Kim Chew, "Minor Sinophone Literature: Diasporic Modernity's Incomplete Journey," in *Global Chinese Literature: Critical Essays*, trans. Andrew Rodekohr, ed. Jing Tsu and David Der-wei Wang (Leiden: Brill, 2010), 19. In this English version, *geren fangyan* is translated as "idiolect," which does not capture the dimension of locality.
105. Ng has said, "I don't think Lin Cantian writes fiction well." See Kho Tong Guan 許通元, "Huang Jinshu zhuanfang" 黃錦樹專訪 [An interview with Ng Kim Chew], *Chao Foon* 蕉風 509 (2015): 56.
106. On how Lin compares literary composition to cultivating a distinctive calligraphic style and writers' personal styles to human countenances, see Cheow Thia Chan 曾昭程, "Hechu mi jiaguo, wendi qiu xiangyi: Zhanqian zuojia Lin Cantian de xiezuo shijian" 何處覓家國, 文地求相宜: 戰前作家林參天的寫作實踐 [In search of home and country, toward the mutual becoming of place and literature: The writing practice of pre–World War II author Lin Cantian], *Lianhe Zaobao* 聯合早報, May 21, 2019.

2. CHANNELING EXEMPLARITY

1. See the section "The promotion of South Seas color" in *Mahua Xinwenxue daxi I · Lilun piping yiji* 馬華新文學大系（一）·理論批評一集 [Compendium of modern Mahua literature, vol. 1: Theory and critique, part 1], ed. Fang Xiu 方修 (Singapore: Shijie shuju, 1972), 119–49.
2. Yu Dafu 郁達夫, "Jige wenti" 幾個問題 [A few questions], in *Mahua Xinwenxue daxi II · Lilun piping erji* 馬華新文學大系（二）·理論批評二集 [Compendium of modern Mahua literature, vol. 2: Theory and critique, part 2], ed. Fang Xiu (Singapore: Shijie shuju, 1971), 444–48.
3. For selected responses to Yu's remarks, see *Mahua Xinwenxue daxi II·Lilun piping erji*, 449–71. For an analysis of why the Mahua writing community was dissatisfied with Yu's advice, see Yeo Song Nian 楊松年, "Cong Yu Dafu 'Jige wenti' yinqi de zhenglun kan dangshi Nanyang zhishifenzi de xintai" 從郁達夫"幾個問題"引起的爭論看當時南洋知識份子的心態 [The polemic of Yu Dafu's "Several Problems" and Chinese intellectuals in Nanyang], *Yazhou wenhua* 亞洲文化 [Asian culture], issue no. 23 (1999): 103–11.
4. Han's real name was Rosalie Matilda Kwanghu Chou 周光瑚. For a concise biography of Han that covers her full writing career, see Cui Feng and Alex Tickell, "Han Suyin: The Little Voice of Decolonizing Asia," *Journal of Postcolonial Writing* 57, no. 2 (2021): 147–49.
5. Yu Dafu, "Jige wenti," 446.
6. Fiona Lee, "Neutralizing English: Han Suyin and the Language Politics of Third World Literature," *Journal of Postcolonial Writing* 57, no. 2 (2021): 226–40.
7. Discussion in this chapter is based on Han Suyin, *And the Rain My Drink* (Boston: Little, Brown and Company, 1956). The original title of this publication was preceded by three ellipsis points, as follows: *… and the Rain My Drink*. To avoid the appearance that words were redacted from the title, I adopt the formulation *And the Rain My Drink* as the novel's title throughout this book. Citations from the novel will henceforth be given in-text in parentheses.
8. For the most comprehensive account of Han's sojourn in Southeast Asia, see Ina Zhang Xing Hong 章星虹, *Han Suyin zai Malaiya: xingyi, xiezuo he shehui canyu* (1952–1964) 韓素音在馬來亞: 行醫、寫作和社會參與 (1952–1964) [Han Suyin in Malaya: Physician, writer, and public intellectual (1952–1964)] (Singapore: Center for Chinese Language and Culture, Nanyang Technological University, and Global Publishing, 2016). I supplement Zhang's account and Han's memoir *My House Has Two Doors* (London: Triad Granada, 1982) with archival findings mainly comprising Han's private correspondences.

9. Han Suyin, "FREEDOM SING MERDEKA," Folder 1(b), Box 18, Han Suyin Collection, Howard Gotlieb Archival Research Center, Boston University (hereafter cited as "Han Suyin Collection").
10. For his specific definition on the "plural society," see J. S. Furnivall, *Netherlands India: A Study of Plural Economy* (Cambridge: Cambridge University Press, 1939), 446.
11. In her memoir, Han claims that she closed her medical practice in 1961 "to document myself fully on China, the Chinese Revolution" (Han Suyin, *My House Has Two Doors*, 405). An archival finding rectifies her mistaken memory: In a 1959 letter, Han's secretary informed her publisher about the clinic's closure (Menina Russell King to Jonathan Cape Ltd., September 22, 1959, Box 72, Han Suyin Collection).
12. On her exchanges with Nanyang University students, see Han Suyin, *My House Has Two Doors*, 106, 282. For an account of her involvement with the institute, see Han, *My House Has Two Doors*, 283–86.
13. "And the Rain My Drink," *The Straits Times*, July 1, 1956.
14. In the early 1960s, Heinemann Education Books Ltd. in London started the African Writers Series that became a towering cultural institution by publishing Anglophone works by literary authors native to Africa. See Alan Hill, "The African Writers Series," *Research in African Literatures* 2, no. 1 (1971): 18–20. For an account of the post–World War II British book trade in relation to its ex-colonies outside Europe, see Alan Hill, "Books for a Commonwealth, Publishing Locally or from London," *Times Literary Supplement*, August 10, 1962.
15. Editorial postscript to Han Suyin, "The Creation of a Malayan Literature," *Eastern World* (May 1957): 21.
16. "Han Suyin Tells the Jungle Girl's Tale," *The Straits Times*, March 10, 1953.
17. Only six out of the thirteen chapters were published in the Chinese edition of *Rain*. See the translator's preface of Han Suyin, *Canfeng yinlu* 餐風飲露 [And the rain my drink], trans. Ly Singko 李星可 (Singapore: Youth Book Company, 1958), 7–8. It remains unclear why the remaining seven chapters, despite being translated according to Ly, were excised from publication. For information on the two-book series, see back matter of Han Suyin, *Qingshan bulao (shangce)* 青山不老（上冊）[The mountain is young, vol. 1], trans. Ly Singko (Singapore: Youth Book Company, 1959).
18. For the list of the banned Beijing, Shanghai, and Hong Kong bookstores, see "Fangmi dianfu xuanchuan, pumie seqing wenhua: Zhengfu yuanyin Buliang Kanwu Faling jinzhi gongchan Zhongguo ji Xianggang wushisanjia chubanwu shu Xing" 防弭顛覆宣傳·撲滅色情文化：政府援引不良刊物法令禁止共產中國及香港五十三家出版物輸星 [Preventing and eliminating subversive propaganda, eradicating

pornographic culture: Government cites the Undesirable Publications Act to proscribe supply to Singapore of fifty three publishers' products from Communist China and Hong Kong], *Nanyang Siang Pau* 南洋商報, May 23, 1958.

19. Tee Kim Tong 張錦忠, *Nanyang lunshu: Mahua wenxue yu wenhua shuxing* 南洋論述：馬華文學與文化屬性 [Studying Southeast Asian Chinese: Essays on Chinese-Malaysian literature and cultural identity] (Taipei: Maitian, 2003), 179–85.

20. Ina Zhang Xing Hong 章星虹, "Shui wei Han Suyin zuo zhongwen fanyi?" 誰為韓素音做中文翻譯？ [Who were the Chinese-language translators of Han Suyin?], *Lianhe Zaobao* 聯合早報, September 30, 2013. For a common bibliographic reference on Mahua writers in which Han is listed, see Ma Lun 馬崙, *Xinma huawen zuojia qunxiang, 1919–1983* 新馬華文作家群像, 1919–1983 [Biographies of Singapore, Malayan and Malaysian Chinese-language writers, 1919–1983] (Singapore: Fengyun Publications, 1984), 337.

21. Emma J. Teng, "On Not Looking Chinese: Does 'Mixed Race' Decenter the Han from Chineseness?" in *Critical Han Studies: The History, Representation, and Identity of China's Majority*, ed. Thomas Mullaney, James Patrick Leibold, Stéphane Gros, and Eric Armand Vanden Bussche (Berkeley: University of California Press, 2012), 64–65.

22. Bill Ashcroft, Gareth Griffiths, and Helen Tiffin, *The Empire Writes Back: Theory and Practice in Postcolonial Literatures*, 2nd ed. (London: Routledge, 2002), 50.

23. Han Suyin to Malcolm MacDonald, August 24, 1963, Box 87, Han Suyin Collection.

24. David Damrosch, *What is World Literature?* (Princeton, NJ: Princeton University Press, 2003), 218.

25. David Damrosch, *What is World Literature?*, 228.

26. David Damrosch, *What is World Literature?*, 213.

27. Editorial postscript to Han Suyin, "The Creation of a Malayan Literature," 21.

28. Han Suyin to Jonathan Cape, February 16, 1953, Box 73, Han Suyin Collection. Emphasis mine.

29. Han Suyin to Jonathan Cape, July 24, 1953, Box 73, Han Suyin Collection.

30. Han Suyin to Jonathan Cape, February 16, 1953, Box 73, Han Suyin Collection.

31. Han Suyin to Hans Taussig, n.d., Box 29, Han Suyin Collection.

32. Han Suyin to Jonathan Cape, June 24, 1955, Box 73, Han Suyin Collection.

33. *Freedom Shout Merdeka* was advertised as the forthcoming volume in the back matter of Han Suyin, *And the Rain My Drink* (London: Jonathan Cape, 1956). See note 7 above regarding the original U.S. publication title, which also applies to this title.

34. In one vignette, Suyin emphatically declares to her interlocutor: "I am a doctor and a writer. I intend to watch what is going on, with cynical compassion."

Box 18, Folder 1(b) "Sequel to *And the Rain My Drink*," Han Suyin Collection. None of extant fragments of *Freedom* suggests that the character finished her book, a situation that mirrors the fate of *Rain*'s sequel in real life.

35. Han Suyin, "Writing about Malaya," *PETIR* [Lightning] (January 1957): 3.
36. Han Suyin, "The Creation of a Malayan Literature," 21.
37. *PETIR*, the People Action Party's periodical, had a multilingual reach. For the Chinese version of Han Suyin's article in the party organ, see Han Suyin 韓素英 [*sic*], "Xie youguan Malaiya de shi" 寫有關馬來亞的事 [Writing about Malaya], trans. Dunbi 鈍筆, *Xingdongbao* 行動報 (January 1957): 4.
38. Han Suyin, *My House Has Two Doors*, 83.
39. Han Suyin to Jonathan Cape, n.d. (but filed under "1954" folder), Box 73, Han Suyin Collection.
40. Han Suyin, "Why I Like Malaya—Home of Many Races," *Malayan Police Magazine* (March 1961): 17.
41. Han Suyin, "Why I Like Malaya," 17.
42. Edward W. Said, *Orientalism* (New York: Vintage Books, 1979), 6. On Han's comments to her Malayan audience, see Han, "Writing About Malaya," 3.
43. Han Suyin to Wren Howard, January 26, 1962, Box 72, Han Suyin Collection.
44. Han Suyin, *My House Has Two Doors*, 110–11. As Zhang Xing Hong points out, this representation of the encounter in her memoir is congruent with the corresponding report in *Nanyang Siang Pau* 南洋商報, one of the most influential Chinese-language newspapers in Singapore. On the same day, however, *The Straits Times*, the main English newspaper in the British colony, claimed that she was appointed as a translator. See Zhang Xing Hong, *Han Suyin zai Malaiya*, 188–89.
45. Mani Mann, "Asia—Above All," magazine interview, unspecified source, dated March 27, 1964, Box 14, Han Suyin Collection. For an analysis of Han's teaching endeavor at Nanyang University, see Ina Zhang, "A Dissenting Voice: The Politics of Han Suyin's Literary Activities in Late Colonial and Postcolonial Malaya and Singapore," *Journal of Postcolonial Writing* 57, no. 2 (2021): 166–67.
46. Mani Mann, "Asia—Above All."
47. Mani Mann, "Asia—Above All."
48. See for instance, her speeches such as "Development of a Malayan Chinese Literature" (1961) and "Some Impressions of Writing in English within the Context of Singapore and Malaya" (1961), found in Box 60 and Box 62, respectively, in the Han Suyin Collection, which I will analyze later in the chapter.
49. "The English Language," a report carrying Han's speech at the Foyles Luncheon in London on October 10, 1958, Box 14, Han Suyin Collection, viii.
50. Bill Ashcroft, Gareth Griffiths, and Helen Tiffin, *Empire Writes Back*, 34.

51. Bill Ashcroft, "Bridging the Silence: Inner Translation and the Metonymic Gap," in *Language and Translation in Postcolonial Literatures: Multilingual Contexts, Translational Texts*, ed. Simona Bertacco (New York: Routledge, 2013), 17.
52. Mani Mann, "Asia Above All."
53. The first study to describe English of the Malay Peninsula appeared in the 1970s, about two decades after *Rain* was published. See Siew-Yue Killingley, "Clause and Sentence Types in Malayan English," *Orbis* 21, no. 2 (1972): 537–48, as quoted in Anthea Fraser Gupta, "The Pragmatic Particles of Singapore Colloquial English," *Journal of Pragmatics* 18, no. 1 (1992): 47.
54. From being theorized as signaling solidarity between interlocutors, to being characterized as serving the pragmatic function of making an assertion, *lah* has become "the most stereotypical feature of the English of Singapore and Malaysia." See Anthea Fraser Gupta, "The Pragmatic Particles of Singapore Colloquial English," 35.
55. On the grammatical idiosyncrasies of Malayan English, which are studied later in the contexts of Malaysian and Singapore English, see John Platt and Heidi Weber, *English in Singapore and Malaysia: Status, Features, Functions* (Kuala Lumpur: Oxford University Press, 1980); and David Deterding, Low Ee Ling, and Adam Brown, eds., *English in Singapore: Research on Grammar* (Singapore: McGraw-Hill Education [Asia], 2003).
56. Han Suyin, Box 18, Folder 1(b) "Sequel to *And the Rain My Drink*," Han Suyin Collection.
57. Han Suyin, "Why I Like Malaya," 17.
58. Hannah Arendt, *The Human Condition*, 2nd ed. (Chicago: University of Chicago Press, 1998), 52. I thank Shuang Shen for referring me to Hannah Arendt's table analogy (Discussant comments at the Inter-University Junior Scholars Workshop, Pennsylvania State University, October 6, 2017).
59. Han Suyin, Box 18, Folder 1(b) "Sequel to *And the Rain My Drink*," Han Suyin Collection.
60. This authorial assertion is only included in the front matter of the title's initial U.K. and U.S. editions, published in 1956 by Jonathan Cape and Little, Brown and Company respectively. Han's British publisher sought counsel on avoiding potential libel liabilities. Letter from H. F. Rubinstein to Wren Howard, September 28, 1955, Box 72, Han Suyin Collection.
61. I thank Philip Holden for sharing this insight (email correspondence, March 10, 2019).
62. Han Suyin, "Some Impressions of Writing in English within the Context of Singapore and Malaya," n.d., Box 62, Han Suyin Collection, 11.
63. Han Suyin, "Writers Must Intervene in Life," March 1960, Box 12, Folder 2, Han Suyin Collection, 5–6.

64. Johannes Fabian, *Time and the Other: How Anthropology Makes its Object* (New York: Columbia University Press, 2002).
65. Han Suyin, "Writing About Malaya," 3.
66. Han Suyin, "Han Suyin Newsletter No. 6 (March 1960)," Box 12, Han Suyin Collection.
67. Fiona Lee, "Epistemological Checkpoint: Reading Fiction as a Translation of History," *Postcolonial Text* 9, no. 1 (2014): 3.
68. Han Suyin to Jonathan Cape, June 24, 1955, Box 73, Han Suyin Collection.
69. Because the incomplete *Freedom* was never published, her extant tale about the "manscape" that is Malaya, as seen through *Rain*, focused primarily on the Chinese community and never ventured into the Malay world that the sequel would have addressed. There is a section entitled "The Malay World" in Han's dossier of notes on *Freedom*. See Han Suyin, "FREEDOM SING MERDEKA," Folder 1(b), Box 18, Han Suyin Collection.
70. For instances from various literatures, see Bill Ashcroft, Gareth Griffiths, and Helen Tiffin, *Empire Writes Back*, 47–50; 7–58.
71. Bill Ashcroft, Gareth Griffiths, and Helen Tiffin, *Empire Writes Back*, 58.
72. Fiona Lee, "Epistemological Checkpoint," 3.
73. Han Suyin, "Development of a Malayan Chinese Literature," 18–19, Box 60, Han Suyin Collection. Emphases mine. The script from public talk is undated, but the date can be inferred from a corresponding news report in 1961. See A. Mahadeva, "Chinese Writers Are Promoting Race Harmony in Malaya," *The Sunday Mail*, January 29, 1961."
74. Han Suyin, *My House Has Two Doors*, 105.
75. Han Suyin, "The Creation of a Malayan Literature," 21. Emphases mine.
76. Han Suyin, "The Creation of a Malayan Literature," 21.
77. Peter Hitchcock, "Decolonizing (the) English," *The South Atlantic Quarterly* 100, no. 3 (2001): 750.
78. Here I have in mind how despite their antithetical stances toward the mainland Chinese polity, Han can be perceived as a predecessor of Ha Jin, who defended the flavor of "foreignness" in his English-language writings. See Ha Jin 哈金, "Wei waiyuqiang bianhu" 為外語腔辯護 [In defense of the foreign accent], in *Zai taxiang xiezuo* 在他鄉寫作 [The writer as migrant], trans. Mingdi 明迪 (Taipei: Linking Publishing, 2010), 137–60.
79. Lian Shisheng 連士升, "Fangwen Zhou Guanghu" 訪問周光瑚 [An interview with Rosalie Matilda Kwanghu Chou], in *Lian Shisheng wenji di'er juan* 連士升文集第二卷 [The Lian Shisheng anthology, vol. 2], ed. Koh Hock Kiat 許福吉 (Beijing: Peking University Press, 2011), 436.
80. Han Suyin, "Plenary Lecture," in *Asian Voices in English*, ed. Mimi Chan and Roy Harris (Hong Kong: Hong Kong University Press, 1991), 20.

81. Han Suyin, Folder 1(b), "Sequel to *And the Rain My Drink*," Box 18, Han Suyin Collection. Emphasis mine.
82. Meir Sternberg, "Polylingualism as Reality and Translation as Mimesis." *Poetics Today* 2, no. 4 (1981): 224.
83. Han Suyin, Folder 1(d), "*And the Rain My Drink* (Sequel to the Book)," Box 18, Han Suyin Collection.
84. Han Suyin, "FREEDOM SING MERDEKA," Box 18, Han Suyin Collection.
85. Han Suyin, "Some Impressions of Writing in English," 9–10. Emphases mine.
86. Han Suyin, "Development of a Malayan Chinese Literature," 5–6.
87. Han Suyin, "Some Impressions of Writing in English," 2, 7.
88. Han Suyin to Liu Pengju, September 6, 1960, Box 79, Han Suyin Collection.
89. Han Suyin, "Development of a Malayan Chinese Literature," 15–16. The *pantun* is a traditional Malay poetic form based on Malay folk songs, usually about love. Subsequent citations from this speech are rendered in-text. Emphases mine.
90. For collated primary materials on the seminal literary debate, see *Xinma huawen wenxue daxi diyiji: Lilun* 新馬華文文學大系第一集: 理論 [Compendium of Singapore, Malayan, and Malaysian Chinese-language literature from Singapore and Malaysia, vol. 1: Theory] ed. Miao Xiu 苗秀 (Singapore: Jiaoyu chubanshe, 1971), 197–278.
91. Han Suyin, "An Outline of Malayan-Chinese Literature," *Eastern Horizon* 3, no. 6 (June 1964): 8.
92. Han Suyin to Menina Russell King, April 5, 1963, Box 74, Han Suyin Collection.
93. Han Suyin, "Asian Writers Who Write in English: English the International Language and History of English," in *Duozhong shijiao: Wenxue yu wenhua bijiao yanjiu lunwenji* 多種視角: 文學與文化比較研究論文集 [Multiple perspectives: An anthology of comparative research on literature and culture], ed. Chang Yaoxin 常耀信 (Tianjin: Nankai daxue chubanshe, 1991), 156–57.
94. Han Suyin, "Nanda de weilai" 南大的未來 [The future of Nanyang University], in *Fuban Nanyang Daxue lunwenji* 復辦南洋大學論文集 [An anthology on the revival of Nanyang University], ed. Tan Kok Chiang 陳國相 (Selangor: Strategic Information and Research Development Centre, 2010), 5.
95. Han Suyin, "Understanding Southeast Asia from the Point of View of the Writer," n.d., Box 62, Han Suyin Collection. The event took place on May 25, 1958, and was reported in *Nanyang Siang Pau* the next day (see Zhang Xing Hong, *Han Suyin zai Malaiya*, 314).
96. Han Suyin, "Understanding Southeast Asia."
97. Han Suyin, "Understanding Southeast Asia."
98. Han Suyin, "Some Impressions of Writing in English," 4. While she protested against linking English reflexively with colonialism, she also objected to the

immediate association of all things Chinese with communism. See Han Suyin, "The Nanyang Students," *Mahasiswa Negara* [University students of the nation] 2, no. 10 (1963): 8.

99. Han Suyin, ""Some Impressions of Writing in English," 4.
100. Han Suyin, "The English Language," vii-viii.
101. Han Suyin, "Some Impressions of Writing in English," 11.
102. Han Suyin, "Some Impressions of Writing in English," 11.
103. Han Suyin, "Some Impressions of Writing in English," 8.
104. Han Suyin, "Some Impressions of Writing in English," 12.
105. Han Suyin, "Development of a Malayan Chinese Literature," 14.
106. Liang Qichao 梁啟超, *Xindalu youji* 新大陸遊記 [Travels to the New World] (Changsha: Hunan renmin chubanshe, 1981), 145.
107. Notably, Singapore after World War II was also the center of vibrant Malay cultural production and hosted many diasporic Malay writers from Malaya. See T. N. Harper, *The End of Empire and the Making of Malaya* (Cambridge: Cambridge University Press, 1999), 300–02; Virginia Matheson Hooker, *Writing a New Society: Social Change through the Novel in Malay* (Honolulu: University of Hawai'i Press, 1999), 183. Yet the coexistence of Malay and Sinophone literary ecologies in Malaya and Singapore remains under-studied.
108. See *Eastern Horizon* 1, no. 13 (1961); and *Eastern Horizon* 2, no. 13 (1963).
109. *Modern Malaysian Chinese Stories*, ed. and tr. Ly Singko (Singapore: Heinemann Educational Books [Asia] Ltd., 1967). The anthology included a foreword by Han that grew out of an article published in 1964: Han Suyin, "An Outline of Malayan Chinese Literature," *Eastern Horizon* 3, no. 6 (1964): 6–16. The Writing in Asia Series was conceived by Leonard Comber (Han's second husband), then based in Singapore as the Southeast Asian representative of Heinemann Education Books Ltd. On his experience of running the Heinemann business in Asia, see Leonard Comber, "Publishing Asian Writers in English," in *Asian Voices in English*, 79–86.
110. Han Suyin, *My House Has Two Doors*, 464–87.
111. Han Suyin to Malcolm MacDonald, August 22, 1966, Box 87, Han Suyin Collection.

3. COSMOPOLITAN VISIONS OF DRIFT

1. Ng Kim Chew, "Wuguoji huawen wenxue: Yige wenxueshi de bijiao gangling" 無國籍華文文學：一個文學史的比較綱領 [Literature in Chinese without nationality: A comparative program for literary history], in *Chongxie Taiwan wenxueshi* 重寫臺灣文學史 [Rewriting Taiwan literary history], ed. Tee Kim Tong 張錦忠 and Ng Kim Chew (Taipei: Maitian, 2007), 123–59.

2. Chiu Kuei-fen 邱貴芬, "Piping yu huiying: Yu Huang Jinshu tan wenxueshi shuxie de baoli wenti" 批評與回應：與黃錦樹談文學史書寫的暴力問題 [Critique and response: Negotiating the question of symbolic violence in literary historiography with Ng Kim Chew], *Wenhua yanjiu* 文化研究 [Router: A journal of cultural studies], no. 2 (2006): 286–87. Chiu translated Huang De-shi's 1943 "Taiwan wenxueshi xushuo" 臺灣文學史序說 [Preface to Taiwan literary history] in Kuei-fen Chiu, "Empire of the Chinese Sign: The Question of Chinese Diasporic Imagination in Transnational Literary Production," *The Journal of Asian Studies* 67, no. 2 (2008): 615.

3. Katherine Brickell and Ayona Datta, "Introduction: Translocal Geographies," in *Translocal Geographies: Spaces, Places, Connections*, ed. Katherine Brickell and Ayona Datta (London: Routledge, 2016), 3.

4. Insofar as the novella is partially set in colonial Malaya, which includes Singapore in ethnic Chinese grassroots imaginaries in the region, it can also be read as "Xinhua literature" 新華文學 [Singapore Chinese-language literature].

5. Shelly Chan, *Diaspora's Homeland: Modern China in the Age of Global Migration* (Durham, NC: Duke University Press, 2018).

6. Wang Anyi 王安憶 et al., "Dangqian wenxue chuangzuozhong de 'qing' yu 'zhong'—wenxue duihualu" 當前文學創作中的"輕"與"重"—文學對話錄 [The lightness and weight of current creative writings: A conversation on literature], *Dangdai zuojia pinglun* 當代作家評論 [Contemporary writers review] 5 (1993): 17.

7. Wang Anyi, "Shangxin Taipingyang" 傷心太平洋 [Sadness of the Pacific], in *Wang Anyi zixuanji zhisan: Xianggang de qing yu ai (zhongpian xiaoshuo juan)* 王安憶自選集之三：香港的情與愛（中篇小說卷）[Wang Anyi self-selected collection III: Love in Hong Kong (volume of novellas)](Beijing: Zuojia chubanshe, 1996), 311, 383. Subsequent references to the novella will appear as in-text citations.

8. Wang Anyi 王安憶, "Wode laili" 我的來歷 [My origins], in *Wutai xiaoshijie: Wang Anyi duanpian xiaoshuo biannian juan'er, 1982–1989* 舞臺小世界：王安憶短篇小說編年卷二，1982–1989 [The stage is a small world: A chronological anthology of Wang Anyi's short stories (vol. 2), 1982–1989] (Beijing: Renmin wenxue chubanshe, 2009), 266.

9. The biographical details of Xiaoping are drawn from Wang Xiaoping 王嘯平, "Wang Anyi zhi fu: Nanyang guiyan de chuanqi" 王安憶之父：南洋歸雁的傳奇 [Wang Anyi's father: The legend of a returning goose from Nanyang], *Shiji* 世紀 [Century], no. 1 (2014): 5–6. On the historical background of the artistic troupe, based in part on Xiaoping's writings in the 1930s and his oral reminiscences, see Yeo Song Nian 楊松年, "Zhanqian Xinma jutuan yanjiu zhiyi: Mahua xunhui gejutuan" 戰前新馬劇團研究之一：馬華巡迴歌劇團 [A study of the Chinese

itinerant drama troupes in Malaya), *Yazhou wenhua* 亞洲文化 [Asian culture], issue no. 13 (1989): 12–40.

10. For a specific study on *guiqiao* writer Wang Xiaoping's trilogy, see Lai Pei-Hsuan 賴佩暄, "Lisan yu guifan: Lun Wang Xiaoping banzizhuanti xiaoshuozhong de liudong shenshi yu jiaguo qinghuai" 離散與歸返：論王嘯平半自傳體小說中的流動身世與家國情懷 [The diaspora and the return: An analysis of Wang Xiaoping's wandering life and feelings about home-country in his semi-autobiographical novels], *Zhongguo xiandai wenxue* 中國現代文學 [Modern Chinese literature] 24 (2013): 167–88.

11. Adam McKeown, "Conceptualizing Chinese Diasporas, 1842 to 1949," *The Journal of Asian Studies* 58, no. 2 (1999): 310.

12. On the notion that characterizes the twin marginalization of Mahua writers in both Malaysian and Taiwan literary spaces, see Tee Kim Tong 張錦忠, "Lisan shuangxiang: Zuowei Yazhou kuaguo huawen shuxie de zaitai Mahua wenxue" 離散雙鄉：作爲亞洲跨國華文書寫的在臺馬華文學 [Double diasporic homelands: Mahua literature in Taiwan as transnational Asian Chinese-language writing], *Zhongguo xiandai wenxue* 中國現代文學 [Modern Chinese literature] 9 (2006): 61–72.

13. For a thorough study on Yu Dafu's Singapore sojourn, see Yeo Mang Thong 姚夢桐, *Yu Dafu lüxin shenghuo yu zuopin yanjiu* 郁達夫旅新生活與作品研究 [A study of Yu Dafu's life and works in Singapore] (Singapore: Singapore Island Society, 1987). For a record of Wang Xiaoping's various meetings with Yu Dafu, see Wang Xiaoping 王嘯平, "Zuojia yu zhanshi—huiyi Yu Dafu xiansheng" 作家與戰士──回憶郁達夫先生 [Writer and fighter: In remembrance of Mr. Yu Dafu], *Shanghai wenxue* 上海文學 [Shanghai literature] 12 (1979): 44–46.

14. For a personal account of Wu Tian's involvement with Mahua literary arts in the late 1930s, see Wang Xiaoping 王嘯平, "Weile bugai wangque de jinian—ji xijujia Wu Tian" 為了不該忘卻的紀念──記戲劇家吳天 [For the sake of remembrance that should not be forgotten—about the dramatist Wu Tian], *Xiju yishu* 戲劇藝術 [Theater arts], no. 4 (1990): 32–35. Wu's political allegiance, a relatively undiscussed but significant aspect of his biography, is briefly recorded in Beijing yuyan xueyuan *Zhongguo wenxuejia cidian* bianweihui 北京語言學院《中國文學家辭典》編委會 [Editorial committee for the *Dictionary of Chinese Literary Figures*, Beijing Language Institute] ed., *Zhongguo wenxuejia cidian (xiandai diyi fence)* 中國文學家辭典（現代第一分冊）[Dictionary of Chinese literary figures (modern period, vol. 1)] (Chengdu: Sichuan renmin chubanshe, 1979), 285–86.

15. A selection of Wang Xiaoping's early works, spanning different genres of writing, written under the pen name "Xiaoping" 嘯平, can be found in various volumes of Fang Xiu, ed., *Mahua Xinwenxue daxi* 馬華新文學大系 [Compendium of modern Mahua literature] (Singapore: Shijie shuju, 1972).

16. Wang Anyi, "Fuqin de shu" 父親的書 [My father's book], written in 1991, later included in her volume of prose essays *Kongjian zai shijian li liutang* 空間在時間裡流淌 [The spaces flowing through time] (Beijing: New Star Press, 2012), 196. The full title of Wang Xiaoping's second novel is *Kezi Nanyang lai* 客自南洋來 [The guest from Nanyang] (Shanghai: Baijia chubanshe, 1990).
17. The phrase is coined by Wang Gungwu who avers that the sense of being Chinese through an association with the idea of China cannot be taken for granted. See Wang Gungwu, "Introduction," in *The Chineseness of China: Selected Essays* (Hong Kong: Oxford University Press, 1991), 2, 6.
18. Wang Anyi, *Wang Anyi Shuo* 王安憶說 [Wang Anyi: Dialogues and speeches] (Changsha: Hunan wenyi chubanshe, 2003), 184.
19. Martin Lewis and Kären Wigen, *The Myth of Continents: A Critique of Metageography* (Berkeley: University of California Press, 1997), 34.
20. Wang Anyi, *Jishi he xugou: Chuangzao shijie fangfa zhi yizhong* 紀實和虛構：創造世界方法之一種 [Documentation and fictionalization: One method of creating the world] (Beijing: Renmin wenxue chubanshe, 1993), 10. The line, which indicates Wang's original representation of her feelings about her personal circumstances in Shanghai, only appears in this edition.
21. Wang Anyi, *Wang Anyi Shuo*, 184.
22. Wang Anyi, "Wutuobang shipian" 烏托邦詩篇 [Utopian verses], in *Wang Anyi zixuanji zhisan: Xianggang de qing yu ai (zhongpian xiaoshuo juan)* 王安憶自選集之三：香港的情與愛（中篇小說卷）[Wang Anyi self-selected collection 3: Love in Hong Kong (volume of novellas)] (Beijing: Zuojia chubanshe, 1996), 257, 303. Subsequent references to the novella will appear as in-text citations.
23. Adam McKeown, "Conceptualizing Chinese Diasporas," 311.
24. In the late 1980s, Wang elucidated her writing tenets in terms of four repudiations, one of which was "avoid the stylization of language" (*buyao yuyan de fenggehua* 不要語言的風格化). See Wang Anyi, "Wode xiaoshuoguan" 我的小說觀 [My perspective on fiction-writing], in *Wang Anyi yanjiu ziliao (shang)* 王安憶研究資料（上）[Research material on Wang Anyi (vol. 1)], ed. Zhang Xinying 張新穎 and Jin Li 金理 (Tianjin: Tianjin renmin chubanshe, 2009), 42.
25. Zheng Wanlong 鄭萬隆, "Zhongguo wenxue yao zouxiang shijie" 中國文學要走向世界 [Chinese literature must join the world], *Zuojia* 作家 [Writer magazine], no. 1 (1986): 70–74.
26. Chen Liao 陳遼, "Zouxiang shijie yihou—tan Xinshiqi Wenxue zai shijie wenxue gejuzhong de dingwei" 走向世界以後—談新時期文學在世界文學格局中的定位 [After having marched toward the world—on the position of literature of the New Era in the world literary order], *Wenyi pinglun* 文藝評論 [Literature and art criticism], no. 4 (1986): 21.

27. Catherine Vance Yeh, "Root Literature of the 1980s: May Fourth as a Double Burden," in *The Appropriation of Cultural Capital: China's May Fourth Project*, ed. Milena Dolezelova-Velingerova, Oldrich Kral, and Graham Sanders (Cambridge, MA: Harvard University Asia Center, 2001), 233.
28. Chen Liao, "Zouxiang shijie yihou," 22. For an account of the two related movements, see Catherine Vance Yeh, "Root Literature of the 1980s."
29. Wang Anyi, "Dalu Taiwan xiaoshuo yuyan bijiao" 大陸臺灣小說語言比較 [The language of fiction in works from mainland China and Taiwan: A comparison], in *Wang Anyi zixuanji zhisi: Piaobo de yuyan (sanwen juan)* 王安憶自選集之四：漂泊的語言（散文卷）[Wang Anyi self-selected collection 4: A language adrift (volume of prose)] (Beijing: Zuojia chubanshe, 1996), 388. Subsequent references to the article will appear as in-text citation.
30. The article's publication trajectory across China and Malaysia is as follows: (1) "Yuyan de mingyun" 語言的命運 [The fate of language], *Haishang wentan* 海上文壇 6 (1992): 77–83; 2) "Yuyan de mingyun (shang, xia)" 語言的命運（上、下）[The fate of language (part 1 and part 2)], *Xingzhou Ribao* 星洲日報 [Sin Chew daily], July 12 and 13, 1993, 3) "Piaobo de yuyan" 漂泊的語言 [A language adrift], in Wang Anyi, *Wang Anyi zixuanji zhisi: Piaobo de yuyan (sanwen juan)*, 214–28. Extracts from this article follow the last version and appear as in-text citation.
31. Wang Anyi et al., "Dangqian wenxue chuangzuozhong de 'qing' yu 'zhong,'" 17.
32. Wang Anyi, "Xiaoshuo de qingjie he yuyan" 小說的情節和語言 [The plot and language of fiction], in *Wang Anyi yanjiu ziliao (shang)*, 108.
33. Wang Anyi et al., "Dangqian wenxue chuangzuozhong de 'qing' yu 'zhong,'" 17.
34. Wang Anyi, *Wang Anyi Shuo*, 83.
35. Wang Anyi, "Xiaoshuo de qingjie he yuyan," 104.
36. Wang Anyi, "Xiaoshuo de qingjie he yuyan," 104.
37. Wang Anyi, "Xiaoshuo de qingjie he yuyan," 107.
38. Wang Anyi, *Wang Anyi Shuo*, 83.
39. Wang Anyi and Zhang Xudong 張旭東, "Lilun yu shijian: Wenxue ruhe chengxian lishi?" 理論與實踐：文學如何呈現歷史？ [Theory and praxis: How does literature represent history?], in *Wang Anyi yanjiu ziliao (shang)*, 340.
40. Laifong Leung, "Wang Anyi: Restless Explorer," in *Morning Sun: Interviews with Chinese Writers of the Lost Generation* (Armonk, NY: M. E. Sharpe, 1994), 185.
41. Wang Anyi, "Guiqu laixi" 歸去來兮 [Longing to return], in *Duyu* 獨語 [Monologue] (Changsha: Hunan wenyi chubanshe, 1998), 27.
42. Zhou Xinmin 周新民 and Wang Anyi, "Haode gushi benshen jiushi haode xingshi: Wang Anyi fangtanlu" 好的故事本身就是好的形式——王安憶訪談錄 [A great story itself comes with a great form: An interview with Wang Anyi], *Xiaoshuo pinglun* 小說評論 [Fiction criticism] 3 (2003): 36.

43. For a comprehensive study on this peculiar national cultural complex of China, see Julia Lovell, *The Politics of Cultural Capital: China's Quest for a Nobel Prize in Literature* (Honolulu: University of Hawai'i Press, 2006).
44. Ng Kim Chew, "M de shizong" M 的失蹤 [Disappearance of M], in *Meng yu zhu yu liming* 夢與豬與黎明 [Dream and swine and aurora] (Taipei: Jiuge, 1994), 10–42.
45. Xuan Sulai 禤素萊, "Kaiting shenxun" 開庭審訊 [The trial], in *Lawei Mahua wenxue: Jiushi niandai Mahua wenxue zhenglunxing keti wenxuan* 辣味馬華文學：九十年代馬華文學爭論性課題文選 [Mahua literature with an edge: Selected essays on topics of controversy in Mahua literature in the 1990s], ed. Chan Yeong Siew 張永修, Teoh Kong Tat 張光達, and Lim Choon Bee 林春美 (Kuala Lumpur: Xuelan'e Zhonghua dahuitang he Malaixiya liutai xiaoyouhui lianhe zonghui, 2002), 73.
46. Xuan Sulai, "Kaiting shenxun," 71.
47. The Japanese scholar Masutani Satoshi, who presented on Mahua literature at the 1991 conference, later clarifies that although Xuan's account was authentic, she was not an eyewitness of the event. Whereas the Mahua literary circle treats Xuan's work as prose essay (*sanwen* 散文) of a reportage nature, he considers Xuan's text to be literary fiction (*xiaoshuo* 小説). See Masutani Satoshi 舛谷銳 and Hee Wai Siam 許維賢, "'Kaiting shenxun': Xuan Sulai buzai xianchang—zoufang Chuangu Rui fujiaoshou"《開庭審訊》：禤素萊不在現場—走訪舛谷銳副教授 ["The trial": Xuan Sulai was absent from the scene—an interview with Associate Professor Masutani Satoshi], *Chao Foon* 蕉風 491 (2004): 49–54.
48. Ng Kim Chew, "Mahua wenxue 'jingdian quexi'" 馬華文學"經典缺席" [The absence of a canon in Mahua literature], in *Lawei Mahua wenxue*, 108.
49. Ng Kim Chew, "Mahua wenxue de bei'ai" 馬華文學的悲哀 [The sad situation of Mahua literature], in *Lawei Mahua wenxue*, 175.
50. Ng Kim Chew, "Dui wenxue de waihang yu dui lishi de wuzhi? Jiu 'Mahua wenxue' da Xiamei" 對文學的外行與對歷史的無知?—就"馬華文學"答夏梅 [A layman to literature who is also ignorant about history? A response to Xiamei on Mahua literature], in *Lawei Mahua wenxue*, 121.
51. Li Tuo 李陀, "Wang Zengqi yu xiandai hanyu xiezuo—jiantan Maowenti" 汪曾祺與現代漢語寫作—兼談毛文體 [Wang Zengqi and writings in modern Chinese—with concurrent thoughts on the "Mao-style prose"], *Huacheng* 花城 [Flower city] 114 (1998): 131.
52. Wang Anyi, "Jiejin shijichu," in *Jiejin shijichu* 接近世紀初 [Approaching the start of a century] (Hangzhou: Zhejiang wenyi chubanshe, 1998), 249.
53. Wang Anyi, "Jiejin shijichu," 250.
54. Ng Kim Chew, "Huawen/Zhongwen: 'Shiyu de nanfang' yu yuyan zaizao" 華文/中文："失語的南方"與語言再造 [Huawen/Zhongwen: 'The South where language

is lost' and linguistic reinvention], in *Mahua wenxue yu Zhongguoxing* 馬華文學與中國性 (Taipei: Yuanzun wenhua, 1998), 53–92.
55. Ng Kim Chew, "Huawen/Zhongwen," 63. I lean primarily on Brian Bernards's translation of this article. See Ng Kim Chew, "Sinophone/Chinese: 'The South Where Language is Lost' and Reinvented," trans. Brian Bernards, in *Sinophone Studies: A Critical Reader*, ed. Shu-mei Shih, Chien-hsin Tsai, and Brian Bernards (New York: Columbia University Press, 2013), 74–92.
56. Ng Kim Chew, "Huawen/Zhongwen," 78.
57. Shang Wei, "Writing and Speech: Rethinking the Issue of Vernaculars in Early Modern China," in *Rethinking East Asian Languages, Vernaculars, and Literacies, 1000–1919*, ed. Benjamin A. Elman (Brill: Leiden, 2014), 256, 258, 295–96.
58. Ng Kim Chew, "Huawen/Zhongwen," 76. I modified Bernards's translation here, mainly substituting "topolect" for "dialect" to foreground the original semantic dimension of locality. See Ng Kim Chew, "Sinophone/Chinese," trans. Brian Bernards, 88. Emphasis mine.
59. Alison M. Groppe, *Sinophone Malaysian Literature: Not Made in China* (Amherst, NY: Cambria Press, 2013), 78–90.
60. Ng Kim Chew, "Huawen/Zhongwen," 54, 61–64, 91–92 (n. 51).
61. Ng Kim Chew, "Huawen/Zhongwen," 62.
62. Ng Kim Chew, "Huawen/Zhongwen," 72.
63. In a 1991 article, Ng also calls Taiwan *huawen* literature based on his perception of historical similarities in the literary developments of Taiwan and Malaysia. See Ng Kim Chew, "Mahua wenxue de yunniangqi" 馬華文學的醞釀期 [The gestation period of Mahua literature], in *Mahua wenxue: Neizai zhongguo, yuyan yu wenxueshi* 馬華文學：內在中國、語言與文學史 [Mahua literature: Internal China, language and literary history] (Kuala Lumpur: Huazi Resource and Research Centre Bhd., 1996), 38, 49–50.
64. Ng Kim Chew, "Zai 'shijie' zhinei de huawen yu 'shijie' zhiwai de huaren" 在"世界"之內的華文與"世界"之外的華人 [The Chinese language within the 'world' and the Chinese people outside the 'world'], in *Mahua wenxue*, 225–26.
65. For a more detailed exposition on the development of his own literary thought, see Ng Kim Chew 黃錦樹, "Nanfang huawen wenxue gongheguo: Yige chuyi" 南方華文文學共和國：一個芻議 [Republic of southern-sinophone literature: A proposal], *Zhongshan renwen xuebao* 中山人文學報 [Sun Yat-sen journal of humanities], issue no. 45 (2018): 12–13.
66. David Der-wei Wang, "Introduction," in *Chinese Literature in the Second Half of a Modern Century: A Critical Survey*, ed. Pang-yuan Chi and David Der-wei Wang (Bloomington: Indiana University Press, 2000), xxxi, xxxiii.
67. David Der-wei Wang, "Introduction," xxxiii.

68. Ng Kim Chew, "Ci de liuwang—Zhang Guixing de xiezuo daolu" 詞的流亡—張貴興的寫作道路 [Words in exile: The path of Zhang Guixing's writing practice], in his *Mahua wenxue yu Zhongguoxing*, 351–78, especially 373–74 (n. 6).
69. See for instance Brian Bernards, "Plantation and Rainforest: Chang Kuei-hsing (Zhang Guixing) and a South Seas Discourse of Coloniality and Nature" in *Sinophone Studies*, 325–38. Shu-mei Shih further opines that Zhang deserves the Nobel Prize in Literature. See Shu-mei Shih, "Comparison as Relation," in *Comparison: Theories, Approaches, Uses*, ed. Rita Felski and Susan Stanford Friedman (Baltimore: Johns Hopkins University Press, 2013), 96.
70. Chen Yingzhen 陳映真, "Wodui Mahua wenxue de guangan" 我對馬華文學的觀感 [My perception of Mahua literature], in *Xinma wenxueshi congtan* 新馬文學史叢談 [Collected writings on Singapore and Malaysian literary history], ed. Fang Xiu 方修 (Singapore: Chunyi tushu maoyi gongsi, 1999), 11.
71. Regarding the ban's impact on the book trade's geographical networks, see Chen Mong Tse 陳蒙志, "Xianggang chuban de bendi shukan" 香港出版的本地書刊 [Singaporean books and journals published in Hong Kong], *Yihe shiji* 怡和世紀 18 (2012): 80–81.
72. See for instance Yang Zonghan 楊宗翰, "Cong Shenzhouren dao Mahuaren" 從神州人到馬華人 [From people of the Divine Land to Malaysian Chinese], in *Chidao huisheng: Mahua wenxue duben II* 赤道回聲：馬華文學讀本 II [Equatorial echoes: A Mahua literature reader 2], ed. Chan Tah Wei 陳大為, Chong Yee-Voon 鍾怡雯 and Woo Kam Lun 胡金倫 (Taipei: Wanjuanlou, 2004), 159.

4. OFF-CENTER ARTICULATIONS

1. Pascale Casanova, *The World Republic of Letters*, trans. M. B. DeBevoise (Cambridge, MA: Harvard University Press, 2004), 83.
2. I use "Taiwan" instead of "Taiwanese" to describe literary production related to the East Asian island for disambiguation purposes. While "Taiwanese" in general refers to something from or related to Taiwan, it also denotes "Taiwanese Hokkien," the language that is a variant of Hokkien from South China. The terms "Taiwanese literature" and "Taiwanese literary space" can thus be construed as language-based categories, the use of which deviates from my place-based focus on Taiwan. For a precedent to my choice of descriptor, see Xiaobing Tang, "On the Concept of Taiwan Literature," in *Writing Taiwan: A New Literary History*, ed. David Der-wei Wang and Carlos Rojas (Durham, NC: Duke University Press, 2007), 51–89.
3. See Ngoi Guat Peng 魏月萍, "Gaobie yu renju: Shahua wenxue de juluo yu lisan changyu" 告別與認據：砂華文學的聚落與離散場域 [Departures and claims: The settlements and diasporic domains of Sarawak Chinese-language literature],

preface to Tian Si 田思, *Shahua wenxue de bentu tezhi* 砂華文學的本土特質 [The native characteristics of Sarawak Chinese-language literature] (Selangor: Mentor Publishing, 2014), 3–7; Zhan Min-xu 詹閔旭, "Zai shijie de bianyuan xiezuo: Li Yongping chengwei Taiwan zuojia zhilu" 在世界的邊緣寫作：李永平成為臺灣作家之路 [Writing in the margin of the world: Li Yongping's road to becoming a Taiwan writer], *Donghua hanxue* 東華漢學 [Dong Hwa journal of Chinese studies], no. 27 (2018): 211–40; Kuei-fen Chiu, "Empire of the Chinese Sign: The Question of Chinese Diasporic Imagination in Transnational Literary Production," *The Journal of Asian Studies* 67, no. 2 (2008): 598–604.

4. Masao Miyoshi, *Off Center: Power and Culture Relations between Japan and the United States* (Cambridge, MA: Harvard University Press, 1991).
5. Mads Rosendahl Thomsen, "Strangeness and World Literature," *CLCWeb: Comparative Literature and Culture* 15, no. 5 (2013): 3, 8, https://doi.org/10.7771/1481-4374.2351.
6. I follow Nick Admussen's English rendition of this Chinese idiom, which he used as the title of his chapbook *Neither Nearing nor Departing* (Greensboro, NC: Two of Cups Press, 2018).
7. For a critique of the "between two worlds" model in the study of migration cultures, see Leslie A. Adelson, *The Turkish Turn in Contemporary German Literature* (New York: Palgrave Macmillan, 2005), 3–5.
8. By "indigeneity," I mean that which is related to the aboriginal populations of Borneo, and not the governance category of *bumiputera* (sons of the soil) that the Malaysian state deployed in 1963 to include the natives in Sabah and Sarawak. For this aspect of Malaysian history, see Rusaslina Idrus, "Malays and Orang Asli: Contesting Indigeneity," in *Melayu: The Politics, Poetics and Paradoxes of Malayness*, ed. Maznah Mohamad and Syed Muhd Khairudin Aljunied (Singapore: National University of Singapore Press, 2011), 113–15. The two concepts (that is, indigenous groups and *bumiputera*) should be kept distinct here, as *River*'s diegesis takes place in 1962, when the Malaysian polity did not exist. Moreover, the story is set in the Indonesian part of Borneo and not in the territories that eventually became Malaysian.
9. M. H. Edney, "British Military Education, Mapmaking, and Military 'Mapmindedness' in the Later Enlightenment," *The Cartographic Journal* 31, no. 1 (1994): 14–20.
10. Pascale Casanova, *World Republic of Letters*, 41.
11. The Malaysian government only recognizes literary works written in the national language of Malay as national literature. In an oft-quoted compliment, Chi Pang-yuan hails the different generations of award-winning Mahua writers in Taiwan as a "powerful and dazzling literary contingent." See Chi Pang-yuan 齊邦媛, "Xu: *Yuxue feifei* yu Mahua wenxue tuxiang" 序：《雨雪霏霏》與馬

華文學圖像 [Preface: *Snowfall in the Clouds* and the picture of Mahua literature], in Li Yongping 李永平, *Yuxue feifei: Poluozhou tongnian jishi* 雨雪霏霏：婆羅洲童年記事 [Snowfall in the clouds: Recollections of a Borneo childhood] (Taipei: Tianxia yuanjian, 2002), vii–viii.
12. Ng Yean Leng 伍燕翎 and Shi Huimin 施慧敏, "Li Yongping fangtanlu (shang)" 李永平訪談錄 (上) [An interview with Li Yongping, part 1], *Xingzhou Ribao* 星州日報 [Sin Chew daily], March 15, 2009.
13. Ng Yean Leng and Shi Huimin, "Li Yongping fangtanlu (shang)."
14. Chen Wanqian 陳宛茜, "Mayi zuojia Li Yongping lai Tai sishinian huo Guojia Wenyijiang" 馬裔作家李永平來臺四十年獲國家文藝獎 [Li Yongping, writer of Malaysian descent, wins National Award for Literary Arts after forty years in Taiwan], *Lianhebao* 聯合報 [United daily news], March 26, 2016.
15. Pascale Casanova, *World Republic of Letters*, 43.
16. Li Yongping, *Dahe jintou (xiajuan): Shan* 大河盡頭（下卷）：山 [Where the Great River ends, vol. 2: The mountain] (Taibei: Maitian, 2010), 26–27. The first volume of the novel is *Dahe jintou (shangjuan): Suliu* 大河盡頭（上卷）：溯流 [Where the Great River ends, vol. 1: Going upstream]. Taipei: Maitian, 2008. Subsequent citations from both volumes will be rendered directly as in-text citations in the format "vol. no: page number."
17. Wang Dewei (David Der-wei Wang) 王德威, "Yuanxiang xiangxiang, langzi wenxue" 原鄉想像，浪子文學 [Imagination of original homeland, literature of a prodigal son], in Li Yongping, *Titto: Li Yongping zixuanji, 1968–2002* 迌迌：李永平自選集，1968–2002 [On gallivanting: Li Yongping's self-selected works, 1968–2002] (Taipei: Maitian, 2003), 11–12.
18. Li Yongping, "Wenzi yinyuan" 文字姻緣 [A predestined relationship with the Chinese script], in Li, *Titto*, 39.
19. David Der-wei Wang, "Introduction: Worlding Literary China," in *A New Literary History of Modern China*, ed. David Der-wei Wang (Boston: Belknap Press, 2017), 5.
20. Rainier Grutman, *Des langues qui résonnent. L'hétérolinguisme au xixe siècle québécois* (Montréal: Fides, 1997), quoted in Reine Meylaerts, "Heterolingualism in/and Translation: How Legitimate Are the Other and His/Her Language? An Introduction," *Target* 18, no.1 (2006): 4.
21. Li Yongping, "Jiantiban xu: Zhi 'zuguo duzhe'" 簡體版序：致"祖國讀者" [Preface to the simplified script version: To "readers in my motherland"], in *Dahe jintou (shangjuan): Suliu* 大河盡頭（上卷）：溯流 [Where the Great River ends, vol. 1: Going upstream] (Shanghai: Shanghai renmin chubanshe: 2011), 16.
22. For an overview of Li Yongping's publication trajectory, see *Jianshan youshi shan: Li Yongping zhuisi jinianhui ji wenxuezhan tekan* 見山又是山：李永平追思紀念會暨文學展特刊 [The mountain is once again the mountain: A special issue

on the memorial service and literary exhibition for Li Yongping], ed. Feng Teping 封德屏 (Taipei: Wenxun zazhishe, 2018), 128–31.

23. Wong Yoon Wah 王潤華 and Kho Tong Guan 許通元, "Cong Poluozhou dao bei Taiwan: Li Yongping de wenxue xinglü" 從婆羅洲到北臺灣：李永平的文學行旅 [From Borneo to North Taiwan: Li Yongping's literary travels], *Chao Foon* 蕉風 511 (2017): 14.

24. Li Yongping, "Daixu: Wode guxiang, wo ruhe jiangshu" 代序：我的故鄉，我如何講述 [In lieu of a preface: How I narrate my homeland], in *Jianshan youshi shan: Li Yongping yanjiu* 見山又是山：李永平研究 [The mountain is once again the mountain: Studies on Li Yongping], ed. Ko Chia-cian 高嘉謙 (Taipei: Maitian, 2017), 11.

25. Li Yongping, "Daixu," 11.

26. Li Yongping, "Daixu," 12.

27. Li Yongping, "Daixu," 12–13.

28. Li Yongping, "Li Yongping da bianzhe wuwen" 李永平答編者五問 [Li Yongping answers five questions from the editor], *Wenxun* 文訊 [Literary information] 29 (1987): 126.

29. Li Yongping, "Jiantiban xu: Yiben xiaoshuode yinguo" 簡體版序：一本小說的因果 [Preface to the simplified script version: The karma of a novel], in *Jiling chunqiu* (Shanghai: Shanghai renmin chubanshe, 2013), 8–10.

30. Li Yongping, preface to second edition of *Jiling chunqiu* 吉陵春秋 [Jiling chronicles] (Taipei: Hongfan shudian, 1986), i.

31. Li Yongping, *Jiling Chunqiu* (1986), i–ii.

32. Toyoda Noriko 豐田周子, "Li Yongping *Jiling chunqiu* de yuedu fangshi: Yi Taiwan wei zhongxin" 李永平《吉陵春秋》的閱讀方式：以臺灣為中心 [Reading *Jiling Chronicles*: How Li Yongping's novel is interpreted in Taiwan], *Taida dongya wenhua yanjiu* 臺大東亞文化研究 [The NTU Journal of East Asian culture] 4 (2017): 30–32.

33. Zhan Min-xu, "Zai shijie de bianyuan," 221.

34. Qiu Miaojin 邱妙津, "Li Yongping: Wodei baziji wuhuadabang zhihou cailaixie zhengzhi" 李永平：我得把自己五花大綁之後才來寫政治 [Li Yongping: I have to tie myself up before I can write about politics], *Xin xinwen zhoukan* 新新聞週刊 [The journalist] 226 (1992): 66. Li Yongping, *Haidong qing: Taibei de yize yuyan* 海東青：臺北的一則寓言 [East Seas turquoise: A fable of Taipei] (Taipei: Lianhe wenxue, 1992).

35. Li Yongping, " Jiantiban xu: Zhi 'zuguo duzhe,'" 17.

36. Tee Kim Tong 張錦忠, *Nanyang lunshu: Mahua wenxue yu wenhua shuxing* 南洋論述：馬華文學與文化屬性 [Studying Southeast Asian Chinese: Essays on Chinese-Malaysian literature and cultural identity] (Taipei: Maitian, 2003), 216.

37. Li Yongping, "Jiantiban xu: Zhi 'zuguo duzhe,'" 16.

38. Zhan Min-xu, "Dahe de lücheng: Li Yongping tan xiaoshuo" 大河的旅程：李永平談小說 [The journey of a Great River: Li Yongping on fiction-writing], *Yinke wenxue shenghuo zazhi* 印刻文學生活雜誌 [INK literary monthly] 58 (June 2008): 180.
39. On the cognate relationship between the two languages, see *The Austronesians: Historical and Comparative Perspectives*, ed. Peter Bellwood, James J. Fox, and Darrell Tryon (Canberra: Australian University E-Press, 2006), 89–91.
40. Despite debates over differences between the terms "native" and "indigenous," I use the terms interchangeably as referential tools to indicate the original inhabitants of Borneo, rather than as theoretical designations to analyze the characteristics of the various social communities. For a sense of the complex polemics in the social sciences such as anthropology and sociology, see André Béteille, "The Idea of Indigenous People," *Current Anthropology* 39, no. 2 (1998): 187–92; and Adam Kuper, "The Return of the Native," *Current Anthropology* 44, no. 3 (2003): 389–402. For a specific engagement with these concepts from the Southeast Asian perspective, which shows awareness of the complexities of the nomenclature, see Geoffrey Benjamin, "On Being Tribal in the Malay World," in *Tribal Communities in the Malay World: Historical, Cultural and Social Perspectives*, ed. Geoffrey Benjamin and Cynthia Chou (Singapore: Institute of Southeast Asian Studies, 2002), 12–17.
41. Adeline Ooi and Dave Lumenta, "The Malaysian Roadless Trip," *The B-Side*, September 2005, 35–36.
42. On the development of indigenous literature and related discourses in Taiwan, see Kuei-fen Chiu, "The Production of Indigeneity: Contemporary Indigenous Literature in Taiwan and Trans-cultural Inheritance," *The China Quarterly* 200 (2009): 1072–75, 1078, 1083.
43. For an incisive analysis of how Li's political consciousness influenced his creative writing, see Ng Kim Chew, "Pibei de gongma: Li Yongping yu Minguo" 疲憊的公馬：李永平與民國 [The exhausted stallion: Li Yongping and Republican China], in *Huawen xiaowenxue de Malaixiya ge'an* 華文小文學的馬來西亞個案 [Minor literature in Chinese: The case of Malaysia] (Taipei: Maitian, 2015), 367–86.
44. I thank Zhan Min-xu for drawing my attention to this detail. For a history of Dong Hwa University's broader academic investment in studies of ethnic relations and cultures in Taiwan, see the following, accessed May 17, 2021, https://cis.ndhu.edu.tw/ezfiles/16/1016/pictures/712/part_135632_4864224_41377.jpg.
45. Kuo Chiang-sheng notes that it was Li's sojourn in east Taiwan, facing the "mountains and lakes" daily, that inspired him to compose *River*. See Kuo Chiang-sheng 郭強生, "Wo-men" 我們 [The three of us], in *Zuihou yitang chuangzuoke* 最後一堂創作課 [The last class on creative writing], ed. Chen Hsia-min 陳夏民 (Taoyuan: Comma Books, 2018), 236.
46. Kuei-fen Chiu, "Production of Indigeneity," 1074.

47. For an elaboration on how these features work to build indigenous subjectivities in Taiwan literature, see Kuei-fen Chiu, "Production of Indigeneity," 1073–74, 1079.
48. For an explication of Taiwan indigenous writers' artistic approach, see Kuei-fen Chiu, "Production of Indigeneity," 1079–82.
49. Kuei-fen Chiu, "Empire of the Chinese Sign," 600–601.
50. For a strong indication that Mahua literature has finally gained recognition as an important component of Taiwan's literary history, see Chen Fangming 陳芳明, *Taiwan Xinwenxueshi (xia)* 臺灣新文學史（下）[A history of Taiwan New Literature (part 2)] (Taipei: Linking Publishing, 2011), 702–14.
51. On the marginalization of Mahua literature during this period, see Ng Kim Chew, *Mahua wenxue yu Zhongguoxing* 馬華文學與中國性 [The spirit of China in Mahua literature] (Taipei: Yuanzun wenhua, 1998), 355.
52. On the contemporaneity of Mahua literature and Taiwan indigenous literature, and their discrepant strategies to gain prominence, see Zhan Min-xu and Hsu Kuo-ming 徐國明, "Dang duozhong huayuyuxi wenxue xiangyu: Guanyu Taiwan yu huayuyuxi shijie de jiuge" 當多種華語語系文學相遇：關於臺灣與華語語系世界的糾葛 [When multiple Sinophone literatures meet: Entanglements between Taiwan and the Sinophone world], *Zhongwai wenxue* 中外文學 [Chung-Wai literary monthly] 44, no. 1 (2015): 25–62.
53. Li claims that he wishes to give voice to indigenous peoples rather than the Chinese. See Zhan Min-xu, "Yu wenxue jieyuan: Li Yongping tan xiezuolu" 與文學結緣：李永平談寫作路 [Creating affective ties with literature: Li Yongping on his writing journey], *Renshe Donghua dianzi jikan* 人社東華電子季刊 [Dong Hwa journal of humanities and social science online] 10 (June 2016), accessed May, 24, 2022, http://journal.ndhu.edu.tw/%E8%88%87%E6%96%87%E5%AD%B8%E7%B5%90%E7%B7%A3%EF%BC%9A%E6%9D%8E%E6%B0%B8%E5%B9%B3%E8%AB%87%E5%AF%AB%E4%BD%9C%E8%B7%AF%E2%94%80%E2%94%80%E8%A9%B9%E9%96%94%E6%97%AD/.
54. In fact, cartographic representations can be considered a notable trope of Mahua writers in Taiwan. Besides Li, in Zhang Guixing's *Houbei* 猴杯 [Monkey cup], for instance, the teacher-protagonist imagines the map of Borneo to be a tree frog, signifying the place as an unpredictable organism that he has to contend with for the rest of the story. See Zhang Guixing, *Houbei* (Taipei: Lianhe wenxue, 2000), 24. Separately, in Zhang's *Qunxiang* 群象 [Elephant herd], one character articulates how Borneo and China both resemble a begonia leaf on a map. See Zhang Guixing, *Qunxiang* (Taipei: Maitian, 2006), 79.
55. Li Yongping, *Haidong qing*, iv, 460–61, 495.
56. Carlos Rojas, "Li Yongping and Spectral Cartography," in *Writing Taiwan*, 324–47.

57. Alison M. Groppe, *Sinophone Malaysian Literature: Not Made in China* (Amherst, NY: Cambria Press, 2013), 187–232.
58. Editors of *Encyclopaedia Britannica*, "Dayak," *Encyclopedia Britannica*, accessed May 17, 2021, https://www.britannica.com/topic/Dayak.
59. Li's debut novella *Poluozhou zhizi* 婆羅洲之子 [Sons of Borneo] (Kuching: Poluozhou wenhuaju, 1968), published in Sarawak, focuses on the Dayak. He confessed later that his knowledge of the Dayak in the 1960s was not "sufficiently comprehensive and deep," which accounted for the tale's generalized treatment of the indigenous group. See Lim Khay Thiong 林開忠, "'Yizu' de zaixian? Cong Li Yongping de *Poluozhou zhizi* yu *Lazi fu* tanqi" "異族"的再現? 從李永平的《婆羅洲之子》與《拉子婦》談起 [The representations of "alien ethnicities?" On Li Yongping's *Sons of Borneo* and *The Bidayuh Woman*] in *Chongxie Mahua wenxueshi lunwenji* 重寫馬華文學史論文集 [Rewriting Mahua literary history], ed. Tee Kim Tong (Nantou: National Chi Nan University Center for Southeast Asian Studies, 2004), 97. He eventually became acquainted with the group's internal differences. The short story "The Bidayuh Woman," which fronts his first collection of works published in Taiwan, depicts a "Land Dayak" character. See Li Yongping, *Lazi fu* 拉子婦 (The Bidayuh woman) (Taipei: Huaxin chuban gongsi, 1976), 1–17.
60. Li Yongping, *Poluozhou zhizi*, 67.
61. Lim Khay Thiong, "'Yizu' de zaixian?," 110.
62. Ng Kim Chew, "Shitou yu nügui—lun *Dahe jintou* zhongde xiangzheng jiaohuan yu siwang" 石頭與女鬼—論《大河盡頭》中的象徵交換與死亡 [Stones and female ghosts: On symbolic exchange and death in *Where the Great River Ends*], *Taiwan wenxue yanjiu xuebao* 臺灣文學研究學報 [Journal of Taiwan literary studies] 14 (2012): 251.
63. Ng Kim Chew, "Shitou yu nügui," 251.
64. Li's strategy has been observed by Ng Kim Chew, "Shitou yu nügui," 247, and Ko Chia-cian, "Xing, qimeng yu lishi zhaiwu: Li Yongping *Dahe jintou* de chuangshang he xushi" 性、啟蒙與歷史債務：李永平《大河盡頭》的創傷和敘事 [Sex, enlightenment, and historical debt: Trauma and narration in Li Yongping's *Where the Great River Ends*], *Taiwan wenxue yanjiu jikan* 臺灣文學研究集刊 [NTU studies in Taiwan literature] 11 (2012): 48. It is worth noting that in *River*, the Malays have also been excluded from the narrative.
65. See Chan Tah Wei 陳大為, "Yueru yinyu de yulin—daodu dangdai Mahua wenxue" 躍入隱喻的雨林—導讀當代馬華文學 [Leaping into the rainforest metaphor—a guide to reading contemporary Mahua literature], *Chengpin haodu* 誠品好讀 [Eslite reader], no. 13 (2001): 33–34.
66. Li once expressed his curiosity about how Zhang can reinvent his writing practice. See Chen Yun-yuan 陳允元, "Qi, beipan yu huijia zhilu: Li Yongping

Yuxuefeifei zhong de shuangxiang zhuiren" 棄、背叛與回家之路：李永平《雨雪霏霏》中的雙鄉追認 [Abandonment, betrayal and home return: The retracement and recognition of dual home countries in Li Yongping's *Snowfall in the Clouds*], *Taiwan wenxue yanjiu xuebao* 臺灣文學研究學報 [Journal of Taiwan literary studies] 13 (2011): 43. But he explicitly declined to compare his works with Zhang's. See Zhan Min-xu, "Yu wenxue jieyuan."

67. In Zhang's novels *Monkey Cup* and *Wosinian de changmianzhong de nanguo gongzhu* 我思念的長眠中的南國公主 [My South Seas sleeping beauty] (Taipei: Maitian, 2001), he designates all indigenous characters as "Dayak," whereas in *Elephant Herd*, he designates them as "Iban."
68. Ko Chia-cian, "Xing, qimeng yu lishi zhaiwu," 45.
69. "Kehua Malaixiya yuanzhumin yangmao de jingdian wenxue juzuo! Li Yongping *Dahe jintou* quantao shangxia chuqi" 刻畫馬來西亞原住民樣貌的經典文學鉅作！李永平《大河盡頭》全套上下出齊 [A canonical magnum opus about Malaysian indigenous tribes! The two-volume novel *Where the Great River Ends* by Li Yongping now out as a set], Maitian, September 7, 2010, http://goo.gl/YtEPE0.
70. Tian Si, *Shahua wenxue de bentu tezhi*, 36.
71. Tian Si, *Shahua wenxue de bentu tezhi*, 47.
72. See the works by Khor Boon Eng 許文榮, especially "Mahua wenxue de ruoshi minzu shuxie: Yige wenxueshi de shiye" 馬華文學的弱勢民族書寫：一個文學史的視野 [Writings about marginalized ethnicities in Mahua literature: A perspective of literary history], *Zhongguo bijiao wenxue* 中國比較文學 [Comparative literature in China] 1 (2011): 82–95.
73. Chong Fah Hing 莊華興, "Liang Fang kuazuqun xiaoshuo de guojia yu meixue shuangzhuti zhuixun" 梁放跨族群小說的國家與美學雙主體追尋 [The pursuit of double subjectivities of nation and aesthetics in Liang Fang's interethnic fiction], in Liang Fang 梁放, *Woceng tingdao nizai fengzhong kuqi* 我曾聽到你在風中哭泣 [I once heard you crying in the wind] (Selangor: Dream Eater Publishing, 2014), ix.
74. See Tian Si, *Shuxie Poluozhou* 書寫婆羅洲 [Writing Borneo] (Sibu: Persatuan Kesusasteraan Zhonghua, 2003).
75. Chong Fah Hing, "Liang Fang kuazuqun xiaoshuo," xi.
76. Ng Yean Leng and Shi Huimin, "Li Yongping fangtanlu (xia)" 李永平訪談錄（下）[An interview with Li Yongping, part 2], *Xingzhou Ribao* [Sin Chew daily], March 22, 2009.
77. On the connotations of physical and intellectual immobility associated with the idea of the "native," see Arjun Appadurai, "Putting Hierarchy in its Place," *Cultural Anthropology* 3, no. 1 (1988): 36–38.
78. Liang Fang, *Woceng tingdao nizai fengzhong kuqi*.

79. It was Ng who first pointed out that Chinese, amid the multilinguality of the storyworld, "is relegated to the realm of near silence." See Ng Kim Chew, "Shitou yu nügui," 245. Ko alternately reads the tale's silence on the entangled Chinese history in Borneo as a sign of Li's diminished anxiety over the loss of Chineseness. See Ko Chia-cian, "Xing, qimeng yu lishi zhaiwu," 48.
80. Shi Wenting 石問亭, "Cun er buzai" 存而不在 [Existing, but not present], in Shen Qingwang 沈慶旺, *Tuibian de shanlin* 蛻變的山林 [The transformation of mountains and rainforests] (Selangor: Mentor Publishing Sdn. Bhd., 2007), 187–88.
81. Chong Fah Hing, *Guojia wenxue: Zaizhi yu huiying* 國家文學：宰制與回應 [National literature: Hegemony and response] (Selangor: Mentor Publishing, 2006), 116–17, 138–39.
82. Chong Fah Hing, "Liang Fang kuazuqun xiaoshuo," xiv–xv.
83. Ngu Ik Tien 吳益婷, "Shahua wenxue lide zuqun guanxi" 砂華文學裏的族群關係 [The ethnic relations in Sarawak Chinese-language literature], *Dangdai pinglun* 當代評論 [Contemporary review] (2015): 35–37.
84. Ng Yean Leng and Shi Huimin, "Li Yongping fangtanlu (xia)."
85. For instance, Li inconsistently attributes the legend of empty canoes traveling upstream toward Batu Tiban to either the Iban or the Kenyah (1: 313; 2: 432, 510). Studies have shown that ethnicities exist in a state of flux, and there is considerable "intricacy and fluidity of social relationships and identities" not captured by "the colonial nomenclature of Malay and Dayak," but the narrator does not demonstrate such knowledge. See James T. Collins, "Contesting Straits-Malayness: The Fact of Borneo," in *Contesting Malayness: Malay Identities Across Boundaries*, ed. Timothy P. Barnard (Singapore: Singapore University Press, 2004), 178–79.
86. Chan Tah Wei, *Zuinianqing de qilin: Mahua wenxue zai Taiwan, 1963–2012* 最年輕的麒麟：馬華文學在臺灣, 1963–2012 [The youngest Kylin: Mahua literature in Taiwan, 1963–2012] (Tainan: Guoli Taiwan wenxueguan, 2012), 42.
87. Tian Si, *Shahua wenxue de bentu tezhi*, 44.
88. For more on how cultural resources in the Mahua literary landscape are unevenly distributed, not just across West Malaysia and East Malaysia, but also within East Malaysia itself, see Chan Tah Wei, *Zuinianqing de qilin*, 23.
89. Zhan Min-xu, "Dahe de lücheng," 179.
90. Li Yongping, "Daixu," 14–15.
91. Li Yongping, "Daixu," 15.
92. Zhan Min-xu, "Dahe de lücheng," 179.
93. Julia Lovell, "Chinese Literature in the Global Canon: The Quest for Recognition," in *Global Chinese Literature: Critical Essays*, ed. Jing Tsu and David Derwei Wang (Leiden: Brill, 2010), 211.
94. Pascale Casanova, *World Republic of Letters*, 83.

CODA: ALWAYS THE INTERNAL OTHER

1. Ho Sok Fong, *Lake Like a Mirror*, trans. Natascha Bruce (London: Granta Books, 2019); Ho Sok Fong, *Lake Like a Mirror*, trans. Natascha Bruce (San Francisco: Two Lines Press, 2020).
2. Before Ho's collection, all titles of Mahua literature in English—by the three authors mentioned—were published by Columbia University Press under the series title "Modern Chinese Literature from Taiwan." See http://cup.columbia.edu/series/modern-chinese-literature-from-taiwan.
3. Julia Lovell, *The Politics of Cultural Capital: China's Quest for a Nobel Prize in Literature* (Honolulu: University of Hawai'i Press, 2006), 30–31.
4. Michael S. Duke, "The Problematic Nature of Modern and Contemporary Chinese Fiction in English Translation," in *Worlds Apart: Recent Chinese Writings and Its Audiences*, ed. Howard Goldblatt (New York: M. E. Sharpe, 1990), 200. The diversification of contemporary Chinese literature in translation is noticeable in the comprehensive "Year-End Roll Call" reports on the annual offerings—"from poetry to sci-fi, from classics to contemporary fiction"— compiled by the translator collective *Paper Republic*, accessed October 11, 2021, https://paper-republic.org/project/year-end-roll-call/.
5. In the United States, for instance, only about 0.7 percent of all books published are translated works of literary fiction and poetry. See "Three Percent: A Resource for International Literature at the University of Rochester," accessed October 24, 2021, http://www.rochester.edu/College/translation/threepercent/about/.
6. Rosa Vieira de Almeida, "Keeping to the Margins: Macau Literature and a Pre-postcolonial 'Poetics of Insignificance,'" in *Reading China Against the Grain: Imagining Communities*, ed. Carlos Rojas and Mei-hwa Sung (London: Routledge, 2020), 112–27. Note that Macau has been overlooked in Ng Kim Chew's conceptualization of the Sinophone (*huawen*) Literary Galapagos.
7. On relooking at regional literatures within China to investigate whether it is the national that constitutes the local in cultural formations, or vice versa, see Li Yi 李怡, "'Difang lujing' ruhe tongda 'xiandai Zhongguo'" "地方路徑"如何通達 "現代中國" [How "local routes" can reach "modern China"], *Dangdai wentan* 當代文壇 [Contemporary literary criticism] 1 (2020): 66–69.
8. David Der-wei Wang 王德威, "Wenxue Dongbei yu Zhongguo xiandaixing— 'Dongbeixue' yanjiu chuyi" 文學東北與中國現代性—"東北學"研究芻議 [Literary Northeast China and Chinese modernity: A preliminary discussion on "Northeast Studies"], *Xiaoshuo pinglun* 小說評論 [Fiction criticism] 1 (2021): 60–75.
9. Besides mainland China, Taiwan's internal regionality has yet to be fully studied as well. For discourses on the significance of non-Taipei sites, see Shen Mian

沈眠, "Zhuanfang *Nanfang conglai buxiaxue* zuozhe Chen Yuxuan: Women yizhi yi Taibei wei zhongxin, dan nanfang guandian ne?" 專訪《南方從來不下雪》作者陳育萱: 我們一直以臺北為中心, 但南方觀點呢? [An interview with Chen Yu-hsuan, author of *It Never Snows in the South*: We have always treated Taipei as the center, but what about the viewpoints of the south?], *Guanjian pinglun* 關鍵評論 [The news lens], March 3, 2020, https://www.thenewslens.com/article/131471, accessed April 12, 2022. For a thought-provoking reflection on the diverse constituents of Singapore Chinese literature, see Yow Cheun Hoe 游俊豪, "Yuanyuan, changyu, xitong: Xinhua wenxueshi de jiegouxing xiezuo," 淵源、場域、系統: 新華文學史的結構性寫作 [Origins, fields, systems: The structural writing of Singapore Chinese literary history], in *Yimin guiji yu lisan lunshu: Xinma huaren zuqun de chongceng mailuo* 移民軌跡與離散論述: 新馬華人族群的重層脈絡 [Migratory routes and diasporic discourses: The layered contexts of ethnic Chinese communities in Singapore and Malaysia] (Shanghai: Shanghai sanlian shudian, 2014), 175–92.

10. For a broad survey on Mahua literature's translingual localization of modernism in world literature during the same period, see Zhou Hau Liew and Zhou Sivan, "Mahua Modernist Poetry as a Translational Practice," *Full Stop Quarterly* 6 (August 2017): 1–10.

11. "Jinmajiang beihou de heima: Tamen laizi Dongnanya" 金馬獎背後的黑馬: 他們來自東南亞 [The dark horses of the Golden Horse Award: Those who come from Southeast Asia], *Guanjian pinglun* 關鍵評論 [The news lens], https://www.thenewslens.com/feature/tghffasean, accessed June 18, 2020. In fact, the increasing significance of Southeast Asia for the geography of Chinese-language film production today harkens back to the second half of twentieth century, when geopolitics reconfigured cultural connections among Sinitic-speaking regions outside China. Recent studies of the earlier period include Jeremy Taylor, *Rethinking Transnational Chinese Cinemas: The Amoy-Dialect Film Industry in Cold War Asia* (New York: Routledge, 2011); and Wai-Siam Hee, *Remapping the Sinophone: The Cultural Production of Chinese-Language Cinema in Singapore and Malaya before and during the Cold War* (Hong Kong: Hong Kong University Press, 2019).

12. For a preliminary study on *xinyao*, see Lily Kong, "Making "Music at the Margins"? A Social and Cultural Analysis of *Xinyao* in Singapore," *Asian Studies Review* 19, no. 3 (1996): 99–124. The latest studies of Chinese popular music have yet to fully consider the transregional making of local acoustic worlds in different Sinitic-speaking regions for a broader cultural history of Chinese music. Southeast Asia is conspicuously absent from the discussion. See, for instance, the two special issues in *China Perspectives*, both edited by Nathanel Amar: "Sinophone Musical Worlds (1): Circulations of Sounds, Affects and Identities,"

China Perspectives 3 (2019), and "Sinophone Musical Worlds (2): The Politics of Chineseness," *China Perspectives* 2 (2020).

13. See Yap Wee Cheng 葉偉征, "Xinjiapo Chaozhou yinyueshe yanjiu" 新加坡潮州音樂社研究 [A study on Teochew music clubs in Singapore], (MA diss., National University of Singapore, 2001).

14. Eric Hayot, "Commentary: On the 'Sainifeng' as a Global Literary Practice," in *Global Chinese Literature: Critical Essays*, ed. Jing Tsu and David Der-wei Wang (Leiden: Brill, 2010), 228. Original emphases. In his article, he quotes from Emily Apter, "Untranslatables: A World System," *New Literary History* 39, no. 3 (2008): 581.

15. To get acquainted with the range of local interpretations, a good place to start will be the eleven-volume *Mahua wenxue piping daxi* 馬華文學批評大系 [Compendium of Mahua literary criticism], ed. Chong Yee-Voon 鍾怡雯 and Chan Tah Wei 陳大為 (Taoyuan: Yuanzhi daxue Zhongguo yuwenxuexi, 2019).

16. Lim Kien Ket 林建國, "Yixing" 異形 [Aliens], *Zhongwai wenxue* 中外文學 [Chung-Wai literary quarterly] 22, no. 3 (1993): 80–82; Tee Kim Tong 張錦忠, "Xiaowenxue, fuxitong: Dongnanya huawen wenxue de (yuyan wenti yu) yiyi" 小文學、複系統：東南亞華文文學的（語言問題與）意義 [Minor literatures and polysystems: The significance (and language problem) of Southeast Asian Chinese literature], in *Dangdai wenxue yu renwen shengtai: 2003nian Dongnanya huawen wenxue guoji xueshu yantaohui lunwenji* 當代文學與人文生態：2003 年東南亞華文文學國際學術研討會論文集 [Contemporary literature and the ecology of the humanities: Proceedings from the 2003 International Symposium on Southeast Asian Chinese Literature], ed. Wu Yaozong 吳耀宗 (Taibei: Wanjuanlou, 2003), 313–27; and Ng Kim Chew 黃錦樹, *Huawen xiaowenxue de Malaixiya ge'an* 華文小文學的馬來西亞個案 [Minor literature in Chinese: The case of Malaysia] (Taipei: Maitian, 2015), 28, 107–19.

17. For instance, see François Paré, *Exiguity: Reflections on the Margins of Literature*, trans. Lin Burman (Waterloo: Wilfrid Laurier University Press, 1997), where Paré departs from the model of resistance by advocating to recognize the regenerative diversity that small literary formations such as Quebec literature and Basque literature offer. In the context of Chinese and Sinophone literatures, see Andrea Bachner, "At the Margins of the Minor: Rethinking Scalarity, Relationality, and Translation," *Journal of World Literature* 2, no. 2 (2017): 139–57, where she emphasizes the invariably comparative positionality of the "minor" by analyzing Taiwanese indigenous literatures, which she conceptualizes as being "ultraminor."

18. Other scholars have created a momentum to theorize the southern character and positionality of Mahua and the historically connected Xinhua (Singapore Chinese-language) literature. See, for instance, how Tee Kim Tong 張錦忠

engages with Ng Kim Chew's literary thought in "Zaina nanfang de guodu: Chidao jifengdai de huawen shuxie" 在那南方的國度：赤道季風帶的華文書寫 [In the southern country: Sinophone writings in the equatorial monsoon belt], in *Nanfang de shehui, xue (xia): Xingdong zuowei lunli* 南方的社會，學（下）：行動作為倫理 [Studying southern societies (part 2): On the ethics of social action], ed. Chao En-chieh 趙恩潔 (New Taipei: Rive Gauche Publishing House, 2020), 51–74; and Lam Lap 林立, "Chaoxiang yige 'Nanyang shixue': Yanjiu Xinjiapo huawen jiutishi zhi wojian" 朝向一個「南洋詩學」：研究新加坡華文舊體詩之我見 [Toward a "Nanyang poetics": My thoughts on studying classical-style Chinese-language poetry in Singapore], in *Cong Quan Tai Shi dao quantaishi guoji xueshu yantaohui lunwenji* 從《全臺詩》到全臺詩國際學術研討會論文集 [Proceedings of archiving Taiwan: The international conference on twenty years of compiling the *Quan Tai Shi*], ed. 黃美娥 Huang Mei-er (Tainan: National Museum of Taiwan Literature, 2020), 753–70.

19. Philip Holden, email correspondence with author, October 8, 2020. I thank Philip Holden for sharing the observation that both Singapore and Peninsular Malaysia map their antipodal locales onto the Republic of Ecuador, which governs the Galapagos, and for pointing out that instead of a critical idiom, the South American archipelago is deployed as a narrative device in the works of Anglophone Singapore writers such as Simon Tay and Amanda Lee Koe.

20. Ng Kim Chew, "Zuowei Taiwan wenxue lilun guanjianci de 'Mahua wenxue'" 作為臺灣文學理論關鍵詞的"馬華文學" [Mahua literature as a keyword for Taiwan literary theory], in *Mahua wenxue piping daxi: Huang Jinshu* 馬華文學批評大系：黃錦樹 [Malaysian Chinese literary criticism: Ng Kim Chew], ed. Chong Yee-Voon and Chan Tah Wei (Taoyuan: Yuanzhi daxue Zhongguo yuwenxuexi, 2019), 326. Emphasis mine.

21. Lim Kien Ket, "Fang Xiu lun" 方修論 [On Fang Xiu], *Zhongwai wenxue* 中外文學 [Chung-Wai literary monthly] 29, no. 4 (2000): 65–98.

22. Antonio Benitez-Rojo, *The Repeating Island: The Caribbean and the Postmodern Perspective (Second Edition)*, trans. James Maraniss (Durham, NC: Duke University Press, 1996), 9.

23. Ng Kim Chew, "Zuowei Taiwan wenxue lilun guanjianci de 'Mahua wenxue,'" 323.

24. Ng Kim Chew, "Zuowei Taiwan wenxue,'" 325.

25. David Der-wei Wang, "Xulun: Huaihaizi Huang Jinshu—Huang Jinshu de Mahua lunshu yu xushu" 序論：壞孩子黃錦樹—黃錦樹的馬華論述與敘述 [Introduction: The enfant terrible Ng Kim Chew—Ng Kim Chew's Mahua discourses and narratives], in Ng Kim Chew, *Youdao zhidao* 由島至島 [From island to island] (Taipei: Maitian, 2002), 12–15. Wang moves on to identifying an enduring dialectic between the Chinese (*hua* 華) and the alien (*yi* 夷) as the fundamental driver of Chinese literary production in non-Chinese settings. For his

interpretation of Chinese literary alterity, he adopts the Mahua scholar Tee Kim Tong's suggestion to translate the "Sinophone" as "huayi feng" 華夷風; see David Der-wei Wang, "Huayi fengqi: Malaixiya yu huayu yuxi wenxue" 華夷風起: 馬來西亞與華語語系文學 [When the wind of the Sinophone blows: Malaysia and Sinophone literature], *Zhongshan renwen xuebao* 中山人文學報 [Sun Yat-sen journal of humanities], issue no. 38 (2015): 1–29. Wang has since reconceptualized the *huayi* dialectic as a "Sinophone/Xenophone" interpretive dyad that considers the longue durée of Chinese civilization and culture. See David Der-wei Wang, "Huayi zhibian: Huayu yuxi yanjiu de xinshijie" 華夷之變: 華語語系研究的新視界 [Sinophone/Xenophone studies: Toward a poetics of wind, sound, and changeability], *Zhongguo xiandai wenxue* 中國現代文學 [Modern Chinese literature] 34 (2018): 1–28.

Bibliography

ARCHIVES

British Library

Xingzhou Ribao (Sin Chew Jit Poh) 星洲日報 (microfilm)
Or MIC 9946 (February 1935)

The National Library, Singapore

Sin Chew Jit Poh (microfilm)
NL11541 (April 18, 1935–May 13, 1935)
A01189142D (October 7, 1936–October 30, 1936)
A01189145G (December 19, 1936–January 18, 1937)

National University of Singapore Central Library

Sin Chew Jit Poh (microfilm)
ZR18842 (May 1–29, 1934)

Howard Gotlieb Archival Research Center, Boston University

The Han Suyin Collection

BOOKS AND ARTICLES

Adelson, Leslie A. *The Turkish Turn in Contemporary German Literature*. New York: Palgrave Macmillan, 2005.

Admussen, Nick. *Neither Nearing nor Departing*. Greensboro, NC: Two of Cups Press, 2018.

Amar, Nathanel. "Sinophone Musical Worlds (1): Circulations of Sounds, Affects and Identities." *China Perspectives* 3 (2019).

———. "Sinophone Musical Worlds (2): The Politics of Chineseness." *China Perspectives* 2 (2020).

Andaya, Barbara Watson, and Leonard Y. Andaya. *A History of Malaysia (Second Edition)*. Honolulu: University of Hawai'i Press, 2001.

Anderson, Benedict. "The Unrewarded: Notes on the Nobel Prize for Literature." *New Left Review* 80 (2013): 99–108.

Appadurai, Arjun. "Putting Hierarchy in Its Place." *Cultural Anthropology* 3, no. 1 (1988): 36–49.

Apter, Emily. *Against World Literature: On the Politics of Untranslatability*. London: Verso, 2013.

Arendt, Hannah. *The Human Condition*, 2nd ed. Chicago: University of Chicago Press, 1998.

Ashcroft, Bill. "Bridging the Silence: Inner Translation and the Metonymic Gap." In *Language and Translation in Postcolonial Literatures: Multilingual Contexts, Translational Texts*, ed. Simona Bertacco, 17–31. New York: Routledge, 2013.

Ashcroft, Bill, Gareth Griffiths, and Helen Tiffin. *The Empire Writes Back: Theory and Practice in Postcolonial Literatures*, 2nd ed. London: Routledge, 2002.

Bachner, Andrea. "At the Margins of the Minor: Rethinking Scalarity, Relationality, and Translation." *Journal of World Literature* 2, no. 2 (2017): 139–57.

Beijing yuyan xueyuan *Zhongguo wenxuejia cidian* bianweihui 北京語言學院《中國文學家辭典》編委會 [Editorial committee for the *Dictionary of Chinese Literary Figures*, Beijing Language Institute], ed. *Zhongguo wenxuajia cidian (xiandai diyi fence)* 中國文學家辭典（現代第一分冊） [Dictionary of Chinese literary figures (modern period, vol. 1)]. Chengdu: Sichuan renmin chubanshe, 1979.

Bellwood, Peter, James J. Fox, and Darrell Tryon, eds. *The Austronesians: Historical and Comparative Perspectives*. Canberra: Australian University E-Press, 2006.

Benitez-Rojo, Antonio. *The Repeating Island: The Caribbean and the Postmodern Perspective (Second Edition)*, trans. James Maraniss. Durham, NC: Duke University Press, 1996.

Benjamin, Geoffrey. "On Being Tribal in the Malay World." In *Tribal Communities in the Malay World: Historical, Cultural and Social Perspectives*, ed. Geoffrey Benjamin and Cynthia Chou, 7–76. Singapore: Institute of Southeast Asian Studies, 2002.

Bernards, Brian. "From Diasporic Nationalism to Transcolonial Consciousness: Lao She's Singaporean Satire, *Little Po's Birthday*." *Modern Chinese Literature and Culture* 26, no. 1 (2014): 1-40.

———. "Malaysia as Method: Xiao Hei and Ethnolinguistic Literary Taxonomy." In *The Oxford Handbook of Modern Chinese Literatures*, ed. Carlos Rojas, and Andrea Bachner, 811–31. Oxford: Oxford University Press, 2016.

———. "Plantation and Rainforest: Chang Kuei-hsing (Zhang Guixing) and a South Seas Discourse of Coloniality and Nature." In *Sinophone Studies: A Critical Reader*, ed. Shu-mei Shih, Chien-hsin Tsai, and Brian Bernards, 325–38. New York: Columbia University Press, 2013.

———. *Writing the South Seas: Imagining the Nanyang in Chinese and Southeast Asian Postcolonial Literature*. Seattle: University of Washington Press, 2015.

Béteille, André. "The Idea of Indigenous People." *Current Anthropology* 39, no. 2 (1998): 187–92.

Brickell, Katherine, and Ayona Datta. "Introduction: Translocal Geographies." In *Translocal Geographies: Spaces, Places, Connections*, ed. Katherine Brickell and Ayona Datta, 3–20. London: Routledge, 2016.

C Jun C 君 (Mr. C) [Liang Shan 梁山]. "Difang zuojia jieshao de shangque" 地方作家介紹的商榷 [A deliberation on the introduction of local writers]. In *Mahua Xinwenxue daxi I·Lilun piping yiji* 馬華新文學大系（一）·理論批評一集 [Compendium of modern Mahua literature, vol. 1: Theory and critique (part 1)], ed. Fang Xiu 方修, 263–65. Singapore: Shijie shuju, 1972.

Casanova, Pascale. *The World Republic of Letters*. Translated by M. B. DeBevoise. Cambridge, MA: Harvard University Press, 2004.

Chan Cheow Thia 曾昭程. "Hechu mi jiaguo, wendi qiu xiangyi: Zhanqian zuojia Lin Cantian de xiezuo shijian" 何處覓家國，文地求相宜：戰前作家林參天的寫作實踐 [In search of home and country, toward the mutual becoming of place and literature: The writing practice of pre–World War II author Lin Cantian]. *Lianhe Zaobao* 聯合早報, May 21, 2019.

Chan, Shelly. *Diaspora's Homelands: Modern China in the Age of Global Migration*. Durham, NC: Duke University Press, 2018.

Chan Tah Wei (Chen Dawei) 陳大為. "Yueru yinyu de yulin—daodu dangdai Mahua wenxue" 躍入隱喻的雨林——導讀當代馬華文學 [Leaping into the rainforest metaphor—a guide to reading contemporary Mahua literature]. *Chengpin haodu* 誠品好讀 [Eslite reader], no. 13 (2001): 32–34.

———. *Zuinianqing de qilin: Mahua wenxue zai Taiwan, 1963–2012* 最年輕的麒麟：馬華文學在臺灣，1963–2012 [The youngest Kylin: Mahua literature in Taiwan, 1963–2012]. Tainan: Guoli Taiwan wenxueguan, 2012.

Cheah, Pheng. *What is a World? On Postcolonial Literature as World Literature*. Durham, NC: Duke University Press, 2016.

Chen Fangming 陳芳明. *Taiwan Xinwenxueshi (xia)* 臺灣新文學史（下）[A history of Taiwan New Literature (part 2)]. Taipei: Linking Publishing, 2011.

Chen Liao 陳遼. "Huawen wenxue yanjiu sanshinian" 華文文學研究三十年 [Studies of literatures in Chinese: A thirty-year review]. *Huawen wenxue* 華文文學 [Literatures in Chinese], no. 2 (2008): 10–14.

———. "Zouxiang shijie yihou—tan Xinshiqi Wenxue zai shijie wenxue gejuzhong de dingwei" 走向世界以後—談新時期文學在世界文學格局中的定位 [After having marched toward the world—on the position of literature of the New Era in the world literary order]. *Wenyi pinglun* 文藝評論 [Literature and art criticism], no. 4 (1986): 20–23.

Chen Mong Tse 陳蒙志. "Xianggang chuban de bendi shukan" 香港出版的本地書刊 [Singapore's books and journals published in Hong Kong]. *Yihe shiji* 怡和世紀 18 (2012): 80–81.

Chen Wanqian 陳宛茜. "Mayi zuojia Li Yongping lai Tai sishinian huo Guojia Wenyijiang" 馬裔作家李永平來臺四十年獲國家文藝獎 [Li Yongping, writer of Malaysian descent, wins National Award for Literary Arts after forty years in Taiwan]. *Lianhebao* 聯合報 [United daily news], March 26, 2016.

Chen Ying 陳穎. "Xiandai Zhongguo zhishi puxizhong de Nanyang, 1911–1937" 現代中國知識譜系中的南洋，1911–1937 [Nanyang in modern China's knowledge system, 1911–1937]. PhD diss., Nanyang Technological University, 2018.

Chen Yingzhen 陳映真. "Wodui Mahua wenxue de guangan" 我對馬華文學的觀感 [My perception of Mahua literature]. In *Xinma wenxueshi congtan* 新馬文學史叢談 [Collected writings on Singapore and Malaysian literary history], ed. Fang Xiu 方修, 5–12. Singapore: Chunyi tushu maoyi gongsi, 1999.

Chen, Yun-yuan 陳允元. "Qi, beipan yu huijia zhilu: Li Yongping *Yuxue feifei* zhong de shuangxiang zhuiren" 棄、背叛與回家之路：李永平《雨雪霏霏》中的雙鄉追認 [Abandonment, betrayal and home return: The retracement and recognition of dual home countries in Li Yongping's *Snowfall in the Clouds*]. *Taiwan wenxue yanjiu xuebao* 臺灣文學研究學報 [Journal of Taiwan literary studies] 13 (2011): 41–67.

Chen Zhengyan 陳征雁. "Mahua xiaoshuojia tan chuangzuo zhi'er" 馬華小說家談創作之二 [Mahua fiction authors on creative writing (part 2)]. In *Xinma huawen wenxue daxi dibaji: Shiliao* 新馬華文文學大系第八集：史料 [Compendium of Singapore, Malayan, and Malaysian Chinese-language literature, vol. 8: Historical material], ed. Zhao Rong 趙戎. 261–65. Singapore: Jiaoyu chubanshe, 1971.

Cheng, Lim-Keak. *Social Change and the Chinese in Singapore: A Socio-economic Geography with Special Reference to Bāng Structure*. Singapore: Singapore University Press, 1985.

Chi Pang-yuan 齊邦媛. "Xu: *Yuxue feifei* yu Mahua wenxue tuxiang" 序：《雨雪霏霏》與馬華文學圖像 [Preface: *Snowfall in the Clouds* and the picture of Mahua literature].

In Li Yongping 李永平, *Yuxue feifei: Poluozhou tongnian jishi* 雨雪霏霏：婆羅洲童年記事 [*Snowfall in the Clouds*: Recollections of a Borneo childhood], i–x. Taipei: Tianxia yuanjian, 2002.

Chiu, Kuei-fen 邱貴芬. "Empire of the Chinese Sign: The Question of Chinese Diasporic Imagination in Transnational Literary Production." *The Journal of Asian Studies* 67, no. 2 (2008): 593–620.

——. "Piping yu huiying: Yu Huang Jinshu tan wenxueshi shuxie de baoli wenti" 批評與回應：與黃錦樹談文學史書寫的暴力問題 [Critique and response: Negotiating the question of symbolic violence in literary historiography with Ng Kim Chew]. *Wenhua yanjiu* 文化研究 [Router: A journal of cultural studies] 2 (2006): 280–91.

——. "The Production of Indigeneity: Contemporary Indigenous Literature in Taiwan and Trans-cultural Inheritance." *The China Quarterly* 200 (2009): 1071–87.

Chong Fah Hing (Zhuang Huaxing) 莊華興. *Guojia wenxue: Zaizhi yu huiying* 國家文學：宰制與回應 [National literature: Hegemony and response]. Selangor: Mentor Publishing, 2006.

——. "Liang Fang kuazuqun xiaoshuo de guojia yu meixue shuangzhuti zhuixun" 梁放跨族群小說的國家與美學雙主體追尋 [The pursuit of double subjectivities of nation and aesthetics in Liang Fang's inter-ethnic fiction]. In Liang Fang 梁放, *Woceng tingdao nizai fengzhong kuqi* 我曾聽到你在風中哭泣 [I once heard you crying in the wind], vii–xxx. Selangor: Dream Eater Publishing, 2014.

——. "Shuide Mahua wenxue yanjiu? Ping Xu Wenrong de *Nanfang xuanhua: Mahua wenxue de zhengzhi dikang shixue*" 誰的馬華文學研究？評許文榮的《南方喧嘩：馬華文學的政治抵抗詩學》 [Whose Mahua literary studies? On Khor Boon Eng's *Uproar in the South: The Poetics of Political Resistance in Mahua Literature*]. *Taiwan dongnanya xuekan* 臺灣東南亞學刊 [Taiwan journal of Southeast Asian studies] 3, no. 1 (2006): 105–09.

Chong Yee-Voon (Zhong Yiwen) 鍾怡雯. "Zhongguo nanyou (lai) wenren yu Mahua sanwen shi" 中國南遊（來）文人與馬華散文史 [Southern-touring (incoming) scholars from China and the history of Mahua prose]. *Zhongguo xiandai wenxue* 中國現代文學 [Modern Chinese literature] 25 (2014): 161–75.

Chong Yee-Voon, and Chan Tah Wei, eds. *Mahua wenxue piping daxi* 馬華文學批評大系 [Compendium of Mahua literary criticism]. 11 vols. Taoyuan: Yuanzhi Daxue Zhongguo yuwenxuexi, 2019.

Chow Tse-tsung 周策縱. "Zongjieci" 總結辭 [Closing remarks]. In *Dongnanya huawen wenxue* 東南亞華文文學 [Chinese literature in Southeast Asia], ed. Wong Yoon Wah 王潤華 and Horst Pastoors, 359–62. Singapore: Goethe-Institut Singapore and Singapore Association of Writers, 1989.

Chui Kwei Chiang 崔貴強. *Xinjiapo huawen baokan yu baoren* 新加坡華文報刊與報人 [The Chinese newspapers and newspapermen of Singapore]. Singapore: Haitian wenhua, 1993.

Collins, James T. "Contesting Straits-Malayness: The Fact of Borneo." In *Contesting Malayness: Malay Identities Across Boundaries*, ed. Timothy P. Barnard, 168–80. Singapore: Singapore University Press, 2004.

Comber, Leon. "Publishing Asian Writers in English." In *Asian Voices in English*, ed. Mimi Chan and Roy Harris, 79–86. Hong Kong: Hong Kong University Press, 1991.

Cui, Feng, and Alex Tickell. "Han Suyin: The Little Voice of Decolonizing Asia." *Journal of Postcolonial Writing* 57, no. 2 (2021): 147–53.

Damrosch, David. *What is World Literature?* Princeton, NJ: Princeton University Press, 2003.

——. "Where is World Literature?" In *Studying Transcultural Literary History*, ed. Gunilla Lindberg-Wada, 211–20. Berlin: De Gruyter, 2012.

Department of Statistics, Malaysia. "Press Release: Current Population Estimates, Malaysia, 2021," July 15, 2021, https://www.dosm.gov.my/v1/index.php?r=column/pdfPrev&id=ZjJOSnpJR21sQWVUcUp6ODRudm5JZz09.

Deterding, David, Low Ee Ling, and Adam Brown, eds. *English in Singapore: Research on Grammar*. Singapore: McGraw-Hill Education (Asia), 2003.

Dirlik, Arif. "Place-based Imagination: Globalism and the Politics of Place." In *Places and Politics in an Age of Globalization*, ed. Roxann Prazniak and Arik Dirlik, 15–51. Lanham, MD: Rowman & Littlefield, 2001.

Du Can 杜殘. "Santan dazhongyu" 三談大眾語 [On mass language, part 3]. In *Mahua Xinwenxue daxi I·Lilun piping yiji* 馬華新文學大系（一）·理論批評一集 [Compendium of modern Mahua literature, vol.1: Theory and critique (part 1)], ed. Fang Xiu 方修, 347–49. Singapore: Shijie shuju, 1972.

Duke, Michael S. "The Problematic Nature of Modern and Contemporary Chinese Fiction in English Translation." In *Worlds Apart: Recent Chinese Writings and Its Audiences*, ed. Howard Goldblatt, 198–227. New York: M. E. Sharpe, 1990.

Edney, M. H. "British Military Education, Mapmaking, and Military 'Mapmindedness' in the Later Enlightenment." *The Cartographic Journal* 31, no. 1 (1994): 14–20.

Editors of *Encyclopedia Britannica*. "Dayak." Brittanica.com, 2021, accessed April 14, 2022, http://www.britannica.com/topic/Dayak.

Evers, Hans-Dieter. "Nusantara: History of a Concept." *Journal of the Malaysian Branch of the Royal Asiatic Society* 89, part 1, no. 310 (2016): 3–14.

Fabian, Johannes. *Time and the Other: How Anthropology Makes its Object*. New York: Columbia University Press, 2002.

Fan Cheng 樊騰. "Wo duiyu dazhongyu wenxue de yijian" 我對於大眾語文學的意見 [My views on literature written in "mass language"]. In *Mahua Xinwenxue daxi I·Lilun piping yiji* 馬華新文學大系（一）·理論批評一集 [Compendium of modern

Mahua literature, vol. 1: Theory and critique (part 1)], ed. Fang Xiu 方修, 337–39. Singapore: Shijie shuju, 1972.

Fang Xiu 方修. *Mahua wenyi sichao de yanbian* 馬華文藝思潮的演變 [The developmental trends of Mahua artistic and literary thought]. Singapore: Wanli wenhua qiye, 1970.

———, ed. *Mahua Xinwenxue daxi* 馬華新文學大系 [Compendium of modern Mahua literature, 10 vols.]. Singapore: Shijie shuju, 1971–1972.

———, ed. *Zhang Tianbai zuopinxuan* 張天白作品選 [A selection of Zhang Tianbai's works]. Singapore: Shanghai shuju, 1979.

"Fangmi dianfu xuanchuan, pumie seqing wenhua: Zhengfu yuanyin Buliang Kanwu Faling jinzhi gongchan Zhongguo ji Xianggang wushisanjia chubanwu shu Xing" 防弭顛覆宣傳‧撲滅色情文化: 政府援引不良刊物法令禁止共產中國及香港五十三家出版物輸星 [Preventing and eliminating subversive propaganda, eradicating pornographic culture: Government cites the Undesirable Publications Act to proscribe supply to Singapore of fifty three publishers' products from Communist China and Hong Kong]. *Nanyang Siang Pau* 南洋商報, May 23, 1958, accessed September 1, 2019, http://eresources.nlb.gov.sg/newspapers/Digitised/Article/nysp19581023-1.2.21.2.

Feiming 廢名 (Qiu Shizhen 丘士珍). "Difang Zuojia Tan" 地方作家談 [On local writers]. In *Mahua Xinwenxue daxi I·Lilun piping yiji* 馬華新文學大系（一）·理論批評一集 [Compendium of modern Mahua literature, vol.1: Theory and critique (part 1)], ed. Fang Xiu, 259–61. Singapore: Shijie shuju, 1972.

Feng Te-ping 封德屏, ed. *Jianshan youshi shan: Li Yongping zhuisi jinianhui ji wenxuezhan tekan* 見山又是山: 李永平追思紀念會暨文學展特刊 [The mountain is once again the mountain: A special issue on the memorial service and literary exhibition for Li Yongping]. Taipei: Wenxun zazhishe, 2018.

Fu Donghua 傅東華. *Shanhutao ji* 山胡桃集 [The hickory collection]. Shanghai: Shenghuo shudian, 1935.

———. "Shijie wenyi de qiantu" 世界文藝的前途 [The future of world literary arts). *Qiantu zazhi* 前途雜誌 [Prospect] 1, no. 1 (1933): 1–10.

Furnivall, J. S. *Netherlands India: A Study of Plural Economy.* Cambridge: Cambridge University Press, 1939.

Ge Kong 哥空. "Yijiusanwu nian Malaiya wentan" 一九三五年馬來亞文壇 (The 1935 Malayan literary circle). In *Mahua Xinwenxue daxi X · Chuban shiliao* 馬華新文學大系（十）·出版史料 [Compendium of modern Malayan Chinese literature, vol. 10: Historical material on publications], ed. Fang Xiu 方修, 468–76. Singapore: Shijie shuju, 1972.

Ge, Liangyan. *Out of the Margins: The Rise of Chinese Vernacular Fiction.* Honolulu: University of Hawai'i Press, 2001.

Goh Leng Hoon 吳龍雲. *Zaoyu bangqun: Bincheng huaren shehui de kuabang zuzhi yanjiu* 遭遇幫群：檳城華人社會的跨幫組織研究 [Encountering dialect groups: A study of cross-*bang* organizations in Penang Chinese society]. Singapore: National University of Singapore Department of Chinese Studies and Global Publishing, 2009.

González, J. A., C. Montes, J. Rodríguez, and W. Tapia. "Rethinking the Galapagos Islands as a Complex Social-ecological System: Implications for Conservation and Management." *Ecology and Society* 13, no. 2 (2008): 13, accessed June 29, 2020, http://www.ecologyandsociety.org/vol13/iss2/art13/.

Groppe, Alison M. *Sinophone Malaysian Literature: Not Made in China*. Amherst, NY: Cambria Press, 2013.

Gupta, Anthea Fraser. "The Pragmatic Particles of Singapore Colloquial English." *Journal of Pragmatics* 18, no. 1 (1992): 31–57.

Ha Jin 哈金. "Wei waiyuqiang bianhu" 為外語腔辯護 [In defense of the foreign accent]. In *Zai taxiang xiezuo* 在他鄉寫作 [The writer as migrant], trans. Mingdi 明迪, 137–60. Taipei: Linking Publishing, 2010.

Han Suyin 韓素音 (漢素音). *And the Rain My Drink*. Boston: Little, Brown and Company, 1956; and London: Jonathan Cape, 1956 [the original title of these two publications was preceded by three ellipsis points, as follows: … *and the Rain My Drink*].

———. "Asian Writers Who Write in English: English the International Language and the History of English." In *Duozhong shijiao: Wenxue yu wenhua bijiao yanjiu lunwenji* 多種視角：文學與文化比較研究論文集 [Multiple perspectives: An anthology of comparative research on literature and culture], ed. Chang Yaoxin 常耀信, 148–60. Tianjin: Nankai daxue chubanshe, 1991.

———. *Canfeng yinlu* 餐風飲露 [And the rain my drink]. Trans. Ly Singko 李星可. Singapore: Youth Book Company, 1958.

———. "The Creation of a Malayan Literature." *Eastern World* (May 1957): 20–21.

———. *My House Has Two Doors*. London: Triad Granada, 1982.

———. "Nanda de weilai" 南大的未來 [The future of Nanyang University]. In *Fuban Nanyang daxue lunwenji* 復辦南洋大學論文集 [An anthology on the revival of Nanyang University], ed. Tan Kok Chiang 陳國相, 3–7. Selangor: Strategic Information and Research Development Centre, 2010.

———. "The Nanyang Students." *Mahasiswa Negara* [University students of the nation] 2, no. 10 (1963): 6–8.

———. "An Outline of Malayan-Chinese Literature." *Eastern Horizon* 3, no. 6 (1964): 6–16.

———. "Plenary Lecture." In *Asian Voices in English*, ed. Mimi Chan and Roy Harris, 17–21. Hong Kong: Hong Kong University Press, 1991.

———. *Qingshan bulao (shangce)* 青山不老（上冊） [The mountain is young, vol. 1], trans. Ly Singko. Singapore: Youth Book Company, 1959.

———. "Why I Like Malaya—Home of Many Races." *Malayan Police Magazine* (March 1961): 16–17.

———. "Writing about Malaya." *PETIR* [Lightning] (January 1957): 3.

———. "Xie youguan Malaiya de shi" 寫有關馬來亞的事 [Writing about Malaya], trans. Dunbi 鈍筆. *Xingdongbao* 行動報 (January 1957): 4.

"Han Suyin Tells the Jungle Girl's Tale." *The Straits Times*, March 10, 1953.

Harper, T. N. *The End of Empire and the Making of Malaya.* Cambridge: Cambridge University Press, 1999.

Hau, Caroline S. *The Chinese Question: Ethnicity, Nation and Region In and Beyond the Philippines.* Singapore: NUS Press, 2014.

Hayot, Eric. "Commentary: On the 'Sainifeng' as a Global Literary Practice." In *Global Chinese Literature: Critical Essays*, ed. Jing Tsu and David Der-wei Wang, 219–28. Leiden: Brill, 2010.

Hee, Wai-Siam 許維賢. *Huayu dianying zai hou-Malaixiya: Tuqiang fengge, huayifeng yu zuozhelun* 華語電影在後馬來西亞：土腔風格、華夷風與作者論 [Post-Malaysian Chinese-language film: Accented style, Sinophone and auteur theory]. Taipei: Linking Publishing, 2018.

———. *Remapping the Sinophone: The Cultural Production of Chinese-Language Cinema in Singapore and Malaya before and during the Cold War.* Hong Kong: Hong Kong University Press, 2019.

Hill, Alan. "The African Writers Series." *Research in African Literatures* 2, no. 1 (1971): 18–20.

———. "Books for a Commonwealth, Publishing Locally or from London," *Times Literary Supplement*, August 10, 1962.

Hillenbrand, Margaret. *Literature, Modernity, and the Practice of Resistance: Japanese and Taiwanese Fiction, 1960–1990.* Leiden: Brill, 2007.

Hitchcock, Peter. "Decolonizing (the) English." *The South Atlantic Quarterly* 100, no. 3 (2001): 749–71.

Hooker, Virginia Matheson. *Writing a New Society: Social Change through the Novel in Malay.* Honolulu: University of Hawai'i Press, 1999.

Ho Sok Fong. *Lake Like a Mirror*, trans. Natascha Bruce. London: Granta Books, 2019.

———. *Lake Like a Mirror*, trans. Natascha Bruce. San Francisco: Two Lines Press, 2020.

Huang, Yu-ting. "The Archipelagos of Taiwan Literature: Comparative Methods and Island Writings in Taiwan." In *Comparatizing Taiwan*, ed. Shu-mei Shih and Ping-hui Liao, 80–99. New York: Routledge, 2015.

Idrus, Rusaslina. "Malays and Orang Asli: Contesting Indigeneity." In *Melayu: The Politics, Poetics and Paradoxes of Malayness*, ed. Maznah Mohamad and Syed Muhd Khairudin Aljunied, 101–23. Singapore: National University of Singapore Press, 2011.

James, Matthew. *Collecting Evolution: The Galapagos Expedition that Vindicated Darwin*. New York: Oxford University Press, 2017.

Jingzi 鏡子. "Fulu: Malaixiya huawen wenxue suishi keneng xiaoshi, er wo ganghao shenzaiqizhong" 附錄：馬來西亞華文文學隨時可能消失，而我剛好身在其中 [Appendix: Mahua literature may disappear anytime, and I happen to be in the midst of it]. In Ng Kim Chew 黃錦樹, *Minguo de manchuan* 民國的慢船 [Slow boat to Republican China], 234–49. Petaling Jaya: Got One Publisher Sdn. Bhd., 2019.

"Jinmajiang beihou de heima: Tamen laizi Dongnanya" 金馬獎背後的黑馬：他們來自東南亞 [The dark horses of the Golden Horse Award: Those who come from Southeast Asia]. *Guanjian pinglun* 關鍵評論 [The news lens], accessed June 18, 2020, https://www.thenewslens.com/feature/tghffasean.

Kenley, David L. *New Culture in a New World: The May Fourth Movement and the Chinese Diaspora in Singapore, 1919–1932*. London: Routledge, 2003.

Kho Tong Guan 許通元. "Yanshao de huajiao *Nongyan*: Lin Cantian shoubu changpian de Mahua wenxue 'jingdianlun'" 延燒的華教《濃煙》：林參天首部長篇的馬華文學"經典論" [The ongoing *Thick Smoke* in Chinese education: Rethinking the discourse of canonicity in Mahua literature through Lin Cantian's first novel]. *Nanfang yanjiu baogao xilie* 南方研究報告系列 [Southern working paper series], no. 2 (2016): 1–27.

———. "Huang Jinshu zhuanfang" 黃錦樹專訪 [An interview with Ng Kim Chew]. *Chao Foon* 蕉風, no. 509 (2015): 52–57.

Khor Boon Eng 許文榮. "Mahua wenxue de ruoshi minzu shuxie: Yige wenxueshi de shiye" 馬華文學的弱勢民族書寫：一個文學史的視野 [Writings about marginalized ethnicities in Mahua literature: A perspective of literary history]. *Zhongguo bijiao wenxue* 中國比較文學 [Comparative literature in China] 1 (2011): 82–95.

Ko Chia-cian (Gao Jiaqian) 高嘉謙. "Xing, qimeng yu lishi zhaiwu: Li Yongping *Dahe jintou* de chuangshang he xushi" 性、啟蒙與歷史債務：李永平《大河盡頭》的創傷和敘事 [Sex, enlightenment, and historical debt: Trauma and narration in Li Yongping's *Where the Great River Ends*]. *Taiwan wenxue yanjiu jikan* 臺灣文學研究集刊 [NTU studies in Taiwan literature] 11 (2012): 35–60.

———. *Yimin, jiangjie yu xiandaixing: Hanshi de nanfang lisan yu shuqing (1895–1945)* 遺民、疆界與現代性：漢詩的南方離散與抒情 (1895–1945) [Loyalists, boundary and modernity: Southbound diaspora and lyricism of classical-style Chinese poetry (1895–1945)]. Taipei: Linking Publishing, 2016.

Kong, Lily. "Making "Music at the Margins"? A Social and Cultural Analysis of *Xinyao* in Singapore." *Asian Studies Review* 19, no. 3 (1996): 99–124.

Krishnaswamy, Revathi. "Toward World Literary Knowledges: Theory in the Age of Globalization." *Comparative Literature* 62, no. 4 (2010): 399–419.

Kuo Chiang-sheng 郭強生. "Women" 我們 [The three of us]. In *Zuihou yitang chuangzuoke* 最後一堂創作課 [The last class on creative writing], ed. Chen Hsia-min 陳夏民, 233–38. Taoyuan: Comma Books, 2018.

Kuo, Huei-Ying. *Networks Beyond Empires: Chinese Business and Nationalism in the Hong-Kong-Singapore Corridor, 1914–1941*. Leiden: Brill, 2014.

Kuo Shiu Nue 郭秀女. "Changpian xiaoshuo *Nongyan* de duocengmian yiyi" 長篇小說《濃煙》的多層面意義 [The multifaceted significance of the novel *Thick Smoke*]. In *Xinma huawen wenxue yanjiu xinguancha* 新馬華文文學研究新觀察 [New observations on Singapore and Malaysian Chinese literary studies], ed. Luo Futeng 羅福騰, 135–76. Singapore: UniSIM Centre for Chinese Studies and Global Publishing, 2012.

Kuper, Adam. "The Return of the Native." *Current Anthropology* 44, no. 3 (2003): 389–402.

Lai Pei-Hsuan 賴佩暄. "Lisan yu guifan: Lun Wang Xiaoping banzizhuanti xiaoshuozhong de liudong shenshi yu jiaguo qinghuai" 離散與歸返：論王嘯平半自傳體小說中的流動身世與家國情懷 [The diaspora and the return: An analysis of Wang Xiaoping's wandering life and feelings about home-country in his semi-autobiographical novels]. *Zhongguo xiandai wenxue* 中國現代文學 [Modern Chinese literature] 24 (2013): 167–88.

Lam Lap 林立. "Chaoxiang yige 'Nanyang shixue': Yanjiu Xinjiapo huawen jiutishi zhi wojian" 朝向一個「南洋詩學」：研究新加坡華文舊體詩之我見 [Toward a "Nanyang poetics": My thoughts on studying classical-style Chinese-language poetry in Singapore]. In *Cong* Quan Tai Shi *dao quantaishi guoji xueshu yantaohui lunwenji* 從《全臺詩》到全臺詩國際學術研討會論文集 [Proceedings of archiving Taiwan: The international conference on twenty years of compiling the *Quan Tai Shi*], ed. Huang Mei-er 黃美娥, 753–70. Tainan: National Museum of Taiwan Literature, 2020.

Lao She 老舍. "Xiaopo de shengri" 小坡的生日 [Little Po's birthday]. In *Lao She wenji: Di'er juan* 老舍文集：第二卷 [An anthology of Lao She's works: vol. 2], 1–146. Beijing: Renmin wenxue chubanshe, 1980.

Lee, Edwin. *Singapore: The Unexpected Nation*. Singapore: Institute of Southeast Asian Studies, 2008.

Lee, Fiona. "Epistemological Checkpoint: Reading Fiction as a Translation of History." *Postcolonial Text* 9, no. 1 (2014): 1–21.

———. "Neutralizing English: Han Suyin and the Language Politics of Third World Literature." *Journal of Postcolonial Writing* 57, no. 2 (2021): 226–40.

Leung, Laifong. *Morning Sun: Interviews with Chinese Writers of the Lost Generation*. Armonk, NY: M. E. Sharpe, 1994.

Lewis, Martin, and Kären Wigen. *The Myth of Continents: A Critique of Metageography*. Berkeley: University of California Press, 1997.

Li Jinzong 李錦宗. *Yunluo de wenxing* 殞落的文星 [The fallen literary stars]. Selangor: Caihong chuban youxian gongsi, 1999.

Li Tuo 李陀. "Wang Zengqi yu xiandai hanyu xiezuo—jiantan Maowenti" 汪曾祺與現代漢語寫作—兼談毛文體 [Wang Zengqi and writings in modern Chinese—with concurrent thoughts on the "Mao-style prose"]. *Huacheng* 花城 [Flower city] 114 (1998): 126–42.

Li Yang 李揚. "'Chengdu moshi' yu wenxue yanjiu shiye de difanghua" "成都模式"與文學研究視野的地方化 [The Chengdu model and localizing the horizon of literary studies]. *Dangdai wentan* 當代文壇 [Contemporary literary criticism] 2 (2020): 91–96.

Li Yi 李怡. "'Difang lujing' ruhe tongda 'xiandai Zhongguo'" "地方路徑"如何通達"現代中國" [How "local routes" can reach "modern China"]. *Dangdai wentan* 當代文壇 [Contemporary literary criticism] 1 (2020): 66–69.

Li Yongping (Li Yung-p'ing) 李永平. *Dahe jintou (shangjuan): Suliu* 大河盡頭（上卷）：溯流 [Where the Great River ends, vol. 1: Going upstream]. Taipei: Maitian, 2008. *Dahe jintou (xiajuan): Shan* 大河盡頭（下卷）：山 [Where the Great River ends, vol. 2: The mountain]. Taipei: Maitian, 2010.

———. "Daixu: Wode guxiang, wo ruhe jiangshu" 代序：我的故鄉，我如何講述 [In lieu of a preface: How I narrate my homeland]. In *Jianshan youshi shan: Li Yongping yanjiu* 見山又是山：李永平研究 [The mountain is once again the mountain: Studies on Li Yongping], ed. Ko Chia-cian 高嘉謙, 9–20. Taipei: Maitian, 2017.

———. *Haidong qing: Taibei de yize yuyan* 海東青：臺北的一則寓言 [East seas turquoise: A fable of Taipei]. Taipei: Lianhe wenxue, 1992.

———. "Jiantiban xu: Yiben xiaoshuode yinguo" 簡體版序：一本小說的因果 [Preface to the simplified script version: The karma of a novel]. In *Jiling chunqiu* 吉陵春秋 [Jiling chronicles], 1-10. Shanghai: Shanghai renmin chubanshe, 2013.

———. "Jiantiban xu: Zhi 'zuguo duzhe'" 簡體版序：致"祖國讀者" [Preface to the simplified script version: To "readers in my motherland"]. In *Dahe jintou (shangjuan): Suliu* 大河盡頭（上卷）：溯流 [Where the Great River ends, vol. 1: Going upstream], 9–21. Shanghai: Shanghai renmin chubanshe: 2011.

———. *Jiling chunqiu* 吉陵春秋 [Jiling chronicles]. Taipei: Hongfan shudian, 1986.

———. *Lazi fu* 拉子婦 [The Bidayuh woman]. Taipei: Huaxin chuban gongsi, 1976.

———. "Li Yongping da bianzhe wuwen" 李永平答編者五問 [Li Yongping answers five questions from the editor]. *Wenxun* 文訊 [Literary information] 29 (1987): 124–27.

———. *Poluozhou zhizi* 婆羅洲之子 [Sons of Borneo]. Kuching: Poluozhou wenhuaju, 1968.

———. "Wenzi yinyuan" 文字姻緣 [A predestined relationship with the Chinese script]. In *Titto: Li Yongping zixuanji, 1968–2002* 迌迌：李永平自選集, 1968–2002

[On gallivanting: Li Yongping's self-selected works, 1968–2002], 27–47. Taipei: Maitian, 2003.

Li Zhongyu 李鍾鈺. "Xinjiapo fengtuji" 新嘉坡風土記 [A record of the local customs of Singapore]. In *Zhongguo gujizhong youguan Xinjiapo Malaixiya ziliao huibian* 中國古籍中有關新加坡馬來西亞資料彙編 [A compilation of materials on Singapore and Malaysia in ancient Chinese books], ed. Yu Dingbang 余定邦 and Huang Chongyan 黃重言, 183–97. Beijing: Zhonghua shuju, 2002.

Lian Shisheng 連士升. "Fangwen Zhou Guanghu" 訪問周光瑚 [An interview with Rosalie Matilda Kwanghu Chou]. In *Lian Shisheng wenji di'er juan* 連士升文集第二卷 [The Lian Shisheng anthology, vol. 2], ed. Koh Hock Kiat 許福吉, 433–36. Beijing: Peking University Press, 2011.

Liang Fang 梁放. *Woceng tingdao nizai fengzhong kuqi* 我曾聽到你在風中哭泣 [I once heard you crying in the wind]. Selangor: Dream Eater Publishing, 2014.

Liang Qichao 梁啟超. *Xindalu youji* 新大陸遊記 [Travels to the New World]. Changsha: Hunan renmin chubanshe, 1981.

Lianqing 鍊青. "Bianzhe di'erci de xianci" 編者第二次的獻辭 [The editor's second pledge]. In *Mahua Xinwenxue daxi X · Chuban shiliao* 馬華新文學大系（十）·出版史料 [Compendium of modern Mahua literature, vol. 10: Historical material on publications], ed. Fang Xiu 方修, 123–26. Singapore: Shijie shuju, 1972.

Liew, Zhou Hau, and Zhou Sivan. "Mahua Modernist Poetry as a Translational Practice." *Full Stop Quarterly* 6 (August 2017): 1–10.

Lim Khay Thiong 林開忠. "'Yizu' de zaixian? Cong Li Yongping de *Poluozhou zhizi* yu *Lazi fu* tanqi" "異族"的再現？從李永平的《婆羅洲之子》與《拉子婦》談起 [The representations of "alien ethnicities?" On Li Yongping's *Sons of Borneo* and *The Bidayuh Woman*]. In *Chongxie Mahua wenxueshi lunwenji* 重寫馬華文學史論文集 [Rewriting Mahua literary history], ed. Tee Kim Tong 張錦忠, 91–114. Nantou: National Chi Nan University Center for Southeast Asian Studies, 2004.

Lim Kien Ket 林建國. "Fang Xiu lun" 方修論 [On Fang Xiu]. *Zhongwai wenxue* 中外文學 [Chung-Wai literary monthly] 29, no. 4 (2000): 65-98.

——. "Yixing" 異形 [Aliens]. *Zhongwai wenxue* 中外文學 [Chung-Wai literary monthly] 22, no. 3 (1993): 73–91.

Lin Cantian 林參天. "Jinbiao" 金錶 [The golden watch]; "Nanyang de nüpengyou" 南洋的女朋友 [Female friends in Nanyang]; and "Yintong" 隱痛 [Hidden pain]. In *Mahua Xinwenxue daxi V·Xiju ji* 馬華新文學大系（五）·戲劇集 [Compendium of modern Mahua literature, vol. 5: Drama], ed. Fang Xiu 方修, 151–63, 133–50; 164–72. Singapore: Shijie shuju, 1972.

——. "Jinian xianfu (san)" 紀念先父（三）[In remembrance of my late father (part 3)]. *Sin Chew Jit Poh*, May 10, 1935.

——. "Jinian xianfu (wu)" 紀念先父（五）[In remembrance of my late father (part 5)]. *Sin Chew Jit Poh*, May 13, 1935.

———. "Jinian xianfu (yi)" 紀念先父（一）[In remembrance of my late father (part 1)]. *Sin Chew Jit Poh*, May 8, 1935.

———. "Malaiya wenyi chenji de yuanyin" 馬來亞文藝沉寂的原因 [The reason for the vapid state of Malayan literary arts]. In *Mahua Xinwenxue daxi I·Lilun piping yiji* 馬華新文學大系（一）·理論批評一集 [Compendium of modern Mahua literature, vol.1: Theory and critique (part 1)], ed. Fang Xiu 方修, 477–81. Singapore: Shijie shuju, 1972.

———. "Nanyang yu dazhong yuwen" 南洋與大眾語文 [Nanyang and a language of the masses]. *Sin Chew Jit Poh* 星洲日報, February 7 and 8, 1935.

———. *Nongyan* 濃煙 [Thick smoke]. Shanghai: Wenxue chubanshe, 1936.

———. *Nongyan* 濃煙 [Thick smoke]. Singapore: Xinjiapo qingnian shuju, 1959.

———. *Rezhang* 熱瘴 [Tropical miasma]. Singapore: Qingnian shuju, 1961.

———. "Tan wode xiezuo" 談我的寫作 [About my writing practice]. In *Xinshengdai (hedingben)* 新生代（合訂本）[Compilation of the "New Generation" literary supplement], ed. Xie Ke 謝克, issue no. 99. Singapore: Xinshengdai chubanshe, 1968.

———. "Wo yu wenxue" 我與文學 [My relationship with literature]. In *Xinshengdai (hedingben)* 新生代（合訂本）[Compilation of the "New Generation" literary supplement], ed. Xie Ke 謝克, issue no. 20. Singapore: Xinshengdai chubanshe, 1968.

Lin Hengnan 林衡南, ed. *Huayi tongyu* 華夷通語 [Language bridger between the Chinese and the non-Chinese], n.p., 1877, accessed September 11, 2019, http://eresources.nlb.gov.sg/printheritage/detail/3b07f148-8b6f-492f-b2fa-7c1c3dc1f188.aspx.

Lin Jin 林錦. *Zhanqian wunian Xinma wenxue lilun yanjiu, 1937–1941* 戰前五年新馬文學理論研究, 1931–1941 [A study on prewar Singapore-Malaya literary theory, 1937–1941]. Singapore: Singapore Tong An Association, 1992.

Lin Mang 林莽 [Lin Cantian]. "Yijiusansi nian Malaiya wentan yipie" 一九三四年馬來亞文壇一瞥 [A glance at the 1934 Malayan literary circle]. In *Mahua Xinwenxue daxi X · chuban shiliao* 馬華新文學大系（十）·出版史料 [Compendium of modern Mahua literature, vol. 10: Historical material on publications], ed. Fang Xiu 方修, 450–54. Singapore: Shijie shuju, 1972.

Lovell, Julia. "Chinese Literature in the Global Canon: The Quest for Recognition." In *Global Chinese Literature: Critical Essays*, ed. Jing Tsu and David Der-wei Wang, 197–217. Leiden: Brill, 2010.

———. *The Politics of Cultural Capital: China's Quest for a Nobel Prize in Literature*. Honolulu: University of Hawai'i Press, 2006.

Ly, Singko, ed. and trans. *Modern Malaysian Chinese Stories*. Singapore: Heinemann Educational Books (Asia) Ltd., 1967.

Ma Lun 馬崙. *Xinma huawen zuojia qunxiang, 1919–1983* 新馬華文作家群像, 1919–1983 [Biographies of Singapore, Malayan, and Malaysian Chinese-language writers, 1919–1983]. Singapore: Fengyun Publications, 1984.

Mahadeva, A. "Chinese Writers are Promoting Race Harmony in Malaya." *The Sunday Mail*, January 29, 1961.

Mahler, Anne Garland. "Global South." In *Oxford Bibliographies in Literary and Critical Theory*, ed. Eugene O'Brien. New York: Oxford University Press, 2017, accessed December 27, 2019, doi: 10.1093/OBO/9780190221911-0055.

Mair, Victor. "What is a Chinese 'Dialect/Topolect'? Reflection on Some Key Sino-English Linguistic Terms." *Sino-Platonic Papers* 29 (1991): 1–31.

Maitian Chuban 麥田出版 [Rye Field Publishing Company]. "Kehua Malaixiya yuanzhumin yangmao de jingdian juzuo! Li Yongping *Dahe jintou* quantao shangxia chuqi" 刻畫馬來西亞原住民樣貌的經典文學鉅作！李永平《大河盡頭》全套上下出齊 [A canonical magnum opus that depicts the ways of Malaysian indigenous peoples! Full set of Li Yongping's *Where the Great River Ends* published], September 7, 2010, http://goo.gl/YtEPEo.

Mak, Lau Fong 麥留芳. *Fangyanqun rentong: zaoqi Xingma huaren de fenlei faze* 方言群認同：早期星馬華人的分類法則 [Dialect group identity: A study of Chinese sub-ethnic groups in early Malaya]. Taipei: Institute of Ethnology, Academia Sinica, 1985.

Massey, Doreen. "Power-Geometry and a Progressive Sense of Place." In *Mapping the Futures: Local Cultures, Global Change*, ed. Jon Bird, Barry Curtis, Tim Putnam, George Robertson, and Lisa Tickner, 59–69. London: Routledge, 1993.

Masutani Satoshi 舛谷銳 and Hee Wai-Siam 許維賢. "'Kaiting shenxun': Xuan Sulai buzai xianchang—zoufang Chuangu Rui fujiaoshou" 《開庭審訊》：襌素萊不在現場—走訪舛谷銳副教授 ("The trial": Xuan Sulai was absent from the scene—an interview with Associate Professor Masutani Satoshi). *Chao Foon* 蕉風 491 (2004): 49–54.

McKeown, Adam. "Conceptualizing Chinese Diasporas, 1842 to 1949." *The Journal of Asian Studies* 58, no. 2 (1999): 306–37.

Meimei 梅梅. "*Nongyan* duhou"《濃煙》讀後 [Reflections after reading *Thick Smoke*]. *Sin Chew Jit Poh* 星洲日報, January 18, 1937.

Meylaerts, Reine. "Heterolingualism in/and Translation: How Legitimate Are the Other and His/Her Language? An Introduction." *Target* 18, no. 1 (2006): 1–15.

Miao Xiu 苗秀. "Daolun" 導論 [Introduction]. In *Xinma huawen wenxue daxi diwuji: Xiaoshuo (er)* 新馬華文文學大系第五集：小說（二）[Compendium of Singapore, Malayan, and Malaysian Chinese-language literature, vol. 5: Fiction (part 2)], ed. Miao Xiu, 1–15. Singapore: Jiaoyu chubanshe, 1971.

Miyoshi, Masao. *Off Center: Power and Culture Relations between Japan and the United States*. Cambridge, MA: Harvard University Press, 1991.

Mo Yimei. *Local Color in Malayan Chinese Fiction: A New Approach (1920–1937)*. Bochum: Brockmeyer, 1992.

Moretti, Franco. *Distant Reading*. London: Verso, 2013.

Ng Kim Chew 黃錦樹. "Ci de liuwang—Zhang Guixing de xiezuo daolu" 詞的流亡—張貴興的寫作道路 [Words in exile: The path of Zhang Guixing's writing practice]; and "Huawen/Zhongwen: 'Shiyu de nanfang' yu yuyan zaizao" 華文／中文: "失語的南方" 與語言再造 [Huawen/Zhongwen: 'The South where language is lost' and linguistic reinvention]. In *Mahua wenxue yu Zhongguoxing* 馬華文學與中國性 [The spirit of China in Mahua literature], 351–78; and 53–92. Taipei: Yuanzun wenhua, 1998.

———. "Dui wenxue de waihang yu dui lishi de wuzhi? Jiu 'Mahua wenxue' da Xiamei" 對文學的外行與對歷史的無知?—就"馬華文學"答夏梅 [A layman to literature who is also ignorant about history? A response to Xiamei on Mahua literature]; "Mahua wenxue de bei'ai" 馬華文學的悲哀 [The sad situation of Mahua literature]; and "Mahua wenxue 'jingdian quexi'" 馬華文學"經典缺席" [The absence of a canon in Mahua literature]. In *Lawei Mahua wenxue: Jiushi niandai Mahua wenxue zhenglunxing keti wenxuan* 辣味馬華文學：九十年代馬華文學爭論性課題文選 [Mahua literature with an edge: Selected essays on topics of controversy in Mahua literature in the 1990s], ed. Chan Yeong Siew 張永修, Teoh Kong Tat 張光達, and Lim Choon Bee 林春美, 116–23; 174–79; and 107–09. Kuala Lumpur: Xuelan'e Zhonghua dahuitang he Malaixiya liutai xiaoyouhui lianhe zonghui, 2002.

———. "Fulu san: Yu Luo Yijun de duitan" 附錄三：與駱以軍的對談 [Appendix 3: A dialogue with Lo Yi-chin]. In *Tu yu huo: Tanah Melayu* 土與火 [Earth and fire: Malay land], 311–23. Taipei: Maitian, 2005.

———. "Fen yu lu—chongshen kaiduan, chongfan 'weishenme Mahua wenxue'" 墳與路—重審開端, 重返"爲什麼馬華文學" [The grave and the road—reassessing the genesis, and returning to the question of "Why Mahua literature"]; "Huawen shaoshu wenxue—lisan xiandaixing de weijing zhi lü" 華文少數文學—離散現代性的未竟之旅 [Minor Sinophone literature: Diasporic modernity's incomplete journey]; and "Pibei de gongma: Li Yongping yu Minguo" 疲憊的公馬：李永平與民國 [The exhausted stallion: Li Yongping and Republican China]. In *Huawen xiaowenxue de Malaixiya ge'an* 華文小文學的馬來西亞個案 [Minor literature in Chinese: The case of Malaysia], 85–104; 107–19; and 367–86. Taipei: Maitian, 2015.

———. *M de shizong* M 的失蹤 [The disappearance of M]. In *Meng yu zhu yu liming* 夢與豬與黎明 [Dream and swine and aurora], 10–42. Taipei: Jiuge, 1994.

———. "Mahua wenxue de yunniangqi" 馬華文學的醞釀期 [The gestation period of Mahua literature]; and "Zai 'shijie' zhinei de huawen yu 'shijie' zhiwai de huaren" 在"世界"之內的華文與"世界"之外的華人 [The Chinese language within the "world" and the Chinese people outside the "world"]. In *Mahua wenxue: Neizai Zhongguo, yuyan yu wenxueshi* 馬華文學：內在中國、語言與文學史 [Mahua literature: Internal China, language, and literary history], 27–54; and 224–27. Kuala Lumpur: Huazi Resource and Research Centre Bhd., 1996.

———. "Meiyou weizhi de weizhi" 沒有位置的位置 [A position that is an inconsequential position]. In *Huo xiaole* 火笑了 [The fire smiled], 285–88. Tapei: Maitian, 2015.

———. "Minor Sinophone Literature: Diasporic Modernity's Incomplete Journey." In *Global Chinese Literature: Critical Essays*, trans. Andrew Rodekohr, ed. Jing Tsu and David Der-wei Wang, 15–28. Leiden: Brill, 2010.

———. "Nanfang huawen wenxue gongheguo: Yige chuyi" 南方華文文學共和國：一個芻議 [Republic of southern-sinophone literature: A proposal]. *Zhongshan renwen xuebao* 中山人文學報 [Sun Yat-sen journal of humanities] issue no. 45 (2018): 1–20.

———. "Shitou yu nügui—lun *Dahe jintou* zhongde xiangzheng jiaohuan yu siwang" 石頭與女鬼—論《大河盡頭》中的象徵交換與死亡 [Stones and female ghosts: On symbolic exchange and death in *Where the Great River Ends*]. *Taiwan wenxue yanjiu xuebao* 臺灣文學研究學報 [Journal of Taiwan literary studies] 14 (2012): 241–63.

———. "Sinophone/Chinese: 'The South Where Language is Lost' and Reinvented." In *Sinophone Studies: A Critical Reader*, trans. Brian Bernards, ed. Shu-mei Shih, Chien-hsin Tsai, and Brian Bernards, 74–92. New York: Columbia University Press, 2013.

———. *Slow Boat to China and Other Stories*, trans. Carlos Rojas. New York: Columbia University Press, 2016.

———. *Women de yanhua* 我們的演化 [Our evolution]. In *Shicha de zengli* 時差的贈禮 [The gift of time-lags], 214–18. Taipei: Maitian, 2019.

———. "Wuguoji huawen wenxue: Yige wenxueshi de bijiao gangling" 無國籍華文文學：一個文學史的比較綱領 [Literature in Chinese without national identity: A comparative program for literary history]. In *Chongxie Taiwan wenxueshi* 重寫臺灣文學史 [Rewriting Taiwan literary history], ed. Tee Kim Tong 張錦忠 and Ng Kim Chew, 123–59. Taipei: Maitian, 2007.

———. *Youling de wenzi* 幽靈的文字 [The script of the spirit]. Kaohsiung: Center for the Humanities, National Sun Yat-sen University, 2019.

———. "Zuowei Taiwan wenxue lilun guanjianci de 'Mahua wenxue'" 作為臺灣文學理論關鍵詞的"馬華文學" [Mahua literature as a keyword for Taiwan literary theory]. In *Mahua wenxue piping daxi: Huang Jinshu* 馬華文學批評大系：黃錦樹 [Mahua literary criticism: Ng Kim Chew], ed. Chan Tah Wei 陳大為 and Chong Yee-Voon 鍾怡雯, 321–26. Taoyuan: Department of Chinese Linguistics and Literature, Yuan Ze University, Taiwan, 2019.

Ng Yean Leng 伍燕翎, and Shi Huimin 施慧敏. "Li Yongping fangtanlu (shang, xia)" 李永平訪談錄（上、下）[An interview with Li Yongping, part 1 and 2]. *Xingzhou Ribao* 星洲日報 [Sin Chew daily], March 15, 2009, http://news.sinchew.com.my/node/106020; *Xingzhou Ribao* [Sin Chew daily], March 22, 2009, http://news.sinchew.com.my/node/107104.

Ngoi Guat Peng (Wei Yueping) 魏月萍. "Gaobie yu renju: Shahua wenxue de juluo yu lisan changyu" 告別與認據：砂華文學的聚落與離散場域 [Departures and claims: The settlements and diasporic domains of Sarawak Chinese-language literature]. In

Tian Si 田思, *Shahua wenxue de bentu tezhi* 砂華文學的本土特質 [The native characteristics of Sarawak Chinese-language literature], 3–7. Selangor, Malaysia: Mentor Publishing, 2014.

Ngu Ik Tien 吳益婷. "Shahua wenxue lide zuqun guanxi" 砂華文學裏的族群關係 [The ethnic relations in Sarawak Chinese-language literature]. *Dangdai pinglun* 當代評論 [Contemporary review] 8 (2015): 33–37.

Nicoll, Allardyce. "Xiju piping gaiguan" 戲劇批評概觀 [An introduction to dramatic theory]. Trans. Lin Cantian. *Sin Chew Jit Poh* 星洲日報, May 20, 1934.

Ooi, Adeline, and Dave Lumenta. "The Malaysian Roadless Trip." *The B-Side* (September 2005), 35–41.

Orsini, Francesca, and Laetitia Zecchini. "The Locations of (World) Literature: Perspectives from Africa and South Asia: Introduction." *Journal of World Literature* 4, no. 1 (2019): 1–12.

Paré, François. *Exiguity: Reflections on the Margins of Literature*. Trans. Lin Burman. Waterloo, ON: Wilfrid Laurier University Press, 1997.

Pickowicz, Paul G. *Marxist Literary Thought in China: The Influence of Ch'ü Ch'iu-pai*. Berkeley: University of California Press, 1981.

Platt, John, and Heidi Weber. *English in Singapore and Malaysia: Status, Features, Functions*. Kuala Lumpur: Oxford University Press, 1980.

Porter, David. "The Crisis of Comparison and the World Literature Debate." *Profession* (2011): 244–58.

Purcell, Victor. *Basic English for Malaya*. Singapore: Lithographies Limited, 1937.

Qiu Miaojin 邱妙津. "Li Yongping: Wodei baziji wuhuadabang zhihou cailaixie zhengzhi" 李永平：我得把自己五花大綁之後才來寫政治 [Li Yongping: I have to tie myself up before I can write about politics]. *Xin xinwen zhoukan* 新新聞週刊 [The journalist] 226 (April 1992): 66.

Quah Sy Ren 柯思仁. *Xiju bainian: Xinjiapo huawen xiju, 1913–2013* 戲聚百年：新加坡華文戲劇, 1913–2013 [SCENES: A hundred years of Singapore Chinese-language theater, 1913–2013). Singapore: Drama Box and National Museum of Singapore, 2013.

Roberts, Brian Russell, and Michelle Ann Stephens. "Archipelagic American Studies: De-continentalizing the Study of American Culture." In *Archipelagic American Studies*, ed. Brian Russell Roberts and Michelle Ann Stephens, 1–54. Durham, NC: Duke University Press, 2017.

Rojas, Carlos. "Language, Ethnicity, and the Politics of Literary Taxonomy: Ng Kim Chew and Mahua Literature." *PMLA* 131, no. 5 (2016): 1316–27.

———. "Li Yongping and Spectral Cartography." In *Writing Taiwan: A New Literary History*, ed. David Der-wei Wang and Carlos Rojas, 324–47. Durham, NC: Duke University Press, 2007.

———. "A ~~World~~ Republic of Southern [Sinophone] Letters." *Modern Chinese Literature and Culture* 30, no. 1 (2018): 42–62 [strikethrough part of original title].

Rubins, Maria. "A Century of Russian Culture(s) 'Abroad:' The Unfolding of Literary Geography." In *Global Russian Cultures*, ed. Kevin M. F. Platt, 21–47. Madison: University of Wisconsin Press, 2019.

Said, Edward W. *Culture and Imperialism*. New York: Vintage Books, 1994.

——. *Orientalism*. New York: Vintage Books, 1979.

——. *Reflections on Exile and Other Essays*. Cambridge, MA: Harvard University Press, 2000.

Seah, Leander. "Between East Asia and Southeast Asia: Nanyang Studies, Chinese Migration, and National Jinan University, 1927–1940." *Translocal Chinese: East Asian Perspectives* 11, no. 1 (2017): 30–56.

Shambaugh, David, ed. "Special Issue: Greater China." *The China Quarterly* 136 (December 1993).

Shang, Wei. "Writing and Speech: Rethinking the Issue of Vernaculars in Early Modern China." In *Rethinking East Asian Languages, Vernaculars, and Literacies, 1000–1919*, ed. Benjamin A. Elman, 254–301. Leiden: Brill, 2014.

Shen Lingxie. "The Sanjiangren in Singapore." *Chinese Southern Diaspora Studies* 5 (2011/2012): 175–96.

Shen Mian 沈眠. "Zhuanfang *Nanfang conglai buxiaxue* zuozhe Chen Yuxuan: Women yizhi yi Taibei wei zhongxin, dan nanfang guandian ne?" 專訪《南方從來不下雪》作者陳育萱: 我們一直以臺北為中心, 但南方觀點呢? [An interview with Chen Yu-hsuan, author of *It Never Snows in the South*: We have always treated Taipei as the center, but what about the viewpoints of the south?]. *Guanjian pinglun* 關鍵評論 [The news lens], March 3, 2020, accessed July 13, 2020, https://www.thenewslens.com/article/131471.

Shi Wenting 石問亭. "Cun er buzai" 存而不在 [Existing, but not present]. In Shen Qingwang 沈慶旺, *Tuibian de shanlin* 蛻變的山林 [The transformation of mountains and rainforests], 184–200. Selangor: Mentor Publishing Sdn. Bhd., 2007.

Shih, Shu-mei. *Visuality and Identity: Sinophone Articulations across the Pacific*. Berkeley: University of California Press, 2007.

——. "Comparison as Relation." In *Comparison: Theories, Approaches, Uses*, ed. Rita Felski and Susan Stanford Friedman, 79–98. Baltimore: Johns Hopkins University Press, 2013.

Shih, Shu-mei, Chien-hsin Tsai, and Brian Bernards, eds. *Sinophone Studies: A Critical Reader*. New York: Columbia University Press, 2013.

Sternberg, Meir. "Polylingualism as Reality and Translation as Mimesis." *Poetics Today* 2, no. 4 (1981): 221–39.

Sulloway, Frank J. "Darwin and the Galapagos." *Biological Journal of the Linnean Society* 21, no. 1–2 (1984): 29–59.

Tan, Chee Beng. *Chinese Peranakan Heritage in Malaysia and Singapore*. Kuala Lumpur: Penerbit Fajar Bakti Sdn. Bhd., 1993.

Tan Swie Hian 陳瑞獻. "Dakewen" 答客問 [Interview by a guest]. In *Jiaofeng* 蕉風 (*Chao Foon*) 225 (1971): 5–18.

Tan Yunshan 譚雲山. "Fu *Nongyan* tiju (youba)" 附《濃煙》題句（有跋） [Attached to poem about *Thick Smoke* (a postscript)]. *Shenzhen daxue Yindu yanjiu tongxun* 深圳大學印度研究通訊 [Newsletter for Indian studies at Shenzhen University] 2 (2010): 33.

Tang, Xiaobing. "On the Concept of Taiwan Literature." In *Writing Taiwan: A New Literary History*, ed. David Der-wei Wang and Carlos Rojas, 51–89. Durham, NC: Duke University Press, 2007.

Taylor, Jeremy. *Rethinking Transnational Chinese Cinemas: The Amoy-Dialect Film Industry in Cold War Asia*. New York: Routledge, 2011.

Tee Kim Tong 張錦忠. "Lisan shuangxiang: Zuowei Yazhou kuaguo huawen shuxie de zaitai Mahua wenxue" 離散雙鄉：作爲亞洲跨國華文書寫的在臺馬華文學 [Double diasporic homelands: Mahua literature in Taiwan as transnational Asian Chinese-language writing]. *Zhongguo xiandai wenxue* [Modern Chinese literature] 9 (2006): 61–72.

———. *Malaixiya huayu yuxi wenxue* 馬來西亞華語語系文學 [Sinophone Malaysian literature]. Selangor: Got One Publisher Sdn. Bhd., 2011.

———. *Nanyang lunshu: Mahua wenxue yu wenhua shuxing* 南洋論述：馬華文學與文化屬性 [Studying Southeast Asian Chinese: Essays on Chinese-Malaysian literature and cultural identity]. Taipei: Maitian, 2003.

———. "Sinophone Malaysian Literature: An Overview." In *Sinophone Studies: A Critical Reader*, ed. Shu-mei Shih, Chien-hsin Tsai, and Brian Bernards, 304–14. New York Columbia University Press, 2013.

———. "Xiaowenxue, fuxitong: Dongnanya huawen wenxue de (yuyan wenti yu) yiyi" 小文學、複系統：東南亞華文文學的（語言問題與）意義 [Minor literatures and polysystems: The significance (and language problem) of Southeast Asian Chinese literature]. In *Dangdai wenxue yu renwen shengtai: 2003nian Dongnanya huawen wenxue guoji xueshu yantaohui lunwenji* 當代文學與人文生態：2003年東南亞華文文學國際學術研討會論文集 [Contemporary literature and the ecology of the humanities: Proceedings from the 2003 International Symposium on Southeast Asian Chinese Literature], ed. Wu Yaozong 吳耀宗, 313–27. Taipei: Wanjuanlou, 2003.

———. "Zaina nanfang de guodu: Chidao jifengdai de huawen shuxie" 在那南方的國度：赤道季風帶的華文書寫 [In the southern country: Sinophone writings in the equatorial monsoon belt]. In *Nanfang de shehui, xue (xia): Xingdong zuowei lunli* 南方的社會，學（下）：行動作為倫理 [Studying southern societes (part 2): On the ethics of social action], ed. Chao En-chieh 趙恩潔, 51–74. New Taipei: Rive Gauche Publishing House, 2020.

Teng, Emma J. "On Not Looking Chinese: Does 'Mixed Race' Decenter the Han from Chineseness?" In *Critical Han Studies: The History, Representation, and Identity of China's Majority*, ed. Thomas Mullaney, James Patrick Leibold, Stéphane Gros, and Eric Armand Vanden Bussche, 45–72. Berkeley: University of California Press, 2012.

Thompson, Lanny. "Heuristic Geographies: Territories and Areas, Islands and Archipelagoes." In *Archipelagic American Studies*, ed. Brian Russell Roberts and Michelle Ann Stephens, 57–73. Durham, NC: Duke University Press, 2017.

Thomsen, Mads Rosendahl. "Strangeness and World Literature." *CLCWeb: Comparative Literature and Culture* 15.5 (2013), accessed 1 July 2019, doi: https://doi.org/10.7771/1481-4374.2351.

Tian Si 田思. *Shahua wenxue de bentu tezhi* 砂華文學的本土特質 [The native characteristics of Sarawak Chinese-language literature]. Selangor: Mentor Publishing, 2014.

——. *Shuxie Poluozhou* 書寫婆羅洲 [Writing Borneo]. Sibu: Persatuan Kesusasteraan Zhonghua, 2003.

Toyoda Noriko 豐田周子. "Li Yongping *Jiling chunqiu* de yuedu fangshi: Yi Taiwan wei zhongxin" 李永平《吉陵春秋》的閱讀方式：以臺灣為中心 [Reading *Jiling Chronicles*: How Li Yongping's novel is interpreted in Taiwan]. *Taida dongya wenhua yanjiu* 臺大東亞文化研究 [The NTU journal of East Asian culture] 4 (2017): 21–36.

Tsu, Jing. "Weak Links, Literary Spaces, and Comparative Taiwan." In *Comparatizing Taiwan*, ed. Shu-mei Shih and Ping-hui Liao, 123–44. New York: Routledge, 2015.

Tu Wei-ming. "Cultural China: The Periphery as Center." In *The Living Tree: The Changing Meaning of Being Chinese Today*, ed. Tu Wei-ming, 1–34. Stanford, CA: Stanford University Press, 1994.

Vieira de Almeida, Rosa. "Keeping to the Margins: Macau Literature and a Pre-postcolonial 'Poetics of Insignificance.'" In *Reading China Against the Grain: Imagining Communities*, ed. Carlos Rojas and Mei-hwa Sung. 112–27. London: Routledge, 2020.

Wang Anyi 王安憶. "Dalu Taiwan xiaoshuo yuyan bijiao" 大陸臺灣小說語言比較 [The language of fiction in works from mainland China and Taiwan: A comparison]; and "Piaobo de yuyan" 漂泊的語言 [A language adrift]. In *Wang Anyi zixuanji zhisi: Piaobo de yuyan (sanwen juan)* 王安憶自選集之四：漂泊的語言（散文卷）[Wang Anyi self-selected collection 4: A language adrift (volume of prose)], 370–88; and 214–28. Beijing: Zuojia chubanshe, 1996.

——. "Fuqin de shu" 父親的書 [My father's book]. In *Kongjian zai shijian li liutang* 空間在時間裡流淌 [The spaces flowing through time], 194–97. Beijing: New Star Press, 2012.

——. ""Guiqu laixi" 歸去來兮 [Longing to return]." In *Duyu* 獨語 [Monologue], 24–28. Changsha: Hunan wenyi chubanshe, 1998.

——. "Jiejin shijichu" 接近世紀初 [Approaching the start of a century]. In *Jiejin shijichu* 接近世紀初 [Approaching the start of a century], 247–55. Hangzhou: Zhejiang wenyi chubanshe, 1998.

———. "Jishi he xugou: Chuangzao shijie fangfa zhi yizhong" 紀實和虛構：創造世界方法之一種 [Documentation and fictionalization: One method of creating the world]. Beijing: Renmin wenxue chubanshe, 1993.

———. "Shangxin Taipingyang" 傷心太平洋 [Sadness of the Pacific]; and "Wutuobang shipian" 烏托邦詩篇 [Utopian verses]. In *Wang Anyi zixuanji zhisan: Xianggang de qing yu ai (zhongpian xiaoshuo juan)* 王安憶自選集之三：香港的情與愛（中篇小說卷）[Wang Anyi self-selected collection 3: Love in Hong Kong (volume of novellas)], 305–83; and 257–304. Beijing: Zuojia chubanshe, 1996.

———. *Wang Anyi Shuo* 王安憶說 [Wang Anyi: Dialogues and speeches]. Changsha: Hunan wenyi chubanshe, 2003.

———. "Wode xiaoshuoguan" 我的小說觀 [My perspective on fiction-writing]; and "Xiaoshuo de qingjie he yuyan" 小說的情節和語言 [The plot and language of fiction]. In *Wang Anyi yanjiu ziliao (shang)* 王安憶研究資料（上）[Research material on Wang Anyi (vol. 1)], ed. Zhang Xinying 張新穎 and Jin Li 金理, 41–43; and 90–108. Tianjin: Tianjin renmin chubanshe, 2009.

———. "Wode laili" 我的來歷 [My origins]. In *Wutai xiaoshijie: Wang Anyi duanpian xiaoshuo biannian juan'er, 1982–1989* 舞臺小世界：王安憶短篇小說編年卷二，1982–1989 [The stage is a small world: A chronological anthology of Wang Anyi's short stories, vol. 2, 1982–1989], 252–76. Beijing: Renmin wenxue chubanshe, 2009.

———. "Yuyan de mingyun" 語言的命運 [The fate of language]. *Haishang wentan* 海上文壇, no. 6 (1992): 77–83.

———. "Yuyan de mingyun (shang, xia)" 語言的命運（上、下）[The fate of language (parts 1 and 2)]. *Xingzhou Ribao* 星洲日報 [Sin Chew daily], July 12 and 13, 1993.

Wang Anyi and Zhang Xudong 張旭東. "Lilun yu shijian: Wenxue ruhe chengxian lishi?" 理論與實踐：文學如何呈現歷史？[Theory and praxis: How does literature represent history?]. In *Wang Anyi yanjiu ziliao (shang)* 王安憶研究資料（上）[Research material on Wang Anyi (vol. 1)], ed. Zhang Xinying and Jin Li, 308–43. Tianjin: Tianjin renmin chubanshe, 2009.

Wang Anyi et al., "Dangqian wenxue chuangzuozhong de 'qing' yu 'zhong'—wenxue duihualu" 當前文學創作中的"輕"與"重"—文學對話錄 [The lightness and weight of current creative writings: A conversation on literature], *Dangdai zuojia pinglun* 當代作家評論 [Contemporary writers review] 5 (1993): 14–23.

Wang, David Der-wei 王德威. "Huayi fengqi: Malaixiya yu huayu yuxi wenxue" 華夷風起：馬來西亞與華語語系文學 [When the wind of the Sinophone blows: Malaysia and Sinophone literature]. *Zhongshan renwen xuebao* 中山人文學報 [Sun Yat-sen journal of humanities], issue no. 38 (2015): 1–29.

———. "Huayi zhibian: Huayu yuxi yanjiu de xinshijie" 華夷之變：華語語系研究的新視界 [Sinophone/Xenophone studies: Toward a poetics of wind, sound, and changeability]. *Zhongguo xiandai wenxue* 中國現代文學 [Modern Chinese literature] 34 (2018): 1–27.

——. "Introduction." In *Chinese Literature in the Second Half of a Modern Century: A Critical Survey*, ed. Pang-yuan Chi and David Der-wei Wang, xiii–xliii. Bloomington: Indiana University Press, 2000.

——. "Introduction: Worlding Literary China." In *A New Literary History of Modern China*, ed. David Der-wei Wang, 1–28. Boston: Belknap Press, 2017.

——. "Xulun: Huaihaizi Huang Jinshu—Huang Jinshu de Mahua lunshu yu xushu" 序論：壞孩子黃錦樹—黃錦樹的馬華論述與敘述 [Introduction: The enfant terrible Ng Kim Chew—Ng Kim Chew's Mahua discourses and narratives], in Ng Kim Chew 黃錦樹, *Youdao zhidao* 由島至島 [From island to island], 11–35. Taipei: Maitian, 2002.

——. "Wenxue Dongbei yu Zhongguo xiandaixing—'Dongbeixue' yanjiu chuyi" 文學東北與中國現代性—"東北學" 研究芻議 [Literary Northeast China and Chinese modernity: A preliminary discussion on "Northeast Studies"]. *Xiaoshuo pinglun* 小說評論 [Fiction criticism] 1 (2021): 60–75.

——. "Yuanxiang xiangxiang, langzi wenxue" 原鄉想像，浪子文學 [Imagination of original homeland, literature of a prodigal son]. In Li Yonging, *Titto: Li Yongping zixuanji, 1968–2002* 迌迌：李永平自選集, 1968–2002 [On gallivanting: Li Yongping's self-selected works, 1968–2002], 11–25. Taipei: Maitian, 2003.

Wang, Gungwu. *The Chineseness of China: Selected Essays*. Hong Kong: Oxford University Press, 1991.

Wang Qiang 王強, ed. *Jindai yuwai youji congkan* 近代域外遊記叢刊 [A series of foreign travelogues in modern times]. Nanjing: Fenghuang chubanshe, 2016.

Wang Xiaoping 王嘯平. *Kezi Nanyang lai* 客自南洋來 [The guest from Nanyang]. Shanghai: Baijia chubanshe, 1990.

——. "Wang Anyi zhi fu: Nanyang guiyan de chuanqi" 王安憶之父：南洋歸雁的傳奇 [Wang Anyi's father: The legend of a returning goose from Nanyang]. *Shiji* 世紀 [Century] 1 (2014): 4–13.

——. "Weile bugai wangque de jinian—ji xijujia Wu Tian" 為了不該忘卻的紀念—記戲劇家吳天 [For the sake of remembrance that should not be forgotten—about the dramatist Wu Tian]. *Xiju yishu* 戲劇藝術 [Theater arts] 4 (1990): 32–35.

——. "Zuojia yu zhanshi—huiyi Yu Dafu xiansheng" 作家與戰士—回憶郁達夫先生 [Writer and fighter: In remembrance of Mr. Yu Dafu]. *Shanghai wenxue* 上海文學 [Shanghai literature] 12 (1979): 44–46.

Warwick Research Collective. *Combined and Uneven Development: Towards a New Theory of World-Literature*. Liverpool: Liverpool University Press, 2015.

Wei Yun 韋量. "Xie *Nongyan* de Lin Cantian" 寫《濃煙》的林參天 [Lin Cantian who wrote *Thick Smoke*]. In *Wenyuan sanye* 文苑散叶 [The scattered leaves in the literary world], 13–17. Kuala Lumpur: Tieshanni chuban youxian gongsi, 1985.

Wong Yoon Wah 王潤華 and Kho Tong Guan 許通元. "Cong Poluozhou dao bei Taiwan: Li Yongping de wenxue xinglü" 從婆羅洲到北臺灣：李永平的文學行旅 (From

Borneo to North Taiwan: Li Yongping's literary travels). *Chao Foon* 蕉風 511 (2017): 8–21.

Wu He. *Remains of Life*, trans. Michael Berry. New York: Columbia University Press, 2017.

Xinshe *Xinma huawen wenxue daxi* bianji weyuanhui 新社新馬華文文學大系編輯委員會 [Editorial committee for compendium of Singapore, Malayan, and Malaysian Chinese-language literature, Journal of the Island Society], ed. *Xinma huawen wenxue daxi* 新馬華文文學大系 [Compendium of Singapore, Malayan, and Malaysian Chinese-language literature], 8 vols. Singapore: Jiaoyu chubanshe, 1971.

Xuan Sulai 禤素萊. "Kaiting shenxun" 開庭審訊 [The trial]. In *Lawei Mahua wenxue: Jiushi niandai Mahua wenxue zhenglunxing keti wenxuan* 辣味馬華文學：九十年代馬華文學爭論性課題文選 [Mahua literature with an edge: Selected essays on topics of controversy in Mahua literature in the 1990s], ed. Chan Yeong Siew 張永修, Teoh Kong Tat 張光達, and Lim Choon Bee 林春美, 68–75. Kuala Lumpur: Xuelan'e Zhonghua dahuitang he Malaixiya liutai xiaoyouhui lianhe zonghui, 2002.

Yang Zonghan 楊宗翰. "Cong Shenzhouren dao Mahuaren" 從神州人到馬華人 (From people from the Divine Land to Malaysian Chinese). In *Chidao huisheng: Mahua wenxue duben II* 赤道回聲：馬華文學讀本 II [Equatorial echoes: A Mahua literature reader 2), ed. Chan Tah Wei 陳大為, Chong Yee-Voon 鍾怡雯, and Woo Kam Lun 胡金倫, 156–82. Taipei: Wanjuanlou, 2004.

Yap Wee Cheng 葉偉征. "Xinjiapo Chaozhou yinyueshe yanjiu" 新加坡潮州音樂社研究 [A study on Teochew music clubs in Singapore]. MA diss., National University of Singapore, 2001.

Yeh, Catherine Vance. "Root Literature of the 1980s: May Fourth as a Double Burden." In *The Appropriation of Cultural Capital: China's May Fourth Project*, ed. Milena Dolezelova-Velingerova, Oldrich Kral, and Graham Sanders. 229–56. Cambridge, MA: Harvard University Asia Center, 2001.

Yen, Ching-hwang. *A Social History of the Chinese in Singapore and Malaya, 1800–1911*. Singapore: Oxford University Press, 1986.

Yeo Mang Thong 姚夢桐. *Yu Dafu lüxin shenghuo yu zuopin yanjiu* 郁達夫旅新生活與作品研究 [A study of Yu Dafu's life and works in Singapore]. Singapore: Singapore Island Society, 1987.

Yeo Song Nian 楊松年. "Cong Yu Dafu 'Jige wenti' yinqi de zhenglun kan dangshi Nanyang zhishifenzi de xintai" 從郁達夫"幾個問題"引起的爭論看當時南洋知識份子的心態 [The polemic of Yu Dafu's "Several Problems" and Chinese intellectuals in Nanyang]. *Yazhou wenhua* 亞洲文化 [Asian culture], issue no. 23 (1999): 103–11.

———. "Zhanqian Xinma jutuan yanjiu zhiyi: Mahua xunhui gejutuan" 戰前新馬劇團研究之一：馬華巡迴歌劇團 [A study of the Chinese itinerant drama troupes in Malaya]. *Yazhou wenhua* 亞洲文化 [Asian culture], issue no. 13 (1989): 12–41.

———. *Zhanqian Xinma wenxue bendi yishi de xingcheng yu fazhan* 戰前新馬文學本地意識的形成與發展 [The formation and development of local consciousness in prewar Singapore and Malayan literature]. Singapore: National University of Singapore Department of Chinese Studies and Global Publishing, 2001.

Yi Duo (Zhao Rong) 以多. "Lun Lin Cantian de xiaoshuo" 論林參天的小說 [On Lin Cantian's fictional works]. In *Xinshengdai (hedingben)* 新生代（合訂本）[Compilation of the "New Generation" literary supplement], issue nos. 61 and 63, ed. Xie Ke 謝克. Singapore: Xinshengdai chubanshe, 1968.

Yijiao 一礁. "Lingling suisui: Gei Zeng Aidi xiansheng" 零零碎碎——給曾艾狄先生 [Some miscellaneous issues: To Mr Zeng Aidi]. In *Mahua Xinwenxue daxi I·Lilun piping yiji* 馬華新文學大系（一）·理論批評一集 [Compendium of modern Mahua literature, vol. 1: Theory and critique (part 1)], ed. Fang Xiu 方修, 307–11. Singapore: Shijie shuju, 1972.

Yildiz, Yasemin. *Beyond the Mother Tongue: The Postmonolingual Condition.* New York: Fordham University Press, 2012.

Yow Cheun Hoe 游俊豪. "Yuanyuan, changyu, xitong: Xinhua wenxueshi de jiegouxing xiezuo," 淵源、場域、系統：新華文學史的結構性寫作 [Origins, fields, systems: The structural writing of Singapore Chinese-language literary history]. In *Yimin guiji yu lisan lunshu: Xinma huaren zuqun de chongceng mailuo* 移民軌跡與離散論述：新馬華人族群的重層脈絡 [Migratory routes and diasporic discourses: The layered contexts of ethnic Chinese communities in Singapore and Malaysia], 175–92. Shanghai: Shanghai sanlian shudian, 2014.

Yu Dafu 郁達夫. "Jige wenti" 幾個問題 [A few questions]. In *Mahua Xinwenxue daxi II·Lilun piping erji* 馬華新文學大系（二）·理論批評二集 [Compendium of modern Mahua literature, vol. 2: Theory and critique (part 2)], ed. Fang Xiu 方修, 444–48. Singapore: Shijie shuju, 1971.

Zhan Min-xu 詹閔旭. "Dahe de lücheng: Li Yongping tan xiaoshuo" 大河的旅程：李永平談小說 [The journey of a Great River: Li Yongping on fiction-writing]. *Yinke wenxue shenghuo zazhi* 印刻文學生活雜誌 [INK literary monthly] 58 (June 2008): 174–83.

———. "Duodi gonggou de huayuyuxi wenxue: Yi Mahua wenxue de Taiwan jingyu weili" 多地共構的華語語系文學：以馬華文學的臺灣境遇為例 [Sinophone literature as multiple forms of place-based production: On the predicament of Mahua literature in Taiwan]. *Taiwan wenxue xuebao* 臺灣文學學報 [Bulletin of Taiwanese literature] 30 (2017): 81–110.

———. "Yu wenxue jieyuan: Li Yongping tan xiezuolu" 與文學結緣：李永平談寫作路 [Creating affective ties with literature: Li Yongping on his writing journey].

Renshe donghua dianzi jikan 人社東華電子季刊 [Dong Hwa journal of humanities and social science online), June 2016, accessed June 22, 2016. http://journal.ndhu.edu.tw/e_paper/e_paper_c.php?SID=167.

———. "Zai shijie de bianyuan xiezuo: Li Yongping chengwei Taiwan zuojia zhilu" 在世界的邊緣寫作：李永平成為臺灣作家之路 [Writing in the margin of the world: Li Yongping's road to becoming a Taiwan writer]. *Donghua hanxue* 東華漢學 [Dong Hwa journal of Chinese studies] 27 (2018): 211–40.

Zhan Min-xu and Wu Chia-rong 吳家榮, eds. Special issue on "Quanqiu nanfang huawen wenxue" 全球南方華文文學 [Global South and Sinophone literature]. *Zhongshan renwen xuebao* 中山人文學報 [Sun Yat-sen journal of humanities], issue no. 51 (2021): 1–154.

Zhan Min-xu and Hsu Kuo-ming 徐國明. "Dang duozhong huayuyuxi wenxue xiangyu: Guanyu Taiwan yu huayuyuxi shijie de jiuge" 當多種華語語系文學相遇：關於臺灣與華語語系世界的糾葛 [When multiple Sinophone literatures meet: Entanglements between Taiwan and the Sinophone world]. *Zhongwai wenxue* 中外文學 [Chung-Wai literary monthly] 44, no. 1 (March 2015): 25–62.

Zhang Guixing (Chang Kuei-hsing) 張貴興. *Houbei* 猴杯 [Monkey cup]. Taipei: Lianhe wenxue, 2000.

———. *Qunxiang* 群象 [Elephant herd]. Taipei: Maitian, 2006.

———. *Wosinian de changmianzhong de nanguo gongzhu* 我思念的長眠中的南國公主 [My South Seas sleeping beauty]. Taipei: Maitian, 2001.

Zhang Hongmin 張宏敏. "'Wenhua Zhongguo' gainian suyuan" "文化中國" 概念溯源 [Tracing the concept of "Cultural China"]. *Shenzhen daxue xuebao* 深圳大學學報 [Journal of Shenzhen University] 28, no. 3 (2011): 56–59.

Zhang, Longxi. "Epilogue: The Changing Concept of World Literature." In *World Literature in Theory*, ed. David Damrosch, 513–23. Western Sussex: Wiley-Blackwell, 2014.

Zhang Xing Hong (Zhang, Ina) 章星虹. "A Dissenting Voice: The Politics of Han Suyin's Literary Activities in Late Colonial and Postcolonial Malaya and Singapore." *Journal of Postcolonial Writing* 57, no. 2 (2021): 155–70.

———. *Han Suyin zai Malaiya: Xingyi, xiezuo he shehui canyu* (1952–1964) 韓素音在馬來亞：行醫, 寫作和社會參與 (1952–1964) [Han Suyin in Malaya: Physician, writer, and public intellectual (1952–1964)]. Singapore: Center for Chinese Language and Culture, Nanyang Technological University, and Global Publishing, 2016.

———. "Shui wei Han Suyin zuo zhongwen fanyi?" 誰為韓素音做中文翻譯？ [Who were the Chinese-language translators of Han Suyin?] *Lianhe Zaobao* 聯合早報, September 30, 2013.

Zhao Rong 趙戎. *Xinma huawen wenyi cidian* 新馬華文文藝辭典 [Dictionary of Singapore-Malaysia Chinese literature]. Singapore: Education Publications Bureau, 1979.

Zheng Wanlong 鄭萬隆. "Zhongguo wenxue yao zouxiang shijie" 中國文學要走向世界 [Chinese literature must join the world]. *Zuojia* 作家 [Writer magazine] 1 (1986): 70–74.

Zhou Xinmin 周新民 and Wang Anyi. "Haode gushi benshen jiushi haode xingshi—Wang Anyi fangtanlu" 好的故事本身就是好的形式—王安憶訪談錄 [A great story itself comes with a great form: An interview with Wang Anyi]. *Xiaoshuo pinglun* 小說評論 [Fiction criticism] 3 (2003): 33–40.

Index

Locators in italics refer to figures.

A Cheng (Zhong Acheng), 139
Admussen, Nick, translation of the Chinese idiom *buji buli*, 239n6
Anderson, Benedict: on nationalization as a kind of seclusion, 12; on Southeast Asian writers as "unrewarded," 2
And the Rain My Drink. See Han Suyin (1916/17–2012)—*And the Rain My Drink* (*Rain*)
Anglophone and Anglophone literature: Han Suyin's advice to Anglophone Malayan writers on writing about Malaya, 78, 92–98, 105–7; Han Suyin's dismantling of barriers between Sinophone and Anglophone cultural spheres in Malaya, 28, 69, 72–73, 111–14, 196, 198; Han Suyin's work understood as world literature, 27–28, 72–73, 78–79, 95–98, 108–14, 202; publishing by Heinemann Education Books Ltd., 225n14;

"vehicular matching" of Anglophone speech in Han Suyin's *Rain*, 101
Apter, Emily, on "untranslatability" as integral to "world forms of literature," 15–16
Arendt, Hannah, metaphor of a table, 90
Ashcroft, Bill, on "inner translation," 88

Bachner, Andrea, on Taiwanese indigenous literatures, 249n17
baihua ("unadorned speech"): *baihuawen* (the written Chinese vernacular) theorized by Ng, 143; depictions of multilingual social realities in *Thick Smoke*, 47–48, 55–57, 59; drama performance in *baihua* vernacular staged in Singapore, 214n6; promotion by the May Fourth New Literature movement, 36, 53; Wang Anyi's "abstract language" (*chouxiang yuyan*) related to, 137–38, 143, 151;

baihua ("unadorned speech") (*continued*)
Wang Anyi's "extremely plain" language (*henbai de hua*) compared with, 138–39

Benitez-Rojo, Antonio, trope of the "repeating island," 204

Bernards, Brian, 237n58; on "Mahua literature" as analytical category for modern Chinese literary studies, 207n4; on "Nanyang" as archipelagic mode of Chinese and Sinophone literary imagination, 8, 209n15

bifocal writing approach. *See* Han Suyin (1916/17–2012)—bifocal writing approach

Borneo: heterolingualism of Li Yongping's *River* set in, 160–70; its topography explored by Li Yongping via the character Yong-the-youth, 158, 169, 178, 182–86, 188–90; Li Yongping's construction of a Borneo literary "nativism," 179; Li Yongping's insider knowledge of, 1, 157–59, 171–72, 175–77, 180; Li Yongping's literary return to, 29, 157–62, 182–85, 192–94; Ng's homogenization of the various native groups in, 179; *peselai* as a custom in, 171–72, 182. *See also* Malaysia—Malaysian Borneo (East Malaysia)

bumiputera (sons of the soil): defined as a postcolonial governance category, 4; indigeneity distinguished from, 239n8

C Jun (Mr. C) [Liang Shan], 218n37

Cantonese, as one of five topolects (dialects) of *huayu* (Chinese language), 60, 86

cartography and cartographic representations: David Wang's mapping world-Chinese literary space, 17, 152; Li Yongping's employment of, 159–60, 169, 177–78; Mahua literature in noncontiguous locales—especially Taiwan and Malaysia, 4, 156, 243n54; Ng's cartographic vision, 7, 10–11, 152

Casanova, Pascale: nation-centric hierarchy of cultural capital, 4, 10, 19, 160, 193–94; privileging of the West in her model of "world literary space," 2, 156, 162, 180; "world literary space" (also called the "World Republic of Letters") identified by, 2, 10, 19, 156, 160, 193–94

Chan, Shelly: "diaspora moments" identified by, 119; on "Nanyang circulations," 38

Chan Tah Wei (Chen Dawei): "literary federation" theorized by, 186; range of local interpretations of Mahua literature compiled and edited by, 249n15

Cheah, Pheng, "literature of the world" defined by, 5

Chen Yingzhen: appearance in Wang Anyi's *Utopian Verses*, 132–33, 139, 154; Mahua literature criticized by, 153–55

Chineseness: "Chineseness of China" constructed as a phrase by Wang Gungwu, 234n17; Han Suyin's binding of the notion of Chineseness to a territorialized identity, 78; the lack of a unitary space of overseas Chineseness, 49; Li Yongping's muting of Chineseness in his diasporic discourse, 174, 176, 183–84, 246n79; in relation to diaspora explored by Wang Anyi, 130–32; the Sinophone defined as on the margins of, 17

Chiu, Kuei-fen: on the development of indigenous literature and related discourses in Taiwan, 173, 174–75, 242n42, 243n47; on Huang De-shi's framework for Taiwan literary history, 116; on Li Yongping's "simultaneous inhabitation" in Mahua and Taiwan literary spaces, 176

Chong Fah Hing (Zhuang Huaxing): epigraph to chapter one, 1, 4–5; on marginalized ethnicities in Mahua literature, 181–82; views on emigrant Mahua writers, 184

Chong Yee-Voon (Zhong Yiwen), 216n22, 249n15

Chow Tse-tsung, 19–20

colonial Malaya: the "Ma" in "Mahua literature" related to, 3–4, 23, 26; partial setting of Wang Anyi's *Shangxin Taipingyang* (Sadness of the Pacific) in, 232n4; translingual literary integration in, 26, 113, 200–201

Comber, Leonard: work for the Special Branch of the Malayan Police, 73; Writing in Asia Series conceived by, 231n109

constitutive others: as components of Mahua literature, 27; framing of Mahua authors as figures of alterity in global Chinese literary production, 118, 157, 205

cosmopolitanism: of the "Galapagos Paradox," 22, 202; Li Yongping's "cosmopolitan development of the Chinese language," 29, 163–65; of Lin's dialectical production of *Thick Smoke*, 42–43, 217–18n36; Tan Swie Hian's highlighting of cosmopolitan energies spanning across Singapore and Malaysia, 198–99; Wang Anyi's pursuit of a "cosmopolitan Chinese literary vernacular," 28–29, 120–21, 138–42

crossings: as an analytical method that can undergird studies on multicultural sites in Southeast Asia, 198; the border-crossing biography of Lin Cantian's *Thick Smoke*, 37, 217–18n36; Ho Sok Fong's transatlantic publication of *Lake Like a Mirror* as a form of, 195–96; simultaneous interaction of Mahua literature with global, local, and other regional scales of literary interests, 22–25, 42–43, 140, 154–55, 193; various types of crossings by Mahua authors, 5, 196

Damrosch, David: epigraph to chapter one, 1; on P. G. Wodehouse, 80, 87–88; world literature defined by, 3, 208n11

Darwin, Charles, 7, 14, 15, 16, 19

Deleuze, Gilles, on "minor literature," 68, 201

diasporas: depicted in Wang Anyi's *Sadness of the Pacific*, 122–26, 130–31, 134, 141–42; "diaspora moments" identified by Shelly Chan, 119; diasporic Mahua writers's *guiqiao xiaoshuo* (novels about or by returned overseas Chinese), 123–24, 128–30; dynamics of topolectal groups in non-China locales, 199; indigeneity in overseas Chinese writers' psyche, 51;

Index 283

diasporas (continued)
    the lack of a unitary space of overseas
        Chineseness, 49; Li Yongping's
        diasporic discourse, 176, 183–84; the
        notion of *bang* as an obstacle to
        solidarity in the Nanyang diaspora,
        46; Sinophone studies' engagement
        with Chinese diaspora studies, 27,
        199; study of Chinese diasporas by
        Adam McKeown, 125, 134
Dirlik, Arif, on the concept of "place-
    based," 26
Duke, Michael S., on the international
    reputation of modern and
    contemporary fiction written in
    Chinese, 195–96

Fabian, Johannes, on "allochronism," 93
Fang Xiu, on the "self-positioning thought
    of Mahua intellectuals," 40, 213n1,
    214n6, 214n7, 215n15, 216n28, 221n67
Feiming (Qiu Shizhen), 1934 debate
    over the recognition of "local
    writers" triggered by, 40–42
Flowers in the Mirror (*Jinghua yuan*)
    by Li Ruzhen: *Thick Smoke*'s
    promotional materials, 31; town
    name in *Thick Smoke* echoes
    locales in, 50
Fu Donghua, Lin Cantian's *Thick Smoke*
    published by, 37, 38, 49
Furnivall, John S., "plural society"
    identified by, 75

Galapagos Paradox, 22, 202
Ge, Liangyan, 54, 64
globality: of Chinese language, 164–65;
    covert globality of Mahua literature,
    22, 202–3; of literary knowledge, 6,
    200, 204; the local-global resonance
    of Han Suyin's cultural discourses,
    72; Malaysia's regional and global
    connectivities, 4, 22–23, 203–4; of the
    readership in Chinese, 210n36;
    simultaneous interaction of Mahua
    literature with global, local, and other
    regional scales of literary interests,
    22–25. *See also* Galapagos Paradox;
    worlding—literary worlding
Groppe, Alison M.: on Li Yongping's
    Snowfall in the Clouds, 178; on
    Mahua writers' "sociolinguistic
    fascination," 43; on Ng Kim Chew's
    "Huawen/Zhongwen" essay, 149
Grutman, Rainier, 163–64
Guattari, Félix, on "minor literature,"
    68, 201

Ha Jin, 229n78
Hainanese, as one of five topolects
    (dialects) of *huayu* (Chinese
    language), 60, 86
Hakka: Li Yongping on writing in, 170;
    as one of five topolects of (dialects)
    huayu (Chinese language), 60, 86
Han Suyin (1916/17–2012): advice to
    Anglophone Malayan writers on
    writing about Malaya, 78, 92–98;
    composition of Anglophone
    literature as world literature, 27–28,
    72–73, 76, 78–79, 95–98, 108–14;
    cooptation into Mahua literary
    space, 76–78; emulation of Chinese
    language in Malaya via her hybrid
    English literary language, 28, 79, 95,
    98, 101–4, 106–7; envisioning of a
    Malayan "pattern" for the world,
    81–82, 84–85; 1955 Hollywood film
    Love Is a Many-Splendored Thing, 76;
    pursuit of real-life speech patterns

and new linguistic relations, 91, 95–96, 100–102, 111, 114

Han Suyin (1916/17–2012)–*And the Rain My Drink* (*Rain*): Chinese publication of only six chapters of, 225n17; place-catalyzed literary language of, 79, 107; publication by Jonathan Cape, 76; self-referential paratext in, 92–94; Sinitic-influenced English in, 28, 95–107

Han Suyin (1916/17–2012)–bifocal writing approach: engagement with paired geographical perspectives, 72–73, 111–12; ethnographic and universal portrayals, 72, 80

Han Suyin (1916/17–2012)–biographical details: husband. *See* Comber, Leonard; lecturer stint at Nanyang University, 85–86, 227n44, 227n45; medical practices in Johor Bahru and Singapore, 73–75, 225n11; Rosalie Matilda Kwanghu Chou as her real name, 92, 224n4; sojourn in Malaya and Singapore, 71, 74f2.1, 114–15

Han Suyin (1916/17–2012)–*Freedom Shout Merdeka*: advertised as sequel to *Rain*, 82, 226n33; scenes in, 74–75, 89, 99, 102, 103; Sinitic-influenced English in, 28; as unfinished manuscript by, 28, 72, 79, 226–27n34, 229n69

Han Suyin (1916/17–2012)–literary worlding by: ambiguous position as both Malayan insider and outsider, 80–82, 94; dismantling of barriers between Sinophone and Anglophone cultural spheres in Malaya, 72–73, 96, 111–14, 196, 198

Han Suyin (1916/17–2012)–speeches by: "The Creation of a Malayan Literature" (1957), 96–97; "Development of a Malayan Chinese Literature" (1961), 95, 104–5, 112, 229n73, 230n89; "Some Impressions of Writing in English within the Context of Singapore and Malaya" (1961), 93, 103–4, 110–11; "Understanding Southeast Asia from the Point of View of the Writer" (1958), 109–10, 230n95

Hayot, Eric, 200

Heinemann Education Books Ltd.: African Writers Series started by, 225n14; *Modern Malaysian Chinese Stories* published by, 113–14, 231n109

heterolingualism: definition by Rainier Grutman, 163–64; of Han Suyin's *Rain*, 94–95, 101–3; of Li Yongping's *River*, 160–70; of Lin Cantian's place-catalyzed literary language, 33–35, 50–52; of Lin Cantian's textualization approach, 54–60

Hitchcock, Peter, on the "logic of imbrication," 96

Ho Sok Fong, *Humian rujing* (*Lake like a mirror*), 195–96

Hokkien (topolect originated from southern Fujian): *Nanyang Siang Pau* as a stronghold for speakers of, 41; as one of five topolects (dialects) of *huayu* (Chinese language), 60, 86; term *titto* (gallivanting) used in Taiwan, 168, 172

Hokkien (topolect originated from southern Fujian)–in Lin Cantian's work: characters Mao Zhendong and Li Mianzhi's lack of proficiency in, 47; representation of Hokkien and Cantonese discourses of daily life, 57–60, 222n80

Huang De-shi, on the corpus that constitutes Taiwan literary history, 116–17

Huang, Yu-ting, 15

huawen. *See* Sinophone (*huawen*)

huawen wenxue. *See* Sinophone literature (*huawen wenxue*)

hybridity: Han Suyin's emulation of Chinese language in Malaya via her hybrid English literary language, 28, 79, 95, 98, 101–4, 106–7; Han Suyin's ideal of the Eurasian and the culturally hybrid Asian, 73, 84, 85, 90–91, 103–4, 108; Han Suyin's ideas on and literary representations of linguistic hybridity, 79, 88, 89, 91, 101, 107; of the human connections and discourse of "diaspora-as-diversity," 134; Latin American literary formation as a product of cultural hybridity described by Ng Kim Chew, 145; Lin Cantian's adoption of a place-evocative mode of linguistic hybridity, 45, 52, 65–66; Lin Cantian's novelistic design of *Thick Smoke*, 34–35; of the literary language of Li Yongping's *River*, 159–60, 164–65, 168–69, 172; "season of hybridity" (*zaji*) in Shanghai's publishing scene, 49

indigeneity: *bumiputera* (sons of the soil) distinguished from groups considered to possess Bornean indigeneity, 4, 239n8; debates over differences between the terms "native" and "indigenous," 242n40; the development of indigenous literature and related discourses in Taiwan, 173, 174–75, 242n42, 243n47; indigenous studies at Taiwan's National Dong Hwa University, 173, 242n44; Li Yongping on using Chinese language to transcribe indigenous languages in *River*, 170; Li Yongping's featuring of indigenous folk customs in *River*, 171–72, 182; Li Yongping's use of literary indigeneity to negotiate his bifurcated authorial identity, 173–80, 182–94, 196; in overseas Chinese writers' psyche, 51. *See also* insiders and inside knowledge; native literary spaces

inner diversity: of China, Europe and Taiwan, 15, 17, 141, 247–48n9; of general literary and cultural formations, 20, 34, 66, 150, 199, 202, 205; of Malaysia and Mahua literature, 5, 24, 40, 47, 49, 110, 121–22, 187, 244n59

insiders and inside knowledge: Han Suyin's ambiguous position as both Malayan insider and outsider, 80–82, 94; Li Yongping's forging of an "insider point of view," 171–72, 183–84; Lin Cantian's fashioning of himself as an insider in both China and Malaya, 27, 63–65

insiders and inside knowledge— participation in two or more literary ecologies: by Han Suyin, 76–77, 113–14; by Li Yongping, 1, 157–59, 175–77, 180; by Lin Cantian, 42–43, 49–50, 66; by Ng Kim Chew, 8, 203–4; by Wang Anyi, 117–22, 153

Japan: anti-Japanese resistance literary movement in Nanyang, 43, 123; specialists of Southeast Asia on Mahua literature, 144–45, 236n47

Kenley, David L., 51
Khoo Seok Wan, 37
Ko Chia-cian (Gao Jiaqian), 180, 244n64, 246n79
Kuo Chiang-sheng, 242n45
Kuo, Huei-Ying, 46, 214n10

Lao She, *Little Po's Birthday* (*Xiaopo de shengri*), 38, 216n23, 219–20n58
Lee, Fiona: on Han Suyin's paratext for *Rain*, 94; on heterolingual rendition in *Rain*, 95; on the local-global resonance of Han Suyin's cultural discourses, 72
Lewis, Martin, and Kären Wigen, 131
Li Tuo, on "Mao-style prose" (*maowenti*), 145
Li Yongping (Li Yung-p'ing) (1947–2017): English translation of his work, 195, 247n2; forging of an "insider point of view" by, 171–72, 183–84, 196; indigeneity used for negotiating his bifurcated authorial identity, 173–80, 182–94; "Lazi Fu" (The Bidayuh woman), 166, 244n59; *Nanyang huayu* used by, 166, 191; "native literary space" of vis-à-vis global Chinese literary production, 159–60; negotiations with *huawen* and *zhongwen*, 165–69; *Poluozhou zhizi* (Sons of Borneo), 166, 179, 244n59; regional categorization of his work, 1; *Yuxue feifei* (Snowfall in the clouds), 168, 177; Zhang Guixing's writing career in Taiwan followed by, 179–80, 244–45n6
Li Yongping (Li Yung-p'ing) (1947–2017)–biographical details: birth in Sarawak, 1; boat trip in Borneo, 157f4.1; "simultaneous inhabitation" in Mahua and Taiwan literary spaces, 1, 157–61, 175–77, 180; sojourn in east Taiwan, 173–75, 242n45
Li Yongping (Li Yung-p'ing) (1947–2017)–*Dahe jintou* (Where the Great River ends): *buji buli* (off-center) dynamic of worlding via composing, 29–30, 158–59, 168–69, 188, 192–94; cartographic representations in, 159–60, 169, 177–78; imaginary conversations with his muse Zhu Ling, 158, 171–72, 174, 175, 178; legend of empty canoes inconsistently attributed by, 246n85; *peselai* trope in, 171–72, 182; the character Yong-the-youth in, 158, 169, 178, 182–85, 188–90
Li Zhongyu, 47
Lian Shisheng, Han Suyin interviewed by, 98
Liang Fang, *Woceng tingdao nizai fengzhong kuqi* (I once heard you crying in the wind), 183
Liang Qichao, 112–13
Liang Shan. *See* C Jun (Mr. C) [Liang Shan]
Lim Kien Ket: on Mahua literary history, 204; on *xiaowenxue* (small literature), 201
Lin Cantian (1904–1972): discourse on his writing endeavor, 221n79; English and Sinitic language mixed in three short plays written by, 37, 215n18; English proficiency and Malay illiteracy of, 221n78; forging of a Malaya-Shanghai connection by, 27, 31, 33–34, 37–38, 42–43, 46–47, 50, 65–66, 196; Hokkien used in his work. *See* Hokkien (topolect originated from southern

Lin Cantian (1904–1972) (continued)
Fujian)—in Lin Cantian's work; promotion of "mass language," 52–53; reputation as "the novelist who specializes in dramatizing problems of overseas Chinese education," 46; *Rezhang* (Tropical miasma), 41–42, 219n52

Lin Cantian (1904–1972)—biographical details: birth and early years in the Chuzhou region of Zhejiang Province, 35–36; impact of the May Fourth Movement on, 31, 36, 61–62; physical characteristics distinguishing him from other *wenren*, 40–41; relocation to Kuala Lumpur, 36; travels to Singapore, 36

Lin Cantian (1904–1972)—*Nongyan* (Thick smoke), 219n47; bifurcated address of both Malayan and Chinese literary spaces, 49–50, 65–66, 203–4; character Li Mianzhi in, 46, 47, 54–55, 214n4; character Mao Zhendong in, 46, 47, 58–59, 214n4; character Selvarajah in, 47–48, 54–56; critical attention hitherto little received by, 33, 43; fictional Malayan town called "The Country of Crying Children" (*ti'er guo*) in, 49–52; Mahua society split along topolectal lines evoked by, 27, 46–49; marketing of, 31, 32f1.1; mass-oriented language derived from the Malayan environment in, 49, 54, 60–61, 221n70; multicultural and multilingual setting of, 35, 37, 44–46; multilingualism as a governing element of the diegesis of, 47–48, 56–59; "Nanyang and a Language of the Masses," 53, 220–21n67; 1934 debate over the recognition of "local writers" and its impact on, 40–43; panoptic narrative voice in, 62–64; place-catalyzed literary language of, 33–35, 50–52; publication in Shanghai, 27, 31, 33, 34, 37–38, 42, 50, 65

Lin Hengnan, *Huayi tongyu* compiled by, 222n84

Literary Galapagos archipelago, Ng Kim Chew's notion of. *See* Ng Kim Chew—Literary Galapagos archipelago

literary worlding. *See* Ng Kim Chew—Literary Galapagos archipelago; worlding—literary worlding

local—as analytical approach: interlocal, 34, 188; local and regional perspectives insufficiently foregrounded in world literary studies, 3, 5–6, 200; translocal, 22, 24, 118, 196

local—as geographical scale: 1934 debate over the recognition of "local writers," 40–43, 217n34; simultaneous interaction of Mahua authorial practices with global and other regional scales of literary interests, 3, 18, 22–25, 26, 27, 72, 132, 193–94, 196, 204

localness: impact of migration on mixes of *huawen* and *zhongwen* in different localities, 151; network of marginalized cultural locales in the Sinophone South (*nanfang huawen*), 21, 24–26, 30, 153, 202–3

Lovell, Julia: on China's obsession with the Nobel Prize in Literature, 144, 236n43; on the "world literary economy," 195

Ly, Singko: translation of Han Suyin's *Rain*, 77–78, 225n17; translation of *Modern Malaysian Chinese Stories*, 231n109

McKeown, Adam, study of Chinese diasporas, 125, 134

Mahua literature (*Mahua wenxue*): as the constitutive other of all place-based literary histories, 27, 118, 157, 205; development of "individualized topolects" (*geren fangyan*) called for by Ng Kim Chew, 67–68; *guiqiao xiaoshuo* (novels about or by returned overseas Chinese), 123–24, 128–29; Ho Sok Fong's transatlantic debut in the English-reading world, 195–96; impact of May Fourth literary figures on. *See* May Fourth New Literature; Wu Tian; Yu Dafu; impact of the Latin American model on, 145–46; Japanese specialists of Southeast Asia on, 144–45, 236n47; Lin Cantian's *Thick Smoke* hailed as the earliest novel in Mahua literary history, 31; *Ma* for "Malaya" in, 3–4, 208n12; post-1937 polemics, 43; as the story of "the unrewarded," 1–3, 12; as a taxonomic category, 25, 26–27, 118–19, 146, 149, 202, 205; zones of contact with its Anglophone audience, 195–96

Mahua literature (*Mahua wenxue*)— discursive reorganization of Chinese literary regions by scholars and critics: Li Yongping, 161–62; Ng Kim Chew, 116–17, 146–51; David Der-wei Wang, 152; Wang Anyi, 117–22

Mahua literature (*Mahua wenxue*)— literary production in Singapore and Malaysia: multiscalar transregionality fostered by Mahua writers grasp of their own marginality, 23–24, 28–30, 143–44, 156–57, 186–88, 193, 196–98, 200–206; Ng Kim Chew's discourse on critical regionalization, 5–12, 18–20, 29, 143–53; 1934 debate over the recognition of "local writers," 40–43; regionalization of colonial Malaya and independent Malaysia as a valid literary terrain, 2–5, 20, 23, 26, 72, 200; Wang Anyi's critical comments about cultural production in Southeast Asia, 28–29, 119–21, 135–37, 153; Wang Xiaoping's contribution to an expanded Singapore and Malaysian Chinese literary history, 123, 128–30, 153

Mair, Victor, 214n3

Malayan English: features of, 89, 92, 103; as a topic for academic study, 88, 228n53, 228n55

Malayan English—as a tool for building grassroots collectivity advocated by Han Suyin, 111, 114; documenting of creolization, 79, 88–92; evolution as literary language, 88–95; place-making, 99, 102–3, 114

Malay language: Chinese-Malay dictionary *Huayi tongyu* compiled by Lin Hengnan, 222n84; Lin Cantian's illiteracy in, 221n78; recognition of literary works written in Malay as national literature by the Malaysian government, 2, 144, 239n11; two modes of transliterating, 45

Malaysia: as a geopolitical unit, 4; crossings by Mahua authors. *See* crossings; dialects of. *See* topolectal (dialect) groups; literary production in Singapore and Malaysia. *See* Mahua literature (*Mahua wenxue*); Ng's satirizing of the debate over a Nobel Prize in Literature for, 144; Peninsular Malaysia (West Malaysia), 4, 186–87; regional and global connectivities of, 4, 19, 22–23, 203–4. *See also* Nanyang (the South Seas)

Malaysia—Malaysian Borneo (East Malaysia), 4; as an exceptional literary locality, 187–88, 246n88; Li Yongping on a boat trip in, 157f4.1; Li Yongping's comprehension of the Dayak in Sarawak, 244n59; Li Yongping's *Poluozhou zhizi* (Sons of Borneo), 166, 179, 244n59; Tian Si's "Writing Borneo" initiative, 181–82, 188; Zhang Guixing's designation of characters as "Dayak" and "Iban," 180, 245n67; Zhang Guixing's rainforest narratives of, 179–80. *See also* Borneo

margins and marginality: Chinese Singaporeans described as like gypsies by Tan Swie Hian, 136–37; Chong Fah Hing on marginalized ethnicities in Mahua literature, 181–82; intermarginal dynamic in the Sinophone South, 21, 24, 193; multiscalar transregionality fostered by Mahua writers grasp of their own marginality, 23–24, 28–30, 143–44, 156–57, 186–88, 193, 196–98, 200–206; nested marginality of Mahua literature, 2, 10–11; network of marginalized cultural locales in the Sinophone South (*nanfang huawen*), 21, 24–26, 30, 153, 202–3; of the Sinophone, 17; Tee Kim Tong on the twin marginalization of Mahua writers in both Malaysian and Taiwan literary spaces, 233n12; unique vantage point for observing globalization of modern Chinese literature, 3, 21

Márquez, Gabriel García, 135, 145

Massey, Doreen, 26

"mass language" (*dazhongyu*): debate associated with the Latinization of the Chinese script in Malaya, 217n34, 220n64; Fan Cheng's discussion of, 54, 221n70; Lin Cantian's employment in *Thick Smoke*, 27, 49, 54, 60–61; Lin Cantian's promotion of, 52–54

Masutani Satoshi, 236n47

May Fourth Movement: ideal of self-determination mirrored by Lin Cantian, 36; Ng Kim Chew on the movement's transformation of vernacular writing, 148

May Fourth New Literature, 62; impact on Li Yongping, 166; individual figures associated with. *See* Lao She; Wu Tian; Yu Dafu; Lin Cantian's encounters with, 31, 36, 49; participation in the diverse and prosperous publishing scene in Shanghai, 49, 62; *yuti wen* (vernacular writing) promoted by. *See baihua* ("unadorned speech")

Miao Xiu, 77, 213n1, 214n6, 230n90

migration: impact on mixes of *huawen* and *zhongwen* in different localities, 151; of Mahua literature to become Taiwan literature, 204; Malaysia as a venue for migratory passages and cultural interactions, 4, 14, 22–23, 204; migratory journey by Han Suyin to Malaya and Singapore, 71, 73, 74f2.1, 114–15; migratory journey by Lin Cantian, 36, 62; migratory journeys of Mahua authors, 22–24; the migratory tendency of literature in the global age, 25; of Wang Anyi's family members reflected in *Sadness of the Pacific*, 122–26, 141–42; Wang Anyi's observation of linguistic mobility accompanying large-scale migration, 136–37

minor literature: Gilles Deleuze and Félix Guattari's concept of, 68, 201; vernacularization of concept by Mahua scholars, 200–201

Miyoshi, Masao, "off center" employed as a term by, 158

Moretti, Franco: archipelagic model of literary cultures, 8; transperipheral movement of forms dismissed by, 11; on world literature as a system of variations, 6

multilinguality: as a major inclination of Mahua literature, 26; of Malaysia, 4

multilinguality—Han Suyin: on the bilingual or trilingual capacity of Nanyang University students, 104; depictions of multilingual diegetic situations, 86–87, 89–90, 91–92, 95, 99, 100–101; on the merits of multilingual national literatures and literary histories, 71, 113

multilinguality—Li Yongping, representation of Bornean multilingualism, 164, 184, 246n79

multilinguality—Lin Cantian: depictions of multilingual social realities in *Thick Smoke*, 47–49, 55–59; multicultural and multilingual setting of *Thick Smoke*, 35, 37, 44–46; representational concerns about, 59, 60, 61, 65, 66

Nanyang (the South Seas): anti-Japanese resistance literary movement in (post-1937), 43, 123; conventional correspondence to Southeast Asia, 8, 31, 117; establishment of the Nanyang Cultural and Education Affairs Bureau, 38; ethno-geographical imaginary of, 4, 209n15; Liang Shan's criticism of Nanyang writers, 218n37; "mass language" movement in, 52–54; rifts among the topolectal groups and native place associations in, 27, 41, 46–49, 217n34; Wang Xiaoping's life in, 123, 128; weak Mahua cultural infrastructure in the 1920s and 1930s in, 27, 41–42

Nanyang Siang Pau (Chinese-language newspaper): as a stronghold for Hokkien speakers, 41; debate over "local writers," 41, 217n34; Han Suyin's negotiation with Lin Yutang reported in, 227n44

native literary spaces: Casanova's concept contrasted with her "world literary space" via Li Yongping's case, 160–62; the "literary federation" theorized by Chan Tah Wei compared with, 186–87; multiscalar transregionality mediated by Mahua literature in, 23–24, 28–30, 143–44, 156–57, 186–88, 193, 196–98, 200, 205–6

Ng Kim Chew: discourse on critical regionalization, 5–12, 18–20, 143–51, 152–53; on early Mahua writers' artistic incompetence, 43–44; English translation of his work, 12, 195, 211n40, 247n2; on the Latin American literary formation, 145–46; "M de shizong" (Disappearance of M), 144, 211n49; root-seeking writers in China as models for, 143, 145–46; *shaoshu wenxue* (minority literature) used as a term by, 201

Ng Kim Chew—Literary Galapagos archipelago, *13*f0.1; comparison across biology (Darwinian ideas) and literary studies elicited by notion of, 7, 14–19, 203; contribution to world literary knowledges, 6–7, 16–17, 204–5; as a heuristic geography, 7; *huawen/zhongwen* discourse, 9–11, 29, 121–22, 146–52; on Mahua literature as a category that stands for all "literatures deficient in resources," 203–5; new cartographical method for representing world-Chinese literary space proposed by, 7, 10–11, 152; Taiwan designated as both a *zhongwen*-producing and *"huawen"*-producing venue in, 149; twin theories of "adaptive radiation" (*fushe shiying*) and "evolution in isolation" (*geli yanhua*), 14–15; on the "'untranslatability' of texts" (*wenben de "bukeyi"*), 15–16, 211n49

Ngu Ik Tien, 184–85

Nobel Prize in Literature: China's quest for recognition via, 144, 146; Gabriel García Márquez winning of (1982), 135; Gao Xingjian's winning of, 191; Li Yongping's missed opportunity to emulate winner William Faulkner, 190; Mo Yan's winning of (2012), 2, 141; Ng's satirizing of the debate over the prize for Malaysia, 144; Southeast Asian writers as "unrewarded" by, 2; Zhang Guixing deemed deserving of the prize, 238n69

Nusantara (the "Malay world"), 209n15; ethno-geographical imaginary of, 4

off-center: Admussen's translation of the Chinese idiom *buji buli*, 239n6; employed as a term by Masao Miyoshi, 158; Li Yongping's approach as a means for reckoning with various literary spaces, 29–30, 158–59, 168–69, 192–94; as relative positionality in connected cultural spheres, 11, 15, 188, 212n61

Paré, François, 249n17

Philippines: incorporation into the transregional dynamics of Li Yongping's *River*, 169; José Rizal's *Noli Me Tángere* (Touch me not), 71–72

place: Arif Dirlik's sense of locality with a flexible and porous boundary, 26; heterolingualism of Lin Cantian's place-catalyzed literary language, 34–35, 51–52; "homeland" as native place and "homeland" as the site of ethnic fraternity explored in Wang Anyi's *Sadness of the Pacific*, 124–26;

Mahua literature as the constitutive other of all place-based literary histories, 27, 118, 157, 205; Massey's temporalized notion of, 26; place-based communities forming their own interpretive traditions, 200–201; place-catalyzed literary language of Han Suyin's *Rain*, 79, 107; sense of place emphasized in Ng Kim Chew's *huawen/zhongwen* discourse, 146–52. *See also* localness

Porter, David, 25

Purcell, Victor, Singapore described as a "harbor of strange tongues," 44

Qing dynasty: fantasy novel *Jinghua yuan*. *See Flowers in the Mirror* (*Jinghua yuan*) by Li Ruzhen; popular fiction and drama of the Ming-Qing period, 62

Qiu Shizhen. *See* Feiming

Qu Qiubai, 62

Quah Sy Ren, 214n6

Rizal, José, 71–72

Roberts, Brian Russell, and Michelle Ann Stephens, 8–9, 212n63

Rojas, Carlos, 13f0.1; on the global readership in Chinese, 210n36; on Li Yongping's spectral cartography about China and Taiwan, 177; on "Mahua literature" as analytical category for modern Chinese literary studies, 207n4; on Ng Kim Chew's interest in islands and archipelagos, 7–8, 13

Rubins, Maria, vision of global Russian culture, 9

Sadness of the Pacific. *See* Wang Anyi (1954–)—*Shangxin Taipingyang* (Sadness of the Pacific)

Said, Edward W.: on the pattern of relative strength between East and West, 84; on the politics of knowledge production, 23–24; on the reassessment of cultural archives, 34

Shanghai: Malaya-Shanghai connection forged by Lin Cantian, 27, 31, 33–34, 37–39, 42–43, 46–47, 50, 62, 196; Nanyang writers ingratiating themselves with the Shanghai literary world, 218n37; publication of Lin Cantian's *Thick Smoke* in, 27, 31, 33, 34, 37–38, 42, 50, 65; "season of hybridity" (*zaji*) for book publishing in, 49, 62; "Shanghainese" as a shorthand for *waijiang ren*, 217n31, 220n58; Shanghai studies as a recognized intellectual rubric, 197; Wang Anyi's rejection of the label of a Shanghai writer, 141; Wang Anyi's representation of personal circumstances in, 132, 234n20; Wang Anyi's writing from the perspective of, 118, 132, 141, 150

Shang, Wei, on the modern view of premodern and early modern Chinese linguistic and writing practices, 147

Shi Wenting, 184, 188

Shih Shu-mei: "Sinophone" coined and defined by, 17; on Zhang Guixing, 238n69

Sin Chew Jit Poh (Chinese-language newspaper): debate over "local writers," 41, 217n34; Yu Dafu's editorship of, 70

Singapore: as the center of Malay cultural production after World War II, 231n107; Chinese-language newspapers in. *See Nanyang Siang Pau*; *Sin Chew Jit Poh*; the first drama performance in *baihua* vernacular staged in Singapore, 214n6; Han Suyin's departure from, 114; inclusion in grassroots imaginaries of colonial Malaya, 232n4; *waijiang xi* preferred over Teochew opera by Teochew merchants in, 199; Yu Dafu's sojourn in, 35, 70, 127, 233n13. *See also* Nanyang (the South Seas)

Singapore Chinese-language literature (*Xinhua wenxue*), 10, 118, 153, 232n4, 247–48n9, 249–50n18

Sinophone (*huawen*): coexistence of Malay and Sinophone literary ecologies in Malaya and Singapore, 231n107; Han Suyin's juxtaposition of the Sinophone with the Anglophone, 27–28, 69, 73, 95–98, 108–14; "huayi feng" suggested as a translation of, 251n25; Ng Kim Chew's *huawen/zhongwen* discourse, 9–11, 29, 121–22, 147–52; in the realm of acoustic arts, 199, 248–49n12; "South" (*nanfang*) and "Sinophone" (*huawen*) as synonymous, 20; as a term privileging the Western context of knowledge production when translated as *huayu yuxi*, 212n60; as a term to render *huawen* and *huayu*, 18, 212n61

Sinophone literature (*huawen wenxue*): divergent implications for knowledge production associated with its alternative translation in Chinese as *huayu yuxi wenxue*, 17–18, 212n60; Macau literature as an instance of, 197, 247n6; Mahua literature as an instance of, 17–18; Ng Kim Chew's conception of Republic of Southern Sinophone Literature, 19–20, 151; Ng Kim Chew's definition of, 9–10; role of translated literature in stimulating the growth of, 77

Sinophone South: adaptation and referencing by authors from different native literary spaces in, 121, 152–53, 203–4; introduced as a term, 5, 20; network of marginalized cultural locales in, 21, 24–26, 30, 153, 202–3; Ng Kim Chew's *nanfang huawen* (Southern Sinophone) translated by the author as, 20, 202, 205; worldliness registered in the fictional practices of authors from, 21–23, 196, 201

Sinophone studies: engagement with Chinese diaspora studies, 27, 199; as a field of study, 3, 29, 122, 152, 153; Ng's discourse on critical regionalization as anticipation of, 143–53; "Sinophone Studies: New Directions" conference (2016), *13*f0.1, 211n46

Southeast Asia: Chinese linguistic and cultural ecologies in and from the region, 68, 121, 136–37, 143, 147, 199, 201; Han Suyin's speech on "Understanding Southeast Asia from the Point of View of the Writer" (1958), 109–10, *109*f2.2, 230n95; Japanese specialists of Southeast Asia on Mahua literature, 144–45, 236n47; lineage of

Chinese-language cinema in Southeast Asia, 222n87, 248n11; Malaysia as a geopolitical unit in, 4; multilingualism of, 5, 28; peripherality of the region in academic disciplines, 6, 248n12; Southeast Asian writers as "unrewarded," 2. *See also* Borneo; Malaysia; Nanyang; Singapore

Sternberg, Meir—critical terminology of "translation mimesis": broad theoretical concern of, 65; introduced, 55; strategies including "selective reproduction," "explicit attribution," and "conceptual reflection" identified in Lin Cantian's *Thick Smoke*, 55–56; "vehicular matching" identified in Han Suyin's *Rain*, 101

Taiwan: as both a *zhongwen*-producing and "*huawen*"-producing venue according to Ng Kim Chew, 149, 237n63; dialect spoken in. *See* Hokkien; internal regionality of, 15, 247–48n9; National Dong Hwa University, 173, 242n44; World Chinese-Language Writers' Association established in, 149

Taiwan literature: Huang De-shi on the corpus that constitutes Taiwan literary history, 116–17; Li Yongping and Zhang Guixing grouped together by Taiwan's leading literary publishers, 179–80; Li Yongping's "simultaneous inhabitation" in Mahua and Taiwan literary spaces, 1, 157–59, 176–77, 180; Ng Kim Chew on the cultural formation of, 9–10, 15, 116, 203–4; novels selected by the National Culture and Arts Foundation initiative (2001), 1–2, 207n3; "Taiwanese literature" distinguished from, 238n2; Zhang Guixing's double inhabitation in Mahua and Taiwan literary spaces, 1, 152, 177, 180

Tan Swie Hian: cosmopolitan energies spanning across Singapore and Malaysia highlighted by, 198–99; marginalized Chinese Singaporeans described as like gypsies by, 136–37; poets from Taiwan and Singapore-Malaysia compared to diverse snails, 15

Tan Yunshan, 33, 223n93; as the archetype for the protagonist Mao Zhendong in *Thick Smoke*, 214n4

Tee Kim Tong: overviews on Mahua literature, 220n64; on the role of translated literature in the growth of Sinophone works, 77; on the southern character of Ng Kim Chew's literary thought, 249–50n18; suggested translation of "Sinophone" as "*huayi feng*," 251n25; on the twin marginalization of Mahua writers in both Malaysian and Taiwan literary spaces, 233n12; on *xiaowenxue* (small literature), 201

Teng, Emma J., 78

Teochew (or Chaozhou): as one of five topolects (dialects) of *huayu* (Chinese language), 60, 86; *waijiang xi* preferred over Teochew opera by Teochew merchants in Singapore, 199

textualization: in Liangyan Ge's study of the *Water Margin* (*Shuihu zhuan*), 54, 64; as a conceptual tool to examine Lin Cantian's *Thick Smoke*, 35, 54–55, 61, 64, 68–69

Index 295

Thick Smoke. See Lin Cantian (1904–1972)—*Nongyan* (Thick smoke)
Thompson, Lanny, on heuristic geographies, 7
Thomsen, Mads Rosendahl, "limited strangeness" employed as a term by, 158
Tian Si, 180–82, 187–88
topolectal (dialect) groups: Lin Cantian's discussion in "Nanyang and a Language of the Masses," 53; Mahua society split along topolectal lines evoked by Lin Cantian in *Thick Smoke*, 27, 46–49; the Malaysian *bang* (*malai bang*) in Taiwan identified by Ng Kim Chew compared to, 67–68; the notion of *bang* among Nanyang Chinese sojourners, 46; rifts among the topolectal groups and native place associations in Nanyang, 40–41, 53, 217n34; Sinophone studies broadened by research on the dynamics of, 27, 199; "southern topolects" in Ng Kim Chew's ideational literary community of the South (*nanfang*), 18–19; "topolect" as a translation for *fangyan* rather than "dialect," 33, 214n3. *See also* Cantonese; Hainanese; Hakka; Hokkien; Teochew (or Chaozhou)
Toyoda Noriko, 167
translational mimesis. *See* Sternberg, Meir—critical terminology of "translation mimesis"
translocatlity. *See* local—as analytical approach
Tu Wei-ming, concept of a "Cultural China," 2–3

vernacular literary language: the first drama performance in *baihua* vernacular staged in Singapore, 214n6; Lin Cantian's reading of "chapter novels" (*zhanghui xiaoshuo*) in premodern vernacular literary language, 36; Ng's discourse on critical regionalization, 143–51, 152–53; of popular fiction and drama of the Ming-Qing period favored by Qu Qiubai, 62; Wang Anyi's pursuit of a "cosmopolitan Chinese literary vernacular," 28–29, 120–21, 138–42; *yuti wen* (vernacular writing) promoted by the May Fourth Movement. *See baihua* ("unadorned speech). *See also baihua* ("unadorned speech"); Hokkien; topolectal (dialect) groups
Vieira de Almeida, Rosa, 197

waijiang ren: in Lao She's *Little Po's Birthday*, 219–20n58; in Lin Cantian's *Rezhang* (Tropical miasma), 219n52; Lin Cantian's identity as, 34, 41; in Lin Cantian's *Thick Smoke*, 46–48, 58–59; prominence in the Chinese-language book trade in Singapore, 217n32; "Shanghainese" as a shorthand for, 217n31, 220n58; Zhao Rong's definition of, 41
Wang Anyi (1954–): Chinese language framed as a "place for wandering" by, 136–37; "cosmopolitan Chinese literary vernacular" pursued by, 28–29, 120–21, 138–42, 196; "The Fate of Language" on the impact of multidirectional linguistic mobility, 120, 135–37, 146; father. *See* Wang

Xiaoping; on her ideal of "abstract language" (*chouxiang yuyan*), 137–39, 151; on Latin American literature as a model, 145–46; root-seeking literature (*xungen wenxue*) pluralized by, 29, 119, 121, 135, 138–42, 146; trip to Singapore and Peninsular Malaysia, 117f3.1, 117–18, 136f3.2

Wang Anyi (1954–)—"The Language of Fiction in Works from Mainland China and Taiwan: A Comparison": on the impact of linguistic mobility, 137, 146; on the limitations of "specific languages" (*juti yuyan*), 137–38; Ng Kim Chew's elaboration on her China-Taiwan analysis, 146–50

Wang Anyi (1954–)—*Shangxin Taipingyang* (Sadness of the Pacific): assertion that islands are interchangeable with continents, 28, 120, 131–33; depiction of Yu Dafu and Wu Tian in, 126–28, 154; *guiqiao* (returned overseas Chinese) foregrounded in, 123–24, 128–30; "homeland" as native place and "homeland" as the site of ethnic fraternity explored in, 124–26; life journey of "my father" (*wo fuqin*) in, 123–30; life journey of "Youngest Uncle" (*xiao shushu*) in, 123, 126, 128; portrayal of the "drifting fate of humanity" in, 120, 123, 126, 131, 133–34; Singapore/colonial Malaya setting of, 118, 232n4

Wang Anyi (1954–)—*Wutuobang shipian* (Utopian verses): Chen Yingzhen's appearance in, 132–33, 154; cosmopolitan Chinese literary vernacular registered in, 139–40; Wang's experience at the 1983 Iowa International Writers' Workshop commemorated in, 132

Wang, David Der-wei, 13f0.1; the alterity of Mahua sociohistorical and literary circumstances identified by, 205; on Chinese literary alterity, 250–51n25; on the Chinese notion of *wen*, 163; on the discursive space of Chinese literary studies, 152; on establishing "Dongbei studies" (*dongbeixue*), 197; on literary worlding, 23; on Li Yongping's "China," 162; modification of Shi Shu-mei's term "Sinophone" to form a new literary cartography, 17

Wang, Gungwu, "Chineseness of China" constructed as a phrase by, 234n17

Wang Wen-hsing, Ng Kim Chew's view of his works of fiction, 15, 149

Wang Xiaoping (pen name Xiaoping): contribution to an expanded Singapore and Malaysian Chinese literary history, 153; early works, 233n15; journey from Singapore to China, 128; life in Nanyang, 123, 128, 153; meeting with Yu Dafu, 126–27, 233n13; semiautobiographical novels written by, 123, 128; Wang Anyi's reconstruction of his life in Nanyang, 123–31

Water Margin (*Shuihu zhuan*), 54, 64

Wei Yun, 40, 77

Where the Great River Ends (River). See Li Yongping (Li Yung-p'ing) (1947–2017)—*Dahe jintou* (Where the Great River ends)

Wong Yoon Wah, on Li Yongping, 165

Index 297

world-Chinese literary space: defined, 3; *shijie huawen wenxue* (world Chinese literature) distinguished from, 208n9; transperipheral relations reflected in Li Yongping's writing practice, 29–30, 156, 158–59, 168–69, 192–94

worlding—literary worlding: analyzed through a multifocal method, 26; definition of, 21–22; by Han Suyin, 108, 113; by Li Yongping, 29, 158–59, 162, 165, 192, 193; by Mahua authors, 202–3; privileging of the West in Casanova's model of world literature, 6, 156; three world-oriented modes of relation-making via literature, 21–25; through rhetorical production, 3; by Wang Anyi, 131, 132. *See also* cartography and cartographic representations; globality; Ng Kim Chew—Literary Galapagos archipelago; Wang, David Der-wei

world literary studies: Casanova on. *See* Casanova, Pascale; important and unconventional questions addressed in *Malaysian Crossings*, 11–12; local and regional perspectives insufficiently foregrounded in, 5–6, 11, 16–17; new historiographical approach to, 202; world-Chinese literary space as a located approach to, 3

Wu He, Ng's view of his works of fiction as untranslatable, 15, 16

Wu Tian: depiction by Wang Anyi in *Sadness of the Pacific*, 126–28, 154; involvement with Mahua literary arts, 127, 233n14

Xiaoping. *See* Wang Xiaoping

Xuan Sulai, 144, 236n47

Yeh, Catherine Vance, 135

Yen Yuan-shu, advice given to Li Yongping, 166, 167, 191

Yi Duo. *See* Zhao Rong (pen name Yi Duo)

Yildiz, Yasemin, 49

Yu Dafu: depiction by Wang Anyi in *Sadness of the Pacific*, 126–28, 154; editorship of *Sin Chew Jit Poh*, 70; as a literary mentor to young Mahua writers, 70–72, 75; meetings with Wang Xiaoping, 233n13; on José Rizal's *Noli Me Tángere* (Touch me not), 71; Singapore sojourn by, 35, 70, 127, 233n13

Zhan Min-xu, 167, 207n3, 243n52

Zhang Guixing (Chang Kuei-hsing): cartographic representations in *Houbei* (Monkey cup), 243n54; deserving of the Nobel Prize in Literature, 238n69; double inhabitation in Mahua and Taiwan literary spaces, 1, 152, 177, 180; English translation of his work, 195, 247n2; rainforest narratives of, 179–80

Zhang, Longxi, 6

Zhang Xing Hong (Zhang, Ina), 77–78, 227n44, 227n45

Zhao Rong (pen name Yi Duo): the narrative voice of Lin Cantian's *Thick Smoke* criticized by, 223n93; on the neglect of *Thick Smoke*'s contribution to Mahua literature, 214n7; on the post-1937 polemics of Mahua literature, 43; *waijiang ren* defined by, 41

GPSR Authorized Representative: Easy Access System Europe, Mustamäe tee 50, 10621 Tallinn, Estonia, gpsr.requests@easproject.com

www.ingramcontent.com/pod-product-compliance
Lightning Source LLC
Chambersburg PA
CBHW031234290426
44109CB00012B/287